T0210552

Lecture Notes in Computer Science   9641

Commenced Publication in 1973
Founding and Former Series Editors:
Gerhard Goos, Juris Hartmanis, and Jan van Leeuwen

Editorial Board

More information about this series at http://www.springer.com/series/7407

Dragan Bošnački · Anton Wijs (Eds.)

Model Checking Software

23rd International Symposium, SPIN 2016
Co-located with ETAPS 2016
Eindhoven, The Netherlands, April 7–8, 2016
Proceedings

 Springer

Editors
Dragan Bošnački
Eindhoven University of Technology
Eindhoven
The Netherlands

Anton Wijs
Eindhoven University of Technology
Eindhoven
The Netherlands

ISSN 0302-9743   ISSN 1611-3349   (electronic)
Lecture Notes in Computer Science
ISBN 978-3-319-32581-1   ISBN 978-3-319-32582-8   (eBook)
DOI 10.1007/978-3-319-32582-8

Library of Congress Control Number: 2016935582

LNCS Sublibrary: SL1 – Theoretical Computer Science and General Issues

Printed on acid-free paper

This Springer imprint is published by Springer Nature
The registered company is Springer International Publishing AG Switzerland

Preface

During the last two decades the SPIN symposiums have established themselves as traditional annual forums for researchers and practitioners for the verification of software systems. The evolution of the SPIN events has to a great extent mirrored the maturing of model checking into a prevailing technology for the formal verification of software systems. The first SPIN workshop was held in Montreal in 1995. The next couple of subsequent editions of SPIN were intended as gatherings for presenting extensions and applications of the model checker SPIN, to which the series owes its name. Starting with the 2000 edition, the scope of the event clearly broadened to include techniques for formal verification and testing in general. In addition the SPIN events aim to promote interaction and exchange of ideas across related software engineering areas, like static and dynamic analysis. To this end, since 1996 SPIN has frequently been collocated with other, related conferences. Finally, since 1999, the proceedings of the SPIN workshops have appeared in Springer's Lecture Notes in Computer Science series.

This volume contains the papers presented at SPIN 2016: the 23rd International SPIN Symposium on Model Checking of Software, held on April 7–8, 2016 in Eindhoven, collocated with the 19th European Joint Conferences on Theory and Practice of Software (ETAPS 2016).

SPIN 2016 received 27 submissions of which 1 was withdrawn in the early phase of the reviewing process. Each submission was reviewed by at least 3 Program Committee members. The Program Committee decided to accept 16 papers, of which 11 regular papers, 1 idea paper, and 4 tool demonstrations. Program Committee members with a possible conflict of interest were excluded for the processing of the corresponding submissions. For each submission, a decision was made by consensus of the reviewers involved and the PC in general. This applied in particular to the borderline papers. Three papers were accepted after an additional shepherding procedure to ensure that the authors had carefully taken the suggestions of the reviewers into account. Besides the accepted papers, the program also included three invited talks by, respectively, Shaz Qadeer (Microsoft Research), Tim Willemse (Eindhoven University of Technology), and Pierre Wolper (University of Liège).

We are very grateful to the members of the Program Committee and the subreviewers who often worked under severe time pressure, as well as to the authors for producing camera ready copies of the papers in a relatively short time. Also, we would like to thank our invited speakers for their valuable contribution to the program. For their support, we thank the members of the SPIN Steering Committee, in particular Gerard Holzmann and Stefan Leue. The latter kindly accepted to act as a technical PC chair for two papers, for which the PC chairs themselves had a conflict of interest. We are indebted to the organizers of the previous edition of the symposium, SPIN 2015, Bernd Fischer and Jaco Geldenhuys. The experience they handed over to us and the suggestions and advice was of tremendous help for the organization. Finally, we would like to thank our colleagues from the Eindhoven University of Technology, Erik de Vink, Hans Zantema, Margje Mommers-Lenders, Mark van den Brand, and Jan Friso Groote for their suggestions and assistance with the local organization.

The SPIN 2016 logo was designed by Ilse Biermans. The symposium was partially supported by the Netherlands Organization for Scientific Research (NWO) and the company Sioux. The submission, reviewing, and discussion processes, as well as the production of the proceedings, were done using the EasyChair conference management system.

March 2016   Dragan Bošnački
                                                                 Anton Wijs

Organization

Steering Committee

Dragan Bošnački	Eindhoven University of Technology, The Netherlands
Susanne Graf	CNRS/VERIMAG, France
Gerard Holzmann (Chair)	NASA/JPL, USA
Stefan Leue	University of Constance, Germany

Program Committee

Jiří Barnat	Masaryk University, Czech Republic
Dragan Bošnački	Eindhoven University of Technology, The Netherlands
Aleksandar Dimovski	IT University of Copenhagen, Denmark
Stefan Edelkamp	University of Bremen, Germany
Bernd Fischer	Stellenbosch University, South Africa
Jaco Geldenhuys	Stellenbosch University, South Africa
Alex Groce	Oregon State University, USA
Jan Friso Groote	Eindhoven University of Technology, The Netherlands
Gerard Holzmann	NASA/JPL, USA
Franjo Ivančić	Google, USA
Alfons Laarman	Technical University of Vienna, Austria
Stefan Leue	University of Constance, Germany
Alberto Lluch Lafuente	Technical University of Denmark, Denmark
Radu Mateescu	INRIA Rhône-Alpes, France
Eric Mercer	Brigham Young University, USA
Pedro Merino	University of Málaga, Spain
Alice Miller	University of Glasgow, UK
Jun Pang	University of Luxembourg, Luxembourg
Corina Pasareanu	CMU/NASA Ames Research Center, USA
Theo Ruys	RUwise, The Netherlands
Jun Sun	Singapore University of Technology and Design, Singapore
Michael Tautschnig	Queen Mary University of London, UK
Mohammad Torabi Dashti	ETH Zürich, Switzerland
Antti Valmari	Tampere University of Technology, Finland
Martin Wehrle	University of Basel, Switzerland
Anton Wijs	Eindhoven University of Technology, The Netherlands
Erika Ábrahám	RWTH Aachen University, Germany

Additional Reviewers

Bey, Alina
Caltais, Georgiana
Cerna, Ivana

Garavel, Hubert
Heidinger, Stephan
Serwe, Wendelin

Invited Papers

On Verification Challenges at the Large Hadron Collider

Tim A.C. Willemse

Eindhoven University of Technology
P.O. Box 513, 5600 MB Eindhoven, The Netherlands

The Large Hadron Collider (LHC) experiment at the European Organization for Nuclear Research (CERN) is built in a tunnel 27 km in circumference and is designed to yield head-on collisions of two proton (ion) beams of 7 TeV each, *i.e.* 14 TeV in total. Next to three 'small' detectors for specialised research, the LHC hosts four large particle detectors: the general purpose detectors for the CMS and ATLAS experiments and the more specialised LHCb and ALICE experiments. The general purpose detectors study a wide range of particles and phenomena produced in the high-energy collisions in the LHC and yielded first evidence of the existence of a particle matching a Higgs boson in 2012. Typically, the experiments are made up of subdetectors, designed to stop, track or measure different particles emerging from the collisions. In 2015, it achieved an unprecedented successful 13 TeV collision, surpassing previous records of 8 TeV (2012) and 7 TeV (2010) collisions. The LHC experiments provide a gold mine of challenges for computer scientists, some of which I will address in this talk.

The Control Software. The Detector Control System takes care of control, configuration, readout and monitoring of the detector status, numerous hardware devices and various kinds of environment variables. The architecture of the control software for all four big LHC experiments is based on the SMI++ framework [3]; this framework views the real world as a collection of objects behaving as finite state machines (FSMs), which are organised hierarchically. A Domain-Specific Language called the State Manager Language (SML) is used to describe the FSMs (which are typically of low complexity) and the entire framework takes care of the interaction between these FSMs. To give an impression of the complexity involved: the control system for the CMS experiment at any time contains between 25,000 and 30,000 FSM nodes, and each FSM contains, on average, 5 *logical* states; this leads to a rather conservative estimate of a state space of somewhere between $10^{25,000}$ and $10^{30,000}$ states.

Despite the modular architecture, the control system occasionally exhibited undesirable behaviours, which had the potential to ruin expensive and difficult experiments. Formal verification techniques were used in an effort to improve its quality. SML and its underlying communication mechanisms were formalised in the process algebraic language mCRL2 [2]. This formalisation facilitated the understanding and enabled automated analyses of the behaviour of small constellations of cooperating FSMs. Not entirely unexpected, the prohibitive size of modest constellations (constellations involving more than 12 FSMs) prevented scaling the analysing to the global control system. On the one hand, the resulting frustration with this state of affairs inspired the development of new theory and tools for the mCRL2 toolset, see [1, 5–7]. On the other hand, the analyses revealed that there were several interesting consistency requirements that could be checked locally, and, indeed, log files of the control system showed that violations of such local consistency requirements had caused prior freezes of the control system. We subsequently developed dedicated verification tools and integrated these in the FSM development environment. Using these tools, we found that in the CMS experiment, up-to 20 % of the non-trivial FSMs violated a local requirement [4].

Data Acquisition. The Worldwide LHC Computing Grid launched in 2002, providing a resource to store, distribute and analyse the mountain of data produced at 6 Gb per second (and soon expected to increase to 25 Gb per second) by the LHC experiments. Among the software frameworks that employ the computing grid is the Distributed Infrastructure with Remote Agent Control (DIRAC) software framework. Programmed in Python, DIRAC provides cooperating distributed services and a plethora of light-weight agents that deliver the workload to the grid resources.

Despite the effort invested in making DIRAC reliable, entities occasionally get into inconsistent states. We reverse engineered several critical subsystems related to DIRAC and used mCRL2 for simulating, visualising and model checking to find race conditions and livelocks, see [8]. These were subsequently confirmed to occur in the real system. These findings led to subsequent improvements in the implementation of DIRAC.

Acknowledgements. Joint work with, a.o., Frank Glege, Robert Gomez-Reino Garrido, Yi-Ling Hwong, Sander Leemans, Gijs Kant, Jeroen Keiren and Daniela Remenska. This research was supported in part by NWO grant number 612.000.937 (VOCHS).

References

1. Cranen, S., Gazda, M., Wesselink, W., Willemse, T.A.C.: Abstraction in fixpoint logic. ACM Trans. Comput. Logic **16**(4), Article 29 (2015)
2. Cranen, S., Groote, J.F., Keiren, J.J.A., Stappers, F.P.M., de Vink, E.P., Wesselink, J.W., Willemse, T.A.C.: An overview of the mCRL2 toolset and its recent advances. In: Proceedings of TACAS 2013. LNCS, vol. 7795, pp. 199–213. Springer, Berlin (2013)
3. Franek, B., Gaspar, C.: SMI++ object-oriented framework for designing and implementing distributed control systems. IEEE Trans. Nuclear Sci. **52**(4), 891–895 (2005)
4. Hwong, Y.L., Keiren, J.J.A., Kusters, V.J.J., Leemans, S., Willemse, T.A.C.: Formalising and analysing the control software of the Compact Muon Solenoid experiment at the Large Hadron Collider. Science of Computer Programming **78**(12), 2435–2452 (2013)
5. Kant, G., van de Pol, J.C.: Generating and solving symbolic parity games. In: Proceedings of GRAPHITE 2014. EPTCS, vol. 159, pp. 2–14 (2014)
6. Keiren, J.J.A., Wesselink, J.W., Willemse, T.A.C.: Liveness analysis for parameterised Boolean equation systems. In: Proceedings of ATVA 2014. LNCS, vol. 8837, pp. 219–234. Springer, Berlin (2014)

7. Koolen, R.P.M., Willemse, T.A.C., Zantema, H.: Using SMT for solving fragments of parameterised Boolean equation systems. In: Proceedings of ATVA 2015, LNCS, vol. 9364, pp. 1–17. Springer, Berlin (2015)
8. Remenska, D., Willemse, T.A.C., Verstoep, K., Templon, J.A., Bal, H.E.: Using model checking to analyze the system behavior of the LHC production grid. Future Generation Comput. Syst. 29(8), 2239–2251 (2013)

Model Checking: What Have We Learned, What Will Machines Learn?

Pierre Wolper

University of Lige, Belgium
Pierre.Wolper@ulg.ac.be
http://montefiore.ulg.ac.be/~pw/

Abstract. Model Checking was introduced more than 30 years ago and, thanks to a steady stream of improvements and new approaches, has developed into a widely used and quite effective tool for verifying some classes of programs. Surveying and reflecting on these developments, this talk attempts to highlight the main lessons learned from the last three decades of research on the topic. Then, looking towards the future, it speculates on what the next decades could bring and on whether it would not be time for machines to do the learning, in order to provide developers with the effective verification assistant they are still waiting for.

Contents

Automated Analysis of Asynchronously Communicating Systems

Lakhdar Akroun[1], Gwen Salaün[1(✉)], and Lina Ye[2]

[1] University of Grenoble Alpes, Inria, LIG, CNRS, Grenoble, France
{lakhdar.akroun,gwen.salaun}@inria.fr
[2] LRI, University Paris-Sud,
CentraleSupélec, CNRS, Université Paris-Saclay, Orsay, France
lina.ye@lri.fr

Abstract. Analyzing systems communicating asynchronously via reliable FIFO buffers is an undecidable problem. A typical approach is to check whether the system is bounded, and if not, the corresponding state space can be made finite by limiting the presence of communication cycles in behavioral models or by fixing the buffer size. In this paper, our focus is on systems that are likely to be unbounded and therefore result in infinite systems. We do not want to restrict the system by imposing any arbitrary bound. We introduce a notion of stability and prove that once the system is stable for a specific buffer bound, it remains stable whatever larger bounds are chosen for buffers. This enables one to check certain properties on the system for that bound and to ensure that the system will preserve them whatever larger bounds are used for buffers. We also prove that computing this bound is undecidable but we show how we succeed in computing these bounds for many examples using heuristics and equivalence checking.

1 Introduction

Most software systems are constructed by reusing and composing existing components or peers. This is the case in many different areas such as component-based systems, distributed cloud applications, Web services, or cyber-physical systems. Software entities are often stateful and therefore described using behavioral models. Moreover, asynchronous communication via FIFO buffers is a classic communication model used for such distributed, communicating systems. A crucial problem in this context is to check whether a new system consisting of a set of interacting peers respects certain properties. Analyzing asynchronously communicating software has been studied extensively in the last 30 years and is known to be undecidable in general [7]. A common approach to circumvent this issue is to bound the state space by restricting the cyclic behaviors or imposing an arbitrary bound on buffers. Bounding buffers to an arbitrary size during the execution is not a satisfactory solution: if at some point buffers' sizes change (due to changes in memory requirements for example), it is not possible to know how the system would behave compared to its former version and new unexpected errors can show up.

© Springer International Publishing Switzerland 2016
D. Bošnački and A. Wijs (Eds.): SPIN 2016, LNCS 9641, pp. 1–18, 2016.
DOI: 10.1007/978-3-319-32582-8_1

In this paper, we propose a new approach for analyzing a set of peers described using Labeled Transition Systems (LTSs), communicating asynchronously via reliable (no loss of messages) and possibly unbounded FIFO buffers. We do not want to restrict the system by imposing any arbitrary bound on cyclic behaviors or buffers. We introduce a notion of stability for the asynchronous versions of the system. A system is stable if asynchronous compositions exhibit the same observable behavior (send actions) from some buffer bound. This property can be verified in practice using equivalence checking techniques on finite state spaces by comparing bounded asynchronous compositions, although the system consisting of peers interacting asynchronously via unbounded buffers can result in infinite state spaces. We prove that once the system is stable for a specific buffer bound, it remains stable whatever larger bounds are chosen for buffers. This enables one to check temporal properties on the system for that bound (using model checking techniques for instance) and ensures that the system will preserve them whatever larger bounds are used for buffers. We also prove that computing this bound is undecidable, but we show how we succeed in computing such bounds in practice for many examples.

Figure 1 gives an example where peers are modeled using LTSs. Transitions are labeled with either send actions (exclamation marks) or receive actions (question marks). Initial states are marked with incoming half-arrows. In the asynchronous composition, each peer is equipped with one input buffer, and we consider only the ordering of the send actions, ignoring the ordering of receive actions. Focusing only on send actions makes sense for verification purposes because: (i) send actions are the actions that transfer messages to the network and are therefore observable, (ii) receive actions correspond to local consumptions by peers from their buffers and can therefore be considered to be local and private information. We can use our approach to detect that when each peer is equipped with a buffer bound fixed to 2, the observable behavior of the system depicted in Fig. 1 is stable. This means that we can check properties, such as the absence of deadlocks, on the 2-bounded asynchronous version of the system and the results hold for any asynchronous version of the system where buffer bounds are greater or equal to 2.

We implemented our approach in a tool that first encodes the peer LTSs and their compositions into process algebra, and then uses heuristics, search algorithms, and equivalence checking techniques for verifying whether the system

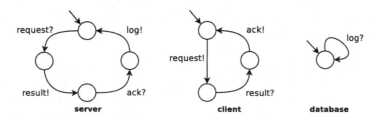

Fig. 1. Motivating example

satisfies the stability property. If this is the case, we return the smallest bound respecting this property. Otherwise, when we reach a certain maximal bound, our check returns an inconclusive result. Heuristics and search algorithms aim at guiding the approach towards the smallest bound satisfying stability whereas equivalence checking techniques are used for checking the stability property given a specific bound k. All the steps of our approach are fully automated (no human intervention). We applied our tool support to more than 300 examples of communicating systems, many of them taken from the literature on this topic. These experiments show that a large number of these examples are stable and can therefore be formally analyzed using our approach.

The contributions of this paper are summarized as follows:

– The introduction of the stability property for asynchronously communicating systems that, once acquired for a bound k, is preserved for upper bounds;
– A proof demonstrating that computing such a bound k is undecidable;
– A fully automated tool support that shows that the bound exists for a majority of our examples.

The organization of the rest of this paper is as follows. Section 2 defines our model for peers and their asynchronous composition. Section 3 presents the stability property and our results on stable systems. Section 4 describes our tool support and experiments we carried out to evaluate our approach. Finally, Sect. 5 reviews related work and Sect. 6 concludes.

2   Communicating Systems

We use Labeled Transition Systems (LTSs) for modeling peers. This behavioral model defines the order in which a peer executes the send and receive actions.

Definition 1. *A peer is an LTS $\mathcal{P} = (S, s^0, \Sigma, T)$ where S is a finite set of states, $s^0 \in S$ is the initial state, $\Sigma = \Sigma^! \cup \Sigma^? \cup \{\tau\}$ is a finite alphabet partitioned into a set of send messages, a set of receive messages, and the internal action, and $T \subseteq S \times \Sigma \times S$ is a transition relation.*

We write $m!$ for a send message $m \in \Sigma^!$ and $m?$ for a receive message $m \in \Sigma^?$. We use the symbol τ for representing internal activities. A transition is represented as $s \xrightarrow{l} s' \in T$ where $l \in \Sigma$. This can be directly extended to $s \xrightarrow{\sigma} s'$, $\sigma \in \Sigma^*$, where $\sigma = l_1, ..., l_n$, $s \xrightarrow{l_1} s_1, ..., s_i \xrightarrow{l_{i+1}} s_{i+1}, ..., s_{n-1} \xrightarrow{l_n} s' \in T$. In the following, for the sake of simplicity, we will denote this by $s \xrightarrow{\sigma} s' \in T^*$.

We assume that peers are deterministic on observable messages meaning that if there are several transitions going out from one peer state, and if all the transition labels are observable, then they are all different from one another. Nondeterminism can also result from internal choices when several transitions (at least two) outgoing from a same state are labeled with τ. Given a set of peers $\{\mathcal{P}_1, \ldots, \mathcal{P}_n\}$, we assume that each message has a unique sender and a unique receiver: $\forall i, j \in [1, n]$, $i \neq j$, $\Sigma_i^! \cap \Sigma_j^! = \emptyset$ and $\Sigma_i^? \cap \Sigma_j^? = \emptyset$. Furthermore, each message is exchanged between two different peers: $\Sigma_i^! \cap \Sigma_i^? = \emptyset$ for all i. We also assume that each send action has a counterpart (receive action) in another peer (closed systems): $\forall i \in [1,n], \forall m \in \Sigma_i^! \implies \exists j \in [1,n], i \neq j, m \in \Sigma_j^?$.

In the asynchronous composition, the peers communicate with each other asynchronously via FIFO buffers. Each peer $\mathcal{P}_i$ is equipped with an unbounded input message buffer Q_i. A peer $\mathcal{P}_i$ can either send a message $m \in \Sigma_i^!$ to the tail of the receiver buffer Q_j of $\mathcal{P}_j$ at any state where this send message is available, read a message $m \in \Sigma_i^?$ from its buffer Q_i if the message is available at the buffer head, or evolve independently through an internal transition. We focus on send actions in this paper. We consider that reading from the buffer is private non-observable information, which is encoded as an internal transition in the asynchronous system.

Definition 2. *Given a set of peers* $\{\mathcal{P}_1, \ldots, \mathcal{P}_n\}$ *with* $\mathcal{P}_i = (S_i, s_i^0, \Sigma_i, T_i)$, *and* Q_i *being its associated buffer, the asynchronous composition* $(P_1|Q_1)|...|(P_n|Q_n)$ *is the labeled transition system* $LTS_a = (S_a, s_a^0, \Sigma_a, T_a)$ *where:*

- $S_a \subseteq S_1 \times Q_1 \times \ldots \times S_n \times Q_n$ *where* $\forall i \in \{1, \ldots, n\}$, $Q_i \subseteq (\Sigma_i^?)*$
- $s_a^0 \in S_a$ *such that* $s_a^0 = (s_1^0, \epsilon, \ldots, s_n^0, \epsilon)$ *(where* ϵ *denotes an empty buffer)*
- $\Sigma_a = \cup_i \Sigma_i$
- $T_a \subseteq S_a \times \Sigma_a \times S_a$, *and for* $s = (s_1, Q_1, \ldots, s_n, Q_n) \in S_a$ *and* $s' = (s_1', Q_1', \ldots s_n', Q_n') \in S_a$, *we have three possible behaviors*
  - $s \xrightarrow{m!} s' \in T_a$ *if* $\exists i, j \in \{1, \ldots, n\}$ *where* $i \neq j : m \in \Sigma_i^! \cap \Sigma_j^?$, *(i)* $s_i \xrightarrow{m!} s_i' \in T_i$, *(ii)* $Q_j' = Q_j m$, *(iii)* $\forall k \in \{1, \ldots, n\} : k \neq j \Rightarrow Q_k' = Q_k$, *and (iv)* $\forall k \in \{1, \ldots, n\} : k \neq i \Rightarrow s_k' = s_k$ *(send action)*
  - $s \xrightarrow{\tau} s' \in T_a$ *if* $\exists i \in \{1, \ldots, n\} : m \in \Sigma_i^?$, *(i)* $s_i \xrightarrow{m?} s_i' \in T_i$, *(ii)* $mQ_i' = Q_i$, *(iii)* $\forall k \in \{1, \ldots, n\} : k \neq i \Rightarrow Q_k' = Q_k$, *and (iv)* $\forall k \in \{1, \ldots, n\} : k \neq i \Rightarrow s_k' = s_k$ *(receive action)*
  - $s \xrightarrow{\tau} s' \in T_a$ *if* $\exists i \in \{1, \ldots, n\}$, *(i)* $s_i \xrightarrow{\tau} s_i' \in T_i$, *(ii)* $\forall k \in \{1, \ldots, n\} : Q_k' = Q_k$, *and (iii)* $\forall k \in \{1, \ldots, n\} : k \neq i \Rightarrow s_k' = s_k$ *(internal action)*

We use $LTS_a^k = (S_a^k, s_a^0, \Sigma_a^k, T_a^k)$ to define the *bounded* asynchronous composition, where each message buffer bounded to size k is denoted Q_i^k, for $i \in [1, n]$. The definition of LTS_a^k can be obtained from Definition 2 by allowing send transitions only if the message buffer of the receiving peer has less than k messages in it. Otherwise, the sender is blocked, *i.e.*, we assume reliable communication without message losses. The k-bounded asynchronous product can be denoted $(P_1|Q_1^k)|...|(P_n|Q_n^k)$ or $(P_1|(Q_1^1| \ldots |Q_1^1))|...|(P_n|(Q_n^1| \ldots |Q_n^1))$, where each peer is in parallel with the parallel composition of k buffers of size one. Let us emphasize that the encoding of an ordered bounded buffer following this pattern based on parallel composition was originally proposed by R. Milner in [36] (see Sects. 1.2 and 3.3 of this book for details). Furthermore, we use $\overline{LTS_a}$ for the asynchronous composition where the receive actions are kept in the resulting LTS ($s \xrightarrow{m?} s' \in \overline{T_a}$, *receive action* rule in Definition 2) instead of being encoded as τ.

3 Stability-Based Verification

In this section, we show that systems consisting of a finite set of peers involving cyclic behaviors and communicating over FIFO buffers may stabilize from a specific buffer bound k. We call this property *stability* and we say that the corresponding systems are *stable*. The class of systems that are stable corresponds to systems whose asynchronous compositions remain the same from some buffer bound when we observe send actions only (we ignore receive actions and buffer contents). Since stable systems produce the same behavior from a specific bound k, they can be analyzed for that bound to detect for instance the presence of deadlocks or to check whether they satisfy any kind of temporal properties. Stability ensures that these properties will be also satisfied for larger bounds. The stability definition relies on branching bisimulation checking [41] (Definition 3). We chose branching bisimulation because in this work receive actions are hidden as internal behaviors, and branching bisimulation is the finest equivalence notion in presence of internal behaviors. This equivalence preserves properties written in ACTL\X logic [33].

Definition 3. *Given two LTSs LTS_1 and LTS_2, they are branching bisimilar, denoted by $LTS_1 \equiv_{br} LTS_2$, if there exists a symmetric relation R (called a branching bisimulation) between the states of LTS_1 and LTS_2 satisfying the following two conditions: (i) The initial states are related by R; (ii) If $R(r,s)$ and $r \xrightarrow{\delta} r\prime$, then either $\delta = \tau$ and $R(r\prime, s)$, or there exists a path $s \xrightarrow{\tau^*} s_1 \xrightarrow{\delta} s\prime$, such that $R(r, s_1)$ and $R(r\prime, s\prime)$. For the sake of simplicity, in the following, $R(r,s)$ is also denoted by $r \equiv_{br} s$.*

Definition 4. *Given a set of peers $\{\mathcal{P}_1, \ldots, \mathcal{P}_n\}$, we say that this system is stable if and only if $\exists k$ such that $LTS_a^k \equiv_{br} LTS_a^q$ $(\forall q > k)$.*

As a first result, we show a sufficient condition to ensure stability: if there exists a bound k such that the k-bounded and the $(k+1)$-bounded asynchronous systems are branching equivalent, then we prove that the system remains stable, meaning that the observable behavior is always the same for any bound greater than k.

Theorem 1. *Given a set of peers $\{\mathcal{P}_1, \ldots, \mathcal{P}_n\}$, if $\exists k \in \mathbb{N}$, such that $LTS_a^k \equiv_{br} LTS_a^{k+1}$, then we have $LTS_a^k \equiv_{br} LTS_a^q, \forall q > k$.*

Proof. We prove the theorem by induction, starting with the following base case: If $LTS_a^k \equiv_{br} LTS_a^{k+1}$ then $LTS_a^k \equiv_{br} LTS_a^{k+2}$. Let us recall that the strong and branching bisimulations are congruences with respect to the operators of process algebras [19], that is, if P and P' are branching bisimilar, then for every Q we have $P|Q \equiv_{br} P'|Q$. Now, suppose that $\exists k \in \mathbb{N}$, such that $LTS_a^k \equiv_{br} LTS_a^{k+1}$, then:

$$(P_1|Q_1^k)|...|(P_n|Q_n^k) \equiv_{br} (P_1|Q_1^{k+1})|...|(P_n|Q_n^{k+1}) \tag{1}$$

A buffer of size k can be written as a parallel composition of k buffers of size 1 (see Sects. 1.2 and 3.3 in [36] for details), hence:

$$(P_1|Q_1^{k+2})|...|(P_n|Q_n^{k+2}) \equiv_{br} (P_1|Q_1^{k+1}|Q_1^1)|...|(P_n|Q_n^{k+1}|Q_n^1) \tag{2}$$

Then, by congruence and using Eq. (1) we have:

$$(P_1|Q_1^{k+2})|...|(P_n|Q_n^{k+2}) \equiv_{br} (P_1|Q_1^k|Q_1^1)|...|(P_n|Q_n^k|Q_n^1) \tag{3}$$

$$(P_1|Q_1^{k+2})|...|(P_n|Q_n^{k+2}) \equiv_{br} (P_1|Q_1^{k+1})|...|(P_n|Q_n^{k+1}) \tag{4}$$

$$(P_1|Q_1^{k+2})|...|(P_n|Q_n^{k+2}) \equiv_{br} (P_1|Q_1^k)|...|(P_n|Q_n^k) \tag{5}$$

The same argument can be used to prove the induction case, *i.e.*, we suppose that $LTS_a^k \equiv_{br} LTS_a^{k+i}$ and we demonstrate that $LTS_a^k \equiv_{br} LTS_a^{k+i+1}$. This proves that if $LTS_a^k \equiv_{br} LTS_a^{k+1}$, then we have $LTS_a^k \equiv_{br} LTS_a^q, \forall q > k$.   ■

The main interest of the stability property is that any temporal property can be analyzed using existing model checking tools on the minimal k-bounded version of the system, and this result ensures that these properties are preserved when buffer bounds are increased or if buffers are unbounded.

Proposition 1. *Given a set of peers $\{\mathcal{P}_1, \ldots, \mathcal{P}_n\}$, if $\exists k$ s.t. $LTS_a^k \equiv_{br} LTS_a^q$ ($\forall q > k$), and for some property P written in $ACTL\backslash X$ logic, $LTS_a^k \models P$, then $LTS_a^q \models P$ ($\forall q > k$).*

Classic properties, such as liveness or safety properties, can be verified considering send actions only. If one wants to check a property involving receive actions, a solution is to replace in the property a specific receive action by one of the send actions (if there is one) occurring next in the corresponding peer LTS.

We prove now that determining whether a system is stable is an undecidable problem. Yet there are many cases in which stability is satisfied and the corresponding bound can be computed in those cases using heuristics, search algorithms, and equivalence checking (see Sect. 4).

To prove that testing the stability is an undecidable problem, we reduce the halting problem of a Turing machine to the test of stability of a set of peers communicating asynchronously. We start the proof with some preliminaries and notation, then we give an overview of the proof. Afterwards, we detail the construction of a system of two peers simulating the Turing machine and finally we prove the undecidability result.

Preliminaries and Notation. The Turing machine used is a deterministic one-way-infinite single tape model. A Turing machine is defined as $M = (Q_M, \Sigma_M, \Gamma_M, q_0, q_{halt}, B, \delta_M)$ where Q_M is the set of states, Σ_M is the input alphabet, Γ_M is the tape alphabet, $q_0 \in Q_M$ is the initial state and q_{halt} is the accepting state. $B \in \Gamma_M$ is the blank symbol and $\delta_M : Q_M \times \Gamma_M \rightarrow Q_M \times \Gamma_M \times \{left, right\}$ is the transition function. The machine M accepts an input word $w = a_1, ..., a_m$ iff M halts on w. If M does not halt on w and the word is not accepted at a state q, then M initiates a loop. This loop reads any symbol and moves to the right. Hence, if the word w is not accepted, then the machine executes an infinite loop by reading symbols and moving to the right. This looping behavior is not usual in classic Turing machines and acceptance semantics, but this simplifies the reduction without modifying the expressiveness of the Turing machine as shown in [18].

A *configuration* of the Turing machine M is a word $uqv\#$ where uv is a word from the tape alphabet, q is a state of M (meaning that M is in the state q and the head pointing on the first symbol of v), and $\#$ is a fixed symbol which is not in Γ_M (used to indicate the end of the word on the tape).

Overview. To facilitate the understanding of the proof, we present the reduction in two phases. In a first phase (i), starting from a Turing machine M and an input word w, we construct a pair of peers P_1 and P_2, such that whenever the machine M halts on w or not, there always exists a k such that $LTS_a^k \equiv_{br} LTS_a$, where LTS_a is the asynchronous product of the system $\{P_1, P_2\}$. In a second phase (ii), we extend P_1 and P_2 respectively to P_1' and P_2', and there exists k such that $LTS_a'^k \equiv_{br} LTS_a'$ iff M does not halt on w, where LTS_a' is the asynchronous product of the system $\{P_1', P_2'\}$.

Phase (i) – Construction of P_1 and P_2. The peer P_1 simulates the execution of the machine M on w while P_2 is used to receive and re-send messages to P_1. A configuration of M of the form $uqv\#$ is encoded with the buffer of P_1 with the content $uheadv\#$. We give in the following the construction of P_1 and P_2.

The peer P_1 is defined as $(S_{P_1}, s_{q_0}, \Sigma_{P_1}, T_{P_1})$ where S_{P_1} is the set of states, s_{q_0} is the initial state where q_0 is the initial state of M. The alphabet $\Sigma_{P_1} = \Sigma_{P_1}^! \cup \Sigma_{P_1}^?$ is defined as follows:

- $\Sigma_{P_1}^! = \Sigma_M \cup \Gamma_M \cup \{head\} \cup \{\#\}$ where all messages sent from P_1 to P_2 are indexed with 2 (*e.g.*, P_1 sends B^2 instead of sending the blank symbol, inversely P_2 sends B^1 instead of sending B to P_1).
- $\Sigma_{P_1}^? = \Sigma_M \cup \Gamma_M \cup \{head\} \cup \{\#\}$ where all messages received from P_2 are indexed with 1.

Now we present how each action of the machine M is encoded.

- For each transition of M of the form $\delta_M(q, a) = (q', a', right)$ we have the following transitions in T_{P_1}: $s_q \xrightarrow{head^1?} s_1 \xrightarrow{a^1?} s_2 \xrightarrow{a'^2!} s_3 \xrightarrow{head^2!} s_{q'}$. If the peer is in the state q and the buffer starts with $head^1 a^1$ then the two messages are read and the peer P_1 sends the next configuration to P_2 as depicted in Fig. 2(a). s_i's are fresh intermediary states.
- For each transition of M of the form $\delta_M(q, a) = (q', a', left)$ and for each $x \in \Gamma_M$ we have the following transitions in T_{P_1}: $s_q \xrightarrow{x^1?} s_1 \xrightarrow{head^1?} s_2 \xrightarrow{a^1?} s_3 \xrightarrow{head^2!} s_4 \xrightarrow{x^2!} s_5 \xrightarrow{a'^2!} s_{q'}$. P_1 starts by reading the letter before $head$, then it reads $head$, the next letter, and sends the new configuration to P_2 as depicted in Fig. 2(b).
- For each state s_q where q is a state of M we have the following cycle in T_{P_1}: $s_q \xrightarrow{head^1?} s_1 \xrightarrow{\#^1?} s_2 \xrightarrow{head^2!} s_3 \xrightarrow{B^2!} s_4 \xrightarrow{\#^2!} s_q$. As depicted in Fig. 2(c),

the configuration of M is extended to the right with a blank symbol. Peer 1 starts by reading the current configuration of the machine, then sends the next configuration of M to P_2 (P_1 adds a blank symbol before #).

– For each letter $x \in \Gamma_M \cup \{\#\}$ and each s_q where q is a state of M, we have the following cycle: $s_q \xrightarrow{x^1?} s_1 \xrightarrow{x^2!} s_q$ where P_1 reads x indexed with 1, then sends x indexed with 2.

Note that at a state s_q representing a state q of the machine M, there is only one outgoing transition labeled with $head^1?$, hence P_1 is deterministic.

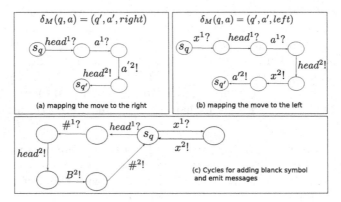

Fig. 2. Mapping the instructions of the machine M to transitions of the peer P_1

The peer P_2 is only used to read and re-send the messages. It is defined as $(S_{P_2}, s_{init}, \Sigma_{P_2}, T_{P_2})$ where S_{P_2} is the set of states and s_{init} is the initial state. P_2 starts by sending the initial configuration of M to P_1, then reaches the state s_{univ}, which contains a set of cycles used to receive any message from P_1 and re-send them. $\Sigma_{P_2} = \Sigma^!_{P_2} \cup \Sigma^?_{P_2}$ is defined as follows:

– $\Sigma^!_{P_2} = \Sigma_M \cup \Gamma_M \cup \{head\} \cup \{\#\}$ where all messages sent from P_2 to P_1 are indexed with 1.
– $\Sigma^?_{P_2} = \Sigma_M \cup \Gamma_M \cup \{head\} \cup \{\#\}$ where all messages received from P_1 are indexed with 2.

P_2 contains the following transitions:

– $s_{init} \xrightarrow{head^1!} s_1 \xrightarrow{a_1^1!} \ldots \xrightarrow{a_n^1!} s_n \xrightarrow{\#^1!} s_{univ} \in T_{P_2}$ where $w = a_1 a_2 \ldots a_n$.
– $s_{univ} \xrightarrow{x^2?} s_1 \xrightarrow{x^1!} s_{univ} \in T_{P_2}$ where x is any symbol in $\Sigma^?_{P_2}$.

Lemma 1. *Given a Turing machine M with an input word w and the peers P_1 and P_2 constructed as above, the system composed of $\{P_1, P_2\}$ is stable whether the machine M halts on w or not.*

Proof. To prove that $\exists k$ such that $LTS_a^k \equiv_{br} LTS_a$, it is sufficient to prove that $\exists k$ such that $LTS_a^k \equiv_{br} LTS_a^{k+1}$ (from Theorem 1). Suppose that M halts on w.

Then, the number of configurations of the machine is finite. Hence, from our construction, the asynchronous product of $\{P_1, P_2\}$ is finite, so there exists a k such that $LTS_a^k \equiv_{br} LTS_a^{k+1}$, hence $LTS_a^k \equiv_{br} LTS_a$.

Now suppose that the machine does not halt on w. Then, the corresponding communicating system executes infinitely two cycles: (1) one adding a blank symbol, (2) another reading blank symbols and moving to the right (which occurs in our construction when the machine does not halt on the input word w). Hence, for a given bound k, the behavior of the system resulting from the execution of one of the two cycles in LTS_a^{k+1} may not be reproduced in LTS_a^k, due to the buffer bound, then $LTS_a^k \not\equiv_{br} LTS_a^{k+1}$. We prove that, with our construction, this case never happens, that is $LTS_a^k \equiv_{br} LTS_a$ when the machine M does not halt on w.

Now we detail the proof for cycles of type (1). The proof for cycles of type (2) is straightforward because those cycles involve receive actions only and do not make the buffer contents increase. Suppose that the machine M does not stop. Let s^k be the state of LTS_a^k representing the configuration of the machine M when starting to execute the infinite loop for the first time. From our construction, at s^k the system can execute the first cycle adding a blank symbol. Note that in s^k the buffer of P_1 is full (size equal to k) and the buffer of P_2 is empty. More precisely, the buffer of P_1 contains the following word: $head^1 \#^1 a_1^1 ... a_m^1$, where $m = k - 2$. It is easy to verify that such a state exists, because at a state s_q representing a state q of the machine M, P_1 can enter two cycles, one starting by reading $head^1$, the other one reading any other symbol. Hence, if the first symbol of the buffer of P_1 is not $head^1$, P_1 reads the symbol and sends it to P_2 which re-sends the symbol to P_1. Thus, in the configuration s^k, the first symbol is $head^1$. Then, P_1 executes the cycle which adds a blank symbol:

$$s^k \xrightarrow{head^1?} s_1 \xrightarrow{\#^1?} s_2 \xrightarrow{head^2!} s_3 \xrightarrow{B^2!} s_4 \xrightarrow{\#^2!} s^{k'}.$$

At $s^{k'}$ the buffer of P_1 contains $k - 2$ messages and the buffer of P_2 three messages. The sum of the two buffers is $k + 1$ messages, due to the addition of the blank symbol, but $s^{k'}$ is still in LTS_a^k. From our construction, at the configuration $s^{k'}$, P_1 sends $a_1^2, ..., a_{m-1}^2$: $s^{k'} \xrightarrow{a_1^2!} s_1 \xrightarrow{a_2^2!} ... \xrightarrow{a_{m-1}^2!} s^{k''}$.

At $s^{k''}$ the buffer of P_2 contains k messages and the buffer of P_1 contains one message. At this configuration, P_1 sends the message a_m^2, and the system reaches a configuration s^{k+1} which is in LTS_a^{k+1} but not in LTS_a^k.

Hence, LTS_a^{k+1} and LTS_a^k can send the same sequences of messages from the initial state to the state $s^{k''}$. Then, LTS_a^{k+1} can send the message a_m^2. Moreover, in the configuration $s^{k''}$, P_2 can read a message (because it is in the state s_{univ}). Thus, in LTS_a^k there is the following sequence: $s^{k''} \xrightarrow{\tau} s_1 \xrightarrow{a_m^1!} s'^k$. With our construction, any sequence of send messages which exceeds the buffer size k can be executed with a buffer size bounded by k. Hence, if the machine does not halt on w, then $\exists k$ such that $LTS_a^k \equiv_{br} LTS_a$.

Note that, since proving $LTS_a^k \equiv_{br} LTS_a^{k+1}$ is sufficient to prove $LTS_a^k \equiv_{br} LTS_a$, we do not need to prove our statement for buffer size containing more than k or $k+1$ messages. The bound k depends on the execution of the machine M and the word w, where k represents the buffer size needed to encode the configuration of the machine M when starting to execute the infinite loop.   ∎

Phase (ii) – Construction of P_1' and P_2'. Until now, whenever the machine M halts on w or not, the system composed of P_1 and P_2 is always stable. Now, we extend P_1 and P_2 respectively to obtain P_1' and P_2' such that the machine M does not halt on w iff the corresponding system (composed of P_1' and P_2') is stable. This is achieved by adding to P_1 the transition system P_a to obtain P_1' and adding to P_2 the transition system P_b to obtain P_2', such that the system $\{P_a, P_b\}$ is not stable. The peers P_a and P_b are not formally defined, we can choose any two peers which are not stable. The additional transitions used to connect P_1 to P_a and P_2 to P_b are listed below:

- s_0 and s_0' are respectively the initial states of P_a and P_b. The messages exchanged between P_a and P_b do not appear in P_1 and P_2.
- $s_{q_{halt}} \xrightarrow{halt!} s_0 \in T_{P_1'}$.
- $s_{univ} \xrightarrow{halt?} s_0' \in T_{P_2'}$.
- $s_0 \xrightarrow{x?} s_0 \in T_{P_1'}$, where x is any letter in $\Sigma_{P_1}^?$.
- $s_0' \xrightarrow{y?} s_0' \in T_{P_2'}$, where y is any letter in $\Sigma_{P_2}^?$.

Lemma 2. *Given a Turing machine M with an input word w and the peers P_1' and P_2' constructed as above, the system composed of $\{P_1', P_2'\}$ is stable iff the machine M does not halt on w.*

Proof. Suppose that the machine M halts on w, then P_1' reaches the state $s_{q_{halt}}$ (see the construction of P_1, which simulates the execution of the machine M) and it sends the message *halt* to P_2'. Hence, it reaches the state s_0. P_2' is in the state s_{univ}, hence, it reads the message *halt* and reaches the state s_0'. At s_0 and s_0', the two peers empty their buffers, start executing P_a and P_b, and thus the stability is violated.

Suppose now that M does not halt on w, then from the construction of P_1 simulating the execution of M, the peer P_1' never reaches the state $s_{q_{halt}}$, and the system executes an infinite loop. Hence, from Lemma 1, the system $\{P_1', P_2'\}$ is stable. $\blacksquare$

We can now formulate one of the main results of this paper, which asserts that testing the stability property in an undecidable problem.

Theorem 2. *Given a set of peers $\{\mathcal{P}_1, \ldots, \mathcal{P}_n\}$, it is undecidable to determine whether the corresponding asynchronous system is stable.*

Proof. The proof is a direct consequence of the construction given above and of both Lemmas 1 and 2. $\blacksquare$

Another result concerns well-formed systems [3]. A system consisting of a set of peers is well-formed iff whenever the size of the buffer, Q_i, of the i-th peer is non-empty, the system can move to a state where Q_i is empty. In other words, well-formedness concerns the ability of a system to eventually consume all messages in any of its buffers. In order to check this property, we have to keep receive messages and thus analyze the system on its asynchronous composition $\overline{LTS_a}$ instead of LTS_a .

Definition 5. *Given a set of peers* $\{\mathcal{P}_1, \ldots, \mathcal{P}_n\}$, *it is well-formed, denoted by* $WF(\overline{LTS_a})$, *if* $\forall s = (s_1, Q_1, \ldots, s_n, Q_n) \in \overline{S_a}, \forall Q_i$, *it holds that if* $|Q_i| > 0$, *then* $\exists s \xrightarrow{\sigma} s\prime \in \overline{T_a}^*$, *where* $s\prime = (s_1\prime, Q_1\prime, \ldots, s_n\prime, Q_n\prime) \in \overline{S_a}, |Q_i\prime| = 0$. *The well-formedness property can be checked with the CTL temporal formula on* $\overline{LTS_a}$: $AG(|Q_i| > 0 \Rightarrow EF(|Q_i| = 0))$.

One can check whether a stable system is well-formed for the smallest k satisfying stability for instance. If a system is both stable and well-formed for this smallest k, then it remains well-formed for larger bound q greater than k.

Theorem 3. *Given a set of peers* $\{\mathcal{P}_1, \ldots, \mathcal{P}_n\}$, *if* $\exists k$ *s.t.* $LTS_a^k \equiv_{br} LTS_a^q$ $(\forall q > k)$ *and* $WF(\overline{LTS_a^k})$, *then we have* $WF(\overline{LTS_a^q})$ $(\forall q > k)$.

Proof. Suppose that there exists a k such that $LTS_a^k \equiv_{br} LTS_a^q$ $(\forall q > k)$. We know from Proposition 1 that the stability preserves properties written in ACTL\X logic, *i.e.*, when the system is stable and $LTS_a^k \models P$, then $LTS_a^q \models P$ $(\forall q > k)$, where P is a property written in this logic. Well-formedness is a property expressed in ACTL\X logic. Hence, $WF(\overline{LTS_a^k})$ implies $WF(\overline{LTS_a^q})$ $(\forall q > k)$ when the system is stable. ∎

4   Tool Support

Figure 3 overviews the main steps of our tool support. Given a set of peer LTSs, we first check as a preprocessing to our approach whether this system is branching synchronizable [34]. Synchronizability is checked comparing the synchronous composition with the 1-bounded asynchronous composition. If the system is synchronizable, the observable behavior for the synchronous and asynchronous composition always remains the same whatever buffer size is chosen. Therefore, the synchronous product can be used for analysis purposes. If the set of peers is not synchronizable, we compute an initial bound k. For that bound, we verify whether the k-bounded asynchronous system is branching equivalent to the $(k+1)$-bounded system. If this is the case, the system is stable for bound k, and properties can be analyzed using that bound. If the equivalence check returns false, we modify k and apply the check again. We repeat the process up to a certain arbitrary bound *kmax* that makes the approach abort inconclusively if attained. All these checks are achieved using compilers, exploration tools, and equivalence checking tools available in CADP [22].

Heuristics and Search Algorithms. Each strategy consists of the computation of an initial bound k and an algorithm calculating the next bound to attempt.

– Strategy #1 starts from bound k equal to one and increment k one by one until obtaining a positive result for the equivalence check or reaching *kmax*.
– Strategy #2 computes the longest sequence of send actions in all peer LTSs, then starts from this number and uses a binary search algorithm. The intuition behind the longest sequence of send actions is that in that case all peers can

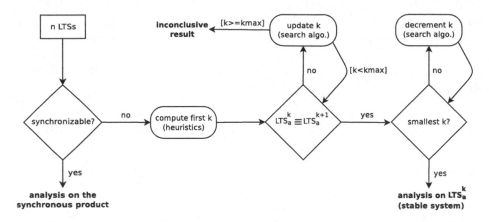

Fig. 3. Methodological aspects

at least send all their messages even if no peer consumes any message from its buffer.

- Strategy #3 uses again the longest sequence of send actions for the initial k, but then progresses by incrementing or decrementing the bound till reaching $kmax$ or the smallest k satisfying stability.
- Strategy #4 computes the maximum between the longest sequence of send actions in all peers and the highest number of send actions destinated to a same peer, and then uses the binary search algorithm (as for #2) for computing the next bounds.
- Strategy #5 uses the same initial k computation as presented for strategy #4, and then increments or decrements the bound till completion of the process as in strategy #3.

Experimental Results. We used a Mac OS laptop running on a 2.3 GHz Intel Core i7 processor with 16 GB of memory and carried out experiments on more than 300 examples. Table 1 presents experimental results for some real-world examples as well as larger (hand-crafted) examples for showing how our approach scales. The table gives for each example the number of peers (P), the total number of states (S) and transitions (T) involved in these peers, the bound k if the system is stable (0 if the synchronous and 1-bounded asynchronous composition are equivalent, and $kmax$ if this upper bound is reached during the analysis process), the size of the k-bounded asynchronous system (minimized modulo branching reduction), and the time for applying the whole process. During our experiments, we used a bound $kmax$ arbitrarily fixed to 10.

Out of the 28 examples presented in the top part of Table 1, 23 can be analyzed using the approach proposed in this paper (10 are synchronizable and 13 are stable). In most cases, LTSs are quite small and computation times reasonable (up to a few minutes). These times increase due to the computation of intermediate state spaces, which grow with the size of the buffer bounds. Examples (29) to (35) show how LTSs and computation time grow mainly with the number of peers.

Table 1. Experimental results

Id	Description	$\|P\|$	$\|S\|/\|T\|$	k	LTS_a^k $\|S\|/\|T\|$	Time (in seconds)				
						#1	#2	#3	#4	#5
(1)	Estelle specification [28]	2	7/9	$kmax$	707/1,751	280	134	302	214	276
(2)	News server [34]	2	9/9	3	14/22	89	180	65	173	85
(3)	Client/server [7]	2	6/10	0	3/4	34				
(4)	CFSM system [28]	2	6/7	$kmax$	393/802	222	107	213	103	212
(5)	Promela program (1) [29]	2	6/6	1	3/4	52	71	67	68	66
(6)	Promela program (2) [30]	2	8/8	$kmax$	275/616	219	107	231	103	228
(7)	Figure 1	3	8/8	1	5/6	87	208	146	208	145
(8)	Web services [20]	3	13/12	0	7/7	44				
(9)	Trade system [17]	3	12/12	0	30/46	44				
(10)	Online stock broker [21]	3	13/16	$kmax$	197/452	>1 h	222	>1 h	223	>1 h
(11)	FTP transfer [6]	3	20/17	2	15/19	91	224	155	215	155
(12)	Client/server [11]	3	14/13	0	8/7	44				
(13)	Mars explorer [8]	3	34/34	2	21/25	93	176	142	170	140
(14)	Online computer sale [14]	3	26/26	0	11/12	69				
(15)	E-museum [12]	3	33/40	3	27/46	146	>1 h	138	243	182
(16)	Client/supplier [10]	3	31/33	0	17/19	44				
(17)	Restaurant service [40]	3	15/16	1	10/12	68				
(18)	Travel agency [39]	3	32/38	0	18/21	44				
(19)	Vending machine [24]	3	15/14	0	8/8	44				
(20)	Travel agency [4]	3	42/57	3	29/42	118	>1 h	113	>1 h	112
(21)	Train station [38]	4	18/18	2	19/26	114	195	137	197	165
(22)	Factory job manager [9]	4	20/20	0	12/15	54				
(23)	Bug report repository [25]	4	12/12	1	7/8	85	221	137	227	136
(24)	Cloud application [27]	4	8/10	$kmax$	26,754/83,200	352	208	339	208	337
(25)	Sanitary agency [37]	4	35/41	3	44/71	144	196	137	196	137
(26)	SQL server [35]	4	32/38	2	22/31	165	195	137	199	170
(27)	SSH protocol [31]	4	26/28	0	16/18	97				
(28)	Booking system [32]	5	45/53	1	27/35	179	285	165	>1 h	>1 h
(29)	Hand-crafted example	5	396/801	4	17,376/86,345	227	>1 h	184	313	189
(30)	——	6	16/18	5	202/559	278	641	188	641	188
(31)	——	7	38/38	6	1,716/6,468	363	763	391	767	393
(32)	——	10	48/47	8	14,904/57,600	624	800	294	804	294
(33)	——	14	85/80	4	19,840/113,520	506	1,449	483	1,442	485
(34)	——	16	106/102	3	22,400/132,400	478	1,620	454	1,621	453
(35)	——	20	128/116	4	80,640/522,480	728	2,194	698	2,183	699

Strategies #2 and #4 are less efficient than the others in terms of performance because binary search may take time before converging to the result and may return high values for k, which implies calculating asynchronous systems with larger state spaces. In contrast, the advantage of binary search is that for non-stable systems, k increases quite fast and quickly reaches $kmax$, see rows (1) and (4) for instance. Strategies #3 and #5 are better than the others in most cases. This gain is not clear for small examples and examples requiring a small buffer bound, but it becomes obvious for examples involving more peers and for those requiring larger buffer bounds, see the hand-crafted examples in Table 1.

Let us focus again on the example presented in Fig. 1 (row (7) in Table 1) in order to illustrate how our approach works in practice using strategy #1. First, we compute the synchronous composition and the 1-bounded asynchronous composition, both are shown in Fig. 4. We can see that these two systems are not equivalent (*i.e.*, not synchronizable) because in the asynchronous composition the client can submit a second request before the server sends its log file to the database. Therefore, we compute the 2-bounded asynchronous composition, which is equivalent to the 1-bounded asynchronous composition. This means that the system is stable from bound 1 and can be analyzed using model checking techniques for that bound and, if the properties are satisfied for that bound, they will be satisfied as well for upper bounds. Note that only send actions are preserved in the asynchronous compositions for comparison purposes. The 1-bounded composition with send and receive actions consists of 16 states and 24 transitions.

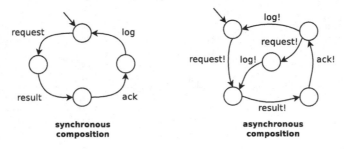

synchronous
composition

asynchronous
composition

Fig. 4. Synchronous (left) and 1-bounded asynchronous (right) compositions

5   Related Work

Brand and Zafiropulo show in [7] that the verification problem for FSMs interacting via (unbounded) FIFO buffers is undecidable. Gouda *et al.* [26] presents sufficient conditions to compute a bound k from which two finite state machines communicating through 1-directional channels are guaranteed to progress indefinitely. Jeron and Jard [28] propose a sufficient condition for testing unboundedness, which can be used as a decision procedure in order to check reachability for CFSMs. Abdulla *et al.* [1] propose some verification techniques for CFSMs. They present a method for performing symbolic forward analysis of unbounded *lossy* channel systems. In [29], the authors present an incomplete boundedness test for communication channels in Promela and UML RT models. They also provide a method to derive *upper bound* estimates for the maximal occupancy of each individual message buffer. Cécé and Finkel [13] focus on the analysis of infinite half-duplex systems and present several (un)decidability results. For instance, they prove that a symbolic representation of the reachability set is computable in polynomial time and show how to use this result to solve several verification problems.

A notion of existential-boundedness was introduced in [23] for communicating automata. The idea is to assume unbounded channels, but to consider only executions that can be rescheduled on bounded ones. Darondeau *et al.* [15] identify a decidable class of systems consisting of non-deterministic communicating processes that can be scheduled while ensuring boundedness of buffers. [16] proposed a causal chain analysis to determine upper bounds on buffer sizes for multi-party sessions with asynchronous communication. Bouajjani and Emmi [5] consider a bounded analysis for message-passing programs, which does not limit the number of communicating processes nor the buffers' size. However, they limit the number of communication cycles. They propose a decision procedure for reachability analysis when programs can be sequentialized. By doing so, program analysis can easily scale while previous related techniques quickly explode.

Compared to all these results, we do not impose any bound on the number of peers, cycles, or buffer bounds. Another main difference is that we do not want to ensure or check (universal) boundedness of the systems under analysis. Contrarily, we are particularly interested in unbounded (yet possibly stable) systems. Existential boundedness in turn assumes structural hypothesis on models, *e.g.*, at most one sending transition and no mix of send/receive actions outgoing from a same state in [15,23], whereas we do not impose any restriction on our LTS models.

In [2], the authors rely on language equivalence and propose a result similar to the stability property introduced here. However, they present this problem as decidable and propose a decision procedure for checking whether a system is stable. We have demonstrated here that the stability problem is undecidable. Since branching bisimulation is a particular case of language equivalence, testing stability is undecidable for language equivalence as well. Moreover, [2] uses LTL logic whereas we consider a finest notion of equivalence in this paper (branching), which allows one to check properties written with ACTL\X logic [33]. The tool support provided in [2] does not provide any result (infinite loop, inconclusive result, or error) for more than half of the examples presented in Table 1.

6   Conclusion

We have presented in this paper a framework for formally analyzing systems communicating via (possibly unbounded) FIFO buffers. This work focuses on cyclic behavioral models, namely Labeled Transition Systems. We have introduced the stability property, which shows that several systems become stable from a specific buffer bound k when focusing on send messages. The stability problem is undecidable in the general case, but for many systems we can determine whether those systems are stable using heuristics, search algorithms, and branching equivalence checking. Experiments showed that many real-world examples satisfy this property and this can be identified in a reasonable time. Model checking techniques can then be used on the asynchronous version of the system with buffers bound to the smallest k satisfying stability. If a stable system satisfies a specific property for that k, the property will be satisfied too if buffer bounds are increased or if buffers are unbounded.

As far as future work is concerned, a first perspective is to investigate whether our results stand or need to be adjusted for different communication models, *e.g.*, when each peer is equipped with one buffer per message type or when each couple of peers in a system is equipped with a specific communication buffer. Many properties on send messages can be formalized using temporal logic and verified using our approach. However, in some cases, one may also want to write properties on receive messages or on both send and receive messages. Thus, we plan to extend our results and define a notion of stability involving not only send actions but also receive actions. A last perspective aims at identifying subclasses of systems preserving the stability property. Such a sufficient condition could be achieved by statically analyzing cycle dependencies.

Acknowledgments. We would like to sincerely thank the anonymous reviewers for their helpful comments on this paper. This work has been supported by the Open-Cloudware project (2012-2015), which is funded by the French *Fonds national pour la Société Numérique* (FSN), and is supported by *Pôles* Minalogic, Systematic, and SCS.

References

1. Abdulla, P.A., Bouajjani, A., Jonsson, B.: On-the-fly analysis of systems with unbounded, lossy FIFO channels. In: Vardi, M.Y. (ed.) CAV 1998. LNCS, vol. 1427, pp. 305–318. Springer, Heidelberg (1998)
2. Basu, S., Bultan, T.: Automatic verification of interactions in asynchronous systems with unbounded buffers. In: Proceedings of ASE 2014, pp. 743–754 (2014)
3. Basu, S., Bultan, T., Ouederni, M.: Deciding choreography realizability. In: Proceedings of the POPL 2012, pp. 191–202. ACM (2012)
4. Bennaceur, A., Chilton, C., Isberner, M., Jonsson, B.: Automated mediator synthesis: combining behavioural and ontological reasoning. In: Hierons, R.M., Merayo, M.G., Bravetti, M. (eds.) SEFM 2013. LNCS, vol. 8137, pp. 274–288. Springer, Heidelberg (2013)
5. Bouajjani, A., Emmi, M.: Bounded phase analysis of message-passing programs. In: Flanagan, C., König, B. (eds.) TACAS 2012. LNCS, vol. 7214, pp. 451–465. Springer, Heidelberg (2012)
6. Bracciali, A., Brogi, A., Canal, C.: A formal approach to component adaptation. J. Softw. Syst. **74**(1), 45–54 (2005)
7. Brand, D., Zafiropulo, P.: On communicating finite-state machines. J. ACM **30**(2), 323–342 (1983)
8. Brogi, A., Popescu, R.: Automated generation of BPEL adapters. In: Dan, A., Lamersdorf, W. (eds.) ICSOC 2006. LNCS, vol. 4294, pp. 27–39. Springer, Heidelberg (2006)
9. Bultan, T., Ferguson, C., Fu, X.: A tool for choreography analysis using collaboration diagrams. In: Proceedings of the ICWS 2009, pp. 856–863. IEEE (2009)
10. Cámara, J., Martín, J.A., Salaün, G., Canal, C., Pimentel, E.: Semi-automatic specification of behavioural service adaptation contracts. Electr. Notes Theor. Comput. Sci. **264**(1), 19–34 (2010)
11. Canal, C., Poizat, P., Salaün, G.: Synchronizing behavioural mismatch in software composition. In: Gorrieri, R., Wehrheim, H. (eds.) FMOODS 2006. LNCS, vol. 4037, pp. 63–77. Springer, Heidelberg (2006)
12. Canal, C., Poizat, P., Salaün, G.: Model-based adaptation of behavioural mismatching components. IEEE Trans. Softw. Eng. **34**(4), 546–563 (2008)

13. Cécé, G., Finkel, A.: Verification of programs with half-duplex communication. Inf. Comput. **202**(2), 166–190 (2005)
14. Cubo, J., Salaün, G., Canal, C., Pimentel, E., Poizat, P.: A model-based approach to the verification and adaptation of WF/.NET components. In: Proceedings of the FACS 2007, vol. 215 of ENTCS, pp. 39–55 (2007)
15. Darondeau, P., Genest, B., Thiagarajan, P.S., Yang, S.: Quasi-static scheduling of communicating tasks. Inf. Comput. **208**(10), 1154–1168 (2010)
16. Deniélou, P.-M., Yoshida, N.: Buffered communication analysis in distributed multiparty sessions. In: Gastin, P., Laroussinie, F. (eds.) CONCUR 2010. LNCS, vol. 6269, pp. 343–357. Springer, Heidelberg (2010)
17. Deniélou, P.-M., Yoshida, N.: Multiparty session types meet communicating automata. In: Seidl, H. (ed.) Programming Languages and Systems. LNCS, vol. 7211, pp. 194–213. Springer, Heidelberg (2012)
18. Finkel, A., McKenzie, P.: Verifying identical communicating processes is undecidable. Theor. Comput. Sci. **174**(1–2), 217–230 (1997)
19. Fokkink, W.: Introduction to Process Algebra. Texts in Theoretical Computer Science, 1st edn. Springer, Heidelberg (2000)
20. X. Fu, T. Bultan, and J. Su. Analysis of Interacting BPEL Web Services. In Proc. of WWW'04, pp. 621–630. ACM Press, (2004)
21. Fu, X., Bultan, T., Su, J.: Conversation protocols: a formalism for specification and verification of reactive electronic services. Theoret. Comput. Sci. **328**(1–2), 19–37 (2004)
22. Garavel, H., Lang, F., Mateescu, R., Serwe, W.: CADP 2010: a toolbox for the construction and analysis of distributed processes. In: Abdulla, P.A., Leino, K.R.M. (eds.) TACAS 2011. LNCS, vol. 6605, pp. 372–387. Springer, Heidelberg (2011)
23. Genest, B., Muscholl, A., Seidl, H., Zeitoun, M.: Infinite-state high-level MSCs: model-checking and realizability. J. Comput. Syst. Sci. **72**(4), 617–647 (2006)
24. Gierds, C., Mooij, A.J., Wolf, K.: Reducing adapter synthesis to controller synthesis. IEEE Trans. Serv. Comput. **5**(1), 72–85 (2012)
25. Gössler, G., Salaün, G.: Realizability of choreographies for services interacting asynchronously. In: Arbab, F., Ölveczky, P.C. (eds.) FACS 2011. LNCS, vol. 7253, pp. 151–167. Springer, Heidelberg (2012)
26. Gouda, M.G., Manning, E.G., Yu, Y.-T.: On the progress of communications between two finite state machines. Inf. Control **63**(3), 200–216 (1984)
27. Güdemann, M., Salaün, G., Ouederni, M.: Counterexample guided synthesis of monitors for realizability enforcement. In: Chakraborty, S., Mukund, M. (eds.) ATVA 2012. LNCS, vol. 7561, pp. 238–253. Springer, Heidelberg (2012)
28. Jéron, T., Jard, C.: Testing for unboundedness of FIFO channels. Theor. Comput. Sci. **113**(1), 93–117 (1993)
29. Leue, S., Mayr, R., Wei, W.: A scalable incomplete test for message buffer overflow in promela models. In: Graf, S., Mounier, L. (eds.) SPIN 2004. LNCS, vol. 2989, pp. 216–233. Springer, Heidelberg (2004)
30. Leue, S., Ştefănescu, A., Wei, W.: Dependency analysis for control flow cycles in reactive communicating processes. In: Havelund, K., Majumdar, R. (eds.) SPIN 2008. LNCS, vol. 5156, pp. 176–195. Springer, Heidelberg (2008)
31. Martín, J.A., Pimentel, E.: Contracts for security adaptation. J. Log. Algebraic Program. **80**(3–5), 154–179 (2011)
32. Mateescu, R., Poizat, P., Salaün, G.: Adaptation of service protocols using process algebra and on-the-fly reduction techniques. In: Bouguettaya, A., Krueger, I., Margaria, T. (eds.) ICSOC 2008. LNCS, vol. 5364, pp. 84–99. Springer, Heidelberg (2008)

33. Nicola, R.D., Vaandrager, F.W.: Action versus state based logics for transition systems. In: Guessarian, Irène (ed.) LITP 1990. LNCS, vol. 469, pp. 407–419. Springer, Heidelberg (1990)
34. Ouederni, M., Salaün, G., Bultan, T.: Compatibility checking for asynchronously communicating software. In: Fiadeiro, J.L., Liu, Z., Xue, J. (eds.) FACS 2013. LNCS, vol. 8348, pp. 310–328. Springer, Heidelberg (2014)
35. Poizat, P., Salaün, G.: Adaptation of open component-based systems. In: Bonsangue, M.M., Johnsen, E.B. (eds.) FMOODS 2007. LNCS, vol. 4468, pp. 141–156. Springer, Heidelberg (2007)
36. Milner, R.: Communication and Concurrency. Prentice-Hall Inc, Upper Saddle River (1989)
37. Salaün, G., Bordeaux, L., Schaerf, M.: Describing and reasoning on web services using process algebra. In: Proceedings of the ICWS 2004, pp. 43–50. IEEE Computer Society (2004)
38. Salaün, G., Bultan, T., Roohi, N.: Realizability of choreographies using process algebra encodings. IEEE Trans. Serv. Comput. **5**(3), 290–304 (2012)
39. Seguel, R., Eshuis, R., Grefen, P.W.P.J.: Generating minimal protocol adaptors for loosely coupled services. In: Proceedings of the ICWS 2010, pp. 417–424. IEEE CS (2010)
40. van der Aalst, W.M.P., Mooij, A.J., Stahl, C., Wolf, K.: Service interaction: patterns, formalization, and analysis. In: Bernardo, M., Padovani, L., Zavattaro, G. (eds.) SFM 2009. LNCS, vol. 5569, pp. 42–88. Springer, Heidelberg (2009)
41. van Glabbeek, R.J., Weijland, W.P.: Branching time and abstraction in bisimulation semantics. J. ACM **43**(3), 555–600 (1996)

Symbolic Game Semantics for Model Checking Program Families

Aleksandar S. Dimovski[(✉)]

IT University of Copenhagen, Copenhagen, Denmark
adim@itu.dk

Abstract. Program families can produce a (potentially huge) number of related programs from a common code base. Many such programs are safety critical. However, most verification techniques are designed to work on the level of single programs, and thus are too costly to apply to the entire program family. In this paper, we propose an efficient game semantics based approach for verifying open program families, i.e. program families with free (undefined) identifiers. We use symbolic representation of algorithmic game semantics, where concrete values are replaced with symbolic ones. In this way, we can compactly represent program families with infinite integers as so-called (finite-state) featured symbolic automata. Specifically designed model checking algorithms are then employed to verify safety of all programs from a family at once and pinpoint those programs that are unsafe (respectively, safe). We present a prototype tool implementing this approach, and we illustrate it with several examples.

1 Introduction

Software Product Line (SPL) [5] is an efficient method for systematic development of a family of related programs, known as *variants* (*valid products*), from a common code base. Each variant is specified in terms of *features* (statically configured options) selected for that particular variant. While there are different implementation strategies, many popular SPLs from system software (e.g. Linux kernel) and embedded software (e.g. cars, phones) domains [18] are implemented using a simple form of two staged computation in preprocessor style, where the programming language is extended with *conditional compilation* constructs (e.g. #ifdef annotations from C preprocessor). At build time, the program family is first configured and a variant describing a particular product is derived by selecting a set of features relevant for it, and only then the derived variant is compiled or interpreted. One of the advantages of preprocessors is that they are mostly independent of the object language and can be applied across paradigms.

Benefits from using program families (SPLs) are multiple: productivity gains, shorter time to market, and greater market coverage. Unfortunately, the complexity created by program families (variability) also leads to problems. The simplest *brute-force approach* to verify such program families is to use a preprocessor to generate all valid products of an SPL, and then apply an existing

© Springer International Publishing Switzerland 2016
D. Bošnački and A. Wijs (Eds.): SPIN 2016, LNCS 9641, pp. 19–37, 2016.
DOI: 10.1007/978-3-319-32582-8_2

single-program verification technique to each resulting product. However, this approach is very costly and often infeasible in practice since the number of possible products is exponential in the number of features. Therefore, we seek for new approaches that rely on finding compact mathematical structures, which take the variability within the family into account, and on which specialized variability-aware verification algorithms can be applied.

In this work, we address the above challenges by using game semantics models. Game semantics [1,14] is a technique for *compositional* modelling of programming languages, which gives models that are fully abstract (sound and complete) with respect to observational equivalence of programs. It has mathematical elegance of denotational semantics, and step-by-step modelling of computation in the style of operational semantics. In the last decade, a new line of research has been pursued, known as *algorithmic game semantics*, where game semantics models are given certain kinds of concrete automata-theoretic representations [8,12,16]. Thus, they can serve as a basis for software model checking and program analysis. The most distinctive property of game semantics is compositionality, i.e. the models are generated inductively on the structure of programs. This is the key to achieve *scalable (modular)* verification, where a larger program is broken down into smaller program fragments which can be modeled and verified independently. Moreover, game semantics yields a very accurate model for any open program with free (undefined) identifiers such as calls to library functions.

In [9], a symbolic representation of algorithmic game semantics has been proposed for second-order Idealized Algol (IA_2). It redefines the (standard) regular-language representation [12] at a more abstract level by using symbolic values instead of concrete ones. This allows us to give a compact representation of programs with infinite integers by using finite-state symbolic automata. Here, we extend the symbolic representation of game semantics models, obtaining so-called *featured symbolic automata*, which are used to compactly represent and verify safety properties of program families.

Motivating Example. To better illustrate the issues we are addressing in this work, we now present a motivating example. Table 1 shows a simple program family M that contains two #if commands. They increase and decrease the local variable x by the value of a non-local expression n, depending on the enabled features. The program uses features $\mathbb{F} = \{A, B\}$ and we assume it has the following set of valid configurations $\mathbb{K} = \{A \wedge B, A \wedge \neg B, \neg A \wedge B, \neg A \wedge \neg B\}$. For each valid configuration a different single program can be generated by appropriately resolving the #if commands. For example, the single program corresponding to the valid configuration $A \wedge B$ will have both features A and B enabled (set to true), which will make both assignment commands in #if-s to be present in the program. Programs for $A \wedge \neg B$ and for $\neg A \wedge B$ are different in one assignment command only, the earlier has the feature A enabled and the command $x := x + n$, whereas the latter has the feature B enabled and the command $x := x - n$. Programs corresponding to all valid configurations are

Table 1. Motivating example: the program family M and its valid products

Program family M:	Config. $A \wedge B$:
$n : \exp \mathsf{int}^n, abort : \mathsf{com}^{abort} \vdash_{\{A,B\}}$	$n : \exp \mathsf{int}^n, abort : \mathsf{com}^{abort} \vdash$
$\mathsf{new}_{\mathsf{int}}\, x := 0 \,\mathsf{in}$	$\mathsf{new}_{\mathsf{int}}\, x := 0 \,\mathsf{in}$
$\texttt{\#if}\,(A)\,\mathsf{then}\, x := x + n;$	$x := x + n;$
$\texttt{\#if}\,(B)\,\mathsf{then}\, x := x - n;$	$x := x - n;$
$\mathsf{if}\,(x = 1)\,\mathsf{then}\, abort : \mathsf{com}$	$\mathsf{if}\,(x = 1)\,\mathsf{then}\, abort : \mathsf{com}$
Configs. $A \wedge \neg B\ (\neg A \wedge B)$:	
$n : \exp \mathsf{int}^n, abort : \mathsf{com}^{abort} \vdash$	Config. $\neg A \wedge \neg B$:
$\mathsf{new}_{\mathsf{int}}\, x := 0 \,\mathsf{in}$	$n : \exp \mathsf{int}^n, abort : \mathsf{com}^{abort} \vdash$
$x := x + n;\ (x := x - n;\ )$	$\mathsf{new}_{\mathsf{int}}\, x := 0 \,\mathsf{in}$
$\mathsf{if}\,(x = 1)\,\mathsf{then}\, abort : \mathsf{com}$	$\mathsf{if}\,(x = 1)\,\mathsf{then}\, abort : \mathsf{com}$

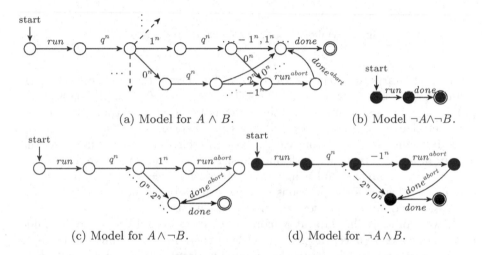

(a) Model for $A \wedge B$.

(b) Model $\neg A \wedge \neg B$.

(c) Model for $A \wedge \neg B$.

(d) Model for $\neg A \wedge B$.

Fig. 1. Automata for valid products of M.

illustrated in Table 1. Thus, to verify our family M we need to build and analyze models of four distinct, but very similar, programs.

We show in Fig. 1, the standard regular-language representation of game semantics for these four programs where concrete values are used [12]. We can see that we obtain regular-languages with infinite summations (i.e. infinite-state automata), since we use infinite integers as data type. Hence, they can be used for automatic verification only if the attention is restricted to finite data types. For example, the model for the product $A \wedge \neg B$ in Fig. 1c illustrates the observable interactions of this term of type com with its environment consisting of free identifiers n and $abort$. So in the model are only represented moves associated with types of n and $abort$ (which are tagged with superscripts n and $abort$, respectively) as well as with the top-level type com of this term. The environment

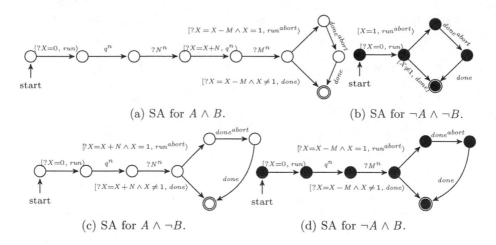

(a) SA for $A \wedge B$. (b) SA for $\neg A \wedge \neg B$.

(c) SA for $A \wedge \neg B$. (d) SA for $\neg A \wedge B$.

Fig. 2. Symbolic automata for valid products of M.

(Opponent) starts the execution of the term by playing the move *run*; when the term (Player) asks for the value of n with the move q^n, the environment can provide any integer as answer. If the answer is 1, the *abort* is run; otherwise the term terminates successfully by reaching the accepting state (shown as double circle in the model). Note that each move represents an observable action that a term of a given type can perform. Thus, for commands we have a move *run* to initiate a command and a move *done* to signal successful termination of a command, whereas for expressions we have a move q to ask for the value of an expression and an integer move to answer the question q.

If we represent the data at a more abstract level and use symbolic values instead of concrete ones, the game models of these four programs can be represented more compactly by finite-state symbolic automata (SA) as shown in Fig. 2. Every letter (label of transition) contains a move and a Boolean condition which represents a constraint that needs to be fulfilled in order for the corresponding move to be performed. Note that so-called *input symbols* of the form $?N$ are used for generating new fresh symbolic names, which bind all occurrences of the symbol N that follow in the play until a new input symbol $?N$ is met. The symbol X is used to keep track of the current value of the local variable x. For example, the answer to the question q^n asked by the term for $A \wedge \neg B$ in Fig. 2c now is a newly instantiated symbol N. If the value of N is 1, the *abort* command is run. We say that "$X_1 = 0 \wedge X_2 = X_1 + N \wedge X_2 = 1$" is a play condition for the play in Fig. 2c: $[X_1 = 0, run\rangle \cdot q^n \cdot N^n \cdot [X_2 = X_1 + N \wedge X_2 = 1, run^{abort}\rangle \cdot done^{abort} \cdot done$. This play is obtained from: $[?X = 0, run\rangle \cdot q^n \cdot ?N^n \cdot [?X = X + N \wedge X = 1, run^{abort}\rangle \cdot done^{abort} \cdot done$, after instantiating its input symbols with fresh symbolic names. We say that one play is *feasible*, only if its play condition is satisfiable (i.e. there exist concrete assignments to symbols that make that condition *true*). This can be checked by calling an SMT solver.

Now, by further enriching letters with feature expressions (propositional formulae defined over the set of features), we can give a more compact single representation of the above related programs to exploit the similarities between them. The feature expression associated with a letter denotes for which valid configurations that letter (in fact, the corresponding move) is feasible. Thus, we can represent all products of M by one compact featured symbolic automaton (FSA) as shown in Fig. 3, which is variability-aware extension of the symbolic automata in Fig. 2. From this model, by exploring all states we can determine for each valid product whether an unsafe behaviour (one that contains *abort* moves) can be exercised. If we find such an unsafe play for a valid product, then we need to check that the play is feasible. If its play condition is satisfiable, the SMT solver will return concrete assignments to symbols which make that condition *true*. In this way, we will generate a concrete counterexample for a valid product. In our example, we can determine that the product $\neg A \wedge \neg B$ is safe, whereas products $A \wedge B$, $A \wedge \neg B$, and $\neg A \wedge B$ are unsafe with concrete counterexamples: $run \cdot q^n \cdot 1^n \cdot q^n \cdot 0^n \cdot run^{abort} \cdot done^{abort} \cdot done$, $run \cdot q^n \cdot 1^n \cdot run^{abort} \cdot done^{abort} \cdot done$, and $run \cdot q^n \cdot -1^n \cdot run^{abort} \cdot done^{abort} \cdot done$, respectively.

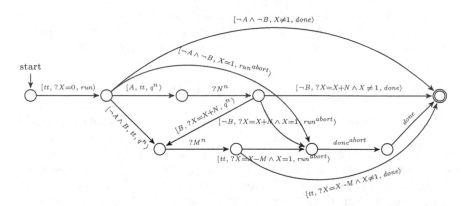

Fig. 3. Featured symbolic automaton for the program family M.

Remark. Alternatively, a program family can be verified by generating a so-called family *simulator* [2], which is a single program where `#if` commands (compile-time variability) are replaced with normal `if` commands and available features are encoded as free (undefined) identifiers. Then the classical (single-system) model checking algorithms [8,9] can be used to verify the generated simulator, since it represents a single program. In case of violation, we will obtain a single counterexample that corresponds to some unsafe products. However, this answer is incomplete (limited) for program families since there might be some safe products and also there might be other unsafe products with different counterexamples. Hence, no conclusive results for all products in a family are reported using this approach. For example, the simulator for the family M is:

n : exp int, *abort* : com, A : exp bool, B : exp bool $\vdash$ new$_{\mathsf{int}}$ $x := 0$ in
    if (A) then $x := x + n$; if (B) then $x := x - n$; if $(x = 1)$ then abort : com

If we generate a (game) model for this term and verify it using algorithms in [8,9], we will obtain a counterexample corresponding only to the product $A \wedge \neg B$.

This leads us to propose an approach that solves the general family-based model checking problem: determine for each product whether or not it is safe, and provide a counterexample for each unsafe product.

Contributions. In this paper, we make the following contributions:

- We introduce a compact symbolic representation, called *featured symbolic automata*, which represent game semantics of so-called *annotative* program families. That is, program families which are implemented by annotating program parts that vary using preprocessor directives.
- We propose specifically designed (family-based) model checking algorithms for verifying featured symbolic automata that represent program families. This allows us to verify safety for all products of a family at once (in a single execution), and to pinpoint the products that are unsafe (resp., safe).
- We describe a prototype tool implementing the above algorithms, and we perform an evaluation to demonstrate the improvements over the brute-force approach where all valid products are verified independently one by one.

2   The Language for Program Families

The standard approach in semantics community is to use meta-languages for the description of certain kinds of computational behaviour. The semantic model is defined for a meta-language, and a real programming language (C, ML, etc.) can be studied by translating it into this meta-language and using the induced model. We begin this section by presenting a meta-language for which algorithmic game semantics can be defined, and then we introduce static variability into it.

Writing Single Programs. We consider the meta-language: Idealized Algol (IA) introduced by Reynolds in [17]. It is a compact language which combines call-by-name typed λ-calculus with the fundamental imperative features and locally-scoped variables. We work with its second-order recursion-free fragment (IA$_2$ for short), because game semantics of this fragment has algorithmic properties.

The data types D are integers and booleans ($D ::= \mathsf{int} \mid \mathsf{bool}$). We have base types B ($B ::= \mathsf{exp} D \mid \mathsf{com} \mid \mathsf{var} D$) and first-order function types T ($T ::= B \mid B \rightarrow T$). The *syntax* of the language is given by:

$$M ::= x \mid v \mid \mathsf{skip} \mid \mathsf{diverge} \mid M \text{ op } M \mid M;\ M \mid \mathsf{if}\ M\ \mathsf{then}\ M\ \mathsf{else}\ M \mid \mathsf{while}\ M\ \mathsf{do}\ M$$
$$\mid M := M \mid !M \mid \mathsf{new}_D\ x := v\ \mathsf{in}\ M \mid \mathsf{mkvar}_D MM \mid \lambda\,x.M \mid MM$$

where v ranges over constants of type D, which includes integers (n) and boolean (tt, ff). The standard arithmetic-logic operations op are employed, as well as the usual imperative and functional constructs. *Well-typed terms* are given by typing judgements of the form $\Gamma \vdash M : T$, where Γ is a type *context* consisting of a finite number of typed free identifiers. Typing rules are given in [1, 17].

The *operational semantics* is defined by a big-step reduction relation: $\Gamma \vdash M, s \Longrightarrow V, s'$, where $\Gamma \vdash M : T$ is a term in which all free identifiers from Γ are variables, and s, s' represent the *state* before and after reduction. The state is a function assigning data values to the variables in Γ. Canonical forms (values) are defined by $V ::= x \mid v \mid \lambda x.M \mid \mathsf{skip} \mid \mathsf{mkvar}_D MN$. Reduction rules are standard (see [1, 17] for details). If M is a closed term (with no free identifiers) of type com, then we abbreviate the relation $M, \emptyset \Longrightarrow \mathsf{skip}, \emptyset$ with $M \Downarrow$. We say that a term $\Gamma \vdash M : T$ is an *approximate* of a term $\Gamma \vdash N : T$, written $\Gamma \vdash M \sqsubseteq N$, if and only if for all terms-with-hole $C[-] : \mathsf{com}$, such that $\vdash C[M] : \mathsf{com}$ and $\vdash C[N] : \mathsf{com}$ are well-typed closed terms of type com, if $C[M] \Downarrow$ then $C[N] \Downarrow$. If two terms approximate each other they are considered *observationally-equivalent*, denoted by $\Gamma \vdash M \cong N$.

Writing Program Families. We use a simple form of two-staged computation to lift IA_2 from describing single programs to program families. The first stage is controlled by a *configuration* k, which describes the set of features that are enabled in the build process. A finite set of Boolean variables describes the available features $\mathbb{F} = \{A_1, \ldots, A_n\}$. A configuration k is a truth assignment (a mapping from $\mathbb{F}$ to $\mathsf{bool} = \{tt, ff\}$) which gives a truth value to any feature. If a feature $A \in \mathbb{F}$ is enabled (included) for the configuration k, then $k(A) = tt$. Any configuration k can also be encoded as a conjunction of propositional formulas: $k(A_1) \cdot A_1 \wedge \ldots \wedge k(A_n) \cdot A_n$, where $tt \cdot A = A$ and $ff \cdot A = \neg A$. We write $\mathbb{K}$ for the set of all *valid configurations* defined over $\mathbb{F}$ for a program family. The set of valid configurations is typically described by a feature model [5, 18], but in this work we disregard syntactic representations of the set $\mathbb{K}$.

The language $\overline{IA_2}$ extends IA_2 with a new compile-time conditional term for encoding multiple variations of a program, i.e. different valid products. The new term "#if ϕ then M else M'" contains a presence condition ϕ over features $\mathbb{F}$, such that if ϕ is satisfied by a configuration $k \in \mathbb{K}$ then M will be included in the resulting product, otherwise M' will be included. The new syntax is:

$$M ::= \ldots \mid \text{\#if } \phi \text{ then } M \text{ else } M' \qquad \phi ::= A \in \mathbb{F} \mid \neg\phi \mid \phi \wedge \phi$$

We add a new syntactic category of feature expressions (i.e. propositional logic formulae over $\mathbb{F}$), $FeatExp(\mathbb{F})$, ranged over by ϕ, to write compile-time conditions over features $\mathbb{F}$. *Well-typed term families* are given by typing judgements of the form $\Gamma \vdash_{\mathbb{F}} M : T$, where $\mathbb{F}$ is a set of available features[1]. Typing rules are those of IA_2 extended with a rule for the new construct:

$$\frac{\Gamma \vdash M : T}{\Gamma \vdash_{\mathbb{F}} M : T} \qquad \frac{\Gamma \vdash_{\mathbb{F}} M : T \qquad \Gamma \vdash_{\mathbb{F}} M' : T \qquad \phi : FeatExp(\mathbb{F})}{\Gamma \vdash_{\mathbb{F}} \text{\#if } \phi \text{ then } M \text{ else } M' : T}$$

---

[1] For the work in this paper, we assume that the set of features $\mathbb{F}$ is fixed and all features are globally scoped.

The semantics of $\overline{\mathrm{IA_2}}$ has two stages: first, given a configuration k compute a single $\mathrm{IA_2}$ term without #if-s; second, evaluate the $\mathrm{IA_2}$ term using the standard $\mathrm{IA_2}$ semantics. The first stage of computation (also called *projection*) is a simple preprocessor from $\overline{\mathrm{IA_2}}$ to $\mathrm{IA_2}$ specified by the projection function π_k mapping an $\overline{\mathrm{IA_2}}$ term family into a single $\mathrm{IA_2}$ term corresponding to the configuration $k \in \mathbb{K}$. The projection π_k copies all basic terms of $\overline{\mathrm{IA_2}}$ that are also $\mathrm{IA_2}$ terms, and recursively pre-processes all sub-terms of compound terms. For example, $\pi_k(\mathsf{skip}) = \mathsf{skip}$ and $\pi_k(M; M') = \pi_k(M); \pi_k(M')$. The interesting case is for the compilation-time conditional term, where one of the two alternative branches is included in the generated valid product depending on whether the configuration k satisfies (entails) the feature expression ϕ, denoted as $k \models \phi$.

We have: $\pi_k(\#\mathsf{if}\ \phi\ \mathsf{then}\ M\ \mathsf{else}\ M') = \begin{cases} \pi_k(M) & \text{if } k \models \phi \\ \pi_k(M') & \text{if } k \not\models \phi \end{cases}$. The variant of a

term family $\Gamma \vdash_\mathbb{F} M : T$ corresponding to the configuration $k \in \mathbb{K}$ can now be defined as: $\Gamma \vdash \pi_k(M) : T$.

3   Symbolic Representation of Game Semantics

In this section we first recall symbolic representation of algorithmic game semantics for $\mathrm{IA_2}$ [9], and then we extend this representation for $\overline{\mathrm{IA_2}}$.

3.1   Symbolic Models of $\mathrm{IA_2}$

Let *Sym* be a countable set of symbolic names, ranged over by upper case letters X, Y, Z. For any finite $W \subseteq Sym$, the function $new(W)$ returns a minimal symbolic name which does not occur in W, and sets $W := W \cup new(W)$. A minimal symbolic name not in W is the one which occurs earliest in a fixed enumeration $X_1, X_2, \dots$ of all possible symbolic names. Let *Exp* be a set of expressions, ranged over by e, inductively generated by using data values ($v \in D$), symbols ($X \in Sym$), and standard arithmetic-logic operations (op). We use a to range over arithmetic expressions (*AExp*) and b over boolean expressions (*BExp*).

Let $\mathcal{A}$ be an alphabet of letters. We define a *symbolic alphabet* $\mathcal{A}^{sym}$ induced by $\mathcal{A}$ as follows: $\mathcal{A}^{sym} = \mathcal{A} \cup \{?X, e \mid X \in Sym, e \in Exp\}$. The letters of the form $?X$ are called *input symbols*. They represent a mechanism for generating new symbolic names, i.e. $?X$ means $\mathsf{let}\ X = new(W)\ \mathsf{in}\ X\ \dots$. We use α to range over $\mathcal{A}^{sym}$. Next we define a *guarded alphabet* $\mathcal{A}^{gu}$ induced by $\mathcal{A}$ as the set of pairs of boolean conditions and symbolic letters: $\mathcal{A}^{gu} = \{[b, \alpha\rangle \mid b \in BExp, \alpha \in \mathcal{A}^{sym}\}$. A guarded letter $[b, \alpha\rangle$ means that α occurs only if b evaluates to true, i.e. $if (b = tt)\ then\ \alpha\ else\ \emptyset$. We use β to range over $\mathcal{A}^{gu}$. We will often write only α for the guarded letter $[tt, \alpha\rangle$. A word $[b_1, \alpha_1\rangle \cdot [b_2, \alpha_2\rangle \dots [b_n, \alpha_n\rangle$ over $\mathcal{A}^{gu}$ can be represented as a pair $[b, w\rangle$, where $b = b_1 \wedge b_2 \wedge \dots \wedge b_n$ is a boolean condition and $w = \alpha_1 \cdot \alpha_2 \dots \alpha_n$ is a word of symbolic letters.

Now, we show how $\mathrm{IA_2}$ terms in β-normal form are interpreted by symbolic regular languages and automata, which will be specified by extended regular expressions R. Each type T is interpreted by a guarded alphabet of moves $\mathcal{A}^{gu}_{[\![T]\!]}$ induced by $\mathcal{A}_{[\![T]\!]}$, which is defined as follows:

$$\mathcal{A}_{[\![\exp D]\!]}=\{q\}\cup\mathcal{A}_{[\![D]\!]}, \mathcal{A}_{[\![\mathsf{com}]\!]}=\{run, done\}, \mathcal{A}_{[\![\mathsf{var}D]\!]}=\{write(a), read, ok, a\mid a\in\mathcal{A}_{[\![D]\!]}\}$$

$$\mathcal{A}^{gu}_{[\![B_1^{\langle 1\rangle}\to\ldots\to B_k^{\langle k\rangle}\to B]\!]} = \sum_{1\leq i\leq k} \mathcal{A}^{gu\,\langle i\rangle}_{[\![B_i]\!]} + \mathcal{A}^{gu}_{[\![B]\!]}$$

where $\mathcal{A}_{[\![\mathsf{int}]\!]} = \mathbb{Z}$, $\mathcal{A}_{[\![\mathsf{bool}]\!]} = \{tt, f\!f\}$, and $+$ denotes a disjoint union of alphabets. Function types are tagged by a superscript $\langle i\rangle$ to keep record from which type, i.e. which component of the disjoint union, each move comes from. The letters in the alphabet $\mathcal{A}_{[\![T]\!]}$ represent the *moves* (observable actions) that a term of type T can perform. Each of moves is either a *question* (a demand for information) or an *answer* (a supply of information). For expressions in $\mathcal{A}_{[\![\exp D]\!]}$, there is a *question* move q to ask for the value of the expression, and values from $\mathcal{A}_{[\![D]\!]}$ to *answer* the question. For commands, there is a *question* move run to initiate a command, and an *answer* move $done$ to signal successful termination of a command. For variables, there are *question* moves for writing to the variable, $write(a)$, which are acknowledged by the *answer* move ok; and there is a *question* move $read$ for reading from the variable, which is *answered* by a value from $\mathcal{A}_{[\![D]\!]}$.

For any (β-normal) term, we define a (symbolic) regular-language which represents its game semantics, i.e. its set of complete plays. Every complete play represents the observable effects of a completed computation of the given term. It is given as a guarded word $[b, w\rangle$, where b is also called *play condition*. Assumptions about a play (computation) to be feasible are recorded in its play condition. For infeasible plays, the play condition is inconsistent (unsatisfiable), thus no assignment of concrete values to symbolic names exists that makes the play condition true. If the play condition is inconsistent, this play is discarded from the final model of the corresponding term. The regular expression for $\Gamma \vdash M : T$, denoted as $[\![\Gamma \vdash M : T]\!]$, is defined over the guarded alphabet: $\mathcal{A}^{gu}_{[\![\Gamma\vdash T]\!]} = \left(\sum_{x:T'\in\Gamma} \mathcal{A}^{gu\,\langle x\rangle}_{[\![T']\!]}\right) + \mathcal{A}^{gu}_{[\![T]\!]}$, where moves corresponding to types of free identifiers are tagged with their names.

The representation of constants is standard:

$$[\![\Gamma\vdash v:\exp D]\!]=q\cdot v \qquad [\![\Gamma\vdash\mathsf{skip}:\mathsf{com}]\!]=run\cdot done \qquad [\![\Gamma\vdash\mathsf{diverge}:\mathsf{com}]\!]=\emptyset$$

Free identifiers are represented by the so-called copy-cat regular expressions, which contain all possible behaviours of terms of that type. For example:

$$[\![\Gamma, x : \exp D_1^{\langle x,1\rangle} \to \ldots \exp D_k^{\langle x,k\rangle} \to \exp D^{\langle x\rangle} \vdash x : \exp D_1^{\langle 1\rangle} \to \ldots \exp D_k^{\langle k\rangle} \to \exp D]\!]$$

$$= q\cdot q^{\langle x\rangle}\cdot\left(\sum_{1\leq i\leq k} q^{\langle x,i\rangle}\cdot q^{\langle i\rangle}.?Z^{\langle i\rangle}\cdot Z^{\langle x,i\rangle}\right)^*.?X^{\langle x\rangle}\cdot X$$

When a call-by-name non-local function x is called, it may evaluate any of its arguments, zero or more times, in an arbitrary order and then it returns any allowable answer from its result type. Note that whenever an input symbol $?X$ (let $X = new(W)$ in X ...) is met in a play, the mechanism for fresh symbol

Table 2. Symbolic representations of some language constructs

$$
\begin{aligned}
&[\![\mathsf{op} : \exp D_1^{\langle 1 \rangle} \times \exp D_2^{\langle 2 \rangle} \to \exp D]\!] = q \cdot q^{\langle 1 \rangle} .? Z^{\langle 1 \rangle} \cdot q^{\langle 2 \rangle} .? Z'^{\langle 2 \rangle} \cdot (Z \text{ op } Z') \\
&[\![; : \mathsf{com}^{\langle 1 \rangle} \times \mathsf{com}^{\langle 2 \rangle} \to \mathsf{com}]\!] = run \cdot run^{\langle 1 \rangle} \cdot done^{\langle 1 \rangle} \cdot run^{\langle 2 \rangle} \cdot done^{\langle 2 \rangle} \cdot done \\
&[\![\mathsf{if} : \mathsf{expbool}^{\langle 1 \rangle} \times \mathsf{com}^{\langle 2 \rangle} \times \mathsf{com}^{\langle 3 \rangle} \to \mathsf{com}]\!] = [tt, run) \cdot [tt, q^{\langle 1 \rangle}) \cdot [tt, ?Z^{\langle 1 \rangle}) \cdot \\
&\qquad\qquad ([Z, run^{\langle 2 \rangle}) \cdot [tt, done^{\langle 2 \rangle}) + [\neg Z, run^{\langle 3 \rangle}) \cdot [tt, done^{\langle 3 \rangle})) \cdot [tt, done) \\
&[\![\mathsf{while} : \mathsf{expbool}^{\langle 1 \rangle} \times \mathsf{com}^{\langle 2 \rangle} \to \mathsf{com}]\!] = [tt, run) \cdot [tt, q^{\langle 1 \rangle}) \cdot [tt, ?Z^{\langle 1 \rangle}) \cdot \\
&\qquad\qquad ([Z, run^{\langle 2 \rangle}) \cdot [tt, done^{\langle 2 \rangle}) \cdot [tt, q^{\langle 1 \rangle}) \cdot [tt, ?Z^{\langle 1 \rangle}))^* \cdot [\neg Z, done) \\
&[\![:= : \mathsf{var} D^{\langle 1 \rangle} \times \exp D^{\langle 2 \rangle} \to \mathsf{com}]\!] = run \cdot q^{\langle 2 \rangle} .? Z^{\langle 2 \rangle} \cdot write(Z)^{\langle 1 \rangle} \cdot ok^{\langle 1 \rangle} \cdot done \\
&[\![! : \mathsf{var} D^{\langle 1 \rangle} \to \exp D]\!] = q \cdot read^{\langle 1 \rangle} .? Z^{\langle 1 \rangle} \cdot Z \\
&\mathsf{cell}_v^{\langle x \rangle} = ([?X{=}v, read^{\langle x \rangle}) \cdot X^{\langle x \rangle})^* \cdot (write(?X)^{\langle x \rangle} \cdot ok^{\langle x \rangle} \cdot (read^{\langle x \rangle} \cdot X^{\langle x \rangle})^*)^*
\end{aligned}
$$

generation is used to instantiate it with a new fresh symbolic name, which binds all occurrences of X that follow in the play until a new $?X$ is met which overrides the previous one. For example, consider a non-local function $f : \mathsf{expint}^{\langle 1 \rangle} \to \mathsf{expint}$. Its symbolic model is: $q \cdot q^{\langle f \rangle} \cdot (q^{\langle f, 1 \rangle} \cdot q^{\langle 1 \rangle} .? Z^{\langle 1 \rangle} \cdot Z^{\langle f, 1 \rangle})^* .? X^{\langle f \rangle} \cdot X$. The play corresponding to f which evaluates its argument two times after instantiating its input symbols is given as: $q \cdot q^{\langle f \rangle} \cdot q^{\langle f, 1 \rangle} \cdot q^{\langle 1 \rangle} \cdot Z_1^{\langle 1 \rangle} \cdot Z_1^{\langle f, 1 \rangle} \cdot q^{\langle f, 1 \rangle} \cdot q^{\langle 1 \rangle} \cdot Z_2^{\langle 1 \rangle} \cdot Z_2^{\langle f, 1 \rangle} \cdot X^{\langle f \rangle} \cdot X$, where Z_1 and Z_2 are two different symbolic names used to denote values of the argument when it is evaluated the first and the second time, respectively.

The representations of some language constructs are given in Table 2. Note that letter conditions different than tt occur only in plays corresponding to "if" and "while" constructs. In the case of "if" command, when the value of the first argument given by the symbol Z is true then its second argument is run, otherwise if $\neg Z$ is true then its third argument is run. A composite term $\mathsf{c}(M_1, \ldots, M_k)$ built out of a language construct "c" and subterms $M_1, \ldots, M_k$ is interpreted by composing the regular expressions for $M_1, \ldots, M_k$ and the regular expression for "c". Composition of regular expressions ($\S$) is defined as "parallel composition plus hiding in CSP" [1]. Conditions of the shared (interacting) guarded letters in the composition are conjoined, along with the condition that their symbolic letters are equal [9]. The $\mathsf{cell}_v^{\langle x \rangle}$ regular expression in Table 2 is used to impose the good variable behaviour on a local variable x introduced using $\mathsf{new}_D \, x := v$ in M. Note that v is the initial value of x, and X is a symbol used to track the current value of x. The $\mathsf{cell}_v^{\langle x \rangle}$ plays the most recently written value in x in response to *read*, or if no value has been written yet then answers *read* with the initial value v. The model $[\![\mathsf{new}_D \, x := v \text{ in } M]\!]$ is obtained by constraining the model of M, $[\![\mathsf{new}_D \, x \vdash M]\!]$, only to those plays where x exhibits good variable behaviour described by $\mathsf{cell}_v^{\langle x \rangle}$, and then by deleting (hiding) all moves associated with x since x is a local variable and so not visible outside of the term [9].

The following formal results are proved in [9]. We define an *effective alphabet* of a regular expression to be the set of all letters that appear in the language denoted by that regular expression. The effective alphabet of a regular expression representing any term $\Gamma \vdash M : T$ contains only a *finite subset* of letters from $\mathcal{A}^{gu}_{[\![\Gamma \vdash T]\!]}$, which includes all constants, symbols, and expressions used for interpreting free identifiers, language constructs, and local variables in M.

Theorem 1. *For any IA_2 term, the set $\mathcal{L}[\![\Gamma \vdash M : T]\!]$ is a symbolic regular-language over its effective (finite) alphabet. Moreover, a finite-state symbolic automata $\mathcal{A}[\![\Gamma \vdash M : T]\!]$ which recognizes it is effectively constructible.*

Suppose that there is a special free identifier abort of type com. We say that a term $\Gamma \vdash M$ is *safe* iff $\Gamma \vdash M[\text{skip/abort}] \sqsubseteq M[\text{diverge/abort}]$; otherwise we say that a term is *unsafe*. Hence, a safe term has no computation that leads to running abort. Let $\mathcal{L}[\![\Gamma \vdash M : T]\!]^{CR}$ denotes the (standard) regular-language representation of game semantics for a term M obtained as in [12], where concrete values are used. Since this representation is fully abstract, and so there is a close correspondence with the operational semantics, the following holds [7].

Proposition 1. *A term $\Gamma \vdash M : T$ is safe iff $\mathcal{L}[\![\Gamma \vdash M : T]\!]^{CR}$ does not contain any play with moves from $\mathcal{A}^{\langle abort \rangle}_{[\![com]\!]}$, which we call unsafe plays.*

The following result [9] confirms that symbolic automata (models) can be used for establishing safety of terms.

Theorem 2. *$\mathcal{L}[\![\Gamma \vdash M : T]\!]$ is safe (all plays are safe) iff $\mathcal{L}[\![\Gamma \vdash M : T]\!]^{CR}$ is safe.*

For example, $[\![\text{abort} : \text{com}^{\text{abort}} \vdash \text{skip} \, ; \, \text{abort} : \text{com}]\!] = run \cdot run^{abort} \cdot done^{abort} \cdot done$, so this term is unsafe.

Since symbolic automata are finite state, we can use model-checking techniques to verify safety of IA_2 terms with integers. The verification procedure proposed in [9] searches for unsafe plays in the symbolic automata representing a term. If an unsafe play is found, it calls an external SMT solver (Yices) to check consistency (satisfiability) of its play condition. If the condition is consistent, then a concrete counterexample is reported. We showed in [9] that the procedure is correct and semi-terminating (terminates for unsafe terms, but may diverge for safe terms) under assumption that constraints generated by any program can be checked for consistency by some (SMT) solver.

Example 1. Consider the term family M from Table 1 in Sect. 1. The symbolic model for the term $A \wedge B$ is given in Fig. 2a. The term asks for a value of the non-local expression n with the move q^n two times, and the environment provides as answers symbols N and M. When the difference $N - M$ is 1, then *abort* command is run. The symbolic model in Fig. 2a contains one unsafe play:$[?X = 0, run \rangle \cdot q^n \cdot ?N^n \cdot [?X = X + N, q^n \rangle \cdot ?M^n \cdot [?X = X - M \wedge X = 1, run^{abort} \rangle \cdot done^{abort} \cdot done$, which after instantiating its input symbols with fresh names becomes: $[X_1 = 0, run \rangle \cdot q^n \cdot N^n \cdot [X_2 = X_1 + N, q^n \rangle \cdot M^n \cdot [X_3 = X_2 - M \wedge X_3 = 1, run^{abort} \rangle \cdot done^{abort} \cdot done$. An SMT solver will inform us that its play condition $(X_1 = 0 \wedge X_2 = X_1 + N \wedge X_3 = X_2 - M \wedge X_3 = 1)$ is satisfiable, yielding a possible assignment of concrete values to symbols: $X_1 = 0, N = 1, X_2 = 1, M = 0$, and $X_3 = 1$. Thus, the corresponding concrete counterexample will be: $run \cdot q^n \cdot 1^n \cdot q^n \cdot 0^n \cdot run^{abort} \cdot done^{abort} \cdot done$. Similarly, concrete counterexamples for terms $A \wedge \neg B$ and $\neg A \wedge B$ can be generated; and it can be verified that the term $\neg A \wedge \neg B$ is safe.　□

3.2   Symbolic Models of $\overline{\text{IA}}_2$

We extend the definition of guarded alphabet $\mathcal{A}^{gu}$ as the set of triples of feature expressions, boolean conditions and symbolic letters:

$$\mathcal{A}^{gu+f} = \{[\phi, b, \alpha\rangle \mid \phi \in FeatExp(\mathbb{F}), b \in BExp, \alpha \in \mathcal{A}^{sym}\}$$

Thus, a guarded letter $[\phi, b, \alpha\rangle$ means that α is triggered only if b evaluates to true in valid configurations $k \in \mathbb{K}$ that satisfy ϕ. That is, every letter is *labelled* with a feature expression that defines products able to perform the letter. As before, we write only α for $[tt, tt, \alpha\rangle$. A word $[\phi_1, b_1, \alpha_1\rangle \cdot [\phi_2, b_2, \alpha_2\rangle \ldots [\phi_n, b_n, \alpha_n\rangle$ over $\mathcal{A}^{gu+f}$ can be written as a triple $[\phi_1 \wedge \ldots \wedge \phi_n, b_1 \wedge \ldots \wedge b_n, \alpha_1 \cdot \ldots \cdot \alpha_n\rangle$. Its meaning is that the word $\alpha_1 \cdot \ldots \cdot \alpha_n$ is feasible only if the condition $b_1 \wedge \ldots \wedge b_n$ is satisfiable, and only for valid configurations that satisfy $\phi_1 \wedge \ldots \wedge \phi_n$. Regular languages and automata defined over $\mathcal{A}^{gu+f}$ are called *featured symbolic*.

We can straightforwardly extend the symbolic representation of all IA_2 terms in the new setting by extending all guarded letters with the value tt for the first (feature expression) component. Now, we are ready to give representation of the compile-time conditional term:

$$[\![\Gamma \vdash_{\mathbb{F}} \texttt{\#if } \phi \texttt{ then } M \texttt{ else } M']\!] = [\![\Gamma \vdash M]\!] \,\mathring{,}\, [\![\Gamma \vdash M']\!] \,\mathring{,}\, [\![\texttt{\#if}]\!]^{\phi}$$

where $\mathring{,}$ is the composition operator, and the interpretation of the compile-time conditional construct parameterized by the feature expressions ϕ is:

$$[\![\texttt{\#if} : \textsf{com}^{\langle 1 \rangle} \times \textsf{com}^{\langle 2 \rangle} \to \textsf{com}]\!]^{\phi} =$$
$$run \cdot \left([\phi, tt, run^{\langle 1 \rangle}\rangle \cdot done^{\langle 1 \rangle} + [\neg\phi, tt, run^{\langle 2 \rangle}\rangle \cdot done^{\langle 2 \rangle}\right) \cdot done$$

That is, the first argument of $\texttt{\#if}$ is run for those configurations that satisfy ϕ, whereas the second argument of $\texttt{\#if}$ is run for configurations satisfying $\neg\phi$.

Again, the effective alphabet of $[\![\Gamma \vdash_{\mathbb{F}} M : T]\!]$ for any $\overline{\text{IA}}_2$ term is a finite subset of $\mathcal{A}^{gu+f}_{[\![\Gamma \vdash_{\mathbb{F}} T]\!]}$. Hence, the automata corresponding to $[\![\Gamma \vdash_{\mathbb{F}} M : T]\!]$ is effectively constructible, and we call it *featured symbolic automata* (FSA). Basically, an FSA is a SA augmented with transitions labelled (guarded) with feature expressions. We denote it as $\mathcal{FSA}[\![\Gamma \vdash_{\mathbb{F}} M : T]\!] = (Q, i, \delta, F)$, where Q is a set of states, i is the initial state, δ is a transition function, and $F \subseteq Q$ is the set of final states. The *purpose of an FSA* is to model behaviours (computations) of the entire program family and *link* each computation to the exact set of products able to execute it. From an FSA, we can obtain the model of one particular product through *projection*. This transformation is entirely syntactical and consists in removing all transitions (moves) linked to feature expressions that are not satisfied by a configuration $k \in \mathbb{K}$.

Definition 1. The projection of $\mathcal{FSA}[\![\Gamma \vdash_{\mathbb{F}} M : T]\!] = (Q, i, \delta, F)$ to a configuration $k \in \mathbb{K}$, denoted as $\mathcal{FSA}[\![\Gamma \vdash_{\mathbb{F}} M : T]\!]\!\mid_k$, is the symbolic automaton $A = (Q, i, \delta', F)$, where $\delta' = \{(q_1, [b, a\rangle, q_2) \mid (q_1, [\phi, b, a\rangle, q_2) \in \delta \wedge k \models \phi\}$.

Theorem 3 (Correctness). $\mathcal{FSA}[\![\Gamma \vdash_{\mathbb{F}} M : T]\!] \mid_k = \mathcal{A}[\![\Gamma \vdash \pi_k(M) : T]\!]$.

Example 2. Consider the term family M from Introduction. Its FSA is given in Fig. 3. Letters represent triples, where the first component indicates which valid configurations can enable the corresponding move. For example, we can see that the unsafe play obtained after instantiating its input symbols with fresh names: $[tt, X_1 = 0, run\rangle \cdot [A, tt, q^n\rangle \cdot N^n \cdot [B, X_2 = X_1 + N, q^n\rangle \cdot M^n \cdot [tt, X_3 = X_2 - M \wedge X_3 = 1, run^{abort}\rangle \cdot done^{abort} \cdot done$, is feasible when $N = 1$ and $M = 0$ for the configuration $A \wedge B$. □

4   Model Checking Algorithms

The *general* model checking problem for program families consists in determining which products in the family are safe, and which are not safe. The goal is to report all products that are not safe and to provide a counterexample for each.

A straightforward but rather naive algorithm to solve the above problem is to check all valid programs individually. That is, compute the projection of each valid configuration, generate its model, and verify it using standard algorithms. This is so-called brute force approach, and it is rather inefficient. Indeed, all programs (exponentially many in the worst case) will be explored in spite of their great similarity. We now propose an alternative algorithm, which explores the set of reachable states in the FSA of a program family rather than the individual models of all its products. We aim to take advantage of the compact structure of FSAs in order to solve the above general model checking problem.

A model checker is meant to perform a search in the state space of the FSA (Q, i, δ, F) and to indicate safe and unsafe products. This boils down to checking if an 'unsafe' state $q' \in Q$ with $q \xrightarrow{[\phi, b, run^{abort}\rangle} q'$ is reachable in the FSA. This can be accomplished with a Breadth-First Search (BFS) in the FSA that encounters all states that are reachable from the initial state and checks whether one of them is 'unsafe'. In this way, the BFS finds the shortest unsafe play for any product. The algorithm is shown in Fig. 4. It maintains a *reachability relation* $R \subseteq Q \times \mathcal{P}(\mathbb{K})$ that stores a set of pairs (q, px) where q is marked as a visited state for the valid products from $px \subseteq \mathbb{K}$; a *queue Queue* that keeps track of all states that still have to be visited (explored), and a *set of counterexamples unsafe*. R is first initialized by the initial state $i \in Q$ that is reachable for all valid products, i.e. $(i, \mathbb{K}) \in R$. For $(q, px) \in R$, we write $R(q)$ for the set of products px. *Queue* supports the operations: *remove* which returns and deletes the first element of *Queue*, and *put* which inserts a new element at the back of *Queue*. In *Queue* along with each state q, we store a trace, $trace(q)$, that shows how q is reached from the initial state i. For each visited state, it is checked whether that state is unsafe (line 6). Each time an unsafe state q is reached, the pair $(e, px') = complete(q, px, trace(q))$ is added to *unsafe* where: 'e' is a complete counterexample generated by looking at the trace kept on *Queue* along with q and by finding the shortest trace from q to an accepting state (by performing an embedded BFS); and px' is the corresponding set of unsafe products. Note that e

---

Input: $\mathcal{FSA}[\![\Gamma \vdash_{\mathbb{F}} M]\!] = (Q, i, \delta, F)$ and valid configs. $\mathbb{K}$
Output: *true* if M is safe; otherwise *false* plus a set of counterexamples
1. $R := \{(i, \mathbb{K})\}$
2. $Queue := [(i, \mathbb{K})]$
3. $unsafe := \emptyset, \mathbb{K}_{unsafe} := \emptyset$
4. **while** $(Queue \neq [\,])$ **do**
5. $\quad (q, px) := remove(Queue)$
6. $\quad$ **if** $(q$ is UNSAFE$)$ **then**
7. $\quad\quad (e, px') := complete(q, px, trace(q))$
8. $\quad\quad unsafe := unsafe \cup (e, px'), \mathbb{K}_{unsafe} := \mathbb{K}_{unsafe} \cup px'$
9. $\quad\quad Queue := Queue - \{(q, px) \in Queue \mid px \subseteq \mathbb{K}_{unsafe}\}$
10. $\quad$ **else** $new := \Big\{(q', px' \backslash R(q')) \mid q \overset{[\phi,b,m]}{\longrightarrow} q', px' = \{k \in px \mid k \models \phi, k \notin \mathbb{K}_{unsafe}\}, px' \backslash R(q') \neq \emptyset\Big\}$
11. $\quad\quad$ **while** $(new \neq \emptyset)$ **do**
12. $\quad\quad\quad (q', px') := remove(new)$
13. $\quad\quad\quad R(q') := R(q') \cup px'$
14. $\quad\quad\quad put((q', px'), Queue)\}$
15. $\quad\quad$ **end**
16. $\quad$ **end**
17. **end**
18. return$(unsafe \neq \emptyset), unsafe$

Fig. 4. Model checking algorithm for verifying safety based on specialized BFS

represents the shortest unsafe play for the products in px'. At each iteration, the BFS calculates the set *new* of unvisited successors of the current state, filtering out states and products that are already visited in R. Assuming that we have a transition $q \overset{[\phi,b,\alpha]}{\longrightarrow} q'$ and the source state q is reachable by products in px, the target state q' is reachable for products in $\{k \in px \mid k \models \phi\}$. Given an FSA as input, the algorithm in Fig. 4 calculates all reachable states from the initial state i. When the search finishes and *unsafe* is empty, the algorithm returns *true*; otherwise it returns *false* and the set *unsafe*.

After having found an unsafe state, our algorithm will continue exploration until the entire model is explored. Since the aim is to identify violating products, it can ignore products that are already known to violate, $\mathbb{K}_{unsafe}$, that is $\cup_{(e,px)\in unsafe} px$. In the BFS, this can be achieved by filtering out states with products $px \subseteq \mathbb{K}_{unsafe}$ as part of the calculation of *new*. This can only eliminate newly discovered states, not those that are already on the queue. States on the queue can be filtered out by removing elements (q, px) for which $px \subseteq \mathbb{K}_{unsafe}$ (line 9).

Compared to the standard BFS, where visited states are marked with Boolean *visited* flags and no state is visited twice, in our algorithm visited states are marked with sets of products (for which those states are visited) and a state can be visited multiple times. This is due to the fact that when the BFS arrives at a state s for the second time, such that $R(q) = px$, $(q, px') \in new$, and

The procedure checks safety of a given term family $\Gamma \vdash_{\mathbb{F}} M : T$.

1 The BFS from Fig. 4 is called with arguments: $\mathcal{FSA}[\![\Gamma \vdash_{\mathbb{F}} M]\!]$ and $\mathbb{K}$.

2 If no unsafe play is found, terminate with answer SAFE.

3 Otherwise, find $\mathbb{K}_{unsafe} = \cup_{(e,px) \in unsafe} px$. For all products in $\mathbb{K} \backslash \mathbb{K}_{unsafe}$ report that they are SAFE. The mechanism for fresh symbol generation is used to instantiate all input symbols in the unsafe plays e, and their conditions are tested for consistency.

4 If the condition of some play e from $(e, px) \in unsafe$ is consistent, report the corresponding products px as UNSAFE with counterexample e. Otherwise generate $\mathbb{K}' \subseteq \mathbb{K}_{unsafe}$ that contains all products associated with inconsistent plays. Then go to Step 1, i.e. call BFS with arguments: $\mathcal{FSA}[\![\Gamma \vdash_{\mathbb{F}} M]\!]$ without all inconsistent unsafe plays and $\mathbb{K}'$.

Fig. 5. Verification procedure (VP)

$px' \not\subseteq px$, then s although already visited, has to be re-explored since transitions that were disallowed for px during the first visit of q might be now allowed for px'.

The complete verification procedure for checking safety of term families is described in Fig. 5. In each iteration, it calls the BFS from Fig. 4 and finds some safe products and (unsafe) products for which a genuine (consistent) counterexample is reported. To prevent the model checker to consider these products (for which conclusive results are previously found), the BFS in the next iteration is called with updated arguments, i.e. only for configurations with no conclusive results. We first show that the projection π_k commutes with our "lifted" verification procedure, which is applied directly on the level of program families.

Theorem 4 (Correctness). $\Gamma \vdash \pi_k(M)$ is safe iff $\mathcal{FSA}[\![\Gamma \vdash_{\mathbb{F}} M]\!]\,|_k$ is safe.

As a corollary of Theorems 2, 3, 4 we obtain that the VP in Fig. 5 returns correct answers for all products. Moreover, it terminates for all unsafe products by generating the corresponding unsafe plays. The VP will find the shortest consistent unsafe play t for each unsafe product after finite number of calls to the BFS, that will first find all inconsistent unsafe plays shorter than t (which are finitely many [9]). However, the VP may diverge for safe products, producing in each next iteration longer and longer unsafe plays with inconsistent conditions.

5 Implementation

We have extended the prototype tool developed in [9] to implement the VP in Fig. 5. That tool [9] converts any single (IA$_2$) term into a symbolic automata representing its game semantics, and then explores the automata for unsafe plays. The extended tool takes as input a term family, and generates the corresponding FSA, which is then explored based on the procedure described in Fig. 5. The tool is implemented in Java along with its own library for working with featured symbolic automata. The tool calls an external SMT solver Yices to determine consistency of play conditions. We now illustrate our tool with an example. The tool, further examples and detailed reports how they execute are available from: http://www.itu.dk/~adim/symbolicgc.htm. Consider the following version of the linear search algorithm, Linear_3.

$$x[k] \ : \ \text{varint}^{x[-]}, \ y \ : \ \text{expint}^y, \ \text{abort} \ : \ \text{com}^{abort} \ \vdash_{\{A,B,C\}}$$
$$\text{new}_{int} \ i := 0 \ \text{in new}_{int} \ j := 0 \ \text{in}$$
$$\#\text{if} \ (A) \ \text{then} \ j := j + 1;$$
$$\#\text{if} \ (B) \ \text{then} \ j := j - 1;$$
$$\#\text{if} \ (C) \ \text{then} \ j := j + 2;$$
$$\text{new}_{int} \ p := y \ \text{in}$$
$$\text{while} \ (i < k) \ \text{do} \ \{$$
$$\quad \text{if} \ (x[i] = p) \ \&\& \ (j = 1) \ \text{then abort else} \ j := j - 1;$$
$$\quad i := i + 1 \ \} \ : \text{com}$$

The term family contains three features A, B, and C, and hence 8 products can be produced. In the above, first depending on which features are enabled some value from -1 to 3 is assigned to j, and then the input expression y is copied into the local variable p. The non-local array x is searched for an occurrence of the value stored in p. If the search succeeds j-times (for $j > 0$), abort is executed.

The arrays are implemented in the symbolic representation by using a special symbol (e.g., k with an initial constraint $k > 0$) to represent the length of an array. A new symbol (e.g., I) is also used to represent the index of the array element that needs to be de-referenced or assigned to (see [9] for details). If we also want to check for array-out-of-bounds errors, we can include in the representation of arrays plays that perform abort moves when $I \geq k$.

If the value read from the environment for y occurs j-times (for $j > 0$) in the array x, then an unsafe behaviour is found in the FSA of the above term family. Hence, all products for which the value assigned to j is less than 1 are safe: $\neg A \wedge \neg B \wedge \neg C$, $\neg A \wedge B \wedge \neg C$, and $A \wedge B \wedge \neg C$. All other products are unsafe. For example, for products $A \wedge B \wedge C$ and $\neg A \wedge \neg B \wedge C$ (for which j is set to 2) the tool reports a counterexample that corresponds to a term with an array of size $k = 2$, where the values read from the environment for $x[0]$, $x[1]$, and y are the same, i.e. the following counterexample is generated: $run \cdot q^y \cdot 0^y \cdot read^{x[0]} \cdot 0^{x[0]} \cdot read^{x[1]} \cdot 0^{x[1]} \cdot run^{abort} \cdot done^{abort} \cdot done$. This counterexample is obtained after 2 iterations of the VP, and it corresponds to a computation which runs the body of 'while' two times. In the first iteration, an inconsistent unsafe play is found (its condition contains $J = 2 \wedge J = 1$, where the symbol J tracks the current value of j). A consistent counterexample is obtained in the first iteration for products $A \wedge \neg B \wedge \neg C$ and $\neg A \wedge B \wedge C$ (for which j is 1), whereas for $A \wedge \neg B \wedge C$ (j is assigned to 3) in the third iteration. The tool diverges for safe terms, producing longer and longer (inconsistent) unsafe plays in each next iteration.

We ran our tool on a 64-bit Intel®Core^{TM} i5 CPU and 8 GB memory. All times are reported as averages over five independent executions. For our experiments, we use four families: Intro is the family from Table 1 in Sect. 1; Linear_3 is

BENCH.	$\mid \mathbb{K} \mid$	family-based approach			brute-force approach		
		TIME	MAX	FINAL	TIME	MAX	FINAL
Intro	4	0.34 s	25	9	0.78 s	68	28
Linear$_3$	8	1.34 s	51	9	3.86 s	336	72
Linear$_4$	16	2.34 s	57	9	7.28 s	720	144
Linear$_5$	32	4.50 s	63	9	16.27 s	1482	288

Fig. 6. Performance comparison for verifying program families.

the above family for linear search with three features; Linear$_4$ is an extended version of Linear$_3$ with one more feature D and command: #if (D) then $j := j + 3$; and Linear$_5$ is Linear$_4$ extended with one additional feature E and command: #if (E) then $j := j - 2$. We restrict our tool to work with bounded number of iterations (10 in this case) since the VP loops for safe terms. For Linear$_4$ the tool reports 13 unsafe products with corresponding counterexamples, whereas for Linear$_5$ 21 unsafe products are found. Figure 6 compares the effect (in terms of TIME, the number of states in the maximal model generated during analysis MAX, and the number of states in the final model FINAL) of verifying benchmarks using our family-based approach vs. using brute-force approach. In the latter case, we first compute all products, generate their models, and verify them one by one by using the tool for single programs [9]. In this case we report the sum of number of states for the corresponding models in all individual products. We can see that the family-based approach is between 2.3 and 3.6 times faster (using considerably less space) than the brute-force. We expect even bigger efficiency gains for families with higher number of products.

6   Related Work and Conclusion

Recently, many so-called lifted techniques have been proposed, which lift existing single-program analysis techniques to work on the level of program families (see [18] for a survey). This includes lifted type checking [3], lifted model checking [4], lifted data-flow analysis [11], etc. Classen et al. have proposed featured transition systems (FTSs) in [4] as the foundation for behavioural specification and verification of variational systems. An FTS, which is feature-aware extension of the standard transition systems, represents the behaviour of all instances of a variational system. They show how the family-based model checking algorithms for verifying FTSs against fLTL properties are implemented in the SNIP model checker. The input language to SNIP is fPromela, which is a feature-aware extension of Promela. In this work, we also propose special family-based model checking algorithms. However, they are not applied on models of variational systems, but on game semantics models extracted from concrete program fragments with #ifdef-s.

The first application of game semantics to model checking was proposed by Ghica and McCusker in [12]. They show how game semantics of IA$_2$ with finite data-types can be represented in a remarkably simple form by regular-languages. Subsequently, several algorithms have been proposed for model checking IA_2 with infinite data types [7,9]. The automata-theoretic representation of game semantics have been also extended to programs with various features: concurrency [13], third-order functions [16], probabilistic constructs [15], nondeterminism [6], etc.

To conclude, in this work we introduce the featured symbolic automata (FSA), a formalism designed to describe the combined game semantics models of a whole program family. A specifically designed model checking technique allows us to verify safety of an FSA. The proposed approach can be extended to support multi-features and numeric features. So-called variability abstractions [10,11] can also be used to define abstract family-based model checking.

References

1. Abramsky, S., McCusker, G.: Linearity, sharing and state: a fully abstract game semantics for idealized algol with active expressions. Electr. Notes Theor. Comput. Sci. **3**, 2–14 (1996)
2. Apel, S., von Rhein, A., Wendler, P., Größlinger, A., Beyer, D.: Strategies for product-line verification: case studies and experiments. In: 35th International Conference on Software Engineering, ICSE 2013, pp. 482–491 (2013)
3. Chen, S., Erwig, M., Walkingshaw, E.: An error-tolerant type system for variational lambda calculus. In: ACM SIGPLAN International Conference on Functional Programming, ICFP 2012, pp. 29–40. ACM (2012)
4. Classen, A., Cordy, M., Schobbens, P.-Y., Heymans, P., Legay, A., Raskin, J.-F.: Featured transition systems: foundations for verifying variability-intensive systems and their application to LTL model checking. IEEE Trans. Softw. Eng. **39**(8), 1069–1089 (2013)
5. Clements, P., Northrop, L.: Software Product Lines: Practices and Patterns. Addison-Wesley, Boston (2001)
6. Dimovski, A.: A compositional method for deciding equivalence and termination of nondeterministic programs. In: Méry, D., Merz, S. (eds.) IFM 2010. LNCS, vol. 6396, pp. 121–135. Springer, Heidelberg (2010)
7. Dimovski, A., Ghica, D.R., Lazić, R.: Data-abstraction refinement: a game semantic approach. In: Hankin, C., Siveroni, I. (eds.) SAS 2005. LNCS, vol. 3672, pp. 102–117. Springer, Heidelberg (2005)
8. Dimovski, A., Lazic, R.: Compositional software verification based on game semantics and process algebra. STTT **9**(1), 37–51 (2007)
9. Dimovski, A.S.: Program verification using symbolic game semantics. Theor. Comput. Sci. **560**, 364–379 (2014)
10. Dimovski, A.S., Al-Sibahi, A.S., Brabrand, C., Wąsowski, A.: Family-based model checking without a family-based model checker. In: Fischer, B., Geldenhuys, J. (eds.) SPIN 2015. LNCS, vol. 9232, pp. 282–299. Springer, Heidelberg (2015)
11. Dimovski, A.S., Brabrand, C., Wasowski, A.: Variability abstractions: trading precision for speed in family-based analyses. In: 29th European Conference on Object-Oriented Programming, ECOOP 2015. LIPIcs, vol. 37, pp. 247–270. Schloss Dagstuhl - Leibniz-Zentrum fuer Informatik (2015)
12. Ghica, D.R., McCusker, G.: The regular-language semantics of second-order idealized algol. Theor. Comput. Sci. **309**(1–3), 469–502 (2003)

13. Ghica, D.R., Murawski, A.S.: Compositional model extraction for higher-order concurrent programs. In: Hermanns, H., Palsberg, J. (eds.) TACAS 2006. LNCS, vol. 3920, pp. 303–317. Springer, Heidelberg (2006)
14. Hyland, J.M.E., Luke Ong, C.-H.: On full abstraction for PCF: I, II, and III. Inf. Comput. **163**(2), 285–408 (2000)
15. Legay, A., Murawski, A.S., Ouaknine, J., Worrell, J.: On automated verification of probabilistic programs. In: Ramakrishnan, C.R., Rehof, J. (eds.) TACAS 2008. LNCS, vol. 4963, pp. 173–187. Springer, Heidelberg (2008)
16. Murawski, A.S., Walukiewicz, I.: Third-order idealized Algol with iteration is decidable. In: Sassone, V. (ed.) FOSSACS 2005. LNCS, vol. 3441, pp. 202–218. Springer, Heidelberg (2005)
17. Reynolds, J.C.: The essence of Algol. In: O'Hearn, P.W., Tennent, R.D. (eds.) Algol-like Languages. Birkhaüser, Basel (1997)
18. Thüm, T., Apel, S., Kästner, C., Schaefer, I., Saake, G.: A classification and survey of analysis strategies for software product lines. ACM Comput. Surv. **47**(1), 6 (2014)

Compositional Semantics and Analysis
of Hierarchical Block Diagrams

Iulia Dragomir[1]([✉]), Viorel Preoteasa[1], and Stavros Tripakis[1,2]

[1] Aalto University, Espoo, Finland
{iulia.dragomir,viorel.preoteasa,stavros.tripakis}@aalto.fi
[2] University of California, Berkeley, USA

Abstract. We present a compositional semantics and analysis framework for hierarchical block diagrams (HBDs) in terms of atomic and composite predicate transformers. Our framework consists of two components: (1) a compiler that translates Simulink HBDs into an algebra of transformers composed in series, in parallel, and in feedback; (2) an implementation of the theory of transformers and static analysis techniques for them in Isabelle. We evaluate our framework on several case studies including a benchmark Simulink model by Toyota.

1   Introduction

Simulink[1] is a widely used tool for modeling and simulating embedded control systems. Simulink uses a graphical language based on *hierarchical block diagrams* (HBDs). HBDs are networks of interconnected *blocks*, which can be either *basic* blocks from Simulink's libraries, or *composite* blocks (*subsystems*), which are themselves HBDs. Hierarchy is the primary *modularization* mechanism that languages like Simulink offer. It allows to structure large models and thus master their complexity, improve their readability, and so on.

In this paper we present a *compositional* semantics and analysis framework for HBDs, including but not limited to Simulink models. By "compositional" we mean exploiting the hierarchical structure of these diagrams, for instance, reasoning about individual blocks and subsystems independently, and then composing the results to reason about more complex systems. By "analysis", we mean different types of checks, including exhaustive verification (model-checking), but also static analysis such as *compatibility checking*, which aims to check whether the connections between two or more blocks in the diagram are valid, i.e., whether the blocks are compatible.

Our framework is based on the theories of *relational interfaces* and *refinement calculus of reactive systems* [19,23]. The framework can express *open*, *non-deterministic*, and *non-input-receptive* systems, and both *safety* and *liveness* properties. As syntax, we use (temporal or non) logic formulas on input,

---

This work has been partially supported by the Academy of Finland, the U.S. National Science Foundation (awards #1329759 and #1139138), and by UC Berkeley's iCyPhy Research Center (supported by IBM and United Technologies).

[1] http://www.mathworks.com/products/simulink/.

D. Bošnački and A. Wijs (Eds.): SPIN 2016, LNCS 9641, pp. 38–56, 2016.
DOI: 10.1007/978-3-319-32582-8_3

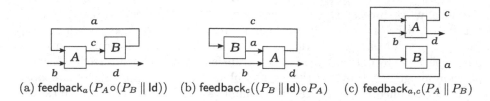

(a) feedback$_a$($P_A \circ (P_B \parallel \mathsf{Id})$) (b) feedback$_c$(($P_B \parallel \mathsf{Id}) \circ P_A$)   (c) feedback$_{a,c}$($P_A \parallel P_B$)

Fig. 1. Three ways to view and translate the same block diagram.

output, and state variables. As semantics we use *predicate* and *property trans-formers* [2,19]. To form complex systems from simpler ones we use composition in *series*, in *parallel*, and in *feedback*. Apart from standard verification (of a system against a property) the framework offers: (1) *compatibility* checking during composition; and (2) *refinement*, a binary relation between components, which characterizes *substitutability* (when can a component replace another one while preserving system properties). Compatibility checking is very useful, as it offers a lightweight alternative to verification, akin to type-checking [23]. Refinement has multiple usages, including compositional and incremental design, and reusability. This makes the framework compelling for application on tools like Simulink, which have a naturally compositional hierarchical language.

In order to define the semantics of HBDs in a compositional framework, one needs to do two things. First, define the semantics of every basic block in terms of an *atomic* element of the framework. We do this by defining for each Simulink basic block a corresponding (atomic) *monotonic predicate transformer* (MPT). Second, one must define the semantics of composite diagrams. We do this by mapping such diagrams to *composite* MPTs (CPTs), i.e., MPTs composed in series, in parallel, or in feedback.

As it turns out, mapping HBDs to CPTs raises interesting problems. For example, consider the block diagram in Fig. 1a. Let P_A and P_B be transformers modeling the blocks A and B in the diagram. How should we compose P_A and P_B in order to get a transformer that represents the entire diagram? As it turns out, there are several possible options. One option is to compose first P_A and P_B in series, and then compose the result in feedback, following Fig. 1a. This results in the composite transformer feedback$_a$($P_A \circ (P_B \parallel \mathsf{Id})$), where $\circ$ is composition in series, $\parallel$ in parallel, and feedback$_x$ is feedback applied on port x. Id is the transformer representing the identity function. A has two outputs and B only one input, therefore to connect them in series we first form the parallel composition $P_B \parallel \mathsf{Id}$, which represents a system with two inputs.

Another option is to compose the blocks in series in the opposite order, P_B followed by P_A, and then apply feedback. This results in the transformer feedback$_c$(($P_B \parallel \mathsf{Id}) \circ P_A$). A third option is to compose the two blocks first in parallel, and then apply feedback on the two ports a, c. This results in the transformer feedback$_{a,c}$($P_A \parallel P_B$). Although semantically equivalent, these three transformers have different computational properties.

Clearly, for complex diagrams, there are many possible translation options. A main contribution of this paper is the study of these options in depth.

Specifically, we present three different translation strategies: *feedback-parallel* translation which forms the parallel composition of all blocks, and then applies feedback; *incremental* translation which orders blocks topologically and composes them one by one; and *feedbackless* translation, which avoids feedback composition altogether, provided the original block diagram has no algebraic loops.

Having defined the compositional semantics of HBDs in terms of CPTs, we turn to analysis. Our main focus in this paper is checking diagram *compatibility*, which roughly speaking means that the input requirements of every block in the diagram are satisfied [19,23]. We check compatibility by (1) *expanding* the definitions of CPTs to obtain an atomic MPT; (2) *simplifying* the formulas in the atomic MPT; and (3) checking satisfiability of the resulting formulas.

We report on a toolset which implements the framework described above. The toolset consists of (1) the SIMULINK2ISABELLE compiler which translates hierarchical Simulink models into CPTs implemented in the Isabelle proof assistant[2], and (2) the implementation of the theory of CPTs, together with expansion and simplification techniques in Isabelle. We evaluate our framework on several case studies, including a Fuel Control System benchmark by Toyota [10,11].

2   Hierarchical Block Diagrams

A *hierarchical block diagram* (HBD) is a network of interconnected blocks.[3] Blocks can be either *basic* blocks (from Simulink libraries), or *composite* blocks (*subsystems*). A basic block is described by: (1) a label, (2) a list of parameters, (3) a list of in- and out-ports, (4) a vector of state variables with predefined initial values (i.e., the local memory of a block) and (5) functions to compute the outputs and next state variables. The outputs are computed from the inputs, current state and parameters. State variables are updated by a function with the same arguments. Subsystems are defined by their label, list of in- and out-ports, and the list of block instances that they contain – both atomic and composite.

Simulink allows to model both discrete and continuous-time blocks. For example, UnitDelay (graphically represented as the $\frac{1}{z}$ block in a Simulink diagram) is a discrete-time block which outputs at step n the input at step $n-1$. An Integrator is a continuous-time block whose output is described by a differential equation solved with numerical methods. We interpret a Simulink model as a discrete-time model (essentially an input-output state machine, possibly infinite-state) which evolves in a sequence of discrete steps. Each step has duration Δt, which is a parameter (user-defined or automatically computed by Simulink based on the blocks' time rates).

Algebraic-Loop-Free Diagrams. In this paper we consider diagrams which are free from *algebraic loops*. By "algebraic loop" we mean a feedback loop resulting in instantaneous cyclic dependencies. More precisely, the way we define and

---

[2] https://isabelle.in.tum.de/.

[3] Our exposition focuses on HBDs as implemented in Simulink, but our method and tool can also be applied to other block-diagram based languages with minor changes.

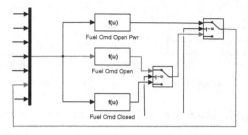

Fig. 2. An extract of Toyota's Simulink Fuel Control System model [10,11]: this diagram is algebraic-loop-free despite the fact that the feedback loop in red is not "broken" by blocks such as Integrator or UnitDelay (Color figure online).

check for algebraic loops is the following: first, we build a directed dependency graph whose nodes are the input/output ports of the diagram, and whose edges correspond to connections or to input-output dependencies within a block; second, we check whether this graph has a cycle. The class of algebraic-loop-free diagrams includes all diagrams whose feedback loops are "broken" by blocks such as Integrator or UnitDelay. The output of such blocks does not depend on their input (it only depends on their state), which prevents a cycle from forming in the dependency graph. For example, the diagram of Fig. 1 is algebraic-loop-free if the output of block B does not depend on its input.

But algebraic-loop-free diagrams can also be diagrams where feedback loops are not broken by Integrators or UnitDelays. An example is shown in Fig. 2. Despite the feedback loop in red, which creates an apparent dependency cycle, this diagram is algebraic-loop-free. The reason is that the Fuel Cmd Open block is the function $\frac{1}{14.7}(-0.366 + 0.08979u_7u_3 - 0.0337u_7u_3^2 + 0.0001u_7^2u_3)$, where $u = (u_1, u_2, ..., u_7)$ is the input vector. This function only depends on variables u_3, u_7 of the vector u, and is independent from u_1, u_2, u_4, u_5, u_6. Since the output of the block does not depend on the 6th input link (i.e., u_6), the cycle is broken. Similarly, the outputs of Fuel Cmd Open Pwr and Fuel Cmd Closed are also independent from u_6, which prevents the other two feedback loops from forming a cyclic dependency. This type of algebraic-loop-free pattern abounds in Simulink models found in the industry.

Running Example. Throughout the paper we illustrate our methods using a simple example of a counter, shown in Fig. 3. This is a hierarchical (two-level) Simulink model. The top-level diagram (Fig. 3a) contains three block instances: the step of the counter as a Constant basic block, the subsystem DelaySum, and the Scope basic block which allows to view simulation results. The subsystem DelaySum (Fig. 3b) contains a UnitDelay block instance which models the state of the counter. UnitDelay can be specified by the formula $a = s \land s' = c$, where c is the input, a the output, s the current state and s' the next state variable. We assume that s is initially 0. The Add block instance adds the two input values and outputs the result in the same time step: $c = f + e$. The *junction* after link a (black dot in the figure) can be seen as a basic block duplicating (or *splitting*) its input to its two outputs: $f = a \land g = a$.

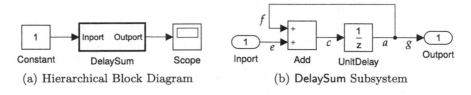

(a) Hierarchical Block Diagram   (b) DelaySum Subsystem

Fig. 3. Simulink model of a counter with step 1.

3   Basic Blocks as Monotonic Predicate Transformers

Monotonic predicate transformers [6] (MPTs) are an expressive formalism, used within the context of programming languages to model non-determinism, correctness (both functional correctness and termination), and refinement [2]. In this paper we show how MPTs can also be used to give semantics to HBDs. We consider basic blocks in this section, which can be given semantics in terms of *atomic* MPTs. In the next section we consider general diagrams, which can be mapped to *composite* MPTs.

3.1   Monotonic Predicate Transformers

A *predicate* on an arbitrary set Σ is a function $q : \Sigma \to$ Bool. Predicate q can also be seen as a subset of Σ: for $\sigma \in \Sigma$, σ belongs to the subset iff $q(\sigma)$ is true. Predicates can be ordered by the subset relation: we write $q \leq q'$ if predicate q, viewed as a set, is a subset of q'. Pred(Σ) denotes the set of predicates $\Sigma \to$ Bool.

A *predicate transformer* is a function $S : (\Sigma' \to$ Bool$) \to (\Sigma \to$ Bool$)$, or equivalently, $S :$ Pred(Σ') $\to$ Pred(Σ). S takes a predicate on Σ' and returns a predicate on Σ. S is *monotonic* if $\forall q, q' : q \leq q' \Rightarrow S(q) \leq S(q')$.

Traditionally, MPTs have been used to model sequential programs using weakest precondition semantics. Given a MPT $S : (\Sigma' \to$ Bool$) \to (\Sigma \to$ Bool$)$, and a predicate $q' : \Sigma' \to$ Bool capturing a set of *final* states, $S(q')$ captures the set of all *initial* states, such that if the program is started in any state in $S(q')$, it is guaranteed to finish in some state in q'. But this is not the only possible interpretation of S. S can also model input-output systems. For instance, S can model a *stateless* system with a single inport ranging over Σ, and a single outport ranging over Σ'. Given a predicate q' characterizing a set of possible *output values*, $S(q')$ characterizes the set of all *input values* which, when fed into the system, result in the system outputting a value in q'. As an example, the identity function can be modeled by the MPT Id : Pred(Σ) $\to$ Pred(Σ), defined by Id$(q) = q$, for any q.

MPTs can also model *stateful* systems. For instance, consider the UnitDelay described in Sect. 2. Let the input, output, and state variable of this system range over some domain Σ. Then, this system can be modeled as a MPT $S :$ Pred($\Sigma \times \Sigma$) $\to$ Pred($\Sigma \times \Sigma$). The Cartesian product $\Sigma \times \Sigma$ captures pairs of *(input, current state)* or *(output, next state)* values. Intuitively, we can think of this system as a function which takes as input (x, s), the input x and the current state s, and returns (y, s'), the output and the next state s', such that $y = s$ and $s' = x$. The MPT S can then be defined as follows:

$$S(q) = \{(x, s) \mid (s, x) \in q\}.$$

In the definition above we view predicates q and $S(q)$ as sets.

Syntactically, a convenient way to specify systems is using formulas on input, output, and state variables. For example, the identity system can be specified by the formula $y = x$, where y is the output variable and x is the input. The UnitDelay system can be specified by the formula $y = s \wedge s' = x$. We next introduce operators which define MPTs from predicates and relations.

For a predicate $p : \Sigma \to \text{Bool}$ and a relation $r : \Sigma \to \Sigma' \to \text{Bool}$, we define the *assert* MPT, $\{p\} : \text{Pred}(\Sigma) \to \text{Pred}(\Sigma)$, and the *non-deterministic update* MPT, $[r] : \text{Pred}(\Sigma') \to \text{Pred}(\Sigma)$, where:

$$\{p\}(q) = (p \wedge q) \quad \text{and} \quad [r](q) = \{\sigma \mid \forall \sigma' : \sigma' \in r(\sigma) \Rightarrow \sigma' \in q\}$$

Transformer $\{p\}$ is used to model non-input-receptive systems, that is, systems where some inputs are illegal [23]. $\{p\}$ constrains the inputs so that they must satisfy predicate p. It accepts only those inputs and behaves like the identity function. That is, $\{p\}$ models a partial identity function, restricted to the domain p. Transformer $[r]$ models an input-receptive but possibly non-deterministic system. Given input σ, the system chooses non-deterministically some output σ' such that $\sigma' \in r(\sigma)$ is true. If no such σ' exists, then the system behaves *miraculously* [2]. In our framework we ensure non-miraculous behavior as explained below, therefore, we do not detail further this term.

3.2 Semantics of Basic Blocks as Monotonic Predicate Transformers

To give semantics to basic Simulink blocks, we often combine $\{p\}$ and $[r]$ using the *serial composition* operator $\circ$, which for predicate transformers is simply function composition. Given two MPTs $S : \text{Pred}(\Sigma_2) \to \text{Pred}(\Sigma_1)$ and $T : \text{Pred}(\Sigma_3) \to \text{Pred}(\Sigma_2)$, their serial composition $(S \circ T) : \text{Pred}(\Sigma_3) \to \text{Pred}(\Sigma_1)$ is defined as $(S \circ T)(q) = S(T(q))$.

For example, consider a block with two inputs x, y and one output z, performing the division $z = \frac{x}{y}$. We want to state that division by zero is illegal, and therefore, the block should reject any input where $y = 0$. This block can be specified as the MPT

$$\text{Div} = \{\lambda(x, y) : y \neq 0\} \circ [\lambda(x, y), z : z = \frac{x}{y}]$$

where we employ lambda-notation for functions.

In general, and in order to ensure non-miraculous behavior, we model non-input-receptive systems using a suitable assert transformer $\{p\}$ such that in $\{p\} \circ [r]$, if p is true for some input x, then there exists output y such that (x, y) satisfies r. MPTs which do not satisfy this condition are not considered in our framework. This is the case, for example, of the MPT $[\lambda(x, y), z : y \neq 0 \wedge z = \frac{x}{y}]$.

For a function $f : \Sigma \to \Sigma'$ the *functional update* $[f] : \mathsf{Pred}(\Sigma') \to \mathsf{Pred}(\Sigma)$ is defined as $[\lambda \sigma, \sigma' : \sigma' = f(\sigma)]$ and we have

$$[f](q) = \{\sigma \mid f(\sigma) \in q\} = f^{-1}(q)$$

Functional predicate transformers are of the form $\{p\} \circ [f]$, and *relational predicate transformers* are of the form $\{p\} \circ [r]$, where p is a predicate, f is a function, and r is a relation. *Atomic predicate transformers* are either functional or relational transformers. Div is a functional predicate transformer which can also be written as $\mathsf{Div} = \{\lambda x, y : y \neq 0\} \circ [\lambda x, y : \frac{x}{y}]$.

For assert and update transformers based on Boolean expressions we introduce a simplified notation that avoids lambda abstractions. If P is a Boolean expression on some variables $x_1, \ldots, x_n$, then $\{x_1, \ldots, x_n : P\}$ denotes the assert transformer $\{\lambda x_1, \ldots, x_n : P\}$. Similarly if R is a Boolean expression on variables $x_1, \ldots, x_n, y_1, \ldots, y_k$ and F is a tuple of expressions on variables $x_1, \ldots, x_n$, then $[x_1, \ldots, x_n \rightsquigarrow y_1, \ldots, y_k : R]$ and $[x_1, \ldots, x_n \rightsquigarrow F]$ are notations for $[\lambda(x_1, \ldots, x_n), (y_1, \ldots, y_k) : R]$ and $[\lambda x_1, \ldots, x_n : F]$, respectively. With these notations the Div transformer becomes:

$$\mathsf{Div} = \{x, y : y \neq 0\} \circ [x, y \rightsquigarrow \frac{x}{y}]$$

Other basic Simulink blocks include constants, delays, and integrators. Let us see how to give semantics to these blocks in terms of MPTs. A constant block parameterized by constant c has no input, and a single output equal to c. As a predicate transformer the constant block has as input the empty tuple (), and outputs the constant c:

$$\mathsf{Const}(c) = [() \rightsquigarrow c]$$

The unit delay block is modeled as the atomic predicate transformer

$$\mathsf{UnitDelay} = [x, s \rightsquigarrow s, x]$$

Simulink includes continuous-time blocks such as the *integrator*, which computes the integral $\int_0^x f$ of a function f. Simulink uses different integration methods to simulate this block. We use the Euler method with fixed time step Δt (a parameter). If x is the input, y the output, and s the state variable of the integrator, then $y = s$ and $s' = s + x \cdot \Delta t$. Therefore, the integrator can be modeled as the MPT

$$\mathsf{Integrator}(\Delta t) = [x, s \rightsquigarrow s, s + x \cdot \Delta t]$$

All other Simulink basic blocks fall within these cases discussed above. Relation (1) introduces the definitions of some blocks that we use in our examples.

$$\mathsf{Add} = [x, y \rightsquigarrow x + y] \qquad \mathsf{Split} = [x \rightsquigarrow x, x] \qquad \mathsf{Scope} = \mathsf{Id}. \tag{1}$$

4   HBDs as Composite Predicate Transformers

4.1   Composite Predicate Transformers

The semantics of basic Simulink blocks is defined using monotonic predicate transformers. To give semantics to arbitrary block diagrams, we map them to *composite predicate transformers* (CPTs). CPTs are expressions over the atomic predicate transformers using *serial, parallel,* and *feedback* composition operators. Here we focus on how these operators instantiate on functional predicate transformers, which are sufficient for this paper. The complete formal definitions of the operators can be found in [7] and in the Isabelle theories that accompany this paper.[4]

Serial composition ∘ has already been introduced in Sect. 3.1. For two functional predicate transformers $S = \{p\} \circ [f]$ and $T = \{p'\} \circ [f']$, it can be shown that their serial composition satisfies:

$$S \circ T = \{p \wedge (p' \circ f)\} \circ [f' \circ f] \tag{2}$$

(2) states that input x is legal for $S \circ T$ if x is legal for S and the output of S, $f(x)$, is legal for T, i.e., $(p \wedge (p' \circ f))(x) = p(x) \wedge p'(f(x))$ is true. The output of $S \circ T$ is $(f' \circ f)(x) = f'(f(x))$.

For two MPTs $S : \mathsf{Pred}(Y) \to \mathsf{Pred}(X)$ and $T : \mathsf{Pred}(Y') \to \mathsf{Pred}(X')$, their parallel composition is the MPT $S \parallel T : \mathsf{Pred}(Y \times Y') \to \mathsf{Pred}(X \times X')$. If $S = \{p\} \circ [f]$ and $T = \{p'\} \circ [f']$ are functional predicate transformers, then it can be shown that their parallel composition satisfies:

$$S \parallel T = \{x, x' : p(x) \wedge p(x')\} \circ [x, x' \rightsquigarrow f(x), f'(x')] \tag{3}$$

(3) states that input (x, x') is legal for $S \parallel T$ if x is a legal input for S and x' is a legal input for T, and that the output of $S \parallel T$ is the pair $(f(x), f'(x'))$.

For $S : \mathsf{Pred}(U \times Y) \to \mathsf{Pred}(U \times X)$ as in Fig. 4a, the feedback of S, denoted $\mathsf{feedback}(S) : \mathsf{Pred}(Y) \to \mathsf{Pred}(X)$ is obtained by connecting output v to input u (Fig. 4b). The feedback operator that we use in this paper is a simplified version of the one defined in [20]. It is specifically designed for a component S having the structure shown in Fig. 4c, i.e., where the first output v depends only on the second input x. We call such components *decomposable*. The result of applying feedback to a decomposable block is depicted in Fig. 4d.

If S is a decomposable functional predicate transformer, i.e., if $S = \{p\} \circ [u, x \rightsquigarrow f'(x), f(u, x)]$, then it can be shown that $\mathsf{feedback}(S)$ is functional and it satisfies:

$$\mathsf{feedback}(S) = \{x : p(f'(x), x))\} \circ [x \rightsquigarrow f(f'(x), x)] \tag{4}$$

That is, input x is legal for the feedback if $p(f'(x), x)$ is true, and the output for x is $f(f'(x), x)$.

---

[4] Available at: http://users.ics.aalto.fi/iulia/sim2isa.shtml.

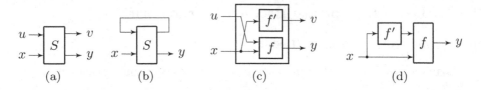

Fig. 4. (a) MPT S, (b) feedback(S), (c) decomposable S, (d) feedback of (c).

The fact that the diagram is algebraic-loop-free implies that whenever we attempt to compute feedback(S), S is guaranteed to be decomposable. However, we only know that $S = \{p\} \circ [h]$ for some p and h, and we do not know what f and f' are. We can compute f and f' by setting $f = snd \circ h$, $f_0 = fst \circ h$, and $f'(x) = f_0(u_0, x)$ for some arbitrary fixed u_0, where fst and snd are the functions that select the first and second elements of a pair, respectively.

As an illustration of how CPTs can give semantics to HBDs, consider our running example (Fig. 3). An example mapping of the DelaySum subsystem and of the top-level Simulink model yields the following two CPTs:

$$\begin{aligned} \text{DelaySum} &= \text{feedback}((\text{Add} \parallel \text{Id}) \circ \text{UnitDelay} \circ (\text{Split} \parallel \text{Id})) \\ \text{Counter} &= (\text{Const}(1) \parallel \text{Id}) \circ \text{DelaySum} \circ (\text{Scope} \parallel \text{Id}) \end{aligned} \quad (5)$$

The Id transformers in these definitions are for propagating the state introduced by the unit delay. Expanding the definitions of the basic blocks, and applying properties (2), (3), and (4), we obtain the *simplified* MPTs for the entire system:

$$\text{DelaySum} = [x, s \rightsquigarrow s, s + x] \qquad \text{and} \qquad \text{Counter} = [s \rightsquigarrow s, s + 1]. \quad (6)$$

4.2 Translating HBDs to CPTs

As illustrated in the introduction, the mapping from HBDs to CPTs is not unique: for a given HBD, there are many possible CPTs that we could generate. Although these CPTs are semantically equivalent, they have different *simplifiability* properties (see Sects. 4.3 and 5). Therefore, the problem of how exactly to map a HBD to a CPT is interesting both from a theoretical and from a practical point of view. In this section, we describe three different translation strategies.

In what follows, we describe how a *flat* (non-hierarchical), *connected* diagram is translated. If the diagram consists of many disconnected "islands", we can simply translate each island separately. Hierarchical diagrams are translated bottom-up: we first translate the subsystems, then their parent, and so on.

Feedback-Parallel Translation. The *feedback-parallel translation* strategy (FPT) first composes all components in parallel, and then connects outputs to inputs by applying feedback operations. FPT is illustrated in Fig. 5a, for the DelaySum component of Fig. 3b. The Split MPT models the junction after link a.

Applying FPT on the DelaySum diagram yields the following CPT:

$$\begin{aligned} \text{DelaySum} = \text{feedback}^3([f, c, a, e, s &\rightsquigarrow f, e, c, s, a] \\ \circ (\text{Add} \parallel \text{UnitDelay} \parallel \text{Split}) \circ [c, a, s', f, g &\rightsquigarrow f, c, a, s', g]) \end{aligned}$$

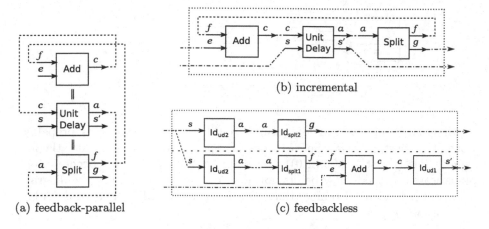

(a) feedback-parallel

(b) incremental

(c) feedbackless

Fig. 5. Translation strategies for the DelaySum subsystem of Fig. 3b.

where $\mathsf{feedback}^3(\cdot) = \mathsf{feedback}(\mathsf{feedback}(\mathsf{feedback}(\cdot)))$ denotes application of the feedback operator 3 times, on the variables f, c, and a, respectively (recall that feedback works only on one variable at a time, the first input and first output of the argument transformer). In order to apply $\mathsf{feedback}^3$ to the parallel composition $\mathsf{Add} \parallel \mathsf{UnitDelay} \parallel \mathsf{Split}$, we first have to reorder its inputs and outputs, such that the variables on which the feedbacks are applied come first in matching order. This is achieved by the *rerouting* transformers $[f, c, a, e, s \rightsquigarrow f, e, c, s, a]$ and $[c, a, s', f, g \rightsquigarrow f, c, a, s', g]$.

Incremental Translation. The *incremental translation* strategy (IT) composes components one by one, after having ordered them in topological order according to the dependencies in the diagram. When composing A with B, a decision procedure determines which composition operator(s) should be applied, based on dependencies between A and B. If A and B are not connected, parallel composition is applied. Otherwise, serial composition is used, possibly together with feedback if necessary.

The IT strategy is illustrated in Fig. 5b. First, topological sorting yields the order $\mathsf{Add}, \mathsf{UnitDelay}, \mathsf{Split}$. So IT first composes Add and $\mathsf{UnitDelay}$. Since the two are connected with c, serial composition is applied, obtaining the CPT

$$\mathsf{ICC1} = (\mathsf{Add} \parallel \mathsf{Id}) \circ \mathsf{UnitDelay}$$

As in the example in the introduction, Id is used here to match the number of outputs of Add with the number of inputs of $\mathsf{UnitDelay}$.

Next, IT composes $\mathsf{ICC1}$ with Split. This requires both serial composition and feedback, and yields the final CPT:

$$\mathsf{DelaySum} = \mathsf{feedback}(\mathsf{ICC1} \circ (\mathsf{Split} \parallel \mathsf{Id}))$$

It is worth noting that composing systems incrementally in this way might result in not the most natural compositions. For example, consider

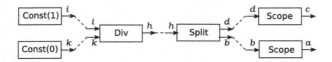

Fig. 6. Diagram ConstDiv.

the diagram from Fig. 6. The "natural" CPT for this diagram is probably: (Const(1) ∥ Const(0)) ∘ Div ∘ Split ∘ (Scope ∥ Scope). Instead, IT generates the following CPT: (Const(1) ∥ Const(0)) ∘ Div ∘ Split ∘ (Scope ∥ Id) ∘ (Id ∥ Scope). More sophisticated methods may be developed to extract parallelism in the diagram and avoid redundant Id compositions like in the above CPT. This study is left for future work.

Feedbackless Translation. Simplifying a CPT which contains feedback operators involves performing decomposability tests, function compositions which include variable renamings, and other computations which turn out to be resource consuming (see Sect. 5). For reasons of scalability, we would therefore like to avoid feedback operators in the generated CPTs. The *feedbackless translation* strategy (NFBT) avoids feedback altogether, provided the diagram is algebraic-loop-free. The key idea is that, since the diagram has no algebraic loops, we should be able to eliminate feedback and replace it with direct operations on current- and next-state variables, just like with basic blocks. In particular, we can *decompose* UnitDelay into two Id transformers, denoted Id_{ud1} and Id_{ud2}: Id_{ud1} computes the next state from the input, while Id_{ud2} computes the output from the current state.

Generally, we decompose all components having multiple outputs into several components having each a single output. For each new component we keep only the inputs they depend on, as shown in Fig. 5c. Thus, the Split component from Fig. 5b is also divided into two Id components, denoted Id_{splt1} and Id_{splt2}.

Decomposing into components with single outputs allows to compute a separate CPT for each of the outputs. Then we take the parallel composition of these CPTs to form the CPT of the entire diagram. Doing so on our running example, we obtain:

$$DelaySum = [s, e \rightsquigarrow s, s, e] \circ \left(\left(Id_{ud2} \circ Id_{splt2}\right) \parallel \left(\left(\left(Id_{ud2} \circ Id_{splt1}\right) \parallel Id\right) \circ Add \circ Id_{ud1}\right)\right)$$

Because Id_{ud1}, Id_{ud2}, Id_{splt1} and Id_{splt2} are all Ids, and $Id \circ A = A \circ Id = A$ and $Id \parallel Id = Id$ (thanks to polymorphism), this CPT is reduced to $DelaySum = [s, e \rightsquigarrow s, s, e] \circ (Id \parallel Add)$. Our tool directly generates this simplified CPT.

4.3   Simplifying CPTs and Checking Compatibility

Once a set of CPTs has been generated, they can be subjected to various static analysis and verification tasks. Currently, our toolset mainly supports static *compatibility* checks, which amount to checking whether any CPT obtained from the diagram is equivalent to the MPT Fail = {x : false}. Fail corresponds to an invalid component, indicating that the composition of two or more blocks in the diagram is illegal [19,23].

Compatibility checking is not a trivial task. Two steps are performed in order to check whether a certain CPT is equivalent to Fail: the CPT is (1) *expanded*, and (2) *simplified*. By *expansion* we mean replacing the serial, parallel, and feedback composition operators by their definitions (2), (3), (4). As a result of expansion, the CPT is turned into an MPT of the form {p} ∘ [f]. By *simplification* we mean simplifying the formulas p and f, e.g., by eliminating internal variables.

5   Implementation and Evaluation

Our framework has been implemented and is publicly downloadable from http:// users.ics.aalto.fi/iulia/sim2isa.shtml. The implementation consists of two components: (1) the SIMULINK2ISABELLE compiler, which takes as input Simulink diagrams and translates them into CPTs, using the strategies described in Sect. 4.2; and (2) an implementation of the theory of CPTs, together with simplification strategies and static analysis checks such as compatibility checks, in the Isabelle theorem prover. In this section we present the toolset and report evaluation and analysis results on several case studies, including an industrial-grade benchmark by Toyota [10,11].

5.1   Toolset

SIMULINK2ISABELLE, written in Python, takes as input Simulink files in XML format and produces valid Isabelle theories that can be subjected to compatibility checking and verification. The compiler currently handles a large subset of Simulink's blocks, including math and logical operators, continuous, discontinuous and discrete blocks, as well as sources, sinks, and subsystems (including enabled and switch case action subsystems). This subset is enough to express industrial-grade models such as the Toyota benchmarks.

During the parsing and preprocessing phase of the input Simulink file, the tool performs a set of checks, including algebraic loop detection, unsupported blocks and/or block parameters, malformed blocks (e.g., a function block referring to a nonexistent input), etc., and issues possible warnings/errors.

SIMULINK2ISABELLE implements all three translation strategies as options -fp, -ic and -nfb, and also takes two additional options: -flat (flatten diagram) and -io (intermediate outputs, applicable to -ic). All options apply to any Simulink model. Option flat flattens the hierarchy of the HBD and produces a single diagram consisting only of basic blocks (no subsystems), on which the translation is then applied. Option io generates and names all intermediate CPTs produced during the translation process. These names are then used in the CPT for the top-level system, to make it shorter and more readable. In addition, the intermediate CPTs can be expanded and simplified incrementally by

Isabelle, and used in their simplified form when computing the CPT for the next level up. This generally results in more efficient simplification. Another benefit of producing intermediate CPTs is the detection of incompatibilities early during the simplification phase. Moreover, this indicates the group of components at fault and helps localize the error.

The second component of our toolset includes a complete implementation of the theory of MPTs and CPTs in Isabelle. In addition, we have implemented in Isabelle a set of functions (keyword **simulink**) which perform expansion and simplification automatically in the generated CPTs, and also generate automatically proved theorems of the simplified formulas. After expansion and simplification, we obtain for the top-level system a single MPT referring only to the external input, output, and state/next state variables of the system (and not to the internal links of the diagram).

For instance, when executed on our running example (Fig. 3) with the IT option, the tool produces the Isabelle code:

$$\textbf{simulink}\ \mathsf{DelaySum} = \mathsf{feedback}((\mathsf{Add} \parallel \mathsf{Id}) \circ \mathsf{UnitDelay} \circ (\mathsf{Split} \parallel \mathsf{Id}))$$
$$\textbf{simulink}\ \mathsf{Counter} = (\mathsf{Const}(1) \parallel \mathsf{Id}) \circ \mathsf{DelaySum} \circ (\mathsf{Scope} \parallel \mathsf{Id})$$

When executed in Isabelle, this code automatically generates the definitions (5) as well as the simplification theorems (6), and automatically proves these theorems. Note that the simplification theorems also contain the final MPT for the entire system. In general, when the diagram contains continuous-time blocks such as Integrator, the final simplified MPT will be parameterized by Δt.

As another example, when we run the tool on the example of Fig. 6, we obtain the theorem ConstDiv = Fail, which states that the system has no legal inputs. This reveals the incompatibility due to performing a division by zero.

5.2   Evaluation

We evaluated our toolset on several case studies, including the Foucault pendulum, house heating and anti-lock braking systems from the Simulink examples library.[5] Due to space limitations, we only present here the results obtained on the running example (Fig. 3) and the Fuel Control System (FCS) model described in [10,11]. FCS solves the problem of maintaining the ratio of air mass and injected fuel at the stoichiometric value [5], i.e., enough air is provided to completely burn the fuel in a car's engine. This control problem has important implications on lowering pollution and improving engine performance. Three designs are presented in [10,11], all modeled in Simulink, but differing in their complexity. The first model is the most complex, incorporating already available subsystems from the Simulink library. The second and third models represent abstractions of this main design, but they are still complicated for verification purposes. The second model is formalized as Hybrid I/O Automata [15], while the third is presented as Polynomial Hybrid I/O Automata [8]. We evaluate our approach on the third model designed with Simulink, available from

---

[5] http://se.mathworks.com/help/simulink/examples.html.

Table 1. Experimental results for the running example (Fig. 3).

		FPT		IT				NFBT
		HBD	FBD	HBD	FBD	IO-HBD	IO-FBD	
Translation	$\mathcal{T}_{trans}$	0.082	0.093	0.081	0.087	0.081	0.085	0.096
	$\mathcal{L}_{cpt}$	722	629	1131	1246	1146	1134	1159
	$\mathcal{N}_{cpt}$	10	9	10	9	14	14	15
Expansion, simplication, and compatibility check	$\mathcal{T}_{simp}$	0.596	0.575	0.184	0.225	0.240	0.279	0.214
	$\mathcal{P}_{simp}$	0.006	0.005	0.005	0.006	0.006	0.007	0.006

Table 2. Experimental results for the FCS model.

		FPT		IT				NFBT
		HBD	FBD	HBD	FBD	IO-HBD	IO-FBD	
Translation	$\mathcal{T}_{trans}$	0.249	0.329	0.213	0.222	0.220	0.260	0.605
	$\mathcal{L}_{cpt}$	18895	17432	87006	116550	86318	108001	46863
	$\mathcal{N}_{cpt}$	127	120	127	120	236	236	269
Expansion, simplification, and compatibility check	$\mathcal{T}_{simp}$	894.472	3471.317	617.873	2439.229	267.052	417.05	57.425
	$\mathcal{P}_{simp}$	7.144	7.267	7.856	7.161	6.742	6.228	5.18
	$\mathcal{L}_{simp}$	158212	158212	157791	157797	127132	127642	122001

http://cps-vo.org/group/ARCH/benchmarks. This model has a 3-level hierarchy with a total of 104 block instances (97 basic blocks and 7 subsystems), and 101 connections, of which 8 feedbacks.

First, we run all three translation strategies on each model using the SIMULINK2ISABELLE compiler. Then, we expand/simplify the CPTs within Isabelle and at the same time check for incompatibilities. The translation strategies are run with the following options: FPT without/with flattening (HBD/FBD), IT without/with flattening and without/with io option (IO), and NFBT. NFBT by construction generates intermediate outputs and does not preserve the structure of the hierarchy in the result, thus, its result is identical with/without the options. The results from the running example are shown in Table 1 and from the FCS model in Table 2.

The notations used in the tables are as follows: (1) $\mathcal{T}_{trans}$: time to generate the Isabelle CPTs from the Simulink model, (2) $\mathcal{L}_{cpt}$: length of the produced CPTs (# characters), (3) $\mathcal{N}_{cpt}$: number of generated CPTs, (4) $\mathcal{T}_{simp}$: total time needed for expansion and simplification, (5) $\mathcal{P}_{simp}$: time to print the simplified formula, (6) $\mathcal{L}_{simp}$: length of the simplified formula (# chars). All times are in seconds. We report separately the time to print the final formulas ($\mathcal{P}_{simp}$), since printing takes significant time in the Isabelle/ML framework.

Let us now focus on Table 2 since it contains the most relevant results due to the size and complexity of the system. Observe that the translation time ($\mathcal{T}_{trans}$)

is always negligible compared to the other times.[6] Also, NFBT generates the most CPTs, which are relatively short compared to the other translations. This is one of the reasons why CPTs produced by NFBT are easier to expand/simplify than those produced by the other methods. The other and main reason is that applying the **feedback** operator requires identifying f and f', computing several function compositions, etc. We note that a Simulink feedback connection can transfer an array of n values, which is translated by our tool as n successive applications of **feedback**.

Readability. An important aspect of the produced CPTs is their *readability*. Defining quantitative readability measures such as number, length, nesting depth, etc., of the generated CPTs, is beyond the scope of this paper. Nevertheless, we can make the following (subjective) observations: (1) IT with option **-io** improves readability as the intermediate outputs allow to parse the result step by step. (2) NFBT reduces readability because this method decomposes blocks and does not preserve the hierarchy of the original model.

Equivalence of the Different Translations. One interesting question is whether the different translation options generate equivalent CPTs. Proving a meta-theorem stating that this is indeed the case for every diagram is beyond the scope of this paper, and part of future work. Nevertheless, we did prove that in the case of the FCS model, the final simplified MPTs resulting from each translation method are all equivalent. These proofs have been conducted in Isabelle.

Analysis. Our tool proves that the final simplified MPT of the entire FCS model is not **Fail**. This proves compatibility of the components in the FCS model. The obtained MPT is functional, i.e., has the form $\{p\} \circ [f]$. Its assert condition p states that the state value of an integrator which is fed into a square root is ≥ 0. We proved in Isabelle that this holds for all $\Delta t > 0$. Therefore, compatibility holds independently of the value of the time step.

We also introduced a fault in the FCS model on purpose, to demonstrate that our tool is able to detect the error. Consider the model fragment depicted in Fig. 7. If the constant *simTime* is mistakenly set to 10, the model contains a division by zero. Our tool catches this error during compatibility checking, in 51.71 s total (including NFBT translation, expansion, and simplification, which results in **Fail**).

Comparison with Simulink. In this work we give semantics of Simulink diagrams in terms of CPTs. One question that may be raised is how the CPT

---

[6] $\mathcal{T}_{\text{trans}}$ for NFBT is almost twice larger than for FPT, IT and IT-IO. The reason is that NFBT executes extra steps, such as splitting blocks with multiple outputs and removing CPTs that are not used in calculating the system's output.

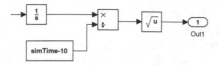

Fig. 7. Part of the FCS model: setting *simTime* to 10 results in incompatibility.

semantics compares to Simulink's own semantics, i.e., to "what the simulator does". Our toolset includes an option to generate simulation code (in Python) from the Isabelle CPTs. Then, we can compare the simulation results obtained from Simulink to those obtained from the CPT-generated simulation code. We performed this comparison for the FCS model: the results are shown in Fig. 8. Since the FCS model is closed (i.e., has no external inputs) and deterministic, it only has a single behavior. Therefore, we only generate one simulation plot for each method. The plot from Fig. 8a is obtained with variable step and the ode45 (Dormand-Prince) solver. The difference between the values computed by Simulink and our simulation ranges from 0 to 6.1487e-05 (in absolute value) for this solver. Better results can be obtained by reducing the step length. For instance, a step of 5e-05 gives an error difference of 2.0354e-06.

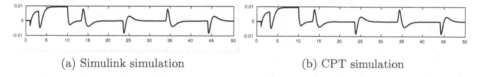

(a) Simulink simulation   (b) CPT simulation

Fig. 8. Simulation plots obtained from Simulink and the simplified CPT for a 50 s time interval and $\Delta t = 0.001$.

6 Related Work

A plethora of work exists on translating Simulink models to various target languages, for verification purposes or for code-generation purposes. Primarily focusing on verification and targeting discrete-time fragments of Simulink, existing works describe translations to BIP [22], NuSMV [17], or Lustre [24]. Other works study transformation of continuous-time Simulink to Timed Interval Calculus [4], Function Blocks [25], I/O Extended Finite Automata [26], or Hybrid CSP [27], and both discrete and continuous time fragments to SpaceEx Hybrid Automata [18]. The Stateflow module of Simulink, which allows to model hierarchical state machines, has been the subject of translation to hybrid automata [1,16].

Contract-based frameworks for Simulink are described in [3,21]. [3] uses pre/post-conditions as contracts for discrete-time Simulink blocks, and SDF graphs [12] to represent Simulink diagrams. Then sequential code is generated from the SDF graph, and the code is verified using traditional refinement-based techniques [2]. In [21] Simulink blocks are annotated with rich types (separate constraints on inputs and outputs, but no relations between inputs and outputs which is possible in our framework). Then the SimCheck tool extracts verification conditions from the Simulink model and the annotations, and submits them to an SMT solver for verification.

Our work offers a compositional framework which allows compatibility checks and refinement, which is not supported in the above works. We also study different translation strategies from HBDs to an algebra with serial, parallel, and feedback composition operators, which, to the best of our knowledge, have not been previously studied.

In [9], the authors propose an n-ary parallel composition operator for the Lotos process algebra. Their motivation, namely, that there may be several different process algebra terms representing a given process network, is similar to ours. But their solution (the n-ary parallel composition operator) is different from ours. Their setting is also different from ours, and results in some significantly different properties. For instance, they identify certain process networks which cannot be expressed in Lotos. In our case, *every* HBD can be expressed as a CPT (this includes HBDs with algebraic loops, even though we do not consider these in this paper).

Modular code generation methods for Simulink models are described in [13,14]. The main technical problem solved there is how to cluster subsystems in as few clusters as possible without introducing false input-output dependencies.

7   Conclusion

In this paper we present a compositional semantics and analysis framework for hierarchical block diagrams such as those found in Simulink and similar tools. Our contributions are the following: (1) semantics of basic Simulink blocks (both stateless and stateful) as atomic monotonic predicate transformers; (2) compositional semantics of HBDs as composite MPTs; (3) three translation strategies from HBDs to CPTs, implemented in the SIMULINK2ISABELLE compiler; (4) the theory of CPTs, along with expansion and simplification methods, implemented in Isabelle; (5) automatic static analysis (compatibility checks) implemented in Isabelle; and (6) proof of concept and evaluation of the framework on a real-life Simulink model from Toyota. Our approach enables compositional and correct-by-construction system design. The top-level MPT, which can be viewed as a formal interface or contract for the overall system, is automatically generated. Moreover, it is formally defined and checked in Isabelle (the theorems are also automatically generated and proved).

As future work, the current code generation process, used to compare the Isabelle code to the Simulink code via simulation, could be extended to also generate proof-carrying, easier-to-certify embedded code, from the Isabelle theories. Other future work directions include: (1) studying other translation strategies; (2) improving the automated simplification methods within Isabelle or other solvers; (3) extending the toolset with automatic verification methods (proving requirements against the top-level MPT); and (4) extending the toolset with fault localization methods whenever the compatibility or verification checks fail.

References

1. Agrawal, A., Simon, G., Karsai, G.: Semantic translation of Simulink/Stateflow models to hybrid automata using graph transformations. Electron. Notes Theor. Comput. Sci. **109**, 43–56 (2004)
2. Back, R.-J., von Wright, J.: Refinement Calculus: A Systematic Introduction. Springer, New York (1998)
3. Boström, P.: Contract-based verification of Simulink models. In: Qin, S., Qiu, Z. (eds.) ICFEM 2011. LNCS, vol. 6991, pp. 291–306. Springer, Heidelberg (2011)
4. Chen, C., Dong, J.S., Sun, J.: A formal framework for modeling and validating Simulink diagrams. Formal Aspects Comput. **21**(5), 451–483 (2009)
5. Cook, J.A., Sun, J., Buckland, J.H., Kolmanovsky, I.V., Peng, H., Grizzle, J.W.: Automotive powertrain control - A survey. Asian J. Control **8**(3), 237–260 (2006)
6. Dijkstra, E.: Guarded commands, nondeterminacy and formal derivation of programs. Comm. ACM **18**(8), 453–457 (1975)
7. Dragomir, I., Preoteasa, V., Tripakis, S.: Translating hierarchical block diagrams into composite predicate transformers. CoRR, abs/1510.04873 (2015)
8. Frehse, G., Han, Z., Krogh, B.: Assume-guarantee reasoning for hybrid I/O-automata by over-approximation of continuous interaction. In: CDC, pp. 479–484 (2004)
9. Garavel, H., Sighireanu, M.: A graphical parallel composition operator for process algebras. In: FORTE XII. IFIP Conference Proceedings, vol. 156, pp. 185–202. Kluwer (1999)
10. Jin, X., Deshmukh, J., Kapinski, J., Ueda, K., Butts, K.: Benchmarks for model transformations and conformance checking. In: ARCH (2014)
11. Jin, X., Deshmukh, J.V., Kapinski, J., Ueda, K., Butts, K.: Powertrain control verification benchmark. In: HSCC, pp. 253–262. ACM (2014)
12. Lee, E., Messerschmitt, D.: Synchronous data flow. Proc. IEEE **75**(9), 1235–1245 (1987)
13. Lublinerman, R., Szegedy, C., Tripakis, S.: Modular code generation from synchronous block diagrams - modularity vs. code size. In: POPL, pp. 78–89. ACM, January 2009
14. Lublinerman, R., Tripakis, S.: Modularity vs. reusability: code generation from synchronous block diagrams. In: DATE, pp. 1504–1509. ACM, March 2008
15. Lynch, N., Segala, R., Vaandrager, F.: Hybrid I/O automata. Inf. Comput. **185**(1), 105–157 (2003)
16. Manamcheri, K., Mitra, S., Bak, S., Caccamo, M.: A step towards verification and synthesis from Simulink/Stateflow models. In: HSCC, pp. 317–318. ACM (2011)
17. Meenakshi, B., Bhatnagar, A., Roy, S.: Tool for translating Simulink models into input language of a model checker. In: Liu, Z., Kleinberg, R.D. (eds.) ICFEM 2006. LNCS, vol. 4260, pp. 606–620. Springer, Heidelberg (2006)
18. Minopoli, S., Frehse, G.: SL2SX Translator: from Simulink to SpaceEx verification tool. In: HSCC (2016)
19. Preoteasa, V., Tripakis, S.: Refinement calculus of reactive systems. In: EMSOFT, pp. 1–10, October 2014

20. Preoteasa, V., Tripakis, S.: Towards compositional feedback in non-deterministic and non-input-receptive systems. CoRR, abs/1510.06379 (2015)
21. Roy, P., Shankar, N.: SimCheck: a contract type system for Simulink. Innovations Syst. Softw. Eng. **7**(2), 73–83 (2011)
22. Sfyrla, V., Tsiligiannis, G., Safaka, I., Bozga, M., Sifakis, J.: Compositional translation of Simulink models into synchronous BIP. In: SIES, pp. 217–220, July 2010
23. Tripakis, S., Lickly, B., Henzinger, T.A., Lee, E.A.: A theory of synchronous relational interfaces. ACM Trans. Program. Lang. Syst. **33**(4), 14:1–14:41 (2011)
24. Tripakis, S., Sofronis, C., Caspi, P., Curic, A.: Translating discrete-time Simulink to Lustre. ACM Trans. Embed. Comput. Syst. **4**(4), 779–818 (2005)
25. Yang, C., Vyatkin, V.: Transformation of Simulink models to IEC 61499 Function Blocks for verification of distributed control systems. Control Eng. Pract. **20**(12), 1259–1269 (2012)
26. Zhou, C., Kumar, R.: Semantic translation of Simulink diagrams to input/output extended finite automata. Discrete Event Dyn. Syst. **22**(2), 223–247 (2012)
27. Zou, L., Zhany, N., Wang, S., Franzle, M., Qin, S.: Verifying Simulink diagrams via a hybrid Hoare logic prover. In: EMSOFT, pp. 9:1–9:10, September 2013

Using SPIN for the Optimized Scheduling of Discrete Event Systems in Manufacturing

Stefan Edelkamp$^{(\boxtimes)}$ and Christoph Greulich

Faculty 3 – Mathematics and Computer Science,
Bremen University, Bremen, Germany
edelkamp@tzi.de

Abstract. A discrete event system (DES) is a dynamic system with discrete states the transitions of which are triggered by events. In this paper we propose the application of the Spin software model checker to a discrete event system that controls the industrial production of autonomous products. The flow of material is asynchronous and buffered. The aim of this work is to find concurrent plans that optimize the throughput of the system. In the mapping the discrete event system directly to the model checker, we model the production line as a set of communicating processes, with the movement of items modeled as channels. Experiments shows that the model checker is able to analyze the DES, subject to the partial ordering of the product parts. It derives valid and optimized plans with several thousands of steps using constraint branch-and-bound.

1 Introduction

Discrete event (dynamic) systems (DES) provide a general framework for systems where the system dynamics not only follow physical laws but also additional firing conditions. DES research is concerned about performance analysis, evaluation, and optimization of DES. As the systems are often only available as computer programs, it turns out to be difficult to describe the dynamics of these systems using closed-form equations.

In many cases, *discrete event system simulation* (DESS) is chosen to describe the DES dynamics and for performance evaluation. Between consecutive events, no change in the system is assumed to occur; thus the simulation can directly jump in time from one event to the next. Each simulation activity is modeled by a process. The idea of a process is similar to the notion in model checking, and indeed one could write process-oriented simulations using independent processes. Most DESS systems store information about pending events in a data structure known as an *event queue*. Each item in the queue would at minimum contain the following information: a timestamp and a piece of software for executing event. The typical operations on an event queue are: inserting a new event and removing the next event (the one with the lowest timestamp) from the queue. It may also be necessary to cancel a scheduled event.

DESS is probably the most widely used simulation technique. Similar approaches are *system dynamics* (SD), and *agent-based simulation* (ABS). As the

D. Bošnački and A. Wijs (Eds.): SPIN 2016, LNCS 9641, pp. 57–77, 2016.
DOI: 10.1007/978-3-319-32582-8_4

name suggests DES model a process as a series of discrete events. They are built using: *entities* (objects that move through the system; *events* (processes which the entities pass through); and *resources* (objects, which are needed to trigger event). SD are related to DES, focusing on *flows* around networks rather than *queueing systems*, it considers: *stocks* (basic stores of objects); *flows* (movement of objects between different stocks in the system); *delays* (between the measuring and then acting on that measurement). ABS is a relatively new technique in OR and consists of: *autonomous agents* (self-directed objects which move about the system) and *rules* (which the agents follow to achieve their objectives). Agents move about the system interacting with each other and the environment. ABS are used to model situations in which the entities have some form of *intelligence*.

Earlier simulation software was efficient but platform-dependent, due to the need for stack manipulation. Modern software systems, however, support lightweight processes or threads. By the growing amount of non-determinism, however, DESS encounters its limits to optimize the concurrent acting of individual processes.

With the advances in technology, more and more complex systems were built, e.g., transportation networks, communication and computer networks, manufacturing lines. In these systems, the main dynamic mechanism in task succession stems from synchronization and competition in the use of common resources, which requires a policy to arbitrate conflicts and define priorities, all kinds of problems generally referred to under the generic terminology of *scheduling*. This type of dynamics hardly can be captured by differential equations or by their discrete time analogues. This is certainly the reason why those systems, which are nevertheless true dynamic systems, have long been disregarded by formal method experts and have been rather considered by operations researchers and specialists of manufacturing with no strong connections with system theory. The dynamics are made up of *events*, which may have a continuous evolution imposed by some called software once they start, but this is not what one is mainly interested in: the primary focus is on the beginning and the end of such events, since ends can cause new beginnings. Hence, the word *discrete* includes *time* and *state*.

In this paper, we utilize the state-of-the-art model checker Spin [25] as a performance analysis and optimization tool, together with its input language Promela to express the flow production of goods. There are several twists needed to adapt *Spin* to the optimization of DES(S) that are uncovered in the sequel of the text. Our running case study is the *Z2*, a physical monorail system for the assembling of tail-lights. Unlike most production systems, Z2 employs agent technology to represent autonomous products and assembly stations. The techniques developed, however, will be applicable to most flow production systems. We formalize the production floor as a system of communicating processes and apply *Spin* for analyzing its behavior. Using optimization mechanisms implemented on top of Spin, additional to the verification of the correctness of the model, we exploit its exploration process for optimization of the production.

For the *optimization via model checking* we use many new language features from the latest version of the Spin model checker including loops and native c-code verification. The optimization approach originally invented for Spin was designed for state space trees [36,37], while the proposed approach also supports state space graphs. Scheduling via model checking has been pioneered by Maler [1], Binksma [7], and Wijs [40].

The paper is structured as follows. First, we introduce discrete event simulation and industrial (flow) production. Then, we review related work including scheduling via model checking. Next, we introduce the industrial case study, and its modeling as well as its simulation as a DES. The simulator is used to measure the increments of the cost function to be optimized. Afterwards, we turn to the intricacies of the Promela model specification, to the parameterization of SPIN, as well as to the novel branch-and-bound optimization scheme. In the experiments, we study the effectiveness of the approach.

2 Preliminaries

2.1 Discrete Event Simulation

An *entity* is an object of interest in the system, and an *attribute* is a (relevant) property of an entity. Attributes are *state variables*, while *activities* form part of the *model specification* and *delays* form part of the simulation result. The *(system) state* is a variable needed to describe the state (e.g., length of a queue), which is aimed to be complete and minimal at any point in time. The occurrence of a *primary event* (e.g. arrival) is scheduled at a certain time, while a *secondary event* (e.g. queueing) is triggered by a certain condition becoming true. An *event* is an occurrence which is instantaneous may change the state of the system. The *(future) event list* PQ controls the simulation: it contains all future events that are scheduled, and is ordered by increasing time of events. Operations on the PQ are: *insert* an event into PQ (at an appropriate position!), *remove* first event from PQ for processing, and *delete* an event from PQ. Thus, PQ is a priorty queue. As operations must be performed efficiently, the common implementation of an event queue is a (binary) *heap*. With such a data structure, access to the next event requires $O(1)$ time, while inserting/deleting an event requires $O(\log(n))$ time, where n is the number of events currently in the queue. Depending on the implementation (e.g., Fibonacci heaps), there are other trade-offs, with constant-time insertion and $O(\log(n))$ (amortized) deletion. The generic DES simulation algorithm looks as follows:

1. IF (PQ empty) THEN exit
2. remove & process 1st primary event e from PQ
3. IF (conditional event e' enabled) THEN remove & process e', goto 3. ELSE goto 1.

We assume exact timing, i.e., deterministic time. However, by different choices points for generating successor events, the simulated DES itself is nondeterministic. Events inserted with priority t are generally assumed to remain unchanged until deletion at time t.

2.2 Flow Manufacturing

Flow manufacturing systems are DES installed for products that are produced in high quantities. By optimizing the flow of production, manufacturers hope to speed up production at a lower cost, and in a more environmentally sound way. In manufacturing practice there are not only series flow lines (with stations arranged one behind the other), but also more complex networks of stations at which assembly operations are performed (assembly lines). The considerable difference from flow lines, which can be analyzed by known methods, is that a number of required components are brought together to form a single unit for further processing at the assembly stations. An assembly operation can begin only if all required parts are available.

Performance analysis of flow manufacturing systems is generally needed during the planning phase regarding the system design, when the decision for a concrete configuration of such a system has to be made. The planning problem arises, e.g., with the introduction of a new model or the installation of a new manufacturing plant. Because of the investments involved, an optimization problem arises. The expenditure for new machines, for buffer or handling equipment, and the holding costs for the expected work-in-process face revenues from sold products. The performance of a concrete configuration is characterized by the throughput, i.e., the number of items that are produced per time unit. Other performance measures are the expected work in process or the idle times of machines or workers.

We consider *assembly-line networks with stations*, which are represented as a directed graph. Between any two successive nodes in the network, we assume a buffer of finite capacity. In the buffers between stations and other network elements, work pieces are stored, waiting for service. At assembly stations, service is given to work pieces. Travel time is measured and overall time is to be optimized.

In a general notation of flow manufacturing, system progress is non-deterministic and asynchronous, while the progress of time is monitored.

Definition 1 (Flow Manufacturing System). *A flow manufacturing system is a tuple $F = (A, E, G, \prec, S, Q)$ where*

- *A is a set of all possible assembling actions*
- *P is a set of n products; each $P_i \in P$, $i \in \{1, \ldots, n\}$, is a set of assembling actions, i.e., $P_i \subseteq A$*
- *$G = (V, E, w, s, t)$ is a graph with start node s, goal node t, and weight function $w : E \to I\!R_{\geq 0}$*
- *$\prec = (\prec_1, \ldots, \prec_n)$ is a vector of assembling plans with each $\prec_i \subseteq A \times A$, $i \in \{1, \ldots, n\}$, being a partial order*
- *$S \subseteq E$ is the set of assembling stations induced by a labeling $\rho : E \to A \cup \{\emptyset\}$, i.e., $S = \{e \in E \mid \rho(e) \neq \emptyset\}$*
- *Q is a set of (FIFO) queues of finite size, i.e., $\forall q \in Q : |q| < \infty$, together with a labeling $\psi : E \to Q$.*

Products P_i, $i \in \{1, \ldots, n\}$, travel through the network G, meeting their assembling plans/order $\prec_i \subseteq A \times A$ of the assembling actions A. For defining the cost function we use the set of predecessor edges $Pred(e) = \{e' = (u, v) \in E \mid e = (v, w)\}$.

Definition 2 (Run, Plan, and Path). *Let $F = (A, E, G, \prec, S, Q)$ be a flow manufacturing system. A run π is a schedule of triples (e_j, t_j, l_j) of edges e_j, queue insertion positions l_j, and execution time-stamp t_j, $j \in \{1, \ldots, n\}$. The set of all runs is denoted as Π. Each run π partitions into a set of n plans $\pi_i = (e_1, t_1, l_1), \ldots, (e_m, t_m, l_m)$, one for each product P_i, $i \in \{1, \ldots, n\}$. Each plan π_i corresponds to a* path, *starting at the initial node s and terminating at goal node t in G.*

The objective in a flow manufacturing system can be formally described as follows.

Definition 3 (Product Objective, Travel and Waiting Time). *The objective for product i is to minimize*

$$\max_{1 \leq i \leq n} wait(\pi_i) + time(\pi_i),$$

over all possible paths with initial node s and goal node t, where

- *$time(\pi_i)$ is the* travel time *of product P_i, defined as the sum of edge costs $time(\pi_i) = \sum_{e \in \pi_i} w(e)$, and*
- *$wait(\pi_i)$ the* waiting time, *defined as $wait(\pi_i) = \sum_{(e,t,l),(e',t',l') \in \pi_i, e' \in Pred(e)} t - (t' + w(e'))$.*

Definition 4 (Overall Objective). *With $cost(\pi_i) = wait(\pi_i) + time(\pi_i)$, as overall objective function we have $\min_{\pi \in \Pi} \max_{1 \leq i \leq n} cost(\pi_i)$*

$$= \min_{\pi \in \Pi} \max_{1 \leq i \leq n} \sum_{e \in \pi_i} w(e)$$
$$+ \sum_{(e,t,l),(e',t',l') \in \pi_i, e' \in Pred(e)} t - (t' + w(e'))$$
$$= \min_{\pi \in \Pi} \max_{1 \leq i \leq n, (e,t,l) \in \pi_i} t + w(e)$$

subject to the side constraints that

- *time stamps on all runs $\pi_i = (e_1, t_1, l_1) \ldots (e_m, t_m, l_m)$, $i \in \{1, \ldots, n\}$ are monotonically increasing, i.e., $t_l \leq t_k$ for all $1 \leq l < k \leq m$.*
- *after assembling all products are complete, i.e., all assembling actions have been executed, so that for all $i \in \{1, \ldots, n\}$ we have $P_i = \cup_{(e_j, t_j, l_j) \in \pi_i} \{\rho(e_j)\}$*
- *the order of assembling product P_i on path $\pi_i = (e_1, t_1, l_1) \ldots (e_m, t_m, l_m)$, $i \in \{1, \ldots, n\}$, is preserved, i.e., for all $(a, a') \in \prec_i$ and $a = \rho(e_j)$, $a' = \rho(e_k)$ we have $j < k$,*
- *all insertions to queues respect their sizes, i.e., for all $\pi_i = (e_1, t_1, l_1) \ldots (e_m, t_m, l_m)$, $i \in \{1, \ldots, n\}$, we have that $0 \leq l_j < |\psi(e_j)|$.*

3   Related Work

One of the most interesting problems in manufacturing is *job shop scheduling* [3].
When solving the scheduling problem, a set of n jobs has to be assigned to a set
of m machines. Consequently, the total number of possible solutions is $(n!)^m$.
The problem complexity grows when the number of required ressources increases,
e.g. by adding specific tools or operators to run machines. For an additional set
k of necessary ressources, the number of possible solution increases to $((n!)^m)^k$
[38]. In the related *flow shop scheduling* problem, a fixed sequence of tasks forms
a job [16]. It is applicable to optimize the so called *makespan* on assembly lines.

Flow line analysis is a more complex setting, often done with queuing theory [8,
33]. Pioneering work in analyzing assembly queuing systems with synchronization
constraints analyzes assembly-like queues with unlimited buffer capacities [22]. It
shows that the time an item has to wait for synchronization may grow without
bound, while limitation of the number of items in the system works as a control
mechanism and ensures stability. Work on assembly-like queues with finite buffers
all assume exponential service times [4,26,30].

A rare example of model checking flow production are timed automata that
were used for simulating material flow in agricultural production [23].

Since the origin of the term artificial intelligence, the automated generation
of plans for a given task has been seen as an integral part of problem solving in
a computer. In *action planning* [35], we are confronted with the descriptions of
the initial state, the goal (states) and the available actions. Based on these we
want to find a plan containing as few actions as possible (in case of unit-cost
actions, or if no costs are specified at all) or with the lowest possible total cost
(in case of general action costs).

The process of fully-automated property validation and correctness verification is referred to as *model checking* [11]. Given a formal model of a system M
and a property specification ϕ in some form of temporal logic like LTL [17], the
task is to validate, whether or not the specification is satisfied in the model,
$M \models \phi$. If not, a model checker usually returns a counterexample trace as a
witness for the falsification of the property.

Planning and model checking have much in common [9,18]. Both rely on the
exploration of a potentially large state space of system states. Usually, model
checkers only search for the existence of specification errors in the model, while
planners search for a short path from the initial state to one of the goal states.
Nonetheless, there is rising interest in planners that prove insolvability [24], and
in model checkers to produce minimal counterexamples [14].

In terms of leveraging state space search, over the last decades there has been
much cross-fertilization between the fields. For example, based on Satplan [28]
bounded model checkers exploit SAT and SMT representations [2,5] of the system
to be verified, while *directed model checkers* [12,29] exploit panning heuristics
to improve the exploration for falsification; partial-order reduction [19,39] and
symmetry detection [15,32] limit the number of successor states, while symbolic
planners [10,13,27] apply functional data structures like BDDs to represent sets
of states succinctly.

4   Case Study

We consider the simulation of the real-world *Z2* production floor unit [34]. The
Z2 unit consists of six workstations where human workers assemble parts of
automotive tail-lights. The system allows production of certain product variations and reacts dynamically to any change in the current order situation, e.g.,
a decrease or an increase in the number of orders of a certain variant. As individual production steps are performed at the different stations, all stations are
interconnected by a monorail transport system. The structure of the transport
system is shown in Fig. 1. On the rails, autonomously moving shuttles carry the
products from one station to another, depending on the products' requirements.
The monorail system has multiple switches which allow the shuttles to enter,
leave or pass workstations and the central hubs. The goods transported by the
shuttles are also autonomous, which means that each product decides on its own
which variant to become and which station to visit. This way, a decentralized
control of the production system is possible.

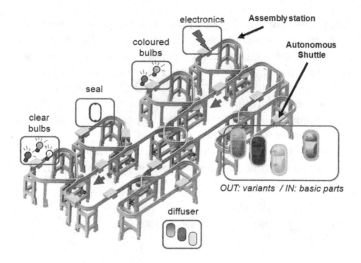

Fig. 1. Assembly scenario for tail-lights.

The modular system consists of six different workstations, each is operated
manually by a human worker and dedicated to one specific production step.
Different parts can be used to assemble different variants of the tail-lights. At the
first station, the basic metal-cast parts enter the monorail on a dedicated shuttle.
The monorail connects all stations, each station is assigned to one specific task,
such as adding bulbs or electronics. Each tail-light is transported from station
to station until it is assembled completely. In the DESS implementation of the
Z2 system, every assembly station, every monorail shuttle and every product is
represented by a software process. Even the RFID readers which keep track of

product positions are represented by software processes, which decide when a shuttle may pass or stop.

Most processes in this DESS resemble simple reflex methods. These processes just react to requests or events which were caused by other processes or the human workers involved in the manufacturing process. In contrast, the processes which represent products are actively working towards their individual goal of becoming a complete tail-light and reaching the storage station. In order to complete its task, each product has to reach sub-goals which may change during production as the order situation may change. The number of possible actions is limited by sub-goals which already have been reached, since every possible production step has individual preconditions.

The product processes constantly request updates regarding queue lengths at the various stations and the overall order situation. The information is used to compute the utility of the expected outcome of every action. High utility is given when an action leads to fulfillment of an outstanding order and takes as little time as possible. Time, in this case, is spent either on actions, such as moving along the railway or being processed, or on waiting in line at a station or a switch.

The Z2 DES was developed strictly for the purpose of controlling the Z2 monorail hardware setup. Nonetheless, due to its hardware abstraction layer [34], the Z2 DES can be adapted into other hardware or software environments. By replacing the hardware with other processes and adapting the monorail infrastructure into a directed graph, the Z2 DES has been transferred to a DESS [21]. Such an environment, which treats the original Z2 modules like black boxes, can easily be hosted by a DESS. Experiments showed how close the simulated and the real-world scenarios match.

For this study, we provided the model with timers to measure the time taken between two graph nodes. Since the hardware includes many RFID readers along

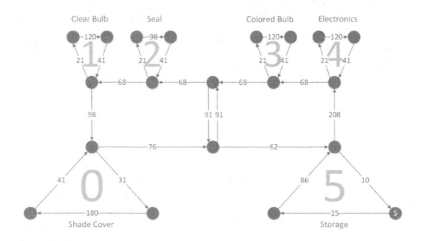

Fig. 2. Weighted graph model of the assembly scenario.

the monorail, which all are represented by an agent and a node within the simulation, we simplified the graph and kept only three types of nodes: switches, production station entrances and production station exits. The resulting abstract model of the system is a weighted graph (see Fig. 2), where the weight of an edge denotes the traveling/processing time of the shuttle between two respective nodes.

5   Promela Specification

Promela is the input language of the model checker Spin[1], the ACM-awarded popular open-source software verification tool, designed for the formal verification of multi-threaded software applications, and used by thousands of people worldwide. Promela defines asynchronously running communicating processes, which are compiled to finite state machines. It has a c-like syntax, and supports bounded channels for sending and receiving messages.

Channels in Promela follow the FIFO principle. Therefore, they implicitly maintain order of incoming messages and can be limited to a certain buffer size. Consequently, we are able to map edges to communication channels. Unlike the original Z2 ABS, the products are not considered to be decision making entities within our Promela model. Instead, the products are represented by messages which are passed along the *node processes*, which resemble switches, station entrances and exits.

Unlike the original DESS, the Promela model is designed to apply a branch-and-bound optimization to evaluate the optimal throughput of the original system. Instead of local decision making, the various processes have certain non-deterministic options of handling incoming messages, each leading to a different system state. The model checker systematically computes these states and memorizes paths to desirable outcomes when it ends up in a final state. As mentioned before, decreasing production time for a given number of products increases the utility of the final state.

We derive a Promela model of the Z2 as follows. First, we define global setting on the number of stations and number of switches. We also define the data type storing the index of the shuttle/product to be byte. In the model, switches are realized as processes and edges between the units by the following channels.

```
chan entrance_to_exit[STATIONS] = [1] of {shuttle};
chan exit_to_switch[STATIONS] = [BUFFERSIZE] of {shuttle};
chan switch_to_switch[SWITCHES] = [BUFFERSIZE] of {shuttle};
chan switch_to_entrance[STATIONS] = [BUFFERSIZE] of {shuttle};
```

As global variables, we have bit-vectors for marking the different assemblies.

```
bit metalcast[SHUTTLES]; bit electronics[SHUTTLES];
bit bulb[SHUTTLES]; bit seal[SHUTTLES]; bit cover[SHUTTLES];
```

---

[1] http://spinroot.com/spin/whatispin.html.

Additionally, we have a bit-vector that denotes when a shuttle with a fully assembled item has finally arrived at its goal location. A second bit-vector is used to set for each shuttle whether it has to acquire a colored or a clear bulb.

```
bit goals[SHUTTLES]; bit color[SHUTTLES];
```

A switch is a process that controls the flow of the shuttles. In the model, a non-deterministic choice is added to either enter the station or to continue traveling onwards on the cycle. Three of four switching options are made available, as immediate re-entering a station from its exit is prohibited.

```
proctype Switch(byte in; byte out; byte station) {
  shuttle s;
  do
  :: exit_to_switch[station]?s; switch_to_switch[out]!s;
  :: switch_to_switch[in]?s; switch_to_switch[out]!s;
  :: switch_to_switch[in]?s; switch_to_entrance[station]!s;
  od
}
```

The entrance of a manufacturing station takes the item from the according switch and moves it to the exit. It also controls that the manufacturing complies with the capability of the station.

First, the assembling of product parts is different at each station, in the stations 1 and 3 we have the insertion of bulbs (station 1 provides colored bulbs, station 3 provides clear bulbs), station 2 assembles the seal, station 4 the electronics and station 0 the cover. Station 5 is the storage station where empty metal casts are placed on the monorail shuttles and finished products are removed to be taken into storage. Secondly, there is a partial order of the respective product parts to allow flexible processing and a better optimization based on the current load of the ongoing production.

```
proctype Entrance(byte station) {
  shuttle s;
  do
  ::    switch_to_entrance[station]?s;
        entrance_to_exit[station]!s
        if
        :: (station == 4) -> electronics[s] = 1;
        :: (station == 3 && !color[s]) -> bulb[s] = 1;
        :: (station == 2)-> seal[s] = 1;
        :: (station == 1 && color[s]) -> bulb[s] = 1;
        :: (station == 0 && seal[s] && bulb[s] && electronics[s])-> cover[s] = 1;
        :: (station == 5 && cover[s]) -> goals[s] = 1;
        :: else
        fi
  od
}
```

An exit is a node that is located at the end of a station, at which assembling took place. It is connected to the entrance of the station and the switch linked to it.

```
proctype Exit(byte station) {
  shuttle s;
  do
  :: entrance_to_exit[station]?s; exit_to_switch[station]!s;
  od
}
```

A *hub* is a switch that is not connected to a station but provides a shortcut in the monorail network. Again, three of four possible shuttle movement options are provided

```
proctype Hub(byte in1; byte out1; byte in2; byte out2) {
  shuttle s;
  do
  ::   switch_to_switch[in1]?s; switch_to_switch[out1]!s;
  ::   switch_to_switch[in1]?s; switch_to_switch[out2]!s;
  ::   switch_to_switch[in2]?s; switch_to_switch[out1]!s;
  od
}
```

In the initial state, we start the individual processes, which represent switches and hereby define the network of the monorail system. Moreover, initially, we have that the metal cast of each product is already present on its carrier, the shuttle. The coloring of the tail-lights can be defined at the beginning or in the progress of the production. Last, but not least, we initialize the process by inserting shuttles on the starting rail (at station 5).

```
init {
  atomic {
    byte i;
    c_code { cost = 0; }
    c_code { best_cost = infinity; }
    for (i : 0 .. (SHUTTLES)/2)){ color[i] = 1; }
    for (i : 0 .. (SHUTTLES-1)) { metalcast[i] = 1; }
    for (i : 0 .. (STATIONS-1)) { run Entrance(i); run Exit(i); }
    run Switch(7,0,5); run Switch(0,1,4);
    run Switch(1,2,3); run Switch(3,4,2);
    run Switch(4,5,1); run Switch(5,6,0);
    run Hub(2,3,8,9); run Hub(6,7,9,8);
    for (i : 0 .. (SHUTTLES-1)) { exit_to_switch[5]!i; }}
}
```

We also heavily made use of the term `atomic`, which enhances the exploration for the model checker, allowing it to merge states within the search. In difference to the more aggressive d_step keyword, in an atomic block all communication queue actions are blocking, so that we chose to use an atomic block around each loop.

6   Optimized Scheduling

Inspired by [7,31,36] we applied and improved branch-and-bound (BnB) optimization. *Branching* is the process of spawning subproblems, while *bounding* refers to ignoring partial solutions that cannot be better than the current best solution. To this end, lower and upper bounds and are maintained as global control values on the solution quality, which improves over time.

For applying BnB to general flow manufacturing systems, we extend depth-first search (DFS) with upper (and lower) bounds. In this context, branching corresponds to the generation of successors, so that DFS can be casted as generating a *branch-and-bound search tree*. One way of obtaining a lower bound L for the problem state u is to apply an *admissible heuristic* h with $L(u) = g(u) + h(u)$, where g denotes the cost for reaching the current node from the root, and h is a function that always underestimates the remaining cost to reach a goal.

As with standard DFS, the first solution obtained might not be optimal. With *depth-first branch-and-bound* (DFBnB), however, the solution quality improves over time together with the global value U until eventually the lower bound $L(u)$ at some node u is equal to U. The pseudo-code of this approach is shown in Algorithm 1. In standard Spin, the trivial heuristic is $h \equiv 0$ used, but in HSF-Spin [12], a few heuristic functions have been implemented. We obtain the following result.

Theorem 1 *(Optimality of Branch-and-Bound for Flow Manufacturing).* For a admissible heuristic function h, the DFBnB procedure in Algorithm 1 will eventually find the optimal solution to the flow manufacturing problem $F = (A, E, G, \prec, S, Q)$.

Proof. We can compute costs for partial runs and extend partial schedules incrementally. The objective function to be minimized over all possible runs Π in the system is monotone increasing. Only inferior paths that cannot be extended to a better path than the currently best known one are pruned. As the state space is finite, the search will eventually terminate and return the optimal solution. q.e.d.

There are different options for finding optimized schedules with the help of a model checker that have been proposed in the literature. First, in the *Soldier* model of [37], rendezvous communication to an additional synchronized process has been used to increase cost, dependent on the transition chosen, together with a specialized LTL property to limit the total cost for the model checking solver. This approach, however, turned out to be limited for our purpose. An alternative proposal for branch-and-bound search is based on the support of native c-code in Spin (introduced in version 4.0) [36]. One running example is the traveling salesman problem (TSP), but the approach is generally applicable to many other optimization problems. However, as implemented, there are certain limitations to the

---

Algorithm 1. DFBnB Algorithm.

DFBnB$(F = (A, E, G, \prec, S, Q))$ **DFS**(F, u, π, U)
    Initialize upper bound U $\pi \leftarrow extend(\pi, u)$
    $\pi' \leftarrow \pi \leftarrow \emptyset$ **if** $(u = (t, \ldots, t))$
    $DFS(F, (s, \ldots, s), 0, U)$ **if** $(cost(\pi) < U)$ $\pi' \leftarrow \pi$; $U \leftarrow cost(\pi)$
    return π' **else for each** v **in** $successors(u)$
                                    if $(cost(\pi) + h(v) < U)$ $DFS(F, v, \pi, U)$

---

scalability of state space problem graphs. Recall that the problem graph induced by the TSP is in fact a tree, generating all possible permutations for the cities.

Following [7,12,36] we applied branch-and-bound optimization within Spin. Essentially, the model checker can find traces of several hundreds of steps and provides trace optimization by finding the shortest path towards a counterexample if ran with the parameter ./pan -i. As these traces are step-optimized, and not cost-optimized, Ruys [36] proposed to introduce a variable *cost* that we extend as follows.

```
c_state "int min_cost" "Hidden"          c_state "int min_cost" "Hidden"
c_code { int cost; }                     c_code { int cost[SHUTTLES]; }
c_track "cost" "sizeof(int)" "Matched"   c_track "cost" STRING "Matched"
```

While the *cost* variable increases the amount of memory required for each state, it also limits the power of Spins built-in duplicate detection, as two otherwise identical states are considered different if reached by different accumulated cost. If the search space is small, so that it can be explored even for the enlarged state vector, then this option is sound and complete, and finally returns the optimal solution to the optimization problem. However, there might be simply too many repetitions in the model so that introducing cost to the state vector leads to a drastic increase in state space size, so that otherwise checkable instances now become intractable. We noticed that even by concentrating on safety properties (such as the failed assertion mentioned), the insertion of costs causes troubles.

6.1 Guarded Branching

For our model, *cost* has to be tracked for every shuttle individually. The variable cost of the most expensive shuttle indicates the duration of the whole production process. Furthermore, the cost total provides insight regarding unnecessary detours or long waiting times. Hence, minimizing both criteria are the optimization goals of this model.

In Promela, every do-loop is allowed to contain an unlimited number of possible options for the model checker to choose from. The model checker randomly chooses between these options, however, it is possible to add an *if*-like condition to an option: If the first statement of a do option holds, Spin will start to execute the following statements, otherwise, it will pick a different option.

Since the model checker explores any possible state of the system, many of these states are technically reachable but completely useless from an optimization point of view. In order to reduce state space size to a manageable level, we add constraints to the relevant receiving options in the do-loops of every node process.

Peeking into the incoming queue to find out, which shuttle is waiting to be received is already considered a complete statement in Promela. Therefore, we exploit C-expressions (c_expr) to combine several operations into one atomic statement. For every station t and every incoming channel q, a function $prerequisites(t, q)$ determines, if the first shuttle in q meets the prerequisites for t, as given by Fig. ??.

```
shuttle s;
do
:: c_expr{prerequisites(Px->q,Px->t)} -> channel[q]?s; channel[out]!;
od
```

At termination of a successful run, we now extend the proposeal of [36]. We use the integer array cost[SHUTTLES] of the Promela model. It enables each process to keep track of its local cost vector and is increased by the cost of each action as soon as the action is executed. This enables the model checker to print values to the output, only if the values of the current max cost and total cost have improved.

```
terminate:
c_code {
  int max = 0, total = 0, j;
  for (j=0; j<SHUTTLES; j++) {
    total += cost[j];
    if (cost[j] > max) max = cost[j]; }
  if (max < min_cost) { min_cost = max; putrail(); Nr_Trails--; };
}
```

For solution reconstruction, we write a file for each new cost value obtained, temporarily renaming the trail file as follows.

```
char mytrailfile[512];
sprintf(mytrailfile, "%s_t%d_st%d.pr", base,min_cost,total);
char* y = mytrailfile;
swap(&TrailFile, &y);
putrail();
swap(&y, &TrailFile);
```

6.2 Process Synchronization

Due to the nature of the state space search of the model checker, processes in the Promela model do not make decisions. Nonetheless, the given model is a distributed DES consisting of a varying number of processes, which potentially influence each other if executed in parallel.

We addressed this problem by introducing an event-based time progress to the Promela model. Whenever a shuttle s travels along one of the edges, the corresponding message is put into a channel and the cost of the respective shuttle is increased by the cost of the given edge.

```
shuttle s;
do
:: c_expr{ canreceive(channel,Px->q,Px->station) }
   -> channel[q]?s
   c_code { cost[s] += Px->c; }
   channel[out] ! s;
od
```

We introduce an atomic C function $canreceive(q)$ that returns true only if the first item s of q has minimal $cost(s)$, changing the receiving constraint to the following.

```
c_code {
int canreceive(int channeltype, int arrayidx, int station) {
  int channelidx = -1;
  switch(channeltype) {
        case xyz: channelidx = now.xyz[arrayidx]; break; [...]
  }
  if(channelidx > -1 && q_len(channelidx) > 0) {
    int shuttle = qrecv(channelidx, 0, 0, 0);
    int minimum = infinity;
    for (int j=0; j<SHUTTLES; j++) {
      if (cost[j] < minimum) minimum = cost[j]; }
    return (minimum == cost[shuttle]); }
  return 0;
}
```

Within Spin, the global Boolean variable `timeout` is automatically set to *true* when all current processes are unable to proceed, e.g., because they cannot receive a message. Consequently, for every shuttle p, all processes will be blocked and `timeout` will be set to *true*. As suggested by Bošnački and Dams [6], we add a process that enforces time progress, whenever `timeout` occurs (*final* is a macro for reaching the goal).

```
active proctype watchdog() {
    do
    ::timeout -> c_code{ increase(); } ; assert(!final);
    od
}
```

Time delay is enforced as follows: if the minimum event in the future event list is blocked (e.g., a shuttle is not first in its queue), we compute the wake-up time of the second best event. If the two are of the same time, a time increment of 1 is enforced. In the other case, the second best event time is taken as the new one for the first. It is easy to see that this strategy eventually resolves all possible deadlocks. Its implementation is as follows.

```
int increase() {
  int j, l = 0, minimum = cost[0];
  for (j=1; j<SHUTTLES; j++)
    if (cost[j] < minimum) { minimum = cost[j]; l = j; }
  int second = infinity;
  for (j=0; j<SHUTTLES; j++) {
    if (cost[j] < second && cost[j] > minimum)
      second = cost[j];  }
  cost[l] = (second == infinity) ? minimum + 1 : second;
}
```

As a summary, the constraint bounded depth-first exploration has turned into the automated generation of the underlying state space of the DES, using c-code to preserve the causality of actions and to simulate the future event list.

7   Evaluation

In this section, we present results of a series of experiments executing two different Promela models. We compare the results of the exploration minimizing local virtual time (LVT) [20] to the ones simulating the discrete event system (DES) described in this paper. For comparison, we also present results of simulation runs of the original implementation on hardware [21].

Unlike the original system, the Promela models do not rely on local decision making but searches for an optimal solution systematically. Therefore, both Promela models resemble a centralized planning approach.

For executing the model checking, we chose version 6.4.3 of Spin. As a compiler we used *gcc* version 4.9.3, with the *posix* thread model. For the standard setting of trace optimization for safety checking (option –DSAFETY), we compiled the model as follows.

```
./spin -a z2.pr;
gcc -O2 -DREACH -DSAFETY -o pan pan.c;
./pan -i -m30000
```

Parameter –i stands for the incremental optimization of the counterexample length. We regularly increased the maximal tail length with option –m, as in some cases of our running example, the traces turned out to be longer than the standard setting of at most 10000 steps. Option –DREACH is needed to warrant minimal counterexamples at the end. To run experiments, we used a common

Table 1. Sequences of events for $n = 3$ products. (*Product* $\Rightarrow$ *Station*, where $\Rightarrow$ indicates a finished production step.)

ABS	LVT	DES
$0 \Rightarrow 4$	$0 \Rightarrow 4$	$0 \Rightarrow 4$
$1 \Rightarrow 2$	$1 \Rightarrow 4$	$1 \Rightarrow 4$
$0 \Rightarrow 3$	$2 \Rightarrow 4$	$2 \Rightarrow 4$
$2 \Rightarrow 1$	$0 \Rightarrow 3$	$0 \Rightarrow 3$
$0 \Rightarrow 2$	$2 \Rightarrow 3$	$1 \Rightarrow 2$
$1 \Rightarrow 4$	$1 \Rightarrow 2$	$2 \Rightarrow 3$
$0 \Rightarrow 0$	$1 \Rightarrow 1$	$0 \Rightarrow 2$
$2 \Rightarrow 4$	$2 \Rightarrow 2$	$1 \Rightarrow 1$
$0 \Rightarrow 5$	$1 \Rightarrow 0$	$2 \Rightarrow 2$
$1 \Rightarrow 1$	$0 \Rightarrow 2$	$0 \Rightarrow 0$
$2 \Rightarrow 2$	$2 \Rightarrow 0$	$1 \Rightarrow 0$
$1 \Rightarrow 0$	$0 \Rightarrow 0$	$2 \Rightarrow 0$
$2 \Rightarrow 0$	$1 \Rightarrow 5$	$0 \Rightarrow 5$
$1 \Rightarrow 5$	$2 \Rightarrow 5$	$1 \Rightarrow 5$
$2 \Rightarrow 5$	$0 \Rightarrow 5$	$2 \Rightarrow 5$

notebook with an Intel(R) Core(TM) i7-4710HQ CPU at 2.50 GHz, 16 GB of RAM and Windows 10 (64 Bit).

For smaller problems we experimented with Spin's parallel BFS (–DBFS_PAR), as it computes optimal-length counterexamples. The hash table is shared based on compare-and-swap (CAS). We also tried supertrace/bitstate hashing (-DBITSTATE) as a trade-off. Unfortunately, BFS interacts with c_track, so we had to drop the experiments for cost optimization. Swarm tree search (./swarm –c3 –m16G –t1 –f) found many solutions, some of them being shorter than the ones offered by option –i (indicating ordering effects), but due to the increased amount of randomness, for the optimized scheduling in general no better results that ordinary DFS were found.

In each experiment run, a number of $n \in \{2 \ldots 20\}$ shuttles carry products through the facility. All shuttles with even IDs acquire clear bulbs, all shuttles with odd IDs acquire colored ones.

A close look at the experiment results of every simulation run reveals that, given the same number of products to produce, all three approaches result in different sequences of events. However, LVT and DES propose the same sequence of production steps for the product of each shuttle. The example given in Fig. 1 shows that for all shuttles $0 \ldots 2$ the scheduling sequence is exactly the same in LVT and DES, while the original ABS often proposes a different schedule. In the given example, both LVT and DES propose a sequence of $4, 2, 1, 0, 5$ for shuttle 1. To the contrary, the ABS approach proposes $2, 1, 4, 0, 5$ for shuttle 1. The same phenomenon can be observed for every $n \in \{2 \ldots 20\}$ number of shuttles.

All three simulation models keep track of the local production time of each shuttle's product. In ABS and LVT simulation, minimizing maximum local production time is the optimization goal. Steady, synchronized progress of time is maintained centrally after every production step. Hence, whenever a shuttle has to wait in a queue, its total production time increases. For the DES model, progress of time is managed differently, as illustrated in Sect. 6.2. Results show that max. production time in DES is lower than LVT and ABS production times in all cases.

For every experiment, the amount of RAM required by DES to determine an optimal solution is slightly lower than the amount required by LVT as shown in Table 2. While the LVT required several iterations to find an optimal solution, the first valid solution found by DES was already the optimal solution in any conducted experiment. However, the LVT model is able to search the whole state space within the 16 GB RAM limit (given by our machine) for $n \leq 3$ shuttles, whereas the DES model is unable to search the whole state space for $n > 2$. For every experiment with $n > 3$ (LVT) or $n > 2$ (DES) shuttles respectively, searching the state space for better results was cancelled, when the 16 GB RAM limit was reached.

Table 2. Simulated production times for n products in the original ABS and Spin simulation, including the amount of RAM required to compute the given result.

Products	ABS	LVT		DES	
	Max. Prod. Time	Max. Prod. Time	RAM	Max. Prod. Time	RAM
2	4:01	3:24	987 MB[a]	2:53	731 MB[a]
3	4:06	3:34	2154 MB[a]	3:04	503 MB
4	4:46	3:56	557 MB	3:13	519 MB
5	4:16	4:31	587 MB	3:25	541 MB
6	5:29	4:31	611 MB	3:34	565 MB
7	5:18	5:08	636 MB	3:45	587 MB
8	5:57	5:43	670 MB	3:55	610 MB
9	6:00	5:43	692 MB	4:06	635 MB
10	6:08	5:43	715 MB	4:15	557 MB
20	9:03	8:56	977 MB	5:59	857 MB

[a] indicates that the whole state space was searched within the given RAM usage

While the experiments indicate that the DES is faster and more memory efficient than the LVT approach, we observe that the mapping cost to time in the DES is limited. Assuming that events are processed by the time stamp while inserted in the priority queue is a limitation. Extensions of the future event list supporting the priority queue operation *increaseKey* have to be looked at. In our experiment if one element in a process queue was delayed, all the ones behind it were delayed as well. While DES and LVT are both sound in resolving deadlocks, LVT has the more accurate representation for the progress of time.

8   Conclusions

Simulation provides a method to approximate the behaviour in a real system (and, hence, can be used for testing scenarios). Constructing the model can prove useful in achieving greater understanding of the system. In this paper, we presented a novel approach for model checking (instead of simulating) DES. The research is motivated by our interest in finding and comparing centralized and distributed solutions to the optimization problems in autonomous manufacturing.

Using model checking for optimizing DES is a relative new playground for formal method tools in form of a new analysis paradigm. The formal model in Promela reflects the routing and scheduling of entities in the DES. Switches of the rail network were modeled as processes, the edges between the switches as communication channels. Additional constraints to the order of production steps enable to carry out a complex planning and scheduling task. Our results clearly indicate a lot of room for improvement in the decentralized solution, since the model checker found more efficient ways to route and schedule the shuttles on several occasions. Furthermore, the model checker could derive optimized plans of several thousand steps.

References

1. Abdeddaïm, Y., Maler, O.: Job-shop scheduling using timed automata. In: Berry, G., Comon, H., Finkel, A. (eds.) CAV 2001. LNCS, vol. 2102, p. 478. Springer, Heidelberg (2001)
2. Armando, A., Mantovani, J., Platania, L.: Bounded model checking of software using SMT solvers instead of SAT solvers. In: Valmari, A. (ed.) SPIN 2006. LNCS, vol. 3925, pp. 146–162. Springer, Heidelberg (2006)
3. Bagchi, T.P.: Multiobjective Scheduling by Genetic Algorithms. Springer, USA (1999)
4. Bhat, U.: Finite capacity assembly-like queues. Queueing Syst. 1, 85–101 (1986)
5. Biere, A., Cimatti, A., Clarke, E., Zhu, Y.: Symbolic model checking without BDDs. In: Cleaveland, W.R. (ed.) TACAS 1999. LNCS, vol. 1579, p. 193. Springer, Heidelberg (1999)
6. Bosnacki, D., Dams, D.: Integrating real time into spin: a prototype implementation. In: Budkowski, S., Cavalli, A., Najm, E. (eds.) FORTE/PSTV, pp. 423–438. Springer, New York (1998)
7. Brinksma, E., Mader, A.: Verification and optimization of a PLC control schedule. SPIN 1885, 73–92 (2000)
8. Burman, M.: New results in flow line analysis. Ph.D. thesis, Massachusetts Institute of Technology (1995)
9. Cimatti, A., Giunchiglia, E., Giunchiglia, F., Traverso, P.: Planning via model checking: a decision procedure for AR. In: Steel, S. (ed.) ECP 1997. LNCS, vol. 1348, pp. 130–142. Springer, Heidelberg (1997)
10. Cimatti, A., Roveri, M., Traverso, P.: Automatic OBDD-based generation of universal plans in non-deterministic domains. In: AAAI, pp. 875–881 (1998)
11. Clarke, E., Grumberg, O., Peled, D.: Model Checking. MIT Press, Cambridge (2000)

12. Edelkamp, S., Lluch-Lafuente, A., Leue, S.: Directed model-checking in HSF-SPIN. In: SPIN, pp. 57–79 (2001)
13. Edelkamp, S., Reffel, F.: OBDDs in heuristic search. In: Herzog, O. (ed.) KI 1998. LNCS, vol. 1504, pp. 81–92. Springer, Heidelberg (1998)
14. Edelkamp, S., Sulewski, D.: Flash-efficient LTL model checking with minimal counterexamples. In: SEFM, pp. 73–82 (2008)
15. Fox, M., Long, D.: The detection and exploration of symmetry in planning problems. In: IJCAI, pp. 956–961 (1999)
16. Garey, M.R., Johnson, D.S., Sethi, R.: The complexity of flowshop and jobshop scheduling. Math. Oper. Res. **1**(2), 117–129 (1976)
17. Gerth, R., Peled, D., Vardi, M., Wolper, P.: Simple on-the-fly automatic verification of linear temporal logic. In: PSTV, pp. 3–18 (1995)
18. Giunchiglia, F., Traverso, P.: Planning as model checking. In: Biundo, S., Fox, M. (eds.) ECP 1999. LNCS, vol. 1809, pp. 1–19. Springer, Heidelberg (2000)
19. Godefroid, P.: Using partial orders to improve automatic verification methods. In: Clarke, E., Kurshan, R.P. (eds.) CAV 1990. LNCS, vol. 531, pp. 176–185. Springer, Heidelberg (1991)
20. Greulich, C., Edelkamp, S.: Branch-and-bound optimization of a multiagent system for flow production using model checking. In: ICAART (2016)
21. Greulich, C., Edelkamp, S., Eicke, N.: Cyber-physical multiagent-simulation in production logistics. In: Müller, J.P., et al. (eds.) MATES 2015. LNCS, vol. 9433, pp. 119–136. Springer, Heidelberg (2015). doi:10.1007/978-3-319-27343-3_7
22. Harrison, J.: Assembly-like queues. J. Appl. Prob. **10**, 354–367 (1973)
23. Helias, A., Guerrin, F., Steyer, J.-P.: Using timed automata and model-checking to simulate material flow in agricultural production systems - application to animal waste management. Comput. Electr. Agric. **63**(2), 183–192 (2008)
24. Hoffmann, J., Kissmann, P., Torralba, Á.: "Distance"? Who cares? tailoring merge-and-shrink heuristics to detect unsolvability. In: ECAI, pp. 441–446 (2014)
25. Holzmann, G.J.: The SPIN Model Checker - Primer and Reference Manual. Addison-Wesley, Boston (2004)
26. Hopp, W., Simon, J.: Bounds and heuristics for assembly-like queues. Queueing Syst. **4**, 137–156 (1989)
27. Jensen, R.M., Veloso, M.M., Bowling, M.H.: OBDD-based optimistic and strong cyclic adversarial planning. In: ECpP (2001)
28. Kautz, H., Selman, B.: Pushing the envelope: planning propositional logic, and stochastic search. In: ECAI, pp. 1194–1201 (1996)
29. Kupferschmid, S., Hoffmann, J., Dierks, H., Behrmann, G.: Adapting an AI planning heuristic for directed model checking. In: Valmari, A. (ed.) SPIN 2006. LNCS, vol. 3925, pp. 35–52. Springer, Heidelberg (2006)
30. Lipper, E., Sengupta, E.: Assembly-like queues with finite capacity: bounds, asymptotics and approximations. Queueing Syst. **1**(1), 67–83 (1986)
31. Liu, W., Gu, Z., Xu, J., Wang, Y., Yuan, M.: An efficient technique for analysis of minimal buffer requirements of synchronous dataflow graphs with model checking. In: CODES+ISSS, pp. 61–70 (2009)
32. Lluch-Lafuente, A.: Symmetry reduction and heuristic search for error detection in model checking. In: MOCHART, pp. 77–86 (2003)
33. Manitz, M.: Queueing-model based analysis of assembly lines with finite buffers and general service times. Comput. Oper. Res. **35**(8), 2520–2536 (2008)
34. Morales Kluge, E., Ganji, F., Scholz-Reiter, B.: Intelligent products - towards autonomous logistic processes - a work in progress paper. In: International PLM Conference (2010)

35. Nau, D., Ghallab, M., Traverso, P.: Automated Planning: Theory and Practice. Morgan Kaufmann Publishers Inc., San Francisco (2004)
36. Ruys, T.C.: Optimal scheduling using branch and bound with SPIN 4.0. In: Ball, T., Rajamani, S.K. (eds.) SPIN 2003. LNCS, vol. 2648, pp. 1–17. Springer, Heidelberg (2003)
37. Ruys, T.C., Brinksma, E.: Experience with literate programming in the modelling and validation of systems. In: Steffen, B. (ed.) TACAS 1998. LNCS, vol. 1384, p. 393. Springer, Heidelberg (1998)
38. Shen, W., Wang, L., Hao, Q.: Planning, agent-based distributed manufacturing process scheduling: a state-of-the-art survey. IEEE Trans. Syst. Man Cybern., Part C (Appl. Rev.) **36**(4), 563–577 (2006)
39. Valmari, A.: A stubborn attack on state explosion. Lect. Notes Comput. Sci. **531**, 156–165 (1991)
40. Wijs, A.: What to do next? analysing and optimising system behaviour in time. Ph.D. thesis, Vrije Universiteit Amsterdam (2007)

River Basin Management with SPIN

María-del-Mar Gallardo, Pedro Merino, Laura Panizo(✉),
and Alberto Salmerón

Andalucía Tech, Dept. de Lenguajes y Ciencias de la Computación,
Universidad de Málaga, Málaga, Spain
{gallardo,pedro,laurapanizo,salmeron}@lcc.uma.es

Abstract. This paper presents the use of the SPIN model checker as the core engine to build Decision Support Systems (DSSs) to control complex river basins during flood situations. Current DSSs in this domain are mostly based on simulators to predict the rainfall and the water flow along the river basin.

In this paper, we propose a scheme that integrates simulators in the water domain with additional logic in PROMELA to represent basin elements, such as dams, their management rules, the evolution of dam parameters (e.g. level or discharge capacity), and user defined constraints in the whole basin over time. Then, we use the exploration capabilities of SPIN to find out which sequences of operations over the dams produce a global behaviour that mitigates the effect of floods according to user defined constraints along the river basin. Although the method is general for any river basin with dams, it has been evaluated in a real basin in the south of Spain.

1 Introduction

Mediterranean countries, like Spain, have built many big dams which ensure the water supply to the population during typical long drought periods, and also limit the damage caused by floods by means of their flood discharge capacity (Spain is the fourth country in number of big dams, following USA, China and India). However, experience has demonstrated [14] that during a flood episode, the incorrect management of a dam can produce disasters worse than if the dam did not exist. This problem is even more complex when there are several dams in the same river basin, because of the difficulty to predict the cumulative effect of water discharging at several points in parallel.

The most common way to manage dams during flood episodes is based on the combination of weather forecasts and ad-hoc decision rules. The dam operators usually estimate the input of water over time (the *input hydrograph*) with official forecasts, and employ a pre-designed catalogue of management rules to decide water discharges. These rules take into account different parameters, e.g. the

This work has been partially funded by the Regional Government of Andalusia under grant P11-TIC-07659, and the European Comission under FP7 Environment project SAID, Grant agreement 619132, and FEDER.

D. Bošnacki and A. Wijs (Eds.): SPIN 2016, LNCS 9641, pp. 78–96, 2016.
DOI: 10.1007/978-3-319-32582-8_5

reservoir level, the weather forecast, the current downstream drainage capacity, etc. One recent trend is the development of software systems that act as reliable Decision Support Systems (DSSs) to assist dam managers in floods [10,11]. These DSSs are based on simulation models that allow a detailed and faithful representation of a real-world system with complex mathematical models. However, they can only show the effect of applying a specific management policy. With this approach, a large number of trials is necessary to establish an optimal policy, which can drastically reduce the time to react to the flood.

In [7], we introduced the use of model checking as a promising novel approach to build more powerful DSSs for flood management in a single dam. The proposal works as follows. We describe the dam's physical components (like spillways to discharge water) with PROMELA as well as a non-deterministic process simulating the dam manager's actions on the physical discharge elements. An external tool provides the representation of the expected input water flow to the dam over time as a hydrograph. Finally, we added constraints to keep the dam level between a minimum and maximum value or to discharge a maximum flow downstream. Constraints are encoded as a *never claim*, a special PROMELA process. SPIN uses these inputs and generates a counterexample that corresponds to the manoeuvres over dams that satisfy the constraints.

Our previous work focused on managing a single dam. Thus, to manage a complex river basin with more than one dam, the dam operators must manually run our DSS for each dam and the hydrologic basin models, appropriately linking the inputs and outputs to simulate the state of the basin. However, this is unfeasible in practice. In this paper, we extend our previous work to use SPIN as the core engine of a DSS for the coordinated management of all the dams in a river basin. We reuse the initial work in [7] to model every dam in the basin in a single PROMELA model, and we integrate an external hydrologic river basin model to simulate the effects of the dams downstream. The constraints over basin locations are checked externally, and the result of the evaluation directly affects the SPIN exploration algorithm. The PROMELA model of the river basin now includes several dams, integrates different external (hydrodynamic) models and safety constraints over the basin, and the management rules modeled as a non-deterministic process. We make extensive use of embedded C code in PROMELA, tracking a minimal number of variables and abstractions to reduce the state space. The embedded C code is also used to deal with discretized continuous variables, and to propagate the effects of dam manoeuvres throughout the basin, using different time references. The output of the verification process is a sequence (or several sequences) of coordinated manoeuvres for all the dams to assist the manager in the decision making process. We have implemented the system for a real river basin in the south of Spain, and validated its performance and usefulness with real scenarios.

To the best of our knowledge, there are no works on the use of model checking to synthesize the manoeuvres in flood episodes. Compared with other works in this domain, like FCROS [9] in Poland, DESMOF [2] in Canada, or IMSFCR [4] in China, our approach offers several novelties. While FCROS and DESMOF only include simulation of flood policies, our DSS and IMSFCR also calculate the necessary operations. IMSFCR makes multi-objective optimisation based on fuzzy iteration, but it does not consider hydrological models downstream.

The rest of the paper is organized as follows. Section 2 provides some background on dam management and presents the case study used in the paper. Section 3 describes our approach based on model checking, while Sect. 4 details how to build the PROMELA models of the river basin. Section 5 explains how to define constraints over the dam parameters and the basin flows. Section 6 is devoted to the evaluation with the case study, and finally Sect. 7 presents the conclusions and future work.

2 Background on Flood Management

Flood management is a complex task, especially in Mediterranean basins, which are characterized by long drought periods and short but intense rainfalls. Dams are an important element in this kind of basin, as they store water for two main purposes: to supply water to the population in drought periods and to control floods. With correct management, a dam can smooth the peak rainfall and avoid downstream flooding.

Dams are equipped with different types of discharge elements. Figure 1 shows the discharge elements of the Conde del Guadalhorce dam, which is included in our case study. Spillways are gates for flood regulation. They usually have the highest discharge capacity. Outflows can be used for flood regulation or other water uses (supply, irrigation or energy production), and their discharge capacity is lower. In general, the outflow capacity of a dam's outlets depends on their location, which is fixed, their opening degree, which is variable, and the dam

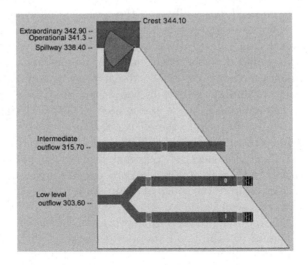

Fig. 1. Dam discharge elements

level, which changes following Eq. 1, where $V(t)$ and $V(t - 1)$ are respectively, the water stored at instant t and $t - 1$, $Inflow(t)$ represents the water input and $Q_{s_i}(t)$ is the water discharged by outlet s_i. Equation 2 shows the discharge capacity of a spillway gate, where h_{s1} and h_{s2} are the water level and the position of the gate evolving over time. The other components, C and L, depend on the geometry of the gates and can be considered constant.

$$V(t) = V(t - 1) + (Inflow(t) - \sum_{i=1}^{n} Q_{s_i}(t)) \tag{1}$$

$$Q_s(t) = CL(\sqrt{h_{s1}(t)^3} - \sqrt{h_{s2}(t)^3}) \tag{2}$$

Basin and dam management are controversial issues, especially in flood scenarios. Dam management has been traditionally carried out by a human operator, who has to manage in parallel the different outflow elements. In addition, a basin can include several dams in parallel and/or cascade, and the management of one dam can have a direct impact on the other dams and on the population downstream. Moreover, in Mediterranean basins, with short and intense rainfalls, dam managers have little time to decide how to operate to ensure dam safety considering the management of the other dams.

2.1 The Guadalhorce Case Study

In this work, the case study is the Guadalhorce River basin, located in the province of Málaga, in the South of Spain. The basin has a total area of $3,175 \text{ km}^2$ and is responsible supplying water to the city of Málaga, a touristic city with a population of more than 500,000 inhabitants. In addition, the basin supplies water and irrigation to other small cities of the province. The Guadalhorce basin has a short concentration time: water flows from the headwater to the mouth in approximately 8 h. Figure 2 shows the basin area. The Guadalhorce is the main river of the basin. Its flow is controlled by means of three dams (Guadalhorce, Guadalteba and Conde del Guadalhorce), which are located at the confluence of the Guadalhorce with the Turón and Guadalteba rivers. The three dams are managed by the Andalusian Regional Ministry (Consejería de Medio Ambiente y Ordenación del Territorio), and are used for flood management and water supply. Table 1 shows the main data of the three dams.

The management of the Guadalhorce and Guadalteba dams is special. These dams are separated by a wall measuring 355 masl (meters above sea level) from the base. During the flood season water is usually over this level and both dams are managed as a single dam. In fact, they have been designed to share the spillway, which is located in the Guadalteba dam. From now on, we will refer to the Conde del Guadalhorce dam as CGH, and to the Guadalhorce and Guadalteba dam jointly as GH-GT. Since the three dams and their outlets are very close, an important aspect of their management is the synchronization of peak discharges to avoid downstream flooding. In the main river channel there are no other dams downstream, but there are many tributaries that flow into the Guadalhorce River. The largest tributaries in volume are the Grande River, which flow

Table 1. Main characteristics of the dams

	Guadalhorce	Guadalteba	Conde G.
Operational level (masl)	362.25	362.25	341.3
Volume at op. level (hm^3)	125.8	153.3	66.5
Extraordinary level	364.0	364.0	342.9
Crest level	367.0	367.0	344.1
Low level outflow			
Number of gates	2	2	2
Level (masl)	302.5	308	304
Spillway			
Number of gates	-	4	2
Level(masl)	-	356	338.4

masl: meters above sea level

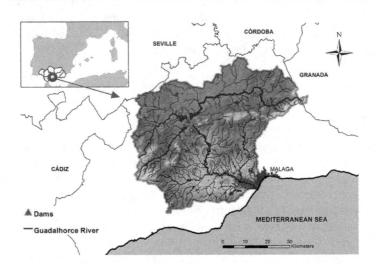

Fig. 2. Guadalhorce river basin

into the Guadalhorce 35 km downstream, and the Campanillas River, which merges near the river mouth.

From the point of view of flood management, the basin has 4 locations in which water flow must be monitored. The first one is La Encantada hydroelectric plant, which is located 7 km downstream of the dams. The second and third locations are at the confluence of the Grande River and the Campanillas River with the main river channel. Finally, the fourth point is the river mouth, which is located in the city of Málaga, near the international airport.

In this work we present a DSS for this basin based on model checking. The dam manager has to define constraints that describe the desired behaviour of the basin for a specific flood episode. Then, the DSS produces a sequence of manoeuvres that satisfies the constraints. Figure 3 shows an example of the results produced by the DSS. At the top, are the level and total outflows of the dams. Then, the evolution of gates' openings is displayed. Finally, on the bottom the water flows in the basin are shown.

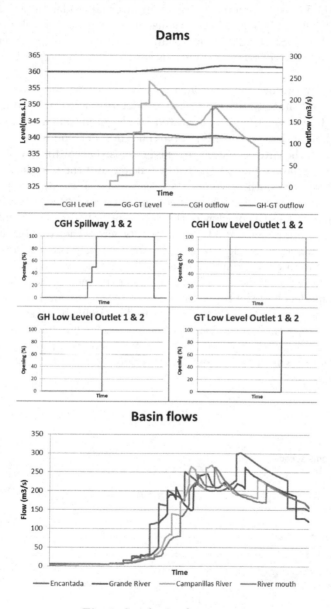

Fig. 3. Synthesis of manouvers

3   Approach with Model Checking

We use model checking in order to synthesize management recommendations that meet the constraints given by the dam manager. We use SPIN [8] as the underlying model checker, and, in consequence, PROMELA as modelling language. In addition, the PROMELA model also uses an external model for the river basin, developed independently. Given a set of constraints over the variables of the dams and the river basin, SPIN will explore exhaustively all possible manoeuvres, and produce a suitable set of recommendations for the dam manager that fulfils the constraints.

Figure 4 shows an overview of our approach, and how the PROMELA model used by SPIN and the external river basin model interact. First, we must model the dam (or dams) which will be operated by the dam manager. The management of the dam outlets is defined in a partially non-deterministic model, which determines when the gates should be opened or closed according to the operation rules, affecting variables such as the water outflow and the dam level over time, and consequently the outflow across the river basin. The latter is provided by an external river basin model, which is not modelled in PROMELA. The external river basin model takes the outflow of the dams and other environmental aspects as input, and computes the flow at several points across the river basin. All these models will be described in Sect. 4. Finally, the user may set restrictions on the outflows of the dam or at points of interest across the river basin, using timed automata, or upper and lower curve bounds, as explained in Sect. 5.

Once the models and the restrictions are in place, the analysis can proceed. The dam manager modelled in SPIN is executed periodically to select and apply one manoeuvre from those available from the rules. The dam model computes the water discharged between manoeuvres. This will serve as input for the external river basin model, which is also executed periodically to compute the outflow along the basin.

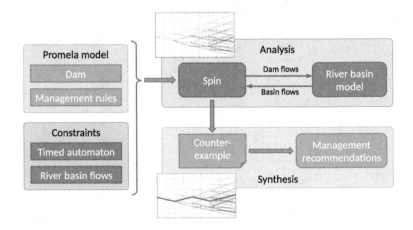

Fig. 4. Overview of synthesis of recommendations for dam management

Depending on the state of the dams and the set of management rules, the management model may have several options available whenever it has to make a decision. These options constitute the state space to be explored. Thanks to the exhaustive exploration provided by SPIN, the analysis can obtain all possible manoeuvres that the dam manager can choose during the course of an episode. If a particular series of actions leads to a state that violates the constraints over the dams or the basin, SPIN will backtrack and try different manoeuvres, until the end of the episode is reached while fulfilling specified constraints. This will produce a counterexample that contains the manoeuvres that satisfy the constraints.

4 Dam and Basin Modelling

The management of the river basin is based on the analysis of a PROMELA basin model against a set of properties that describes the constraints of dam and basin parameters, such as dam level or water flow. It is worth noting that some of these parameters have a continuous evolution over time and have to be properly represented to avoid state-space explosion problems.

The global model of the basin comprises different sub-models, such as the model of the dams and their outlets, or the model of the water flow downstream. As mentioned above, in this work, we have used PROMELA as the modelling language, embedding C code to describe some complex mathematical equations. In addition, we have used C code to embed the interaction with external models developed by third parties.

In this section, we describe the main structure of these sub-models, and some specific issues for the case study.

4.1 Dam Model

There are two main aspects that must be taken into account by a dam model. First, it must describe the evolution of the main variables of the dam over time and how they are related, e.g. the relation between dam volume and dam level (dam's bathymetry), the relation of the stored water volume and the water inflow and outflow over time, etc. Second, it must provide a mechanism to change the state of the dam outlets, i.e. their opening degree, during the analysis.

In [7], we presented a simplified version of a dam model. We describe the dam as a PROMELA proctype that receives commands from the dam manager (another proctype) to change the opening degree of the outlets. After updating the state of the outlets, the model computes the flow discharged by means of embedded C code that describes the outlet equations. In this work, we have improved the dam model such that it is now possible to describe and analyze the behaviour of dams with more outlets, more outlet opening degrees, and longer flood episodes. In addition, we also allow non operative outlets, i.e. outlets whose state cannot be changed. Figure 5 shows the skeleton of the dam model used in the case study.

To reduce the state space to be explored, we make extensive use of embedded C code, and export some of the C variables into SPIN's state. Some of these variables have been declared as UnMatched, i.e. outside the scope of SPIN's state matching algorithm, to reduce the of number states. In other cases, we have abstracted the values of several UnMatched variables into a single variable in SPIN's state. For instance, the current opening degree of each gate of an outlet is UnMatched, but we include a single matched variable that abstracts these values. This abstract variable only provides the number of gates that are opened or closed, and not which ones are opened or close, which is not of interest from the point of view of the exploration. However, if SPIN backtracks, the exact state of each gate will be recovered.

Finally, we have defined a systematic way of defining this kind of dam model, which has been implemented in a prototype tool as part of the SAID project [1]. Using this tool, it is possible to easily develop models of new dams without errors.

4.2   River Basin Model

To manage a complete river basin, we need a hydrological model that simulates the water inflow to the dams and the flow downstream. There exist different hydrological models and simulation engines that fulfil our needs. In particular, other partners in the SAID project have used a basin model through the WiMMed tool [5, 13]. Instead of translating these models to PROMELA code, we treat them as black boxes that produce the required output given the appropriate inputs, such as the outflows from the dams and the environmental inflows.

Before the analysis, we first run the black box to produce the inflow hydrographs of the dams for the particular flood episode we are analysing. These inflow hydrographs are independent of the manoeuvres performed during the analysis. Then, during the analysis with SPIN, the black box model will be executed periodically using embedded C code to simulate the water flow downstream for different sets of manoeuvres. The model will return the resulting hydrographs at predefined locations in the basin, showing how the manoeuvres affect the flow along the river basin.

While the PROMELA model tries different manoeuvres with a short time period, e.g. every hour, external river basin models are usually meant to simulate longer periods of time, e.g. several days. Executing the external river basin model for each new manoeuvre to find out their effect downstream can be very time consuming. To solve this problem, we use a longer period to execute the external model, i.e. the external model will be executed after the management model has selected the manoeuvres for the past few hours.

In addition, we are only interested in the portion of the simulation which was affected by the chosen manoeuvres. The external model provides hydrographs at several points of interest along the river basin, which are increasingly further away from the dam. Although the distances are constant, the time elapsed between the manoeuvres and the water affecting these points downstream varies

```
1    /* Macro definition */
2    #define action_spill_gg(id,ap)
3      c_code{if(spill_gg_enabled[PDam->id]==1){spill_gg_opening[PDam->id]=ap;}}
4    #define outflow_spill_gg(id)
5      c_code{spill_gg_outflow[PDam->id]=spill_gg_contribution
6      (spill_gg_opening[PDam->id],dam_h_gg,1);}
7    #define update_state_spill_gg
8      c_code{now.spill_gg_outlet_type_state = update_outlet_type_state
9      (&spill_gg_opening, MAX_SPILL_GG);}
10   ...
11   /* GH-GT Dam variables*/
12   c_track "&dam_h_gg" "sizeof(double)" "UnMatched";
13   c_track "&dam_v_gg" "sizeof(double)" "Matched";
14   c_track "&inflow_gg" "sizeof(double)" "UnMatched";
15   c_track "&outflow_gg" "sizeof(double)" "UnMatched";
16   /*Spillway GH-GT Dam - Variables*/
17   c_track "&spill_gg_outflow" "sizeof(spill_gg_outflow)" "UnMatched";
18   c_track "&spill_gg_opening" "sizeof(spill_gg_opening)" "UnMatched";
19   c_track "&spill_gg_enabled" "sizeof(spill_gg_enabled)" "UnMatched";
20   int spill_gg_outlet_type_state;
21   mtype={spill_gg_ap0, spill_gg_ap1, spill_gg_ap2, spill_gg_ap3};
22   chan cmd_spill_gg[MAX_SPILL_GG] = [1] of {mtype};
23   /* LLO GH-GT Dam - Variables */
24   ...
25   /* CGH Dam and outlets variables */
26   ...
27   proctype Dam() provided(current==1)
28   {
29     int id;
30     atomic{
31       do
32       ::(c_expr{t==0})-> break;
33       ::else ->   id = 0;
34         do  /* Spillway GH-GT Dam - Command reception */
35         ::(id<MAX_SPILL_GG)->
36             if
37             ::(cmd_spill_gg[id]?[spill_gg_ap0])-> cmd_spill_gg[id]?_;
38                 action_spill_gg(id,SPILL_GG_AP0);
39             ::(cmd_spill_gg[id]?[spill_gg_ap1])-> cmd_spill_gg[id]?_;
40                 action_spill_gg(id,SPILL_GG_AP1);
41             ::(cmd_spill_gg[id]?[spill_gg_ap2])-> cmd_spill_gg[id]?_;
42                 action_spill_gg(id,SPILL_GG_AP2);
43             ::(cmd_spill_gg[id]?[spill_gg_ap3])-> cmd_spill_gg[id]?_;
44                 action_spill_gg(id,SPILL_GG_AP3);
45             ::else -> skip;
46             fi;
47             id= id +1;
48         ::else-> id=0; break;
49         od;
50         do /* Spillway GH-GT Dam - workout outflow */
51         ::(id<MAX_SPILL_GG)-> outflow_spill_gg(id); id=id+1;
52         ::else-> id=0; break;
53         od;
54       update_state_spill_gg;
55   /* Rest of outlets GH-GT and CGH Dams */
56   ...
57         current=_pid+1;
58       od;
59     current=_pid+1;
60   };
61   }
```

Fig. 5. PROMELA dam model

dynamically depending on several conditions. For our analysis, we use the estimated minimum of these times for each point (provided together with the river basin model) to determine which part of the basin flows can be safely analyzed. If a property is violated in this part, SPIN will backtrack and try another set of manoeuvres, as explained previously.

It is worth noting that we do not check the constraints in a portion of the basin flows that has not been affected by the water discharged from the dam. If we did, SPIN could detect a constraint violation in an unaffected portion of the basin flows, and then incorrectly assume that the chosen manoeuvres had a negative impact. This would lead to backtracking and choosing a different set of manoeuvres, while in reality the discarded set could be valid. If these manoeuvres did in fact have a negative impact, this will be eventually detected by the analysis, and they will be discarded during backtracking.

This approach to timing can be seen in Fig. 6, which shows a dam and two points (#1 and #2) along the river basin. The Y axis shows the minimum distance in hours between the dam and the two points. The dots along the dam line represent manoeuvres chosen by the management model. The dashed lines show the minimum time it takes the water released from the dam to reach and influence the two basin points. For instance, water released in t_0 will reach points #1 and #2 at t_0' and t_0'' at the earliest, respectively. A flow is shown for each element above its line, e.g. showing how the peak discharge in the dam is smoothed as it flows downstream. Also note that any flow from the river basin model before t_0' and t_0'' will not be affected by any of the manoeuvres.

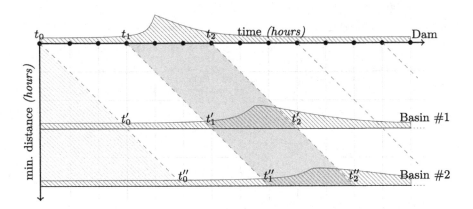

Fig. 6. Timeline of different basin elements

In this example, the dam manager chooses a manoeuvre every hour, but the external model is executed every three hours. Between t_1 (inclusive) and t_2 (non-inclusive) the manager performs three manoeuvres. The shaded area shows the part of the river basin that will be affected by these manoeuvres, i.e. interval $[t_1', t_2')$ for point #1 and $[t_1'', t_2'')$ for point #2. The constraints set by the user in the river basin will be checked for these intervals. If one of the constraints is not met in these intervals, SPIN will backtrack and try a different set of manoeuvres. If the water is slower than the minimum time, possible constraint violations will be detected later, but will result in backtracking to try new manoeuvres as well.

4.3 Management Rules

The management rules define how the dam manager has to act in flood episodes. These rules are included in the dam manual and consider average and maximum rainfalls. Rules are usually described as *if-then* statements to simplify their application during flood episodes. Our objective is to provide the dam (basin) manager with a set of manoeuvres that leave the basin and its dams in a safe and desired state. To this end, we have extended and modelled the management rules defined for the three dams of the Guadalhorce basin. Figure 7 shows the skeleton of the current management rule model. It describes most of the original if-then rules included in the dam manual. For instance, line 12 implements a rule that closes all outlets if the dam level is under $NMN\_C - SHELTER$ and the dam level is decreasing. In addition, this model monitors the dams and operates (or not) periodically to model the real management and also reduce the state space. In this case study, the model can operate the dams each one or two hours (e.g. lines 24 and 28) depending on dam's state.

The management rule model includes non-deterministic choices, making it possible to synthesize manoeuvres that satisfy different constraints. The number of non-deterministic choices directly affects the state space of the model. In addition, the coding of the model directly affects the analysis performance and the results. For instance, we have used the order of non-deterministic choices to first explore sequences of manoeuvres with a lower cost; that is, the DSS will return solutions with fewer operations if possible, which are more suitable in real flood management. Thus, this model can be refined to produce appropriate manoeuvres in a short period of time with the resources available.

5 Constraints for Synthesis of Management Decisions

The objective of our DSS is to provide different alternatives to manage the dams of the basin in flood episodes. Given a particular flood scenario, the DSS has to synthesize a set of manoeuvres that preserve the safety of the dams and the basin. For each scenario, we describe the safety of the dams and the basin as a set of constraints. For instance, during the flood season it is desirable to maintain dam levels lower than in other seasons, and keep the flow at the river mouth under a threshold to avoid flooding the airport. These constraints are then transformed into safety properties that are analyzed on the model using SPIN. The non-deterministic behaviour of the operation rule model, presented in Sect. 4.3, allows the DSS to come up with different basin management alternatives.

In [6], we described the constraints as LTL formulas that SPIN automatically translates to a *never claim* proctype that represents the Büchi automaton

```
1    #define wait(x) if ::c_expr{PRules->x<t}->set(t_user, x);current=1;
2                      ::else-> break; fi
3    c_decl{ double last_dam_h_c,last_dam_h_gg, QNMN_C, QNMN_GG;}
4    c_track "&last_dam_h_c" "sizeof(double)" "UnMatched";
5    c_track "&last_dam_h_gg" "sizeof(double)" "UnMatched";
6    proctype Rules() provided(current==_pid)
7    {
8      atomic{
9        do
10       ::(1)->
11         if /* Rules for CGH Dam */
12         :: c_expr{(dam_h_c<NMN_C-SHELTER_C)&&(dam_h_c<=last_dam_h_c)}->
                    cmd_spill_c[0]!spill_c_ap0; /* ... close all */
13         :: c_expr{(dam_h_c<NMN_C)&&(dam_h_gg>NMN_GG)}-> /* close all to let
                    GH_GT discharge */
14         :: c_expr{(dam_h_c>=NME_C)&&(dam_h_c>last_dam_h_c)}-> cmd_spill_c[0]!
                    spill_c_ap3; /* ... open all */
15         ::else->   /* Open non-deterministically CGH Dam outlets */
16         fi;
17         if /* Rules for GH-GT */
18         ::c_expr{(dam_h_gg<NMN_GG-SHELTER_GG)&&(dam_h_gg<=last_dam_h_gg)}->
19                /* close all */
20                wait(120);
21         ::c_expr{(dam_h_gg<NMN_GG-SHELTER_GG)&&(dam_h_gg>last_dam_h_gg)&&
22                (inflow_gg<QNMN_GG)}&&(spill_gg_outlet_type_state != 0)->
23                /* close spillway */
24                wait(120);
25         ::c_expr{(dam_h_gg>=NME_GG)&&(dam_h_gg>last_dam_h_gg)}-> /* open all */
26                wait(120);
27         ::else-> /* Open non-deterministically GH-GT Dam outlets */
28         wait(60);
29         fi;
30       od;
31       current = 1;
32     }
33   }
```

Fig. 7. PROMELA operation rules

associated with the LTL. However, LTL is not suitable for describing properties that refer to precise time instants. In [12], we defined the constraints as Timed Automata [3], which are automata extended with real-valued clocks, and we proposed a translation from Timed Automata to never claim, using a discretized clock variable. In both cases, constraints were always relative to dam parameters, such as the dam level or the outflow. The state space of the discretized automaton is a subset of the original, thus we ensure that in this discrete time instant the dam model satisfies the constraints. However, given the nature of the variables modeled (dam level, water flow, etc.) and the small time step used, the evolution of variables can be considered lineal between two time instants, which allow us to guarantee that the constraints are also satisfied between two discrete time instants.

In this work, we allow the definition of constraints over dam parameters and flows at locations of interest in the river basin. The evaluation of these two types of constraints is slightly different. We use the approach presented in [12] to define and evaluate constraints over dam parameters. In this case, the constraint is described as a timed automaton and translated into a never claim with an acceptance state that is only reached if the constraint is satisfied. When SPIN analysis reaches the acceptance state, the analysis ends and returns the

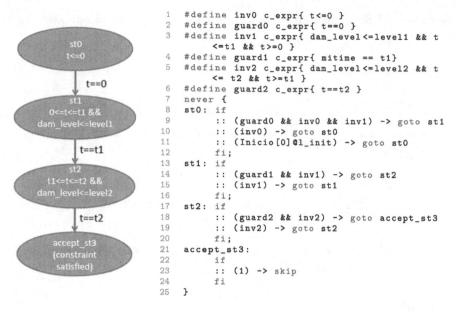

```
1   #define invO c_expr{ t<=0 }
2   #define guardO c_expr{ t==0 }
3   #define inv1 c_expr{ dam_level<=level1 && t
            <=t1 && t>=0 }
4   #define guard1 c_expr{ mitime == t1}
5   #define inv2 c_expr{ dam_level<=level2 && t
            <= t2 && t>=t1 }
6   #define guard2 c_expr{ t==t2 }
7   never {
8   stO: if
9      :: (guardO && invO && inv1) -> goto st1
10     :: (invO) -> goto stO
11     :: (Inicio[0]@l_init) -> goto stO
12     fi;
13  st1: if
14     :: (guard1 && inv1) -> goto st2
15     :: (inv1) -> goto st1
16     fi;
17  st2: if
18     :: (guard2 && inv2) -> goto accept_st3
19     :: (inv2) -> goto st2
20     fi;
21  accept_st3:
22         if
23         :: (1) -> skip
24         fi
25  }
```

Fig. 8. Constraint described as (a) timed automaton and (b) never claim

sequence of states leading to this *error* state. The sequence of states includes the scheduling of manoeuvres performed by the operation rule model. Figure 8 shows an example of a timed automaton and never claim used to synthesize a set of manoeuvres. The constraint is to maintain the dam_level under a threshold level1 in period $[0, t1]$ and under threshold level2 in period $[t1, t2]$. When the never claim reaches the state accept_st3, the analysis will stop and return the execution trace of the basin model, including the management rules applied to dams.

To analyze constraints over basin flows, we have to extend this approach. The main reason is that the external hydrological model returns the temporal evolution of the flows for future time instants that are not easily synchronized with the timing of the PROMELA model. The constraints over basin flows are described as curves that serve as the upper or lower limit for some of these flows. In Sect. 4.2 we explained how the hydrological model is periodically executed to compute the effects of the manoeuvres downstream. Figure 9 shows how the external model is called (line 5) and how the constraints over basin flows are evaluated (line 7). When execution of the external hydrological model finishes, its results are stored in hidden C structures. These values are checked by the function basin_check_constraints, which compares the results against the constraints set by the user. Only the interval affected by the manoeuvres since the last time the external model was executed is checked, taking into account the distance from the dams to each basin point of interest. Observe that the function is called using the primitive c_expr instead of c_code. If the checks succeed, the analysis can continue, but if the checks fail, the instruction is not executable and SPIN has to backtrack to a state where different operation rules can be selected.

```
1    proctype Timer()
2    { ...
3    if
4    :: (t_basin == 0) ->
5       c_code { basin_execute_model(t, cycles); }; /* Run hydrological model */
6       /* Check constraints over basin flows; block if not satisfied */
7       c_expr { basin_check_constraints(t-BASIN_TIME_STEPS, BASIN_TIME_STEPS) };
8       set(t_basin, BASIN_TIME_STEPS)
9    :: else -> skip
10   fi;
11   ... }
```

Fig. 9. Evaluation of constraints over basin flows

When constraints are only specified over the basin flows, the never claim has to check that time t reaches the end of the episode.

6   Evaluation

In this section, we analyze a flood episode of 60 h to evaluate the performance of the DSS. Figure 10 shows the dam inflows and their initial state. Since the levels of the Guadalhorce and Guadalteba were above the separation wall, we can manage them as a single dam.

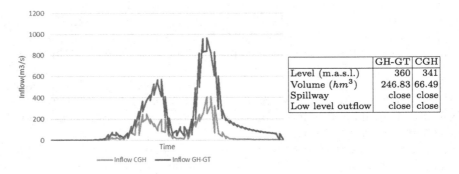

	GH-GT	CGH
Level (m.a.s.l.)	360	341
Volume (hm^3)	246.83	66.49
Spillway	close	close
Low level outflow	close	close

Fig. 10. Flood episode (a) inflow and (b) initial dam state

Using this initial configuration and the inflow hydrographs, we carry out different analyses. The first one checks that the model (PROMELA plus embedded C code) does not end in invalid states. For this analysis there are no constraints over the basin or the dam, thus SPIN explores all the possible execution branches produced by the non-deterministic behaviour of the management rule model. The analysis ends without errors, and we have obtained 15 different manoeuvre sets for this episode.

The following analyses include constraints to synthesize specific manoeuvres. To this end, we configure SPIN to analyze the system plus a never claim, and to stop when the first error occurs. Constraints can be defined over dam parameters and the basin flows, in an independent or combined way. The objective of the second analysis is to limit the outflow of GH-GT and CGH to under $310\,\mathrm{m}^3/\mathrm{s}$, and the flow at the four locations to under $310\,\mathrm{m}^3/\mathrm{s}$. Figure 11 shows the never claim used to describe these constraints. The analysis ends with an error, which means that there is at least one set of manoeuvres that satisfies the constraint. Figure 3 shows the evolution of dam parameters, the flow downstream in different locations, and the manoeuvres of the different outlets. In this case, the spillway of the GH-GT dam remains closed, and the other gates are opened at different degrees over time.

```
1   #define inv0 c_expr{t <= 0}
2   #define inv1 c_expr{outflow_c < 310 && outflow_gg < 310 && t <= 3600}
3   #define guard0 c_expr{t == 0}
4   #define guard1 c_expr{t == 3600}
5   never {
6   st0:
7     if
8     :: (guard0 && inv0 && inv1)->goto st1
9     :: (inv0)->goto st0
10    :: (Inicio[0]@l_init)->goto st0
11    fi;
12  st1:
13    if
14    :: (guard1 && inv1)->goto accept_st2
15    :: (inv1)->goto st1
16    fi;
17  accept_st2:
18    if
19    :: (1) -> skip
20    fi
21  }
```

Fig. 11. Never claim for constant constraints

The last analysis uses variable constraints to synthesize manoeuvres. There are two ways of defining variable constraints over dam parameters. The first approach is to define constraints as curves that define the upper and lower bounds of the parameters. These curves are stored in UnMatched C structures. The never claim is modified to compare the parameter with the curves. For example, the definition of inv1 in Fig. 11 can be modified to check that outflow_c is always under the curve stored in curve[0] as follows:

```
#define inv1 e_expr{outflow_c< curve[0][t]}
```

The second approach is to define constraints as a timed automaton that represents sequences of intervals. This approach does not require C structures, which reduces the memory and time required. The timed automaton is transformed into a never claim, as explained in Sect. 5. We use this approach to restrict the level of CGH dam at four different time intervals. Figure 12 shows the timed automaton that represent the variable constraint. The analysis ends with an

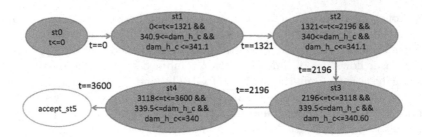

Fig. 12. Timed automaton for variable constraints

Table 2. SPIN statistics

	Invalid end state	Const. constraint	Var. constraint
Depth	421573	432403	432393
States stored	102530	10834	12018
States matched	1	0	1
Atomic steps	3989109	421565	467584
Memory usage (MB)			
For states	17.133	2.104	2.300
For hash table	2.000	2.000	2.000
For DFS stack	26.703	26.703	26.703
Other(proc and chan stacks)	29.821	30.127	30.127
Total memory	75.773	61.027	61.222
Time (sec)			
Total elapsed time	175	19.2	22.4
External model	89.6	9.1	10.6

error that corresponds to the manoeuvres, which are very similar to the previous ones. In this case, the CGH spillway is completely open in two steps, while in the previous analysis, it is opened in three steps. Since the spillways are the gates with greatest discharge capacity, this small change has a great influence on constraint satisfaction.

Table 2 shows the statistics of SPIN for each analysis. Note that the state space is fairly small, this is thanks to the use of UnMatched C variables and the abstraction of outlet states described in Sect. 4.1. The time elapsed in each analysis depends on the calls to the external model. We have measured the execution time of the external model to determine how much time is spent on these calls. Observe that the depth in the second and third analysis has increased, because of the interleaved execution of the PROMELA model and the never claim that defines the constraints. Finally, note that the number of matched states is 0 or 1, which means that there are no repeated states. This is mainly because of a global timer in the PROMELA model, which is defined as a C Matched variable that counts the number of minutes of the flood episode. In addition, when SPIN backtracks to a state, the management rule model operates the dam outlets in a different way, which causes a different evolution of the other model variables.

7   Conclusions and Future Work

We have provided a complete case study to show how the SPIN model checker can be a central part of future DSSs to help in mitigating the effects of floods. The methodology to generate the dam and management rule models, which exports a reduced number of C variables into SPIN's state, and reduces the interleaving of the different process, makes the approach effective enough regarding to both the effort to write the PROMELA models for each specific river basin and also to the time needed to synthesize the appropriate manoeuvres. Since the simulators for hydrologic models are integrated as a black box, more accurate versions of such simulators can be easily integrated. This novel application domain opens the use of the SPIN model checker as a central component of (commercial) DSSs demanded by the authorities that manage big dams in many countries. This is a real need identified in the current European Research Project SAID (Smart wAter management with Integrated DSSs) [1]. In the final stage of the project the DSS will be fully operative, and the dam manager will evaluate the quality of synthesized manoeuvres and the time required.

The work could be further extended to introduce additional optimisation when there are many dams in cascade in the same basin. We are also working on a different way of building the models in order to exploit parallel execution of SPIN for very complex river basins.

References

1. SAID Project 12 Feb 2015. http://www.said-project.eu
2. Ahmad, S., Simonovic, S.: An intelligent decision support system for management of floods. Water Resour. Manage. **20**, 391–410 (2006)
3. Alur, R., Dill, D.: The theory of timed automata. In: Huizing, C., de Bakker, J.W., Rozenberg, G., de Roever, W.-P. (eds.) REX 1991. LNCS, vol. 600, pp. 45–73. Springer, Heidelberg (1992)
4. Cheng, C.T., Chau, K.W.: Flood control management system for reservoirs. Environ. Model. Softw. **19**(12), 1141–1150 (2004)
5. Díaz, M., Soler, E., Romero, S., Gallardo, M.M., Merino, P., Panizo, L., Salmerón, A.: Technical specification of the DSS for flood management. Deliverable 1.3, SAID Project (2015)
6. Gallardo, M.M., Merino, P., Panizo, L., Linares, A.: Developing a decision support tool for dam management with spin. In: Alpuente, M., Cook, B., Joubert, C. (eds.) FMICS 2009. LNCS, vol. 5825, pp. 210–212. Springer, Heidelberg (2009)
7. Gallardo, M.M., Merino, P., Panizo, L., Linares, A.: A practical use of model checking for synthesis: generating a dam controller for flood management. Softw. Pract. Experience **41**(11), 1329–1347 (2011)
8. Holzmann, G.: The SPIN Model Checker: Primer and Reference Manual. Addison-Wesley Professional, Reading (2003)

9. Karbowski, A.: Fc-ros - decision support system for reservoir operators during flood. Environ. Softw. **6**(1), 11–15 (1991)
10. Labadie, J.W.: Optimal operation of multireservoir systems: state-of-the-art review. J. Water Resour. Plan. Manage. **130**(2), 93–111 (2004)
11. McCartney, M.P.: Decision support systems for dam planning and operation in Africa. International Water Managment Institute, Colombo (2007)
12. Panizo, L., Gallardo, M.M., Merino, P., Sanán, D., Linares, A.: Dam management based on model checking techniques. In: 8th International Conference on Software Engineering and Formal Methods. SEFM 2010: Proceedings of the Posters and Tooldemo Session, pp. 9–13. CNR, Pisa, Italy, Sept. 2010
13. Polo, M., Herrero, J., Aguilar, C., Millares, A., Moñino, A., Nieto, S., Losada, M.: Wimmed, a distributed physically-based watershed model (i): Description and validation. Environmental Hydraulics: Theoretical, Experimental & Computational Solutions, pp. 225–228 (2010)
14. Pottinger, L.: A Flood of Dam Safety Problems, 8 Sept. 2010. https://www.internationalrivers.org/resources/a-flood-of-dam-safety-problems-1700

ESBMC^{QtOM}: A Bounded Model Checking Tool to Verify Qt Applications

Mário Garcia$^{(\boxtimes)}$, Felipe Monteiro, Lucas Cordeiro, and Eddie de Lima Filho

Electronic and Information Research Centre,
Federal University of Amazonas, Manaus, Brazil
marioangelpg@gmail.com

Abstract. We integrate a simplified model of the Qt framework, named as Qt operational model (QtOM), into the efficient SMT-based context-bounded model checker (ESBMC++), which results in ESBMC^{QtOM}. In particular, ESBMC^{QtOM} is a bounded model checking tool to verify Qt-based applications, which focuses on the verification of code properties, such as invalid memory access and containers usage, through pre- and postconditions, data usage evaluation, and simulation features. Experimental results show that ESBMC^{QtOM} can be effectively and efficiently applied to verify Qt-based consumer electronics applications.

1 Introduction

Currently, in order to be competitive, consumer electronics companies tend to provide devices with reduced prices, which are produced in large scale. As a consequence, profit margins tend to be small, which, in turn, acts as a feedback to the production process. In particular, such products must be as robust and bug-free as possible, given that even medium product-return rates tend to be unacceptable. This way, it is important to adopt reliable verification methods, with the goal of ensuring system correctness and avoiding losses [1].

Model checking [1] is an interesting approach, due to the possibility of auto-mated verification, which makes such a process cheap and simple. Nonetheless, the employed verifier should provide support regarding target language and sys-tem properties, which even include linked libraries and development frameworks. For instance, a checker based on satisfiability modulo theories (SMT), such as the efficient SMT-based context-bounded model checker (ESBMC++) [2], can be employed to verify C/C++ code, but it does not support specific frameworks, such as Qt [3]. The same happens to Java PathFinder [4], with respect to multi-media home platform applications [5] and programs developed for the Android operating system [6]. The former are even verified with a specific test suite, which relies on a specialized library; however, such a problem could be overcome through an abstract representation of the associated libraries, known as opera-tional model (OM) [7]. Indeed, it must approximate the behavior of the original modules to provide the same inputs and outputs to the main application.

The present work provides a Qt framework OM, which checks properties related to Qt modules, named as Qt Operational Model (QtOM). QtOM was

© Springer International Publishing Switzerland 2016
D. Bošnački and A. Wijs (Eds.): SPIN 2016, LNCS 9641, pp. 97–103, 2016.
DOI: 10.1007/978-3-319-32582-8_6

integrated into ESBMC++, which gave rise to ESBMC^{QtOM}, in order to verify specific properties in Qt/C++ programs. It is worth noticing that the combination between ESBMC++ and OMs has been previously applied to verify Qt/C++ programs [8]; however, the present work largely extended that, in order to verify specific properties related to Qt structures, via pre and postconditions. Besides, two real-world applications were included in the current benchmark set.

Contributions. The present paper extends a previously published work [8]. Here, implementation and usage aspects are tackled and, in particular, QtOM now includes new features from the Qt Essentials modules [3], in order to verify two Qt-based applications: *Locomaps* [9] and *GeoMessage* [10], which were not part of the previous benchmark set [8]. Besides, sequential and associative Qt containers [2] were also included into QtOM. To the best of our knowledge, there is no other bounded model checker for Qt-based programs, regarding consumer electronics devices. All benchmarks, OMs, tools, and experimental results, associated with the current evaluation, are available on a supplementary web page[1].

2   Qt Operational Model (QtOM)

QtOM strictly provides the same behavior of the Qt framework, while presenting a simplified implementation focused on property verification [8], and can be split into functionality modules [3]. The QtOM Core module [3], as also happens to Qt, contains all non-graphical core classes (including containers) and presents a complete abstraction for the graphical user interface part.

QtCore also comprises container classes, which implement template-based containers for general purpose, similar to what is offered by the standard template libraries (STL). For instance, `QVector<QWidget>` or `QStack<QWidget>` could be used for implementing a dynamic array of QWidgets. The former is similar to the STL counterpart, while the latter provides a last in, first out semantics with new methods, such as `QStack::push()`.

Figure 1 shows the integration of QtOM into ESBMC++, *i.e.*, ESBMC^{QtOM}, where gray boxes represent the respective OM, the white ones show inputs and outputs, the dotted ones belong to ESBMC++, and elements connected through dotted arrows represent the components used to build QtOM. The first step is the parser, where ESBMC++ translates the input code into an intermediate representation (IR) tree, where each language structure is correctly identified, by means of QtOM. The latter considers each library and its associated classes, including attributes, method signatures, and function prototypes, through assertions, as shown in Fig. 2. Indeed, assertions are of paramount importance, given that they ultimately allow formal property verification.

Hence, QtOM aids the parser process to build a C++ IR with all necessary assertions to verify Qt-specific properties. After that, the remaining verification flow is normally carried out, as described by Cordeiro *et al.* [11].

It is clear that the usefulness of the proposed methodology relies on the fact that QtOM correctly represents the original Qt libraries. In that sense,

---

[1] http://esbmc.org/qtom/.

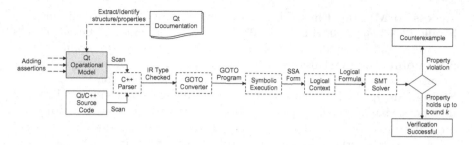

Fig. 1. Connecting QtOM to ESBMC++ architecture.

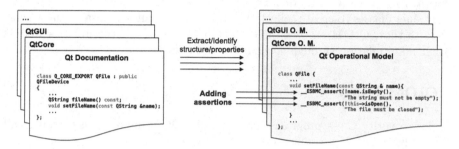

Fig. 2. QtOM development process.

all developed QtOM modules were manually verified and exhaustively compared with the original ones, in order to guarantee the same behavior. Besides, although QtOM is a new implementation, it consists in constructing a simplified model of the related libraries, using the same language and through the original code and documentation, which tends to reduce the resulting number of errors.

Even so, one may also argue that conformance testing regarding OMs [12] would be a better approach, which is true; however, that option is not available in the present case, albeit it is an interesting possibility for future work.

3   QtOM Features

Through the integration of QtOM into ESBMC++, ESBMC^{QtOM} is able to properly identify Qt/C++ programs and verify all default properties that it can handle, such as under- and overflow arithmetic, pointer safety, memory leaks, array bounds, and atomicity [2]. Additionally, in order to ensure the correct usage of the Qt methods, pre- and postconditions check the following properties:

- **Invalid Memory Access.** QtOM assertions ensure that only valid memory addresses are accessed, through operations with arrays, objects, and pointers.
- **Time-Period Values.** Some Qt features, such as those offered by the `QTime` class, need time-period specifications to be properly executed. This way, QtOM ensures that only valid time parameters are considered.

- **Access to Missing Files.** The Qt framework provides a set of libraries to handle files (*e.g.*, `QIODevice` and `QFile`). As a consequence, QtOM checks the access and manipulation of all handled files, in a given program.
- **Null Pointers.** QtOM also covers pointer manipulation, by adding assertions to ensure that `NULL` pointers are not used in invalid operations.
- **String Manipulation.** Unicode character string representations and a set of methods to handle them are provided by the `QString` class. As such structures are widely used by several Qt classes and Qt-based applications, QtOM checks pre and postconditions, for each method from that library, with the goal of ensuring correct string manipulation.
- **Container Usage.** The `QtCore` module provides a set of template-based container classes to create collections and provide uniform data management. Due to that, QtOM ensures the correct usage of such structures, as well as their manipulation through specialized methods.

4   QtOM Usage

In order to verify C++ programs based on the Qt framework, users must call the ESBMC++ v1.25.4 command-line version, using

esbmc<file>.cpp − −unwind $<k>$ −I $<$ path − to − QtOM $>$ −I $<$ path − to − C + + − OM $>$,

where $<file>$.*cpp* is the Qt/C++ code to be verified, $<k>$ is the maximum loop unrolling, and $<path − to − QtOM>$ and $<path − to − C + + − OM>$ are the locations of the QtOM files and the C++ OM [2], respectively. Thenceforth, the verification process is completely automatic, *i.e.*, if no bug is found, up to a k-depth unwinding, then ESBMC^{QtOM} reports *VERIFICATION SUCCESSFUL*; otherwise, it reports *VERIFICATION FAILED*, along with a counterexample, which contains all necessary information for detecting and reproducing the respective error.

5   Verifying Qt Applications with ESBMC^{QtOM}

5.1   Locomaps Application

ESBMC^{QtOM} was applied to verify a Qt sample application called *Locomaps* [9], which demonstrates satellite, terrain, street maps, tiled map service planning, and Qt Geo GPS Integration, among other features. By means of a unique source code, such an application can be cross-compiled and run on Mac OS X, Linux, and Windows. It contains two classes and 115 Qt/C++ code lines, using five different APIs from the Qt framework: `QApplication`, `QCoreApplication`, `QDesktopWidget`, `QtDeclarative`, and `QMainWindow`.

5.2   GeoMessage Application

Another verification was performed on a real-world Qt application called *GeoMessage* simulator, which provides messaging for applications and system components, in the ArcGIS platform [10]. It receives XML files as input and generates, in different frequencies, User Datagram Protocol (UDP) broadcast datagrams, as an output to ArcGIS's applications and system components.

GeoMessage is also cross-platform and contains 1209 Qt/C++ code lines, using 20 different Qt APIs, which cover several features, such as events, file handling, and widgets. It is worth noticing that *GeoMessage* uses `QMutex` and `QMutexLocker`, which are related to the Qt Threading module (classes for concurrent programs). Such classes were used to lock/unlock mutexes, in *GeoMessage*, and, most importantly, ESBMC^{QtOM} is able to properly verify their structures; however, it does not provide full support to the Qt Threading module yet.

5.3   Verification Results

During the verification of *Locomaps* and *GeoMessage*, the following properties were checked: array-bound violations, under- and overflow arithmetic, division by zero, pointer safety, and other specific properties defined in QtOM (cf. Sect. 3). Furthermore, ESBMC^{QtOM} was able to fully identify the verified source code, using five different QtOM modules for *Locomaps* and twenty for *GeoMessage*, *i.e.*, one for each original counterpart. The verification process was totally automatic and took approximately 6.7 s, for generating 32 verification conditions (VCs) for *Locomaps*, and 16 s, regarding 6421 VCs for *GeoMessage*, on a standard PC desktop. Additionally, ESBMC^{QtOM} was able to find similar bugs in both applications, which were confirmed by the respective developers.

Figure 3 shows a code fragment from *Locomaps*, which uses the `QApplication` class present in the `QtWidgets` module. In that particular case, if the *argv* parameter is not correctly initialized, then the constructor called by object *app* does not execute properly and the application crashes (see line 2, in Fig. 3). In order to verify this property, ESBMC^{QtOM} checks two assertions regarding (input) parameters, as can be seen in Fig. 4 (see lines 4 and 5), while evaluating them as preconditions. A similar problem was also found in the *GeoMessage* application. One way to fix such a bug is to check, with conditional statements, whether *argv* and *argc* are valid arguments, before using them in an operation.

```
1  int main(int argc, char *argv[]) {
2      QApplication app(argc, argv);
3      return app.exec();
4  }
```

Fig. 3. Code fragment from the main file of the *Locomaps* benchmark.

```
1   class QApplication {
2     ...
3     QApplication( int & argc, char ** argv ){
4     __ESBMC_assert(argc > 0, ''Invalid parameter'');
5     __ESBMC_assert(argv != NULL, ''Invalid pointer'');
6     this->str = argv;
7     this->_size = strlen(*argv);
8     ...
9   }
10    ...
11  };
```

Fig. 4. Operational model for the *QApplication*() constructor.

6   Conclusions

ESBMC^{QtOM} was presented as an SMT-based BMC tool, which employs an operational model (QtOM) to verify Qt-based applications. In particular, QtOM comprises a simple representation of Qt, including several pre- and postconditions, data storage evaluation (*e.g.*, container checks), and simulation features (*e.g.*, string and file manipulation), which are used to check code properties, such as invalid memory access, time-period values, and container usage.

Additionally, a Qt touch screen program for browsing maps, satellite, and terrain data [9] and another application that provides messaging for the ArcGIS platform [10] were successfully verified, in the context of consumer electronics devices. For the best of our knowledge, there is no other approach, employing BMC, that is able to verify Qt-based applications. For future work, the developed QtOM will be extended (support to more modules), with the goal of increasing the Qt framework coverage. Besides, conformance testing procedures will be developed for validating QtOM, which could also be applied to Qt modules.

References

1. Berard, B., Bidoit, M., Finkel, A.: Systems and Software Verification: Model-Checking Techniques and Tool. Springer Publishing, Heidelberg (2010)
2. Ramalho, M., et al.: SMT-based bounded model checking of C++ programs. In: ECBS, pp. 147–156 (2013)
3. The Qt Framework. http://www.qt.io/qt-framework/, April 2015
4. Mehlitz, P., Rungta, N., Visser, W.: A hands-on Java pathfinder tutorial. In: ICSE, pp. 1493–1495 (2013)
5. Piesing, J.: The DVB multimedia home platform (MHP) and related specifications. Proc. IEEE **94**(1), 237–247 (2006)
6. van der Merwe, H., et al.: Execution and property specifications for JPF-Android. ACM SIGSOFT Softw. Eng. Notes **39**(1), 1–5 (2014)
7. van der Merwe, H., et al.: Generation of library models for verification of Android applications. ACM SIGSOFT Softw. Eng. Notes **40**(1), 1–5 (2015)

8. Monteiro, F., Cordeiro, L., de Lima Filho, E.: Bounded model checking of C++ programs based on the Qt Framework. In: GCCE, pp. 179–180 (2015)
9. Spatial Minds and CyberData Corporation: Locomaps. https://github.com/craig-miller/locomaps. Accessed 10 Sept 2015
10. Environmental Systems Research Institute: GeoMessage Simulator. https://github.com/Esri/geomessage-simulator-qt. Accessed 15 Sept 2015
11. Cordeiro, L., Fischer, B., Marques-Silva, J.: SMT-based bounded model checking for embedded ANSI-C software. IEEE TSE **38**(4), 957–974 (2012)
12. de la Cámara, P., Castro, J., Gallardo, M., Merino, P.: Verification support for ARINC-653-based avionics software. JSTVR **21**(4), 267–298 (2011)

Autonomous Agent Behaviour Modelled in PRISM – A Case Study

Ruth Hoffmann[1]([✉]), Murray Ireland[1], Alice Miller[1], Gethin Norman[1], and Sandor Veres[2]

[1] University of Glasgow, Glasgow G12 8QQ, Scotland
ruth.hoffmann@glasgow.ac.uk
[2] University of Sheffield, Sheffield S1 3JD, UK

Abstract. Formal verification of agents representing robot behaviour is a growing area due to the demand that autonomous systems have to be proven safe. In this paper we present an abstract definition of autonomy which can be used to model autonomous scenarios and propose the use of small-scale simulation models representing abstract actions to infer quantitative data. To demonstrate the applicability of the approach we build and verify a model of an unmanned aerial vehicle (UAV) in an exemplary autonomous scenario, utilising this approach.

1 Introduction

Autonomous systems have the ability to decide at run-time what to do and how to do it. A critical question is how this decision making process is implemented.

Increasingly, autonomous systems are being deployed within the public domain (e.g. driverless cars, delivery drones). Naturally, there is concern that these systems are reliable, efficient and - most of all - safe. Although testing is a necessary part of this process, simulation and formal verification are key tools, especially at the early stages of design where experimental testing is both infeasible and dangerous. Simulation allows us to view the continuous dynamics and monitor behaviour of a system. On the other hand, model checking allows us to formally verify properties of a finite representation. Whereas the simulation model is close to an implementation, simulation runs are necessarily incomplete. Verification models, on the other hand, require us to abstract more coarsely.

The decisions made by an autonomous agent depend on the current state of the environment, specifically in terms of data perceived by the agent from its sensors. If model checking is to be used for the verification of autonomous systems we must reflect the uncertainty associated with the state of the environment by using probabilistic model checking.

We propose a framework for analysing autonomous systems, specifically to investigate decision-making, using probabilistic model checking of an abstract model where quantitative data for abstract actions is derived from small-scale simulation models. We illustrate our approach for an example system composed of a UAV searching for and collecting objects in an arena. The simulation models

© The Author(s) 2016
D. Bošnački and A. Wijs (Eds.): SPIN 2016, LNCS 9641, pp. 104–110, 2016.
DOI: 10.1007/978-3-319-32582-8_7

for abstract actions are generated using the object-oriented framework Simulink and the abstract models are specified and verified using the probabilistic model checker PRISM. In our example, autonomous decision making involves making a weighted choice between a set of possible actions, and is loosely based on the Belief-Desire-Intention architecture [7].

Previous work in which model checking is used to verify autonomy includes [3] in which the decision making process is verified in isolation, while our aim is to integrate this process with the autonomous agent as a whole. Other research includes an investigation of the cooperative behaviour of robots, where each robot is represented by a hybrid automaton [1], and verification of a consensus algorithm using experimental verification and an external observer [2].

2   Autonomy

In order to formally define autonomous behaviour, we introduce finite state machines which abstract the autonomous actions independent of the agent type.

Before we give the formal definitions we require the following notation. For a finite set of variables V, a valuation of V is a function s mapping each variable in V to a value in its finite domain. Let $val(V)$ be the set of valuations of V. For any $s \in val(V)$, $v \in V$ and value x of V, let $s[v:=x]$ and $s[v \pm x]$ be the valuations where for any $v' \in V$ we have $s[v:=x](v') = x$ and $s[v \pm x](v') = s(v') \pm x$ if $v'=v$ and $s[v:=x](v') = s[v \pm x](v') = s(v')$ otherwise. For a finite set X, a probability distribution over X is a function $\mu : X \to [0,1]$ such that $\sum_{x \in X} \mu(x) = 1$. Let $Dist(X)$ be the set of distributions over X.

Definition 1. A *probabilistic finite-state machine* is a tuple $\mathcal{M}=(V,I,A,T)$ where: V is a finite set of *variables*; $I \subseteq val(V)$ a set of *initial states*; A a finite set of *actions* and $T : val(V) \times A \to Dist(S)$ a (partial) *transition function*.

The set of states of $\mathcal{M}=(V,I,A,T)$, denoted S, is the set of valuations $val(V)$ of V. Let $A(s)$ denote the actions available from state s, i.e. the actions $a \in A$ for which $T(s,a)$ is defined. In state s an action is chosen non-deterministically from the available actions $A(s)$ and, if action a is chosen, the transition to the next state is made according to the probability distribution $T(s,a)$. A probabilistic finite-state machine describes a system without autonomy, we introduce this through a weight function adding decision making to the finite-state machine.

Definition 2. An *autonomous* probabilistic finite-state machine is a tuple $\mathcal{A} = (V,I,A,T,w)$ where (V,I,A,T) is a probabilistic finite-state machine and w is a *weight function* $w : val(V) \times A \to [0,1]$ such that for any $s \in val(V)$ and $a \neq b \in A$ we have $w(s,a) \neq w(s,b)$ and $w(s,a)>0$ implies $a \in A(s)$.

In an autonomous machine the non-determinism in the first step of a transition is removed. More precisely, if a machine $\mathcal{A}=(V,I,A,T,w)$ is in state s, then the action performed is that with the largest weight, that is the action:

$$a_{s,w} = \arg \max\{w(s,a) \mid a \in A(s)\}.$$

Requiring the weights for distinct actions and the same state to be different ensures this action is always well defined. Having removed the non-determinism through the introduction of a weight function, the semantics of an autonomous finite state machine is a discrete time Markov chain.

3   UAV Example

In this case study we consider a specific example (a simple search and retrieve example, with a UAV in a finite sized arena) to demonstrate our approach.

The UAV first takes off and checks whether the system and sensors are functional. If the UAV detects an issue in the system, then it returns to base. Otherwise it will proceed to search for a given number of objects. When an object is found, the UAV positions itself above the object and descends until the grabber can pick it up. The UAV then ascends to transportation height and transports the object to the deposit site. There is the possibility that the UAV will drop its object along the way and need to retrieve it. Once the UAV is above the deposit site, it releases the object and ascends back to search height. It will then decide whether it continues the search or returns to the base and complete the mission. During operation, the UAV may return to base to recharge if it is low on battery, or conduct an emergency landing, due to an internal system error. If the mission time limit is reached, the UAV abandons the mission and returns to base. Figure 1 represents this scenario, showing the different modes of the UAV and progression between the modes.

We represent this scenario using a autonomous finite-state machine $\mathcal{A}$. The variables V of $\mathcal{A}$ are given by:

- obj the number of objects which have not been found;
- $pos=(pos_x, pos_y)$ the position of the UAV in the arena;
- $ret=(ret_x, ret_y)$ the return coordinates when search is interrupted;
- m the current mode of the UAV;
- t the mission time;
- b the battery charge level.

Each state $s \in val(V)$ of $\mathcal{A}$ is a valuation of these variables. The transition and weight functions T and w are based on Fig. 1. We focus on the target approach and search modes of the UAV.

In the target approach mode ($m=4$), the UAV positions itself above an observed object and we denote this abstract action by *Approach*. Thus, the weight function is $w(s, Approach)=1$ for all states s such that $s(m)=2$, and for any such state s we have for any $s' \in S$:

$$T(s, Approach)(s') = \begin{cases} 1 & \text{if } s' = s[m:=5][t+T_{ap}][b-B_{ap}] \\ 0 & \text{otherwise} \end{cases}$$

where T_{ap} and B_{ap} are the time and battery charge used approaching the object, and $m=5$ is the mode for descending. The abstract action *Approach* models

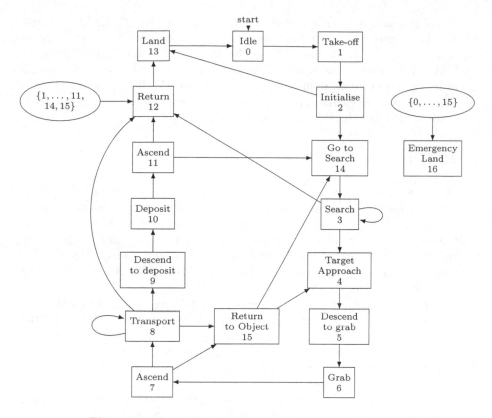

Fig. 1. The finite state machine representing the scenario.

several different operations of the UAV including the use of its camera and navigational system. A small-scale simulation model was built for this abstract action to provide the required quantitative data.

When the UAV is in search mode ($m=3$) there are two actions that can occur: *Search* and *BatteryLow* with the UAV continuing search if the battery charge level is above a certain threshold, and returning to base otherwise. The weight function for the *Search* action from any state s such that $s(m)=3$ is given by:

$$w(s, Search) = \begin{cases} 0 & \text{if } s(b) \leq B_{low} \\ 1 & \text{if } s(b) > B_{low} \end{cases}$$

and for the *BatteryLow* action we have $w(s, BatteryLow) = 1-w(s, Search)$. Concerning the transition function we have for any $s' \in S$:

$$T(s, Search)(s') = \begin{cases} 1 - \alpha & \text{if } s' = s[pos:=\Delta pos][t+\Delta t][b-\Delta b] \\ \alpha & \text{if } s' = s[pos:=\Delta pos][ret:=\Delta pos][m:=4][t+\Delta t][b-\Delta b] \\ 0 & \text{otherwise} \end{cases}$$

and $T(s, BatteryLow)(s)=1$ if $s'=s[pos:=\Delta pos][ret:=\Delta pos][m:=12][t+\Delta t][b-\Delta b]$ and
0 otherwise, where Δpos denotes the movement from one discrete square in
the arena to the next, Δt and Δb are the time and battery consumption of
the UAV while moving one square. The UAV has probability α of finding an
object in a given position, if an object is found the UAV changes to mode $m=4$
and ret is set to the current coordinates, as the search has been interrupted.
If no object is found, the UAV continues searching.

4   Results

We have modelled our scenario in the probabilistic model checker PRISM [5],
building small-scale simulation models to determine individual abstract actions
to generate probabilistic and timing values. To encode the timing values in
PRISM as integer variables we take the floor and ceiling, introducing non-
determinism into the model and upper and lower bounds for properties [4]. The
experiments were performed on a computer with 16GB RAM and a 2.3 GHz
Intel Core i5 processor.

The main properties of interest concern the UAV successfully completing the
mission (finding and depositing all objects within the time limit) and failing the
mission (either due to an emergency landing, missing some objects or running
out of time). We have also considered other properties including how often the
UAV drops an object and how often it recharges during a mission, more details
can be found in the repository [6].

We have analysed two scenarios where there are 3 objects and a time limit of
900s, and 2 objects and a time limit of 500s respectively. For the first scenario
the model has 116 191 709 states, was built in 488s and verifying a property
varied between 298s and 813s. This is far more efficient than running Monte
Carlo simulations, as simulating 10 000 runs of the same scenario takes over
two weeks. For the second scenario the model has 35 649 503 states and model
construction time was 77s.

For the first scenario, the maximum and minimum probabilities of the UAV
completing a mission are 0.7610 and 0.6787 respectively. The maximum and

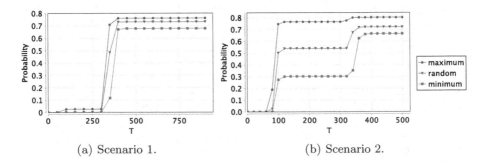

(a) Scenario 1.   (b) Scenario 2.

Fig. 2. Probability of completing the mission successfully by deadline T .

minimum probabilities of running out of time are negligible, searching the arena and missing some objects are 0.2617 and 0.1808, and 0.0628 and 0.0552 for performing an emergency landing. Figure 2 shows the maximum and minimum probability of a successful mission within a time bound as well as the results obtained when the non-determinism is replaced by a uniform random choice. The probability increases after a threshold time as the UAV has to search a proportion of the arena before finding all objects.

5 Conclusions

We have proposed using small-scale simulation models to inform probabilistic models used for verification. The simulation models can be used to provide quantitative data for abstract actions. The probabilistic models can be used for fast property specific verification, that is not possible using simulations alone.

Our approach is highly adaptable; once the initial small-scale simulation and probabilistic models have been set up, different decision algorithms can be easily substituted and analysed. Our example illustrates the use of a weight function for decision making. In a more extensive scenario the weight function would be more complex (e.g. involving current values associated with all sensors and guiding systems). Our use of non-determinism when approximating quantitative data obtained from the small-scale simulation models allows us to provide an range of uncertainty for our results. We aim to formally prove a link between the simulation and the abstract model to allow us to infer results from the abstract model for the actual system. To allow the analysis of more complex scenarios we plan to incorporate abstraction techniques.

Acknowledgments. This work was supported by the Engineering and Physical Sciences Research Council [grant number EP/N508792/1].

References

1. Chaimowicz, L., Campos, M.F.M., Kumar, V.: Hybrid systems modeling of cooperative robots. In: Proceedings International Conference Robotics and Automation (ICRA 2003), pp. 4086–4091. IEEE Press, New York (2003)

2. Cook, J., Hu, G.: Experimental verification and algorithm of a multi-robot cooperative control method. In: Proceedings IEEE/ASME International Conference Advanced Intelligent Mechatronics (AIM 2010), pp. 109–114. IEEE Press, New York (2010)
3. Dennis, L., Fisher, M., Lincoln, N., Lisitsa, A., Veres, S.: Practical verification of decision-making in agent-based autonomous systems. Autom. Softw. Eng., pp. 1–55 (2014). http://link.springer.com/article/10.1007/s10515-014-0168-9
4. Kattenbelt, M., Kwiatkowska, M., Norman, G., Parker, D.: A game-based abstraction-refinement framework for Markov decision processes. Formal Methods Syst. Des. **36**(3), 246–280 (2010)
5. Kwiatkowska, M., Norman, G., Parker, D.: PRISM 4.0: verification of probabilistic real-time systems. In: Gopalakrishnan, G., Qadeer, S. (eds.) CAV 2011. LNCS, vol. 6806, pp. 585–591. Springer, Heidelberg (2011)
6. PRISM model repository (2016). http://dx.doi.org/10.5525/gla.researchdata.274
7. Veres, S., Molnar, L., Lincoln, N., Morice, C.: Autonomous vehicle control systems - a review of decision making. Proc. Inst. Mech. Eng. Part I: J. Syst. Control Eng. **225**(2), 155–195 (2011)

Certification for μ-Calculus
with Winning Strategies

Martin Hofmann[1], Christian Neukirchen[1(✉)], and Harald Rueß[2]

[1] Department of Informatics, Ludwig-Maximilians-Universität, Munich, Germany
hofmann@ifi.lmu.de, chneukirchen@gmail.com
[2] Fortiss, An-Institut Technische Universität München,
Guerickestr. 25, 80805 Munich, Germany
ruess@fortiss.org

Abstract. We define memory-efficient certificates for μ-calculus model checking problems based on the well-known correspondence between μ-calculus model checking and winning certain parity games. Winning strategies can be independently checked, in low polynomial time, by observing that there is no reachable strongly connected component in the graph of the parity game whose largest priority is odd. Winning strategies are computed by fixpoint iteration following the naive semantics of μ-calculus. We instrument the usual fixpoint iteration of μ-calculus model checking so that it produces evidence in the form of a winning strategy; for a formula ϕ with fixed alternation depth, these winning strategies can be computed in polynomial time in $|S|$ and in space $O(|S|^2|\phi|^2)$, where $|S|$ is the size of the state space and $|\phi|$ the length of the formula ϕ. On the technical level our work yields a new, simpler, and immediate constructive proof of the correspondence between μ-calculus and parity games. A prototypical implementation of a μ-calculus model checker generating these certificates has been developed.

1 Introduction

We address the problems (1) of constructing concise certificates for μ-calculus model checking problems, and (2) for efficiently and independently checking these certificates by means of a trustworthy checker. Our main result here is an effective and low overhead instrumentation of the usual fixpoint iteration of μ-calculus model checking [3] for generating certificates that are independently checkable in low polynomial time.

There are a number of results and algorithms for constructing witnesses and counterexamples of various forms for different sublogics, including *LTL*, *ACTL*, *CTL*, *CTL**, or the μ-calculus [1,6,7,14,24,27,33,34]. For example, for linear temporal logic (*LTL*) restricted to the temporal operators F, U and X, a positive certificate can be given by a finite *path*. Model checkers for *CTL** (for example, SMV) are capable of generating *counterexamples* [7] in the form of

C. Neukirchen—The author was supported by DFG Graduiertenkolleg 1480 (PUMA).

© Springer International Publishing Switzerland 2016
D. Bošnački and A. Wijs (Eds.): SPIN 2016, LNCS 9641, pp. 111–128, 2016.
DOI: 10.1007/978-3-319-32582-8_8

a *lasso*; that is, infinite sequences of states $s_0, \ldots, s_i, (s_{i+1}, \ldots, s_k)^\omega$ which end up repeating periodically after some prefix of length i. Whereas lasso-shaped sequences refute properties assumed for *all* possible paths, they fail, for example, in falsifying conjectured *existence* of certain paths. *Witnesses* for full *CTL* have been proposed by Shankar and Sorea [27,29]. These results are based on a symbolic representation of witnesses that enables the extraction of explicit witnesses (and counterexamples) for full *CTL* model checking.

Local model checking procedures for determining whether finite-state systems have properties expressible in the μ-calculus incrementally construct tableau proofs [8,31,35]. These tableaux can be proof-checked independently, but the size of the constructed tableaux may grow exponentially in the number of states of the underlying transition system. Based on the tableau method of local μ-calculus model checking, Kick [18] proposes an optimized construction by identifying isomorphic subproofs. Namjoshi [20] introduces the notion of a *certifying model checker* that can generate independently checkable witnesses for properties verified by a model checker. He defines witnesses for properties of labelled transition systems expressed in the μ-calculus based on parity games over alternating tree automata. These developments rely on μ-calculus signatures [32] for termination, and are also based on the correspondence between μ-calculus model checking with winning parity games [12].

The developments in this paper can certify full μ-calculus model checking problems. Moreover, in order to certify that a given formula does *not* hold for some state, the result of checking the *dual formula* (cf. Lemma 1) is certified instead. In this way, certificates of the dual formula may be regarded as *generalized counterexamples* of the original formula.

Our approach of instrumenting μ-calculus model checking fixpoint iteration with the computation of witnesses, including the underlying notion and algebra of *partial winning strategies*, is novel. Moreover, in contrast to the previous work on local μ-calculus model checking, the witnesses generated by our global model checking algorithm are rather space-efficient, as they can be represented in space in $O(|S|^2|\phi|^2)$, where $|S|$ is the size of the state space and $|\phi|$ is the length of the formula ϕ.

Our constructions build on the well-known equivalence of model checking for the μ-calculus with winning corresponding parity games [12,13,34]. Because of the determinacy of parity games (see [19]), players of these games may restrict themselves to considering memoryless strategies only. In particular, there are no draws and exactly one of the players has a winning strategy for each vertex of the game graph. Algorithms for generating witnesses for players of parity games and their complexity are described by Jurdziński [17].

On the technical level our work can be seen as a new, simpler, and immediately constructive proof of the correspondence between μ-calculus and parity games. Winning strategies are computed by fixpoint iteration following the naive semantics of μ-calculus. No complex auxiliary devices such as signatures [32] or alternating automata [12] are needed. It should be possible to instrument existing implementations (such as the one integrated in the PVS theorem prover [23]) of μ-calculus based on fixpoint iteration to generate these certificates.

Roadmap. This paper is structured as follows. In Sects. 2 and 3 we summarize some standard developments for the μ-calculus in order to keep the paper self-contained. Section 3 also contains a low polynomial-time checker for certificates which is inspired by the standard algorithm for checking for nonemptiness of Streett automata. Section 4 elaborates the correspondence between μ-calculus and winning parity games and in particular contains a new constructive proof of the correspondence (Theorem 2). Section 5 provides the technical details, first, of the central notion of *partial winning strategies*, and, second, for instrumenting the usual μ-calculus fixpoint iteration with the computation of partial winning strategies. For ease of exposition of this algorithm, we choose *systems of equations* as an alternative representation of μ-calculus formulas. The corresponding implementation of a witness-generating μ-calculus model checker is presented in Sect. 6, and the feasibility of our approach is demonstrated by means of selected benchmark examples. Concluding remarks, including further applications of our technical results on witness-generation and -checking, are presented in Sect. 7.

An earlier version of this paper, without implementation and the use of equation systems, has been presented at the VeriSure 2013 workshop (associated with CAV 2013) [16].

2 Syntax and Semantics

We assume variables $X \in \mathcal{X}$, propositions $p \in \mathcal{P}$, and actions $a \in \mathcal{A}$.

2.1 μ-Calculus Formulas

Definition 1. *The set of μ-calculus formulas is given by the grammar*

$$\phi ::= X \mid p \mid \neg p \mid \langle a \rangle \phi \mid [a]\phi \mid \phi_1 \wedge \phi_2 \mid \phi_1 \vee \phi_2 \mid \mu X . \phi \mid \nu X . \phi$$

The set of free variables $FV(\phi) \subseteq \mathcal{X}$, the size $|\phi|$ of a formula, and the substitution $\phi[Z := \psi]$ of formula ψ for any free occurrence $Z \in FV(\phi)$ are defined in the usual way. Note that negation is allowed for propositions only, hence all syntactically valid formulas are monotonic in their free variables and no considerations of polarity need to be taken into account.

The notations $Q \in \{\mu, \nu\}$, $M \in \{[a], \langle a \rangle \mid a \in \mathcal{A}\}$, $* \in \{\wedge, \vee\}$ are used to simplify inductive definitions.

The semantics of μ-calculus formulas is given in terms of labelled transition systems (LTS), consisting of a nonempty set of states S, and a family of left-total[1] relations $\xrightarrow{a} \in S \times S$ for each action $a \in \mathcal{A}$ and, finally, an assignment $T \in S \to 2^{\mathcal{P}}$ which tells for each state s which atomic propositions $p \in \mathcal{P}$ are true in that state. If T is an LTS, we use $\mathcal{S}(T)$ for its set of states; $\xrightarrow{a}_T$ or simply $\xrightarrow{a}$ for its transition relation and T itself for its interpretation of atomic propositions.

---

[1] Left-total means for all $s \in S$ there exists $s' \in S$ with $s \to s'$.

$$[\![X]\!]\eta = \eta(X)$$
$$[\![p]\!]\eta = \{s \mid p \in T(s)\} \qquad\qquad [\![\neg p]\!]\eta = \{s \mid p \notin T(s)\}$$
$$[\![\phi_1 \vee \phi_2]\!]\eta = [\![\phi_1]\!]\eta \cup [\![\phi_2]\!]\eta \qquad\qquad [\![\phi_1 \wedge \phi_2]\!]\eta = [\![\phi_1]\!]\eta \cap [\![\phi_2]\!]\eta$$
$$[\![\langle a\rangle\phi]\!]\eta = pre(\xrightarrow{a})([\![\phi]\!]\eta) \qquad\qquad [\![[a]\phi]\!]\eta = \widetilde{pre}(\xrightarrow{a})([\![\phi]\!]\eta)$$
$$[\![\mu X.\phi]\!]\eta = lfp(U \mapsto [\![\phi]\!]\eta[X := U]) \qquad [\![\nu X.\phi]\!]\eta = gfp(U \mapsto [\![\phi]\!]\eta[X := U])$$

Fig. 1. Set semantics of μ-calculus formulas.

Fix a transition system T and put $S = \mathcal{S}(T)$. For η a finite partial function from $\mathcal{X}$ to 2^S with $FV(\phi) \subseteq dom(\eta)$ we define $[\![\phi]\!]\eta \subseteq S$ as in Fig. 1.

The sets $pre(\xrightarrow{a})([\![\phi]\!]\eta)$ and $\widetilde{pre}(\xrightarrow{a})([\![\phi]\!]\eta)$ respectively denote the *preimage* and the *weakest precondition* of the set $[\![\phi]\!]\eta$ with respect to the binary relation $\xrightarrow{a}$; formally:

$$s \in pre(\xrightarrow{a})([\![\phi]\!]\eta) \;\; iff \;\; \exists t \in S.\ s \xrightarrow{a} t \; and \, t \in [\![\phi]\!]\eta$$
$$s \in \widetilde{pre}(\xrightarrow{a})([\![\phi]\!]\eta) \;\; iff \;\; \forall t \in S.\ s \xrightarrow{a} t \; implies \, t \in [\![\phi]\!]\eta$$

Given the functional $F(U) = [\![\phi]\!]\eta[X := U]$, $lfp(F)$ and $gfp(F)$ respectively denote the least and the greatest fixpoints of F, with respect to the subset ordering on 2^S. By Knaster-Tarski, these fixpoints exist, since F is monotone.

Proposition 1. $[\![QX.\phi]\!]\eta = [\![\phi[X := QX.\phi]]\!]\eta$.

By the monotonicity of F, $\emptyset \subseteq F(\emptyset) \subseteq F^2(\emptyset) \subseteq \ldots$ and $S \supseteq F(S) \supseteq F^2(S) \supseteq \ldots$. Moreover, if S is finite then we have

$$[\![\mu X.\phi]\!]\eta = \{s \in S \mid \exists t \leq |S|.\ s \in F^t(\emptyset)\},$$
$$[\![\nu X.\phi]\!]\eta = \{s \in S \mid \forall t \leq |S|.\ s \in F^t(S)\}.$$

Therefore, in case S is finite, the iterative algorithm in Fig. 2 computes $[\![\phi]\!]\eta$.

Proposition 2. $[\![\phi]\!]\eta = sem(\phi, \eta)$.

Lemma 1. $s \notin [\![\phi]\!]\eta$ iff $s \in [\![\phi^*]\!]\eta'$, where $\eta'(X) = S\backslash\eta(X)$ and ϕ^* is the dual of ϕ given by

$$(X)^* = X$$
$$(p)^* = \neg p \qquad\qquad (\neg p)^* = p$$
$$(\phi_1 \wedge \phi_2)^* = \phi_1^* \vee \phi_2^* \qquad\qquad (\phi_1 \vee \phi_2)^* = \phi_1^* \wedge \phi_2^*$$
$$([a]\phi)^* = \langle a\rangle\phi^* \qquad\qquad (\langle a\rangle\phi)^* = [a]\phi^*$$
$$(\mu X.\phi)^* = \nu X.\phi^* \qquad\qquad (\nu X.\phi)^* = \mu X.\phi^*.$$

$$sem(X, \eta) = \eta(X)$$
$$sem(p, \eta) = T(p)$$
$$sem(\neg p, \eta) = S \setminus T(p)$$
$$sem(\mu X.\phi, \eta) = \text{ITER}_X(\phi, \eta, \emptyset)$$
$$sem(\nu X.\phi, \eta) = \text{ITER}_X(\phi, \eta, S)$$
$$sem(\phi_1 \wedge \phi_2, \eta) = sem(\phi_1, \eta) \cap sem(\phi_2, \eta)$$
$$sem(\phi_1 \vee \phi_2, \eta) = sem(\phi_1, \eta) \cup sem(\phi_2, \eta)$$
$$sem([a]\phi, \eta) = \widetilde{pre}(\xrightarrow{a})(sem(\phi, \eta))$$
$$sem(\langle a \rangle \phi, \eta) = pre(\xrightarrow{a})(sem(\phi, \eta))$$

$$\text{ITER}_X(\phi, \eta, U) = \textit{if } U = U' \textit{ then } U \textit{ else } \text{ITER}_X(\phi, \eta, U')$$
$$\textit{where } U' := sem(\phi, \eta[X := U])$$

Fig. 2. Fixpoint iteration for computing the semantics of μ-calculus formulas.

2.2   Ordered Systems of Equations

We now use an alternate representation of μ-calculus formulas considering them to be an *ordered system of equations* [26]. Under this point of view, a formula ϕ is represented by a set of equations $(X = \phi_X)_{X \in \mathcal{X}}$, with one formula ϕ_X for each variable X occurring in ϕ, together with a strict partial order of variables $\succ \subseteq \mathcal{X} \times \mathcal{X}$.

To do this, we assume that every fixpoint quantifier binds a different variable; if needed this can be ensured by α-renaming. For example, we replace $\mu X.X \wedge \nu X.X$ with $\mu X.X \wedge \nu Y.Y$. For each variable X we denote $q_X \in \{\mu, \nu\}$ the kind of quantifier that it stems from.

We then replace each fixpoint formula by the (unique) variable it introduces and thereafter give for each fixpoint formula a defining equation. Formally, for any subformula ψ of ϕ let $\hat{\psi}$ denote the formula obtained by replacing each fixpoint subformula by the variable it binds. The equation system then contains one equation $X = \hat{\psi}$ for each fixpoint subformula $QX.\psi$, with $q_X = Q$.

In parallel, we build the strict partial order $\succ$ of variables. For each variable X bound by a fixpoint subformula $QX.\psi$ and each variable Y bound by a fixpoint subformula of ψ, i.e. all Y bound below X, we set $X \succ Y$.

For example let

$$\phi := \nu Z.(b \vee (\mu X.X \vee [a]Z)) \wedge [a]Z$$

We have $\hat{\phi} = (b \vee (\mu X.X \vee [a]Z)) \wedge [a]Z = (b \vee X) \wedge [a]Z$ so the equations are

$$Z = (b \vee X) \wedge [a]Z \tag{i}$$
$$X = X \vee [a]Z \tag{ii}$$

Moreover, $q_Z = \nu$, $q_X = \mu$, and $Z \succ X$.

The order $\succ$ is relevant for the restoration of the original formula: had we instead set $X \succ Z$, we would retrieve

$$\mu X.X \vee [a](\nu Z.(b \vee X) \wedge [a]Z).$$

It is now clear that such systems of equations together with $\succ$ are in 1-1 correspondence with formulas.

In case the formula does not start with a quantifier, a fresh variable needs to be introduced and bound to the formula in the first place. Since this variable is not used anywhere else, either μ or ν can be chosen.

This representation is advantageous for our implementation as it avoids the need for syntactic substitution of fixpoint formulas for their variables.

We extend $[\![-]\!]\eta$ to formulas ψ appearing in a given equation system according to the following clause, under the condition that $\{\, X \mid X \succ Y, Y \in FV(\psi)\,\} \subseteq \mathrm{dom}(\eta)$, i.e. all variables of higher priority reachable from the right hand side of the equation are already bound in η.

$$[\![X]\!]\eta = \begin{cases} \mathit{lfp}(U \mapsto [\![\phi_X]\!]\eta[X{:=}U]) & \text{if } X \notin \mathrm{dom}(\eta) \text{ and } q_X = \mu \\ \mathit{gfp}(U \mapsto [\![\phi_X]\!]\eta[X{:=}U]) & \text{if } X \notin \mathrm{dom}(\eta) \text{ and } q_X = \nu \end{cases}$$

In particular, the following is then obvious, starting from an empty environment:

Lemma 2. *Let ϕ be a formula and let X be the toplevel variable of the representation of ϕ as an equation system. Then $[\![X]\!] = [\![\phi]\!]$.*

Remark. It is possible to extend the semantics to the case where the relations $\xrightarrow{a}$ are not necessarily total: The semantics carries over without changes.

The restriction to total relations is a standard one and it is vindicated by the following translation from the general case to the one treated here:

Given a LTS T with a not necessarily total $\xrightarrow{a}$ we build a new LTS T' with an additional distinguished state, $\mathcal{S}(T') = \mathcal{S}(T) \cup \{\mho\}$, then extend $\xrightarrow{a}$ with extra edges from any state to $\mho$ ($\xrightarrow{a}_{T'} = \xrightarrow{a}_T \cup\{\,(s,\mho) \mid s \in \mathcal{S}(T')\,\}$) so that $\xrightarrow{a}_{T'}$ now is total. We also add a proposition $p_\mho$ which is true at state $\mho$ and nowhere else.

We can now define a translation $\widehat{\phi}$ for formulas by setting

$$\widehat{\langle a \rangle \phi} = \langle a \rangle \neg p_\mho \wedge \widehat{\phi} \qquad\qquad \widehat{[a]\phi} = [a]p_\mho \vee \widehat{\phi}.$$

The translation is homomorphically extended to all other connectives. It is then easy to see that $\forall s \in \mathcal{S}(T) : s \in [\![\phi]\!]_T \iff s \in [\![\widehat{\phi}]\!]_{T'}$.

3   Parity Games

A *parity game* is given by the following data:

- a (finite or infinite) set of positions *Pos* partitioned into proponent's (Player 0) and opponent's (Player 1) positions: $Pos = Pos_0 + Pos_1$;
- a left-total edge relation $\rightarrow \,\subseteq Pos \times Pos$;
- a function $\Omega \in Pos \rightarrow \mathbb{N}$ with a finite range; we call $\Omega(p)$ the priority of position p.

The players move a token along the edge relation $\rightarrow$. When the token is on a position in Pos_0 then proponent decides where to move next and likewise for opponent.

In order to formalize the notion of "to decide" we must introduce strategies. Formally, a strategy for a player $i \in \{0, 1\}$ is a function σ that for any nonempty string $\vec{p} = p(0) \dots p(n)$ over *Pos* such that $p(k) \rightarrow p(k+1)$ for $k = 0 \dots n - 1$ and $p(n) \in Pos_i$ associates a position $\sigma(\vec{p}) \in Pos$ such that $p(n) \rightarrow \sigma(\vec{p})$.

Given a starting position p and strategies σ_0 and σ_1 for the two players one then obtains an infinite sequence of positions (a "play") $p(0), p(1), p(2), \dots$ by

$$p(0) = p$$
$$p(n+1) = \sigma_i(p(0) \dots p(n)) \quad \text{where } p(n) \in Pos_i$$

We denote this sequence by $play(p, \sigma_0, \sigma_1)$.

The play is won by proponent (Player 0) if the largest number that occurs infinitely often in the sequence $\Omega(play(p, \sigma_0, \sigma_1))$ is even and it is won by opponent if that number is odd. Note that $\Omega(-)$ is applied component-wise and that a largest priority indeed exists since Ω has finite range.

Player i wins from position p if there exists a strategy σ_i for Player i such that for all strategies σ_{1-i} of the other player (Player $1 - i$) Player i wins $play(p, \sigma_0, \sigma_1)$. We write W_i for the set of positions from which Player i wins.

A strategy σ is *positional* if $\sigma(p(0) \dots p(n))$ only depends on $p(n)$. Player i *wins positionally* from p when the above strategy σ_i can be chosen to be positional.

The following is a standard result [19].

Theorem 1. *Every position p is either in W_0 or in W_1 and Player i wins positionally from every position in W_i.*

Example 1. Figure 3 contains a graphical display of a parity game. Positions in Pos_0 and Pos_1 are represented as circles and boxes, respectively, and labelled with their priorities. Formally, $Pos = \{a, b, c, d, e, f, g, h, i\}$; $Pos_0 = \{b, d, f, h\}$; $Pos_1 = \{a, c, e, g, i\}$; $\Omega(a) = 3, \dots$, and $\rightarrow = \{(a, b), (b, f), \dots\}$.

In the right half of Fig. 3 the winning sets are indicated and corresponding positional winning strategies are given as fat arrows. The moves from positions that are not in the respective winning set are omitted but can of course be filled-in in an arbitrary fashion.

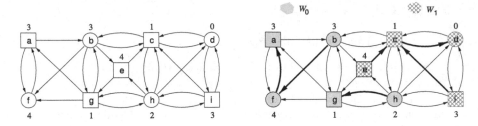

Fig. 3. A parity game and its decomposition into winning sets.

3.1   Certification of Winning Strategies

Given a parity game with finitely many positions, presented explicitly as a finite labelled graph, and a partition of *Pos* into V_0 and V_1 we are now looking for an easy-to-verify certificate as to the fact that $V_0 = W_0$ and $V_1 = W_1$.

In essence, such a certificate will consist of a positional strategy σ_i for each Player i such that i wins using σ_i from every position p in V_i. Clearly, this implies $V_i = W_i$ and the above theorem asserts that in principle such certificates always exist when $V_i = W_i$. However, it remains to explain how we can check that a given positional strategy σ_i wins from a given position p.

We first note that for this it is enough that it wins against any adversarial positional strategy because the "optimal" counterstrategy, i.e., the one that wins from all adversarial winning positions is positional (by Theorem 1). Thus, given a positional strategy σ_i for Player i we can remove all edges from positions $p' \in Pos_i$ that are not chosen by the strategy and in the remaining game graph look for a cycle whose largest priority has parity $1-i$ and is reachable from p. If there is such a cycle then the strategy was not good and otherwise it is indeed a winning strategy for Player i.

Naive enumeration of all cycles in the graph will result in having to check exponentially many cycles in the worst-case. However, the check can be performed in polynomial time [17], using the standard algorithm for nonemptiness of Streett automata [2] of which the problem at hand is actually an instance. This algorithm uses a decomposition of the graph into nontrivial strongly connected components (SCC).

If every reachable SCC only has positions whose priority has parity i then obviously the strategy is good for Player i. Next, if there is a reachable SCC where the *highest* priority has parity $1-i$, the strategy is bad, since this particular position can be reached infinitely often.

Otherwise, the highest priority in each SCC has parity i and of course player $1-i$ can win only if it is possible for them to avoid those nodes. Thus, we remove those nodes and decompose the resulting graph in SCCs again and start over.

For our implementation, we use a variant of this algorithm based on Dijkstra's algorithm for SCC as presented by [9,10]. In contrast to other efficient algorithms for this problem (such as [15]), it has the benefit of being *on-the-fly* and does not require precomputation of the parity game graph. The checking algorithm is described in more detail in Sect. 6.

Example 2. After removing the edges not taken by Player 0 according to their purported winning strategy we obtain the following graph:

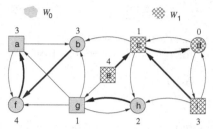

We see that the two reachable SCC from W_0 are $\{a, b, f\}$ and $\{g, h\}$. The first one contains the cycles a, f and a, b, f which both have largest priority 4. The other one is itself a cycle with largest priority 2.

Likewise, adopting the viewpoint of Player 1, after removing the edges not taken by their strategy we obtain

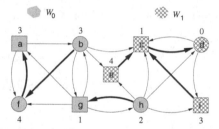

and find the reachable (from W_1) SCCs to be $\{c, d, i\}$. The only cycles therein are d, e and d, e, i. Both are good for Player 1.

4   Game-Theoretic Characterization of μ-Calculus

Fix an LTS T and a μ-calculus formula ϕ. We first translate ϕ into an equation system (as explained in Sect. 2.2) over the variables $\mathcal{X}$ written as $X = \phi_X$ where $X \in \mathcal{X}$ and $q_X \in \{\mu, \nu\}$.

We also fix a function $\Omega : \mathcal{X} \to \mathbb{N}$ such that

- $q_X = \mu \Rightarrow \Omega(X)$ odd;
- $q_X = \nu \Rightarrow \Omega(X)$ even;
- $X \succ Y \Rightarrow \Omega(X) > \Omega(Y)$.

If in addition η is an environment with $\mathrm{dom}(\eta) \subseteq \mathcal{X}$ we define the game $G(T, \phi, \eta)$ as follows:

Positions are pairs (s, ψ) where $s \in S$ and ψ is a subformula of the right-hand sides of the equation system and $FV(\psi) \subseteq \mathrm{dom}(\eta)$. In positions of the form (s, ψ) where ψ starts with $\vee$ or $\langle a \rangle$, it is proponent's (Player 0) turn. The possible moves for proponent to choose from are:

$$(s, \psi_1 \vee \psi_2) \rightsquigarrow (s, \psi_1)$$
$$(s, \psi_1 \vee \psi_2) \rightsquigarrow (s, \psi_2)$$
$$(s, \langle a \rangle \psi) \rightsquigarrow (t, \psi) \qquad \text{where } s \xrightarrow{a}_T t.$$

In positions of the form (s, ψ) where ψ starts with $\wedge$ or $[a]$ it is the opponent's turn. The possible moves for opponent to choose from are:

$$(s, \psi_1 \wedge \psi_2) \rightsquigarrow (s, \psi_1)$$
$$(s, \psi_1 \wedge \psi_2) \rightsquigarrow (s, \psi_2)$$
$$(s, [a] \psi) \rightsquigarrow (t, \psi) \qquad \text{where } s \xrightarrow{a}_T t.$$

From all other positions there is exactly one move so it does not matter to which player they belong. We fix them to be proponent's positions for definiteness. These unique moves are:

$$(s, X) \rightsquigarrow (s, \phi_X) \qquad \text{when } X \notin \mathrm{dom}(\eta)$$
$$(s, X) \rightsquigarrow (s, X) \qquad \text{when } X \in \mathrm{dom}(\eta)$$
$$(s, p) \rightsquigarrow (s, p)$$
$$(s, \neg p) \rightsquigarrow (s, \neg p)$$

The priorities $\Omega(s, \phi)$ on these positions are defined as follows:

$$\Omega(s, p) = \begin{cases} 0 & \text{if } p \in T(s) \\ 1 & \text{if } p \notin T(s) \end{cases}$$

$$\Omega(s, \neg p) = \begin{cases} 1 & \text{if } p \in T(s) \\ 0 & \text{if } p \notin T(s) \end{cases}$$

$$\Omega(s, X) = \begin{cases} \Omega(X) & \text{if } X \notin \mathrm{dom}(\eta) \\ 0 & \text{if } s \in \eta(X) \\ 1 & \text{if } s \notin \eta(X) \end{cases}$$

$$\Omega(s, \phi) = 0 \quad \text{otherwise}$$

The cases for predicates p, $\neg p$ and concrete sets X, i.e., where $X \in \mathrm{dom}(\eta)$ are clear. They are winning positions iff the associated state s satisfies the corresponding predicate.

The variables $X \notin \mathrm{dom}(\eta)$ on the other hand are understood as abbreviations of the fixpoint formula they represent. Upon reaching such a position the fixpoint is unrolled and such unrolling is signalled by the priority $\Omega(X)$.

Example 3. Let $\phi = \mu X. p \vee \langle a \rangle X$ which asserts that a state where p is true can be reached.

Define the transition system T by $\mathcal{S}(T) = \{s, t\}$ and $T(s) = \emptyset$ and $T(t) = \{p\}$ and $\xrightarrow{a}_T = \{(s,s), (s,t), (t,t)\}$. The associated game graph is as follows:

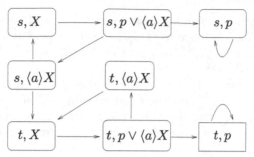

The priorities of the positions labelled $(s, X), (t, X), (s, p)$ are 1; the priorities of the four other positions are 0.

Player 0 wins from every position except (s, p). The winning strategy moves to $(s, \langle a \rangle X)$ and then (t, X) and then (t, p). Note that a strategy that moves from $(s, \langle a \rangle X)$ to (s, X) loses even though it never leaves the winning set W_0. Thus, in order to compute winning strategies it is not enough to choose any move that remains in the winning set.

Theorem 2. *Fix a formula ϕ_0 and an environment η.*
If $s \in [\![\phi_0]\!]\eta$ then proponent wins $G(T, \eta)$ from (s, ϕ_0).

Before proving this, we note that the converse is in this case actually a relatively simple consequence.

Corollary 1. *If proponent wins $G(T, \eta)$ from (s, ϕ) then $s \in [\![\phi]\!]\eta$.*

Proof. Suppose that proponent wins $G(T, \eta)$ from (s, ϕ) and $s \notin [\![\phi]\!]\eta$. We then have $s \in [\![\phi^*]\!]\eta'$ using Lemma 1 for the formal dualisation for formulas and complementation for environments. Thus, by the theorem, proponent wins $G(T, \eta')$ from (s, ϕ^*). However, it is easy to see that a winning strategy for proponent in $G(T, \eta')$ from (s, ϕ^*) is tantamount to a winning strategy for opponent in $G(T, \eta)$ from (s, ϕ); so we get a contradiction using Theorem 1. □

Proof (of Theorem 2). The proof of Theorem 2 now works by structural induction on the equation system generated by ϕ_0. We note that this induction preserves the invariant $\{ X \mid X \succ Y, Y \in FV(\phi) \} \subseteq \text{dom}(\eta)$, such that $[\![\phi]\!]\eta$ is always well-defined.

For a variable X, there are three cases, the latter ones are the interesting ones, as X denotes a fixpoint there:
(i) $X \in \text{dom}(\eta)$, then obviously $G(T, \eta)$ agrees with $[\![X]\!]\eta$.
(ii) $X \notin \text{dom}(\eta)$ and $q_X = \mu$. Then we define

$$U := \{ t \mid proponent\ wins\ G(T, \eta)\ from\ (t, X) \}.$$

We must show that $[\![\phi_X]\!]\eta \subseteq U$. By definition of $[\![\phi_X]\!]\eta$ it suffices to show that $[\![\phi_X]\!]\eta[X \mapsto U] \subseteq U$. Thus, suppose that $t \in [\![\phi_X]\!]\eta[X \mapsto U]$. By the induction hypothesis this means that proponent wins $G(T, \eta[X \mapsto U])$ from (t, ϕ_X). (Now $\eta(X)$ is bound while recursing the subformulas of lower priority, preserving the condition on η.)

Call the corresponding winning strategy σ. We should prove that proponent also wins from (t, X). We move to (t, ϕ_X) and then play according to σ. If we never reach a position (t', X), then by the definition of $G(T, \eta[X \mapsto U])$ we actually have won $G(T, \eta)$.

The first time, if ever, that we reach a position (t', X), we know by the definition of U that $t' \in U$ and therefore we win $G(T, \eta)$ from (t', X), so we abandon σ and continue play according to the strategy embodied in the latter statement. This then ensures winning from (t, X) since finite prefixes do not affect the winning condition.

(iii) $X \notin \text{dom}(\eta)$ and $q_X = \nu$. Let $U := [\![X]\!]\eta \ (= [\![\nu X.\phi_X]\!]\eta)$. We define a winning strategy for positions of the form (t, X) where $t \in U$ as follows. First, we move (forcedly) to (t, ϕ_X). We know that $t \in [\![\phi_X]\!]\eta[X \mapsto U]$ by unwinding so that, inductively, we have a strategy that allows us to either win right away, or move to another position (t', X) where $t' \in U$ and all priorities encountered on the way are smaller than the one of X due to the definition of priorities, and since all higher occurring priorities are bound in η, thus not resulting in a loop.

We start over and unless we eventually do win right away at some point we would have seen the priority of X itself infinitely often which is the largest and even.   □

We remark that while the previous result is well-known the proof presented here is quite different from the ones in the standard literature, e.g. [4], which use the order-theoretic concept of signatures, also known as rankings. Those proofs are less compositional than ours, in the sense that they do not proceed directly by structural induction on formulas but rather on the global development of all the fixpoints.

It is essentially this new compositional proof which allows us to instrument the usual fixpoint iteration so as to compute winning strategies alongside as we now detail.

5   Computing Winning Strategies via Fixpoint Iteration

5.1   Fixpoint Iteration

It is well-known that the fixpoint iteration in Fig. 2 computes $[\![\phi]\!]\eta$ in the finite case. Our goal is to somehow instrument this algorithm so that it produces evidence in the form of a winning strategy. In instrumenting this algorithm to produce evidence in the form of a winning strategy it is not enough to simply compute the winning sets using $\text{SEM}(-, -)$ and then simply choose moves that do not leave the winning set. This is because of Example 3 which show that a strategy that never leaves the winning set may nonetheless be losing.

Instead we will use the construction from the proof of Theorem 2. Some care needs to be taken with the exact setup of the input and output data formats;

in particular, our algorithm will return partial winning strategies (that win on a subset of the whole winning set) but only require sets of states (rather than partial winning strategies) as the values of free variables.

5.2 Partial Winning Strategies

A *partial winning strategy* is a partial function Σ mapping positions of the game $G(T, \eta)$ to elements of S extended with $\{1, 2, *\}$; it must satisfy the following conditions:

STAR. If $\Sigma(\phi, s) = *$ then all immediate successors of (ϕ, s) are in $\mathrm{dom}(\Sigma)$;

OR. If $\Sigma(\phi, s) = i \in \{1, 2\}$ then ϕ is of the form $\phi_1 \vee \phi_2$ and $(\phi_i, s) \in \mathrm{dom}(\Sigma)$;

DIA. If $\Sigma(\phi, s) = s' \in S$ then ϕ is of the form $\langle a \rangle \psi$ and $s \xrightarrow{a} s'$ and $(\psi, s') \in \mathrm{dom}(\Sigma)$.

WIN. Player 0 wins from all the positions in $\mathrm{dom}(\Sigma)$ and the obvious strategy induced by Σ is a winning strategy for Player 0 from those positions.

Note that the empty function (denoted $\{\}$) is in particular a partial winning strategy. To illustrate the notation we describe a (partial) winning strategy for the entire winning set for Example 3:

$$\Sigma(\phi, s) = * \qquad \Sigma(\phi, t) = *$$
$$\Sigma(P \vee \langle a \rangle \phi, s) = 2 \qquad \Sigma(P \vee \langle a \rangle \phi, t) = 1$$
$$\Sigma(\langle a \rangle \phi, s) = t \qquad \Sigma(P, t) = *, \qquad \text{and undefined elsewhere.}$$

So, $\mathrm{dom}(\Sigma) = \{(\phi, s), \ldots, (P, t)\}$ and, indeed, Player 0 wins from all these positions by following the advice given by Σ. Of course, $\Sigma'(P, t) = *$ and undefined elsewhere is also a partial winning strategy albeit with smaller domain of definition.

Updating of winning strategies. Suppose that Σ and Σ' are partial winning strategies. A new partial winning strategy $\Sigma + \Sigma'$ with $\mathrm{dom}(\Sigma + \Sigma')$ is defined by

$$(\Sigma + \Sigma')(\phi, s) = if \ (\phi, s) \in \mathrm{dom}(\Sigma) \ then \ \Sigma(\phi, s) \ else \ \Sigma'(\phi, s).$$

Lemma 3. $\Sigma + \Sigma'$ *is a partial winning strategy and* $\mathrm{dom}(\Sigma + \Sigma') = \mathrm{dom}(\Sigma) \cup \mathrm{dom}(\Sigma')$

Proof. A play following $\Sigma + \Sigma'$ will eventually remain in one of Σ or Σ'; this, together with the fact that initial segments do not affect the outcome of a game implies the claim. $\qquad \square$

5.3   Computing Winning Strategies by Fixpoint Iteration

For any LTS T, formula ϕ and environment η with $\mathrm{dom}(\eta) \supseteq FV(\phi)$ we define a partial winning strategy $\mathrm{SEM}(\phi)_\eta$ by the following clauses:

$$\mathrm{SEM}(X)_\eta = \{\, (X, s) \mapsto * \mid s \in \eta(X) \,\} \qquad\qquad \text{if } X \in \mathrm{dom}(\eta)$$

$$\mathrm{SEM}(p)_\eta = \{\, (p, s) \mapsto * \mid p \in T(s) \,\}$$

$$\mathrm{SEM}(\neg p)_\eta = \{\, (p, s) \mapsto * \mid p \notin T(s) \,\}$$

$$\mathrm{SEM}(\phi \wedge \psi)_\eta = \mathrm{SEM}(\phi)_\eta + \mathrm{SEM}(\psi)_\eta$$
$$+ \{\, (\phi \wedge \psi, s) \mapsto * \mid (\phi, s) \in \mathrm{dom}(\mathrm{SEM}(\phi)_\eta)$$
$$\wedge\, (\psi, s) \in \mathrm{dom}(\mathrm{SEM}(\psi)_\eta) \,\}$$

$$\mathrm{SEM}(\phi \vee \psi)_\eta = \mathrm{SEM}(\phi)_\eta + \mathrm{SEM}(\psi)_\eta$$
$$+ \{\, (\phi \vee \psi, s) \mapsto 1 \mid (\phi, s) \in \mathrm{dom}(\mathrm{SEM}(\phi)_\eta) \,\}$$
$$+ \{\, (\phi \vee \psi, s) \mapsto 2 \mid (\psi, s) \in \mathrm{dom}(\mathrm{SEM}(\psi)_\eta) \,\}$$

$$\mathrm{SEM}([a]\phi)_\eta = \mathrm{SEM}(\phi)_\eta$$
$$+ \{\, ([a]\phi, s) \mapsto * \mid (\phi, s) \in \mathrm{dom}(\mathrm{SEM}(\phi)_\eta) \,\}$$

$$\mathrm{SEM}(\langle a\rangle\phi)_\eta = \mathrm{SEM}(\phi)_\eta$$
$$+ \{\, (\langle a\rangle\phi, s) \mapsto s' \mid s \xrightarrow{a} s' \wedge (\phi, s') \in \mathrm{dom}(\mathrm{SEM}(\phi)_\eta) \,\}$$

$$\mathrm{SEM}(X = \phi_X)_\eta = \mathrm{SHIFT}(\nu X.\phi_X, \mathrm{SEM}(\phi_X)_{\eta[X := sem(\phi_X, \eta)]}) \quad \text{if } q_X = \nu$$

$$\mathrm{SEM}(X = \phi_X)_\eta = \mathrm{SHIFT}(\mu X.\phi_X, \mathrm{ITER}_X(\phi_X, \eta, \{\})) \quad\quad \text{if } q_X = \mu$$

$$\mathrm{ITER}_X(\phi, \eta, \Sigma) = \text{let } \Sigma' := \mathrm{SEM}(\phi)_{\eta[X := \{s \mid (\phi, s) \in \mathrm{dom}(\Sigma)\}]} \text{ in}$$
$$\text{if } \mathrm{dom}(\Sigma) = \mathrm{dom}(\Sigma') \text{ then } \Sigma \text{ else } \mathrm{ITER}_X(\phi, \eta, \Sigma')$$

$$\mathrm{SHIFT}(QX.\phi, \Sigma) = \Sigma + \{\, (QX.\phi, s) \mapsto * \mid (\phi, s) \in \mathrm{dom}(\Sigma) \,\}$$

Of particular interest is the SHIFT function: since the only possible moves for $QX.\phi$ formulas are to move to the subformula ϕ, we need to adjust the domain of the winning strategy under construction to only allow this move when the strategy will win for the subformula already.

Note how the fixpoint iteration in ITER_X stops when the domain of the partial winning strategy does not change anymore. Since the greatest fixpoint for $\nu X.\phi$ cannot be calculated from above in terms of winning strategies (which can only grow according to our definitions), the winning set (and thus, domain of the winning strategy) is computed using the set semantics $sem(-, -)$ instead.

The following Lemma and Theorem are now immediate from these definitions and Lemma 3.

Lemma 4. $\{\, s \mid (\phi, s) \in \mathrm{dom}(\mathrm{SEM}(\phi)_\eta) \,\} = [\![\phi]\!]\eta.$

Theorem 3. $\mathrm{SEM}(\phi)_\eta$ *is a winning strategy for* $G(T, \phi, \eta)$.

Proposition 3. *Given a formula ϕ with fixed alternation depth, $\mathrm{SEM}(\phi)_\eta$ can be computed in polynomial time in $|S|$ and in space $O(|S|^2|\phi|^2)$, where $|S|$ is the size of the state space and $|\phi|$ the length of the formula ϕ.*

Proof. The computation of SEM$(\phi)_\eta$ follows the one of $[\![\phi]\!]\eta$ hence the time bound. Just like in the usual implementations of fixpoint iteration one only needs to remember the result of the last iteration. Storing a single partial winning strategy requires space $O(|S|^2|\phi|)$ (associating at most one state to each pair of state and subformula) and the recursion stack during traversal of subformulas is limited by $|\phi|$ thus requiring us to store $O(\phi)$ partial winning strategies at any one time. This yields the announced space bound.   □

6   Implementation and Evaluation

We have developed an implementation [22] of both computation and checking of certificates in OCaml. Winning strategies are kept abstract, only exposing an `assoc` function to look up a possible move given a model and particular state. Computation of winning strategies happens by fixpoint iteration using a recursive function, just like presented in Sect. 5.3.

Two algorithms for checking certificates are implemented: "Check", a naive, recursive one with worst-case exponential time, and "Check SCC", a more intricate one using strongly-connected components to detect cycles. Both algorithms operate *on-the-fly* and do not need to pre-compute or even keep the parity game graph in memory.

The algorithm "Check SCC" is a variant of Dijkstra's algorithm for detecting strongly connected components and can be found in [9,10].

This algorithm works as follows [25]: During a depth-first search of the graph, we keep a stack of strongly connected components that have been found. Upon finding an edge back into a SCC that closes a cycle, we merge all SCC that are part of the cycle, since using the cycle we can now move from every SCC into any other, i.e. their union is actually one SCC.

We provide three benchmarks that give insight into the algorithms at work.

The "Flower" benchmark is a parity game (from [5]) translated into a μ-calculus formula, which shows the exponential runtime of fixpoint iteration for μ-calculus. However, the certificates can be checked in polynomial time.

The "Circle" benchmark measures the overhead of the algorithms. It consists of a single cycle that needs to be traversed to check for a reachability property. In this case, runtime is linear, and checking is very fast.

The "Braid" benchmark focuses on checking complexity. This family of graphs has exponentially many cycles, thus the simple checker requires exponential time. The SCC algorithm is not affected and checks these strategies in linear time (Table 1).

Table 1. Runtimes on a AMD Phenom II X4 920 (2.80 GHz)

Problem		States	sem [s]	SEM [s]	Check [s]	Check SCC [s]
Flower	8	16	0.179	0.203	0.009	0.040
Flower	10	20	3.166	1.960	0.071	0.419
Flower	12	24	32.269	11.688	0.287	2.061
Flower	14	28	320.931	61.733	1.298	10.829
Flower	16	32	3196.043	326.666	6.131	58.871
Circle	100	100	0.003	0.001	0.001	0.001
Circle	1000	1000	0.109	0.018	0.005	0.006
Circle	10000	10000	15.763	3.398	0.054	0.057
Circle	100000	100000	2027.584	811.041	0.581	0.582
Braid	6	12	0.001	0.005	1.282	0.009
Braid	8	16	0.002	0.003	31.062	0.013
Braid	10	20	0.002	0.006	711.002	0.020
Braid	100	200	0.663	0.993	—	3.674

7   Conclusion

Our main result is an effective and low overhead instrumentation of the usual fixpoint iteration of μ-calculus model checking [3] for generating certificates or counterexamples that are independently checkable in low polynomial time. The notion of *partial winning strategies* is central to our developments and also seems to be novel.

We have implemented our witness-generating algorithms and demonstrated the feasibility of our approach by means of a collection of benchmark examples. For simple formulas, manual inspection of the generated certificates yields counterexamples similar to those generated by SMV, but algorithmic approaches for extracting explicit counterexamples in general needs further investigation.

There are numerous applications for our certifying μ-calculus model checker. In particular, it should be possible to generate checkable certificates for the bisimulation between programs and for model checking problems for both linear time temporal logics and computation tree logics [11] as the basis for assurance cases and certification arguments for safety-critical systems. Moreover, certificates for μ-calculus model checking might also be used as the basis of symmetric abstraction-refinement-based model checking engines for the full μ-calculus based on refining over-approximations using *spurious counterexamples* and relaxing under-approximations using *dubious witnesses* along the lines of [29,30], for sending code together with proofs of arbitrary safety and liveness properties, which are then checked by code consumers according to the *proof-carrying code* paradigm of [21], and for synthesizing *correct-by-construction* controllers from these certificates [30].

Our developments may also form the underpinning for a sound integration of μ-calculus model checking into other verification systems such as PVS [23]. Using

Shankar's kernel of truth [28] approach, which is based on checking the verification and on verifying the checker, certificates are generated using an untrusted implementation of our μ-calculus model checking algorithms, and certificates are then checked by means of an executable PVS function, which itself is verified in a trusted kernel of PVS.

References

1. Biere, A., Zhu, Y., Clarke, E.: Multiple state and single state tableaux for combining local and global model checking. In: Olderog, E.-R., Steffen, B. (eds.) Correct System Design. LNCS, vol. 1710, pp. 163–179. Springer, Heidelberg (1999)
2. Bloem, R., Gabow, H.N., Somenzi, F.: An algorithm for strongly connected component analysis in $n \log n$ symbolic steps. Formal Methods Syst. Des. **28**(1), 37–56 (2006)
3. Bradfield, J., Stirling, C.: Modal mu-calculi. Stud. Logic Pract. Reasoning **3**, 721–756 (2007)
4. Bradfield, J., Stirling, C.: Modal logics and mu-calculi: an introduction. In: Bergstra, J., Ponse, A., Smolka, S. (eds.) Handbook of Process Algebra, pp. 293–330. Elsevier, Amsterdam (2001)
5. Buhrke, N., Lescow, H., Vöge, J.: Strategy construction in infinite games with streett and rabin chain winning conditions. In: Margaria, T., Steffen, B. (eds.) TACAS. LNCS, vol. 1055, pp. 207–225. Springer, Heidelberg (1996)
6. Clarke, E., Jha, S., Lu, Y., Veith, H.: Tree-like counterexamples in model checking. In: Proceedings of the 17th Annual IEEE Symposium on Logic in Computer Science, pp. 19–29. IEEE (2002)
7. Clarke, E., Grumberg, O., McMillan, K., Zhao, X.: Efficient generation of counterexamples and witnesses in symbolic model checking. In: Proceedings of the 32nd Annual ACM/IEEE Design Automation Conference, pp. 427–432. ACM (1995)
8. Cleaveland, R.: Tableau-based model checking in the propositional mu-calculus. Acta Informatica **27**(8), 725–747 (1990)
9. Duret-Lutz, A.: Contributions à l'approche automate pour la vérification de propriétés de systèmes concurrents. Ph.D. thesis, Université Pierre et Marie Curie (Paris 6) July 2007. https://www.lrde.epita.fr/~adl/th.html
10. Duret-Lutz, A., Poitrenaud, D., Couvreur, J.-M.: On-the-fly emptiness check of transition-based streett automata. In: Liu, Z., Ravn, A.P. (eds.) ATVA 2009. LNCS, vol. 5799, pp. 213–227. Springer, Heidelberg (2009)
11. Emerson, E., Jutla, C., Sistla, A.: On model-checking for fragments of μ-calculus. In: Courcoubetis, C. (ed.) CAV 1993. LNCS, vol. 697, pp. 385–396. Springer, Heidelberg (1993)
12. Emerson, E., Jutla, C.: Tree automata, mu-calculus and determinacy. In: Proceedings of the 32nd Annual Symposium on Foundations of Computer Science (FOCS 1991), pp. 368–377. IEEE (1991)
13. Grädel, E.: Back and forth between logic and games. In: Apt, K., Grädel, E. (eds.) Lectures in Game Theory for Computer Scientists, pp. 99–138. Cambridge University Press, Cambridge (2011)
14. Gurfinkel, A., Chechik, M.: Proof-like counter-examples. In: Garavel, H., Hatcliff, J. (eds.) TACAS 2003. LNCS, vol. 2619, pp. 160–175. Springer, Heidelberg (2003)

15. Henzinger, M.R., Telle, J.A.: Faster algorithms for the nonemptiness of streett automata and for communication protocol pruning. In: Karlsson, R., Lingas, A. (eds.) SWAT 1996. LNCS, vol. 1097, pp. 16–27. Springer, Heidelberg (1996)
16. Hofmann, M., Rueß, H.: Certification for μ-calculus with winning strategies. ArXiv e-prints, January 2014
17. Jurdziński, M.: Algorithms for solving parity games. In: Apt, K., Grädel, E. (eds.) Lectures in Game Theory for Computer Scientists, pp. 74–98. Cambridge University Press, Cambridge (2011)
18. Kick, A.: Generation of counterexamples for the μ-calculus. Technical report iratr-1995-37, Universität Karlsruhe, Germany (1995)
19. Martin, D.A.: Borel determinacy. Ann. Math. **102**(2), 363–371 (1975)
20. Namjoshi, K.S.: Certifying model checkers. In: Berry, G., Comon, H., Finkel, A. (eds.) CAV 2001. LNCS, vol. 2102, pp. 2–13. Springer, Heidelberg (2001)
21. Necula, G.: Proof-carrying code. In: Proceedings of the 24th ACM SIGPLAN-SIGACT Symposium on Principles of Programming Languages, pp. 106–119. ACM (1997)
22. Neukirchen, C.: Computation of winning strategies for μ-calculus by fixpoint iteration. Master's thesis, Ludwig-Maximilians-Universität München, November 2014
23. Owre, S., Rushby, J.M., Shankar, N.: PVS: a prototype verification system. In: Kapur, D. (ed.) CADE 1992. LNCS, vol. 607, pp. 748–752. Springer, Heidelberg (1992)
24. Peled, D.A., Pnueli, A., Zuck, L.D.: From falsification to verification. In: Hariharan, R., Mukund, M., Vinay, V. (eds.) FSTTCS 2001. LNCS, vol. 2245, pp. 292–304. Springer, Heidelberg (2001)
25. Renault, E., Duret-Lutz, A., Kordon, F., Poitrenaud, D.: Three SCC-based emptiness checks for generalized Büchi automata. In: McMillan, K., Middeldorp, A., Voronkov, A. (eds.) LPAR 2013. LNCS, vol. 8312, pp. 668–682. Springer, Heidelberg (2013)
26. Seidl, H.: Fast and Simple Nested Fixpoints. Universität Trier, Mathematik/Informatik, Forschungsbericht 96-05 (1996)
27. Shankar, N., Sorea, M.: Counterexample-driven model checking (revisited version). Technical report SRI-CSL-03-04, SRI International (2003)
28. Shankar, N.: Rewriting, inference, and proof. In: Ölveczky, P.C. (ed.) WRLA 2010. LNCS, vol. 6381, pp. 1–14. Springer, Heidelberg (2010)
29. Sorea, M.: Dubious witnesses and spurious counterexamples. UK Model Checking Days, York (2005). http://www.cs.man.ac.uk/~msorea/talks/york.pdf
30. Sorea, M.: Verification of real-time systems through lazy approximations. Ph.D. thesis, University of Ulm, Germany (2004)
31. Stirling, C., Walker, D.: Local model checking in the modal mu-calculus. In: Díaz, J., Orejas, F. (eds.) TAPSOFT 1989. LNCS, vol. 351, pp. 369–383. Springer, Heidelberg (1989)
32. Streett, R.S., Emerson, E.A.: The propositional mu-calculus is elementary. In: Paredaens, J. (ed.) Automata, Languages and Programming. LNCS, vol. 172, pp. 465–472. Springer, Heidelberg (1984)
33. Tan, L., Cleaveland, W.R.: Evidence-based model checking. In: Brinksma, E., Larsen, K.G. (eds.) CAV 2002. LNCS, vol. 2404, pp. 455–470. Springer, Heidelberg (2002)
34. Vardi, M., Wilke, T.: Automata: from logics to algorithms. In: WAL, pp. 645–753 (2007)
35. Winskel, G.: A note on model checking the modal ν-calculus. Theor. Comput. Sci. **83**(1), 157–167 (1991)

Real-Time Strategy Synthesis for Timed-Arc Petri Net Games via Discretization

Peter Gjøl Jensen[✉], Kim Guldstrand Larsen, and Jiří Srba

Department of Computer Science, Aalborg University,
Selma Lagerlöfs Vej 300, 9220 Aalborg East, Denmark
{pgj,kgl,srba}@cs.aau.dk

Abstract. Automatic strategy synthesis for a given control objective can be used to generate correct-by-construction controllers of reactive systems. The existing symbolic approach for continuous timed games is a computationally hard task and current tools like UPPAAL TiGa often scale poorly with the model complexity. We suggest an explicit approach for strategy synthesis in the discrete-time setting and show that even for systems with closed guards, the existence of a safety discrete-time strategy does not imply the existence of a safety continuous-time strategy and vice versa. Nevertheless, we prove that the answers to the existence of discrete-time and continuous-time safety strategies coincide on a practically motivated subclass of urgent controllers that either react immediately after receiving an environmental input or wait with the decision until a next event is triggered by the environment. We then develop an on-the-fly synthesis algorithm for discrete timed-arc Petri net games. The algorithm is implemented in our tool TAPAAL and based on the experimental evidence, we discuss the advantages of our approach compared to the symbolic continuous-time techniques.

1 Introduction

Formal methods and model checking techniques have been traditionally used to verify whether a given system model complies with its specification. However, when we consider formal (game) models where both the controller and the environment can make choices, the question now changes to finding a controller strategy such that any behaviour under such a fixed strategy complies with the given specification. The model checking approach can be used as a try-and-fail technique to check whether a given controller is correct but automatic synthesis of a controller correct-by-construction, as already proposed by Church [12,13], is a more difficult problem as illustrated by the SYNTCOMP competition and SYNT workshop [1]. This area has recently seen renewed interest, partly given the rise in computational power that makes the synthesis feasible. We focus on the family of timed systems, where for the model of timed automata [2] synthesis has already been proposed [33] and implemented [4,11].

In the area of model checking, symbolic continuous-time on-the-fly methods were ensuring the success of tools such as Kronos [9], UPPAAL [5], Tina [6]

© Springer International Publishing Switzerland 2016
D. Bošnački and A. Wijs (Eds.): SPIN 2016, LNCS 9641, pp. 129–146, 2016.
DOI: 10.1007/978-3-319-32582-8_9

and Romeo [21], utilizing the zone abstraction approach [2] via the data structure DBM [16]. These symbolic techniques were recently employed in on-the-fly algorithms [28] for synthesis of controllers for timed games [4,11,33]. While these methods scale well for classical reachability, the limitation of symbolic techniques is more apparent when used for liveness properties and for solving timed games. We have shown that for reachability and liveness properties, the discrete-time methods performing point-wise exploration of the state-space can prove competitive on a wide range of problems [3], in particular in combination with additional techniques as time-darts [25], constant-reducing approximation techniques [7] and memory-preserving data structures as PTrie [24].

In this paper, we benefit from the recent advances in the discrete-time verification of timed systems and suggest an on-the-fly point-wise algorithm for the synthesis of timed controllers relative to safety objectives (avoiding undesirable behaviour). The algorithm is described for a novel game extension of the well-studied timed-arc Petri net formalism [8,23] and we show that in the general setting the existence of a controller for a safety objective in the discrete-time setting does not imply the existence of such a controller in the continuous-time setting and vice versa, not even for systems with closed guards—contrary to the fact that continuous-time and discrete-time reachability problems coincide for timed models [10], in particular also for timed-arc Petri nets [30]. However, if we restrict ourselves to the practically relevant subclass of urgent controllers that either react immediately to the environmental events or simply wait for another occurrence of such an event, then we can use the discrete-time methods for checking the existence of a continuous-time safety controller on closed timed-arc Petri nets. The algorithm for controller synthesis is implemented in the tool TAPAAL [15], including the memory optimization technique via PTrie [24], and the experimental data show a promising performance on a large data-set of infinite job scheduling problems as well as on other examples.

Related Work. An on-the-fly algorithm for synthesizing continuous-time controllers for both safety, reachability and time-optimal reachability for time automata was proposed by Cassez et al. [11] and later implemented in the tool UPPAAL TiGa [4]. This work is based on the symbolic verification techniques invented by Alur and Dill [2] in combination with ideas on synthesis by Pnueli et al. [33] and on-the-fly dependency graph algorithms suggested by Liu and Smolka [28]. For timed games, abstraction refinement approaches have been proposed and implemented by Peter et al. [31,32] and Finkbeiner and Peter [19] as an attempt to speed up synthesis, while using the same underlying symbolic representation as UPPAAL TiGa. These abstraction refinement methods are complementary to the work presented here. Our work uses the formalism of timed-arc Petri nets that has not been studied in this context before and we rely on the methods with discrete interpretation of time as presented by Andersen et al. [3]. As an additional contribution, we implement our solution in the tool TAPAAL, utilizing memory reduction techniques by Jensen et al. [24], and compare the performance of both discrete-time and continuous-time techniques.

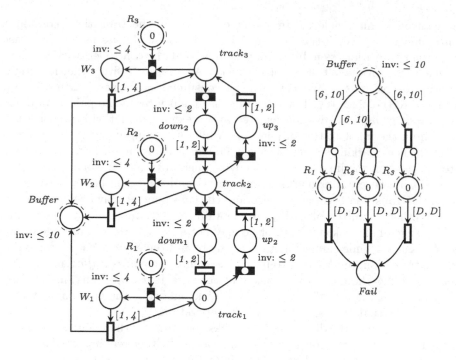

Fig. 1. A timed-arc Petri net game model of a harddisk

Control synthesis and supervisory control was also studied for the family of Petri net models [17,18,34,36] but these works do not consider the timing aspects.

2 Motivating Example of Disk Operation Scheduling

We shall now provide an intuitive description of the timed-arc Petri net game of *disk operation scheduling* in Fig. 1, modelling the scheduler of a mechanical harddisk drive (left) and a number of read stream requests (right) that should be fulfilled within a given deadline D. The net consists of *places* drawn as circles (the dashed circle around the places R_1, R_2, R_3 and *Buffer* simply means that these places are shared between the two subnets) and *transitions* drawn as rectangles that are either filled (controllable transitions) or framed only (environmental transitions). Places can contain *tokens* (like the places R_1 to R_3 and the place $track_1$) and each token carries its own age. Initially all token ages are 0. The net also contains *arcs* from places to transitions (input arcs) or transitions to places (output arcs). The input arcs are further decorated with *time intervals* restricting the ages of tokens that can be consumed along the arc. If the time interval is missing, we assume the default $[0, \infty]$ interval not restricting the ages of tokens in any way.

In the initial *marking* (token configuration) depicted in our example, the two transitions connected by input arcs to the place $track_1$ are *enabled* and the controller can decide to *fire* either of them. As the transitions contain a white circle, they are *urgent*, meaning that time cannot pass as long at least one urgent transition is enabled. Suppose now that the controller decides to fire the transition on the left of the place $track_1$. As a result of firing the transition, the two tokens in R_1 and $track_1$ will be consumed and a new token of age 0 produced to the place W_1. Tokens can be also transported via a pair of an input and output *transport arcs* (not depicted in our example) that will transport the token from the input to the output place while preserving its age.

In the new marking we just achieved, no transition is enabled due to the time interval $[1, 4]$ on the input arc of the environmental transition connected to the place W_1. However, after one time unit passes and the token in W_1 becomes of age 1, the transition becomes enabled and the environment may decide to fire it. On the other hand, the place W_1 also contains an *age invariant* ≤ 4, requiring that the age of any token in that place may not exceed 4. Hence after age of the token reaches 4, time cannot progress anymore and the environment is forced to fire the transition, producing two fresh tokens into the places *Buffer* and $track_1$. Hence, reading the data from track 1 of the disk takes between 1 ms to 4 ms (depending on the actual rotation of the disk) and it is the environment that decides the actual duration of the reading operation.

The idea is that the disk has three tracks (positions of the reading head) and at each track $track_i$ the controller has the choice of either reading the data from the given track (assuming there is a reading request represented by a token in the place R_i) or move the head to one of the neighbouring tracks (such a mechanical move takes between 1 ms to 2 ms). The reading requests are produced by the subnet on the right where the environment decides when to generate a reading request in the interval between 6 ms to 10 ms. The number of tokens in the right subnet represents the parallel reading streams. The net also contains *inhibitor arcs* with a cirle-headed tip that prohibit the environmental transitions from generating a reading request on a given track if there is already one. Finally, if the reading request takes too long and the age of the token in R_i reaches the age D, the environment has the option to place a token in the place *Fail*.

The control synthesis problem asks to find a strategy for firing the controllable transitions that guarantees no failure, meaning that irrelevant of the behaviour of the environment, the place *Fail* never becomes marked (safety control objective). The existence of such a control strategy depends on the chosen value of D and the complexity of the controller synthesis problem can be scaled by adding further tracks (in the subnet of the left) or allowing for more parallel reading streams (in the subnet on the right). In what follows, we shall describe how to automatically decide in the discrete-time setting (where time can be increased only by nonnegative integer values) whether a controller strategy exists. As the controllable transitions are urgent in our example, the existence of such a discrete-time control strategy implies also the existence of a continuous-time control strategy where the environment is free to fire transitions after an arbitrary delay taken from the dense time domain.

3   Definitions

Let $\mathbb{N}_0 = \mathbb{N} \cup \{0\}$ and $\mathbb{N}_0^{\infty} = \mathbb{N}_0 \cup \{\infty\}$. Let $\mathbb{R}^{\geq 0}$ be the set of all nonnegative real numbers. A *timed transition system* (TTS) is a triple $(S, Act, \rightarrow)$ where S is the set of states, Act is the set of actions and $\rightarrow \subseteq S \times (Act \cup \mathbb{R}^{\geq 0}) \times S$ is the transition relation written as $s \xrightarrow{a} s'$ whenever $(s, a, s') \in \rightarrow$. If $a \in Act$ then we call it a *switch transition*, if $a \in \mathbb{R}^{\geq 0}$ we call it a *delay transition*. We also define the set of *well-formed closed time intervals* as $\mathcal{I} \stackrel{\text{def}}{=} \{[a, b] \mid a \in \mathbb{N}_0, b \in \mathbb{N}_0^{\infty}, a \leq b\}$ and its subset $\mathcal{I}^{\text{inv}} \stackrel{\text{def}}{=} \{[0, b] \mid b \in \mathbb{N}_0^{\infty}\}$ used in age invariants.

Definition 1 (Timed-Arc Petri Net). *A timed-arc Petri net (TAPN) is a 9-tuple $N = (P, T, T_{urg}, IA, OA, g, w, Type, I)$ where*

- *P is a finite set of places,*
- *T is a finite set of transitions such that $P \cap T = \emptyset$,*
- *$T_{urg} \subseteq T$ is the set of urgent transitions,*
- *$IA \subseteq P \times T$ is a finite set of input arcs,*
- *$OA \subseteq T \times P$ is a finite set of output arcs,*
- *$g : IA \rightarrow \mathcal{I}$ is a time constraint function assigning guards to input arcs such that*
  - *if $(p, t) \in IA$ and $t \in T_{urg}$ then $g((p, t)) = [0, \infty]$,*
- *$w : IA \cup OA \rightarrow \mathbb{N}$ is a function assigning weights to input and output arcs,*
- *$Type : IA \cup OA \rightarrow \textbf{Types}$ is a type function assigning a type to all arcs where $\textbf{Types} = \{Normal, Inhib\} \cup \{Transport_j \mid j \in \mathbb{N}\}$ such that*
  - *if $Type(z) = Inhib$ then $z \in IA$ and $g(z) = [0, \infty]$,*
  - *if $Type((p, t)) = Transport_j$ for some $(p, t) \in IA$ then there is exactly one $(t, p') \in OA$ such that $Type((t, p')) = Transport_j$,*
  - *if $Type((t, p')) = Transport_j$ for some $(t, p') \in OA$ then there is exactly one $(p, t) \in IA$ such that $Type((p, t)) = Transport_j$,*
  - *if $Type((p, t)) = Transport_j = Type((t, p'))$ then $w((p, t)) = w((t, p'))$,*
- *$I : P \rightarrow \mathcal{I}^{inv}$ is a function assigning age invariants to places.*

Remark 1. Note that for transport arcs we assume that they come in pairs (for each type $Transport_j$) and that their weights match. Also for inhibitor arcs and for input arcs to urgent transitions, we require that the guards are $[0, \infty]$. This restriction is important for some of the results presented in this paper and it also guarantees that we can use DBM-based algorithms in the tool TAPAAL [15].

Before we give the formal semantics of the model, let us fix some notation. Let $N = (P, T, T_{urg}, IA, OA, g, w, Type, I)$ be a TAPN. We denote by $\bullet x \stackrel{\text{def}}{=} \{y \in P \cup T \mid (y, x) \in IA \cup OA, \ Type((y, x)) \neq Inhib\}$ the preset of a transition or a place x. Similarly, the postset is defined as $x^{\bullet} \stackrel{\text{def}}{=} \{y \in P \cup T \mid (x, y) \in (IA \cup OA)\}$. Let $\mathcal{B}(\mathbb{R}^{\geq 0})$ be the set of all finite multisets over $\mathbb{R}^{\geq 0}$. A *marking* M on N is a function $M : P \longrightarrow \mathcal{B}(\mathbb{R}^{\geq 0})$ where for every place $p \in P$ and every token $x \in M(p)$ we have $x \in I(p)$, in other words all tokens have to satisfy the age invariants. The set of all markings in a net N is denoted by $\mathcal{M}(N)$.

We write (p, x) to denote a token at a place p with the age $x \in \mathbb{R}^{\geq 0}$. Then $M = \{(p_1, x_1), (p_2, x_2), \ldots, (p_n, x_n)\}$ is a multiset representing a marking M with n tokens of ages x_i in places p_i. We define the size of a marking as $|M| = \sum_{p \in P} |M(p)|$ where $|M(p)|$ is the number of tokens located in the place p.

Definition 2 (Enabledness). *Let* $N = (P, T, T_{urg}, IA, OA, g, w, Type, I)$ *be a TAPN. We say that a transition* $t \in T$ *is* enabled *in a marking* M *by the multisets of tokens* $In = \{(p, x_p^1), (p, x_p^2), \ldots, (p, x_p^{w((p,t))}) \mid p \in {}^{\bullet}t\} \subseteq M$ *and* $Out = \{(p', x_{p'}^1), (p', x_{p'}^2), \ldots, (p', x_{p'}^{w((t,p'))}) \mid p' \in t^{\bullet}\}$ *if*

- *for all input arcs except the inhibitor arcs, the tokens from* In *satisfy the age guards of the arcs, i.e.*

$$\forall p \in {}^{\bullet}t.\ x_p^i \in g((p,t))\ for\ 1 \leq i \leq w((p,t))$$

- *for any inhibitor arc pointing from a place* p *to the transition* t, *the number of tokens in* p *is smaller than the weight of the arc, i.e.*

$$\forall (p,t) \in IA.\ Type((p,t)) = Inhib \Rightarrow |M(p)| < w((p,t))$$

- *for all input arcs and output arcs which constitute a transport arc, the age of the input token must be equal to the age of the output token and satisfy the invariant of the output place, i.e.*

$$\forall (p,t) \in IA.\forall (t,p') \in OA.\ Type((p,t)) = Type((t,p')) = Transport_j$$
$$\Rightarrow \left(x_p^i = x_{p'}^i \wedge x_{p'}^i \in I(p') \right)\ for\ 1 \leq i \leq w((p,t))$$

- *for all normal output arcs, the age of the output token is 0, i.e.*

$$\forall (t,p') \in OA.\ Type((t,p')) = Normal \Rightarrow x_{p'}^i = 0\ for\ 1 \leq i \leq w((t,p')).$$

A given TAPN N defines a TTS $T(N) \stackrel{\text{def}}{=} (\mathcal{M}(N), T, \rightarrow)$ where states are the markings and the transitions are as follows.

- If $t \in T$ is enabled in a marking M by the multisets of tokens In and Out then t can *fire* and produce the marking $M' = (M \setminus In) \uplus Out$ where $\uplus$ is the multiset sum operator and $\setminus$ is the multiset difference operator; we write $M \stackrel{t}{\rightarrow} M'$ for this switch transition.
- A time *delay* $d \in \mathbb{R}^{\geq 0}$ is allowed in M if
  - $(x + d) \in I(p)$ for all $p \in P$ and all $x \in M(p)$, and
  - if $M \stackrel{t}{\rightarrow} M'$ for some $t \in T_{urg}$ then $d = 0$.
  By delaying d time units in M we reach the marking M' defined as $M'(p) = \{x + d \mid x \in M(p)\}$ for all $p \in P$; we write $M \stackrel{d}{\rightarrow} M'$ for this delay transition.

Let $\rightarrow \stackrel{\text{def}}{=} \bigcup_{t \in T} \stackrel{t}{\rightarrow} \cup \bigcup_{d \in \mathbb{R}^{\geq 0}} \stackrel{d}{\rightarrow}$. By $M \stackrel{d,t}{\rightarrow} M'$ we denote that there is a marking M'' such that $M \stackrel{d}{\rightarrow} M'' \stackrel{t}{\rightarrow} M'$.

The semantics defined above in terms of timed transition systems is called the *continuous-time semantics*. If we restrict the possible delay transitions to take values only from nonnegative integers and the markings to be of the form $M : P \longrightarrow \mathcal{B}(\mathbb{N}_0)$, we call it the *discrete-time semantics*.

3.1   Timed-Arc Petri Net Game

We shall now extend the TAPN model into the game setting by partitioning the set of transitions into the controllable and uncontrollable ones.

Definition 3 (Timed-Arc Petri Net Game). *A Timed-Arc Petri Net Game (TAPG) is a TAPN with its set of transitions T partitioned into the controller T_{ctrl} and environment T_{env} sets.*

Let G be a fixed TAPG. Recall that $\mathcal{M}(G)$ is the set of all markings over the net G. A *controller strategy* for the game G is a function

$$\sigma : \mathcal{M}(G) \to \mathcal{M}(G) \cup \{wait\}$$

from markings to markings or the special symbol *wait* such that

- if $\sigma(M) = wait$ then either M can delay forever ($M \xrightarrow{d}$ for all $d \in \mathbb{R}^{\geq 0}$), or there is $d \in \mathbb{R}^{\geq 0}$ where $M \xrightarrow{d} M'$ and for all $d'' \in \mathbb{R}^{\geq 0}$ for all $t \in T_{ctrl}$ we have that if $M' \xrightarrow{d''} M''$ then $M'' \xrightarrow{t} \!\!\!\!/\,$, and
- if $\sigma(M) = M'$ then there is $d \in \mathbb{R}^{\geq 0}$ and there is $t \in T_{ctrl}$ where $M \xrightarrow{d,t} M'$.

Intuitively, a controller can in a given marking M either decide to wait indefinitely (assuming that it is not forced by age invariants or urgency to perform some controllable transition) or it can suggest a delay followed by a controllable transition firing. The environment can in the marking M also propose to wait (unless this is not possible due to age invariants or urgency) or suggest a delay followed by firing of an uncontrollable transition. If both the controller and environment propose transition firing, then the one preceding with a shorter delay takes place. In the case where both the controller and the environment propose the same delay followed by a transition firing, then any of these two firings can (nondeterministically) happen. This intuition is formalized in the notion of *plays* following a fixed controller strategy that summarize all possible executions for any possible environment.

Let $\pi = M_1 M_2 \ldots M_n \ldots \in \mathcal{M}(G)^{\omega}$ be an arbitrary finite or infinite sequence of markings over G and let M be a marking. We define the concatenation of M with π as $M \circ \pi = M M_1 \ldots M_n \ldots$ and extend it to the sets of sequences $\Pi \subseteq \mathcal{M}(G)^{\omega}$ so that $M \circ \Pi = \{M \circ \pi \mid \pi \in \Pi\}$.

Definition 4 (Plays According to the Strategy σ). *Let G be a TAPG, M a marking on G and σ a controller strategy for G. We define a function $\mathbb{P}_\sigma : \mathcal{M}(G) \to 2^{\mathcal{M}(G)^{\omega}}$ returning for a given marking M the set of all possible plays starting from M under the strategy σ.*

- *If $\sigma(M) = wait$ then $\mathbb{P}_\sigma(M) = \{M \circ \mathbb{P}_\sigma(M') \mid d \in \mathbb{R}^{\geq 0}, \ t \in T_{env}, \ M \xrightarrow{d,t} M'\} \cup X$ where $X = \{M\}$ if $M \xrightarrow{d}$ for all $d \in \mathbb{R}^{\geq 0}$, or if there is $d' \in \mathbb{R}^{\geq 0}$ such that $M \xrightarrow{d'} M'$ and $M' \xrightarrow{d''} \!\!\!\!/\,$ for any $d'' > 0$ and $M' \xrightarrow{t} \!\!\!\!/\,$ for any $t \in T_{env}$, otherwise $X = \emptyset$.*

– If $\sigma(M) \neq wait$ then according to the definition of controller strategy we have $M \xrightarrow{d,t} \sigma(M)$ and we define $\mathbb{P}_\sigma(M) = \{M \circ \mathbb{P}_\sigma(\sigma(M))\} \cup \{M \circ \mathbb{P}_\sigma(M') \mid d' \leq d, t' \in T_{env}, M \xrightarrow{d',t'} M'\}$.

The first case says that the plays from the marking M where the controller wants to wait consist either of the marking M followed by any play from a marking M' that can be reached by the environment from M after some delay and firing a transition from T_{env}, or a finite sequence finishing the marking M if it is the case that M can delay forever, or we can reach a deadlock where no further delay is possible and no transition can fire.

The second case where the controller suggests a transition firing after some delay, contains M concatenated with all possible plays from $\sigma(M)$ and from $\sigma(M')$ for any M' that can be reached by the environment before or at the same time the controller suggests to perform its move.

We can now define the safety objectives for TAPGs that are boolean expressions over arithmetic predicates which observe the number of tokens in the different places of the net. Let φ be so a boolean combination of predicates of the form $e \bowtie e$ where $e ::= p \mid n \mid e + e \mid e - e \mid e * e$ and where $p \in P$, $\bowtie \in \{<, \leq, =, \neq, \geq, >\}$ and $n \in \mathbb{N}_0$. The semantics of φ in a marking M is given in the natural way, assuming that p stands for $|M(p)|$ (the number of tokens in the place p). We write $M \models \varphi$ if φ evaluates in the marking M to true. We can now state the safety synthesis problem.

Definition 5 (Safety Synthesis Problem). *Given a marked TAPG G with the initial marking M_0 and a safety objective φ, decide if there is a controller strategy σ such that*

$$\forall \pi \in \mathbb{P}_\sigma(M_0). \forall M \in \pi. M \models \varphi. \tag{1}$$

If Eq. (1) holds then we say that σ is a winning controller strategy *for the objective φ.*

4   Controller Synthesis in Continuous vs. Discrete Time

It is known that for classical TAPNs the continuous and discrete-time semantics coincide up to reachability [30], which is what safety synthesis reduces to if the set of controllable transitions is empty. Contrary to this, Fig. 2a and b show that this does not hold in general for safety strategies.

For the game in Fig. 2a, there exists a strategy for the controller and the safety objective $Bad \leq 0$ but this is the case only in the continuous-time semantics as the controller has to keep the age of the token in place P_1 strictly below 1, otherwise the environment can mark the place Bad by firing U_1. However, if the controller fires transition C_1 without waiting, U_2 becomes enabled and the environment can again break the safety. Hence it is impossible to find a discrete-time strategy as even the smallest possible delay of 1 time unit will enable U_1. However, if the controller waits an infinitesimal amount (in the continuous

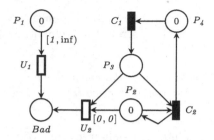

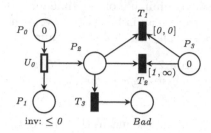

(a) A TAPG where $Bad \leq 0$ can be guaranteed by the controller under the continuous-time semantics but not under the discrete-time semantics by exploiting Zeno behavior.

(b) A TAPG where $Bad \leq 0$ can be guaranteed by the controller under the discrete-time semantics but not under the continuous-time semantics.

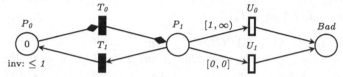

(c) A TAPG where $Bad \leq 0$ can be guaranteed by the controller under the continuous-time semantics but not under the discrete-time semantics (without exploiting Zeno behavior).

Fig. 2. Difference between continuous and discrete-time semantics

semantics) and fires C_1, then U_2 will not be enabled as the token in P_2 aged slightly. The controller can now fire C_2 and repeat this strategy over and over in order to keep the token in P_1 from ever reaching the age of 1.

The counter example described before relies on Zeno behaviour, however, this is not needed if we use transport arcs that do not reset the age of tokens (depicted by arrows with diamond-headed tips), as demonstrated in Fig. 2c. Here the only winning strategy for the controller to avoid marking the place Bad is to delay some fraction and then fire T_0. Any possible integer delay (1 or 0) will enable the environment to fire U_0 or U_1 before the controller gets to fire T_1. Hence we get the following lemma.

Lemma 1. *There is a TAPG and a safety objective where the controller has a winning strategy in the continuous-time semantics but not in the discrete-time semantics.*

Figure 2b shows, on the other hand, that a safety strategy guaranteeing $Bad \leq 0$ exists only in the discrete-time semantics but not in the continuous-time one where the environment can mark the place Bad by initially delaying 0.5 and then firing U_0. This will produce a token in P_1 which restricts the time from progressing further and thus forces the controller to fire T_3 as this is the only enabled transition. On the other hand, in the discrete-time semantics the environment can either fire U_0 immediately but then T_1 will be enabled, or it can wait (a minimum of one time unit), however then T_2 will be enabled. Hence the controller can in both cases avoid the firing of T_3 in the discrete-time semantics. This implies the following lemma.

Lemma 2. *There is a TAPG and a safety objective where the controller has a winning strategy in the discrete-time semantics but not in the continuous-time semantics.*

This indeed means that the continuous and discrete-time semantics are incomparable and it makes sense to consider both of them, depending on the concrete application domain and the fact whether we consider discretized or continuous time. Nevertheless, there is a practically relevant subclass of the problem where we consider only urgent controllers and where the two semantics coincide. We say that a given TAPG is with an *urgent controller* if all controllable transitions are urgent, formally $T_{ctrl} \subseteq T_{urg}$.

Theorem 1. *Let G be a TAPG with urgent controller and let φ be a safety objective. There is a winning controller strategy for G and φ in the discrete-time semantics iff there is a winning controller strategy for G and φ in the continuous-time semantics.*

Proof (Sketch). The existence of a winning controller strategy in the continuous-time semantics clearly implies the existence of such a strategy also in the discrete-time because here the environment is restricted to playing only integer delays and the controller can always react to these according to the continuous-time strategy that exists by our assumption. Because the controller is making only urgent choices or waits for the next environmental move, all transitions happen in the discrete-time points.

For the other direction, we prove the converse via the use of linear programming as used e.g. in [30]. Assuming that the urgent controller does not have a winning strategy in the continuous-time semantics, we will argue that the controller does not have a winning strategy in the discrete-time semantics either. Due to the assumption, we know that the environment can in any current marking choose a real-time delay and an uncontrollable transition in such a way that irrelevant of what the controller chooses, it eventually reaches a marking violating the safety condition φ. Such an environmental strategy can be described as a finite tree where nodes are markings, edges contain the information about the delay and transition firing, the branching describes all controller choices and each leaf of the tree is a marking that satisfies $\neg\varphi$. The existence of this environmental strategy follows from the determinacy of the game that guarantees that one of the players must have a winning strategy (to see this, we realize that the environmental strategy contains only finite branches, all of them ending in a marking satisfying $\neg\varphi$, and hence we have an instance of an open game that is determined by the result of Gale and Stewart [20]—see also [22]).

As we assume that the environment can win in the continuous-time semantics, the delays in the tree may be nonnegative real numbers (controller's moves in the tree are always with delay 0). Our aim is to show that there is another winning tree for the environment, however, with integer delays only. This can be done by replacing the delays in the tree by variables and reformulating the firing conditions of the transitions in the tree as a linear program. Surely, the constraints in the linear program have, by our assumption, a nonnegative real solution. Moreover, the constraint system uses only closed difference constraints (nonstrictly bounding the difference of two variables from below or above) and we can therefore reduce the linear program to a shortest-path problem with integer weights only and this implies that an integer solution exists too [14]. This means that there is a tree describing an environmental winning strategy using only integer delays and hence the controller does not have a winning strategy in the discrete-time setting. The technical details of the proof are provided in the full version of the paper.   □

5   Discrete-Time Algorithm for Controller Synthesis

We shall now define the discrete-time algorithm for synthesizing controller strategies for TAPGs. As the state-space of a TAPG is infinite in several aspects (the number of tokens in reachable markings can be unbounded and even for bounded nets the ages of tokens can be arbitrarily large), the question of deciding the existence of a controller strategy is in general undecidable (already the classical reachability is undecidable [35] for TAPNs).

We address the undecidability issue by enforcing a given constant k, bounding the number of tokens in any marking reached by the controller strategy. This means that instead of checking the safety objective φ, we verify instead the safety objective $\varphi_k = \varphi \wedge k \geq \sum_{p \in P} p$ that at the same time ensures that the total number of tokens is at most k. This will, together with the extrapolation technique below, guarantee the termination of the algorithm.

5.1   Extrapolation of TAPGs

We shall now recall a few results from [3] that allow us to make finite abstractions of bounded nets (in the discrete-time semantics). The theorems and lemmas in the rest of this section hold also for continuous-time semantics, however, the finiteness of the extrapolated state space is not guaranteed in this case.

Let $G = (P, T, T_{env}, T_{ctrl}, T_{urg}, IA, OA, g, w, Type, I)$ be a TAPG. In [3] the authors provide an algorithm for computing a function $C_{max} : P \rightarrow (\mathbb{N}_0 \cup \{-1\})$ returning for each place $p \in P$ the maximum constant associated to this place, meaning that the ages of tokens in place p that are strictly greater than $C_{max}(p)$ are irrelevant. The function $C_{max}(p)$ for a given place p is computed by essentially taking the maximum constant appearing in any outgoing arc from p and in the place invariant of p, where a special care has to be taken for places with outgoing transport arcs (details are discussed in [3]). In particular, places where $C_{max}(p) = -1$ are the so-called *untimed* places where the age of tokens is not relevant at all, implying that all the intervals on their outgoing arcs are $[0, \infty)$.

Let M be a marking of G. We split it into two markings $M_>$ and $M_\le$ where $M_>(p) = \{x \in M(p) \mid x > C_{max}(p)\}$ and $M_\le(p) = \{x \in M(p) \mid x \le C_{max}(p)\}$ for all places $p \in P$. Clearly, $M = M_> \uplus M_\le$.

We say that two markings M and M' in the net G are equivalent, written $M \equiv M'$, if $M_\le = M'_\le$ and for all $p \in P$ we have $|M_>(p)| = |M'_>(p)|$. In other words M and M' agree on the tokens with ages below the maximum constants and have the same number of tokens above the maximum constant.

The relation $\equiv$ is an equivalence relation and it is also a timed bisimulation (see e.g. [27]) where delays and transition firings on one side can be matched by exactly the same delays and transition firings on the other side and vice versa.

Theorem 2 ([3]). *The relation $\equiv$ is a timed bisimulation.*

We can now define canonical representatives for each equivalence class of $\equiv$.

Definition 6 (Cut). *Let M be a marking. We define its canonical marking $cut(M)$ by $cut(M)(p) = M_\le(p) \uplus \underbrace{\{ C_{max}(p) + 1, \ldots, C_{max}(p) + 1 \}}_{|M_>(p)| \; times}$.*

Lemma 3 ([3]). *Let M, M_1 and M_2 be markings. Then (i) $M \equiv cut(M)$, and (ii) $M_1 \equiv M_2$ if and only if $cut(M_1) = cut(M_2)$.*

5.2   The Algorithm

After having introduced the extrapolation function *cut* and our enforcement of the k-bound, we can now design an algorithm for computing a controller strategy σ, provided such a strategy exists.

Algorithm 1 describes a discrete-time method to check if there is a controller strategy or not. It is centered around four data structures: *Waiting* for storing markings to be explored, *Losing* that contains marking where such a strategy does not exist, *Depend* for maintaining the set of dependencies to be reinserted to the waiting list whenever a marking is declared as losing, and *Processed* for already processed markings. All markings in the algorithm are always considered modulo the *cut* extrapolation. The algorithm performs a forward search by repeatedly selecting a marking M from *Waiting* and if it can determine that the controller cannot win from this marking, then M gets inserted into the set *Losing* while the dependencies of M are put to the set *Waiting* in order to backward propagate this information. If the initial marking is ever inserted to the set *Losing*, we can terminate and announce that a controller strategy does not exist. If this is not the case and there are no more markings in the set *Waiting*, then we terminate with success. In this case, it is also easy to construct the controller strategy by making choices so that the set *Losing* is avoided.

Theorem 3 (Correctness). *Algorithm 1 terminates and returns tt if and only if there is a controller strategy for the safety objective $\varphi_k = \varphi \wedge k \ge \sum_{p \in P} p$.*

Algorithm 1. Safety Synthesis Algorithm

Input: A TAPG $G = (P, T, T_{env}, T_{ctrl}, T_{urg}, IA, OA, g, w, Type, I)$, initial
    marking M_0, a safety objective φ and a bound k.
Output: tt if there exists a controller strategy ensuring φ and not exceeding k
    tokens in any intermediate marking, ff otherwise

1 **begin**
2 | $Waiting := Losing := Processed = \emptyset; \; \varphi_k = \varphi \wedge k \geq \sum_{p \in P} p;$
3 | $M \leftarrow cut(M_0); \; Depend[M] \leftarrow \emptyset;$
4 | **if** $M \not\models \varphi_k$ **then**
5 | | $Losing \leftarrow \{M\}$
6 | **else**
7 | | $Waiting \leftarrow \{M\}$
8 | **while** $Waiting \neq \emptyset \wedge cut(M_0) \notin Losing$ **do**
9 | | $M \leftarrow pop(Waiting);$
10 | | $Succs_{env} := \{cut(M') \mid t \in T_{env}, \; M \xrightarrow{t} M'\};$
11 | | $Succs_{ctrl} := \{cut(M') \mid t \in T_{ctrl}, \; M \xrightarrow{t} M'\};$
12 | | $Succs_{delay} := \begin{cases} \emptyset & \text{if } M \xcancel{\xrightarrow{1}} \\ \{cut(M')\} & \text{if } M \xrightarrow{1} M' \end{cases}$
13 | | **if** $\exists M' \in Succs_{env} \; s.t. \; M' \not\models \varphi_k \vee M' \in Losing$ **then**
14 | | | $Losing \leftarrow Losing \cup \{M\};$
15 | | | $Waiting \leftarrow (Waiting \cup Depend[M]) \setminus Losing;$
16 | | **else**
17 | | | **if** $Succs_{ctrl} \cup Succs_{delay} \neq \emptyset \wedge \forall M' \in Succs_{ctrl} \cup Succs_{delay}.$
                       $M' \not\models \varphi_k \vee M' \in Losing$ **then**
18 | | | | $Losing \leftarrow Losing \cup \{M\};$
19 | | | | $Waiting \leftarrow (Waiting \cup Depend[M]) \setminus Losing;$
20 | | | **else**
21 | | | | **if** $M \notin Processed$ **then**
22 | | | | | **foreach** $M' \in (Succs_{ctrl} \cup Succs_{env} \cup Succs_{delay})$ **do**
23 | | | | | | **if** $M' \notin Losing \wedge M' \models \varphi_k$ **then**
24 | | | | | | | $Depend[M'] \leftarrow Depend[M'] \cup \{M\};$
25 | | | | | | | $Waiting \leftarrow Waiting \cup \{M'\};$
26 | | $Processed \leftarrow Processed \cup \{M\};$
27 | **return** tt if $cut(M_0) \notin Losing$, else ff

---

6   Experiments

The discrete-time controller synthesis algorithm was implemented in the tool
TAPAAL [15] and we evaluate the performance of the implementation by comparing it to UPPAAL TiGa [4] version 0.18, the state-of-the-art continuous-time
model checker for timed games. The experiments were run on AMD Opteron

Table 1. Time in seconds to find a controller strategy for the disk operation scheduling for the smallest D where such a strategy exists.

1 Stream	$D = 133$	$D = 173$	$D = 213$	$D = 253$	$D = 293$	$D = 333$	$D = 373$
Tracks	70	90	110	130	150	170	190
TAPAAL	30.14s	69.78s	128.58s	216.44s	316.71s	491.65s	665.34s
UPPAAL	36.41s	76.63s	193.37s	351.17s	509.46s	1022.83s	1604.04s
2 Streams	$D = 19$	$D = 27$	$D = 35$	$D = 43$	$D = 51$	$D = 59$	$D = 67$
Tracks	6	8	10	12	14	16	18
TAPAAL	1.98s	7.34s	30.73s	101.92s	210.25s	398.00s	768.11s
UPPAAL	19.11s	93.46s	436.15s	1675.85s	3328.66s	☻	☻
3 Streams	$D = 17$	$D = 21$	$D = 25$	$D = 29$	$D = 35$	$D = 39$	$D = 43$
Tracks	3	4	5	6	7	8	9
TAPAAL	2.20s	16.52s	72.41s	244.28s	885.60s	(2132.71s)	☻
UPPAAL	885.56s	☻	☻	☻	☻	☻	☻

6376 processor limited to using 16 GB of RAM[1] and with one hour timeout (denoted by ☻).

6.1 Disk Operation Scheduling

In the disk operation scheduling model presented in Sect. 2 we scale the problem by changing the number of tracks and the number of simultaneous read streams. A similar model using the timed automata formalism was created for UPPAAL TiGa. We then ask whether a controller exists respecting a fixed deadline D for all requests. For each instance of the problem, we report the computation time for the smallest deadline D such that it is possible to synthesize a controller. Notice that the disk operating scheduling game net has an urgent controller, hence the discrete and continuous-time semantics coincide.

The results in Table 1 show that our algorithm scales considerably better than TiGa (that suffers from the large fragmentation of zone federations) as the number of tracks increases and it is significantly better when we add more read streams (and hence increase the concurrency and consequently the number of timed tokens/clocks).

6.2 Infinite Job Shop Scheduling

In our second experiment, infinite job shop scheduling, we consider the duration probabilistic automata [29]. Kempf et al. [26] showed that "non-lazy" schedulers are sufficient to guarantee optimality in this class of automata. Here non-lazy means that the controller only chooses what to schedule at the moment when a running task has just finished (the time of this event is determined by the

---

[1] UPPAAL TiGa only exists in a 32 bit version, but for none of the tests the 4 GB limit was exceeded for UPPAAL TiGa.

Table 2. Results for infinite scheduling of DPAs. The first row in each age-instance is TAPAAL, the second line is UPPAAL TiGa. The format is (X) Ys where X the number of solved instances (within 3600 s) out of 100 and Y is the median time needed to solve the problem. The largest possible constant for each row is given as an upper bound of the deadline D.

2 Processes/7-13 tokens

Max Age	10 Tasks		12 Tasks		14 Tasks		16 Tasks		18 Tasks	
5	(100)	63s	(100)	141s	(100)	283s	(100)	570s	(100)	829s
$D \leq 144$	(100)	100s	(98)	413s	(85)	1201s	(35)	⏱	(18)	⏱
10	(100)	318s	(100)	882s	(96)	1555s	(65)	2911s	(14)	⏱
$D \leq 288$	(96)	221s	(69)	1443s	(43)	⏱	(16)	⏱	(1)	⏱
15	(99)	1054s	(78)	2521s	(19)	⏱	(14)	⏱	(2)	⏱
$D \leq 432$	(87)	315s	(60)	1960s	(19)	⏱	(8)	⏱	(0)	⏱
20	(80)	2479s	(22)	⏱	(14)	⏱	(3)	⏱	(2)	⏱
$D \leq 576$	(90)	554s	(66)	2914s	(34)	⏱	(4)	⏱	(1)	⏱

3 Processes/10-19 tokens

Max Age	2 Tasks		3 Tasks		4 Tasks		5 Tasks		6 Tasks	
5	(100)	2s	(100)	39s	(99)	402s	(66)	1884s	(38)	⏱
$D \leq 57$	(99)	16s	(69)	1827s	(4)	⏱	(0)	⏱	(0)	⏱
10	(100)	15s	(97)	484s	(47)	⏱	(20)	⏱	(6)	⏱
$D \leq 114$	(98)	32s	(52)	3338s	(6)	⏱	(0)	⏱	(0)	⏱
15	(100)	51s	(69)	1373s	(28)	⏱	(4)	⏱	(0)	⏱
$D \leq 171$	(98)	27s	(50)	⏱	(1)	⏱	(0)	⏱	(0)	⏱

4 Processes/13-25 tokens

Max Age	2 Tasks		3 Tasks		4 Tasks		5 Tasks		6 Tasks	
5	(92)	215s	(30)	⏱	(7)	⏱	(1)	⏱	(0)	⏱
$D \leq 66$	(3)	⏱	(0)	⏱	(0)	⏱	(0)	⏱	(0)	⏱
10	(60)	2286s	(11)	⏱	(2)	⏱	(0)	⏱	(0)	⏱
$D \leq 132$	(0)	⏱	(0)	⏱	(0)	⏱	(0)	⏱	(0)	⏱

environment). We consider here a variant of this problem that should guarantee an infinite (cyclic) scheduling where all processes that share various resources and must meet their deadlines. The countdown of a process is started when its first task is initiated and the process deadline is met if the process is able to execute its last task within the deadline. After such a completed cycle, the process starts from its initial configuration and the deadline-clock is restarted. The task of the controller is now to find a schedule such that all processes always meet their deadline. The problem can be modelled using urgent controller, so the discrete and continuous-time semantics again coincide.

The problem is scaled by the number of parallel processes, number of tasks in each processes and the size of constants used in guards (excepted the deadline D that contains a considerably larger constant). For each set of scaling parameters, we generated 100 random instances of the problem and report on the number of cases where the tool answered the synthesis problem (within one hour deadline) and if more than 50 instances were solved, we also compute the median of the running time.

The comparison with UPPAAL TiGa in Table 2 shows a similar trend as in the previous experiment. Our algorithm scales nicely as we increase the number of tasks as well as the number of processes. This is due to the fact that the zone fragmentation in TiGa increases with the number of parallel components and more distinct guards. When scaling the size of constants, the performance of the discrete-time method gets worse and eventually UPPAAL TiGa can solve more instances.

7   Conclusion

We introduced timed-arc Petri net games and showed that for urgent controllers, the discrete and continuous-time semantics coincide. The presented discrete-time method for solving timed-arc Petri net games scales considerably better with the growing size of problems, compared to the existing symbolic methods. On the other hand, symbolic methods scale better with the size of the constants used in the model. In the future work, we may try to compensate for this drawback by using approximate techniques that "shrink" the constants to reasonable ranges while still providing conclusive answers in many cases, as demonstrated for pure reachability queries in [7]. Another future work includes the study of different synthesis objectives, as well as the generation of continuous-time strategies from discrete-time analysis techniques on the subclass of urgent controllers.

Acknowledgments. The research leading to these results has received funding from the EU FP7 FET projects CASSTING and SENSATION, the project DiCyPS funded by the Innovation Fund Denmark, the Sino Danish Research Center IDEA4CPS and the ERC Advanced Grant LASSO. The third author is partially affiliated with FI MU, Brno, Czech Republic.

References

1. SYNT 2015. Electronic Proceedings in Theoretical Computer Science (2015). http://formal.epfl.ch/synt/2015/
2. Alur, R., Dill, D.L.: A theory of timed automata. Theoret. Comput. Sci. **126**(2), 183–235 (1994)
3. Andersen, M., Larsen, H.G., Srba, J., Sørensen, M.G., Haahr Taankvist, J.: Verification of liveness properties on closed timed-arc Petri nets. In: Kučera, A., Henzinger, T.A., Nešetřil, J., Vojnar, T., Antoš, D. (eds.) MEMICS 2012. LNCS, vol. 7721, pp. 69–81. Springer, Heidelberg (2013)
4. Behrmann, G., Cougnard, A., David, A., Fleury, E., Larsen, K.G., Lime, D.: UPPAAL-TiGa: time for playing games!. In: Damm, W., Hermanns, H. (eds.) CAV 2007. LNCS, vol. 4590, pp. 121–125. Springer, Heidelberg (2007)
5. Behrmann, G., David, A., Larsen, K.G., Hakansson, J., Petterson, P., Yi, W., Hendriks, M.: UPPAAL 4.0. In: Third International Conference on Quantitative Evaluation of Systems, pp. 125–126 (2006)
6. Berthomieu, B., Vernadat, F.: Time Petri nets analysis with TINA. In: Third International Conference on Quantitative Evaluation of Systems, pp. 123–124. IEEE Computer Society (2006)

7. Birch, S.V., Jacobsen, T.S., Jensen, J.J., Moesgaard, C., Nørgaard Samuelsen, N., Srba, J.: Interval abstraction refinement for model checking of timed-arc Petri nets. In: Legay, A., Bozga, M. (eds.) FORMATS 2014. LNCS, vol. 8711, pp. 237–251. Springer, Heidelberg (2014)

8. Bolognesi, T., Lucidi, F., Trigila, S.: From timed Petri nets to timed LOTOS. In: Proceedings of the IFIP WG6.1 Tenth International Symposium on Protocol Specification, Testing and Verification X, North-Holland, pp. 395–408 (1990)

9. Bozga, M., Daws, C., Maler, O., Olivero, A., Tripakis, S., Yovine, S.: Kronos: a model-checking tool for real-time systems. In: Hu, A.J., Vardi, M.Y. (eds.) CAV 1998. LNCS, vol. 1427, pp. 546–550. Springer, Heidelberg (1998)

10. Bozga, M., Maler, O., Tripakis, S.: Efficient verification of timed automata using dense and discrete time semantics. In: Pierre, L., Kropf, T. (eds.) CHARME 1999. LNCS, vol. 1703, pp. 125–141. Springer, Heidelberg (1999)

11. Cassez, F., David, A., Fleury, E., Larsen, K.G., Lime, D.: Efficient on-the-fly algorithms for the analysis of timed games. In: Abadi, M., Alfaro, L. (eds.) CONCUR 2005. LNCS, vol. 3653, pp. 66–80. Springer, Heidelberg (2005)

12. Church, A.: Application of recursive arithmetic to the problem of circuit synthesis. J. Symbolic Logic **28**(4), 289–290 (1963)

13. Church, A.: Logic, arithmetic, and automata. In: Proceedings of the International Congress of Mathematicians (Stockholm, 1962), pp. 23–35. Institute Mittag-Leffler (1963)

14. Cormen, T.H., Leiserson, C.E., Rivest, R.L., Stein, C.: Introduction to Algorithms, Third Edition, 3rd edn. The MIT Press (2009). ISBN: 0262033844 9780262033848

15. David, A., Jacobsen, L., Jacobsen, M., Jørgensen, K.Y., Møller, M.H., Srba, J.: TAPAAL 2.0: integrated development environment for timed-arc Petri nets. In: Flanagan, C., König, B. (eds.) TACAS 2012. LNCS, vol. 7214, pp. 492–497. Springer, Heidelberg (2012)

16. Dill, D.L.: Timing assumptions and verification of finite-state concurrent systems. In: Sifakis, J. (ed.) CAV 1989. LNCS, vol. 407, pp. 197–212. Springer, Heidelberg (1990)

17. Finkbeiner, B.: Bounded synthesis for Petri games. In: Meyer, R., et al. (eds.) Olderog-Festschrift. LNCS, vol. 9360, pp. 223–237. Springer, Heidelberg (2015)

18. Finkbeiner, B., Olderog, E.: Petri games: synthesis of distributed systems with causal memory. In: Proceedings Fifth International Symposium on Games, Automata, Logics and Formal Verification, vol. 161 of EPTCS, pp. 217–230 (2014)

19. Finkbeiner, B., Peter, H.-J.: Template-based controller synthesis for timed systems. In: Flanagan, C., König, B. (eds.) TACAS 2012. LNCS, vol. 7214, pp. 392–406. Springer, Heidelberg (2012)

20. Gale, D., Stewart, F.M.: Infinite games with perfect information. In: Contributions to the Theory of Games. Annals of Mathematics Studies, no. 28, vol. 2, pp. 245–266. Princeton University Press, Princeton, N.J (1953)

21. Gardey, G., Lime, D., Magnin, M., Roux, O.H.: Romeo: a tool for analyzing time Petri nets. In: Etessami, K., Rajamani, S.K. (eds.) CAV 2005. LNCS, vol. 3576, pp. 418–423. Springer, Heidelberg (2005)

22. Gurevich, Y.: Games people play. In: Lane, S.M., Siefkes, D. (eds.) The Collected Works of J. Richard Büchi, pp. 517–524. Springer, Berlin (1990)

23. Hanisch, H.-M.: Analysis of place/transition nets with timed arcs and its application to batch process control. In: Marsan, M.A. (ed.) ICATPN 1993. LNCS, vol. 691, pp. 282–299. Springer, Heidelberg (1993)

24. Jensen, P.G., Larsen, K.G., Srba, J., Sørensen, M.G., Taankvist, J.H.: Memory efficient data structures for explicit verification of timed systems. In: Badger, J.M., Rozier, K.Y. (eds.) NFM 2014. LNCS, vol. 8430, pp. 307–312. Springer, Heidelberg (2014)

25. Jørgensen, K.Y., Larsen, K.G., Srba, J.: Time-darts: a data structure for verification of closed timed automata. In: Proceedings Seventh Conference on Systems Software Verification, vol. 102 of EPTCS, pp. 141–155. Open Publishing Association (2012)

26. Kempf, J.-F., Bozga, M., Maler, O.: As soon as probable: optimal scheduling under stochastic uncertainty. In: Piterman, N., Smolka, S.A. (eds.) TACAS 2013 (ETAPS 2013). LNCS, vol. 7795, pp. 385–400. Springer, Heidelberg (2013)

27. Larsen, K.G., Wang, Y.: Time-abstracted bisimulation: implicit specifications and decidability. Inf. Comput. **134**(2), 75–101 (1997)

28. Liu, X., Smolka, S.A.: Simple linear-time algorithms for minimal fixed points (extended abstract). In: Larsen, K.G., Skyum, S., Winskel, G. (eds.) ICALP 1998. LNCS, vol. 1443, pp. 53–66. Springer, Heidelberg (1998)

29. Maler, O., Larsen, K.G., Krogh, B.H.: On zone-based analysis of duration probabilistic automata. In: Proceedings 12th International Workshop on Verification of Infinite-State Systems, vol.39 of EPTCS, pp. 33–46 (2010)

30. Mateo, J.A., Srba, J., Sørensen, M.G.: Soundness of timed-arc workflow nets in discrete and continuous-time semantics. Fundamenta Informaticase **140**(1), 89–121 (2015)

31. Peter, H.: Component-based abstraction refinement for timed controller synthesis. In: IEEE, pp. 364–374. IEEE Computer Society (2009)

32. Peter, H.-J., Ehlers, R., Mattmüller, R.: Synthia: verification and synthesis for timed automata. In: Gopalakrishnan, G., Qadeer, S. (eds.) CAV 2011. LNCS, vol. 6806, pp. 649–655. Springer, Heidelberg (2011)

33. Pnueli, A., Asarin, E., Maler, O., Sifakis, J.: Controller synthesis for timed automata. System Structure and Control. Citeseer, Elsevier (1998)

34. Raskin, J.F., Samuelides, M., Begin, L.V.: Petri games are monotone but difficult to decide. Technical report, Université Libre De Bruxelles (2003)

35. Ruiz, V.V., Cuartero Gomez, F., de Frutos Escrig, D.: On non-decidability of reachability for timed-arc Petri nets. In: Proceedings of the 8th International Workshop on Petri Nets and Performance Models, pp. 188–196 (1999)

36. Zhou, Q., Wang, M., Dutta, S.P.: Generation of optimal control policy for flexible manufacturing cells: a Petri net approach. Int. J. Adv. Manuf. Technol. **10**(1), 59–65 (1995)

Finite-Horizon Bisimulation Minimisation for Probabilistic Systems

Nishanthan Kamaleson$^{(\boxtimes)}$, David Parker, and Jonathan E. Rowe

School of Computer Science, University of Birmingham, Birmingham, UK
nxk249@cs.bham.ac.uk

Abstract. We present model reduction techniques to improve the efficiency and scalability of verifying probabilistic systems over a finite time horizon. We propose a finite-horizon variant of probabilistic bisimulation for discrete-time Markov chains, which preserves a bounded fragment of the temporal logic PCTL. In addition to a standard partition-refinement based minimisation algorithm, we present on-the-fly finite-horizon minimisation techniques, which are based on a backwards traversal of the Markov chain, directly from a high-level model description. We investigate both symbolic and explicit-state implementations, using SMT solvers and hash functions, respectively, and implement them in the PRISM model checker. We show that finite-horizon reduction can provide significant reductions in model size, in some cases outperforming PRISM's existing efficient implementations of probabilistic verification.

1 Introduction

Probabilistic verification is an automated technique for the formal analysis of quantitative properties of systems that exhibit stochastic behaviour. A probabilistic model, such as a Markov chain or a Markov decision process, is systematically constructed and then analysed against properties expressed in a formal specification language such as temporal logic. Mature tools for probabilistic verification such as PRISM [15] and MRMC [13] have been developed, and the techniques have been applied to a wide range of application domains, from biological reaction networks [11] to car airbag controllers [1].

A constant challenge in this area is the issue of scalability: probabilistic models, which are explored and constructed in an exhaustive fashion, are typically huge for real-life systems, which can limit the practical applicability of the techniques. A variety of approaches have been proposed to reduce the size of these models. One that is widely used is *probabilistic bisimulation* [18], an equivalence relation over the states of a probabilistic model which can be used to construct a smaller *quotient* model that is equivalent to the original one (in the sense that it preserves key properties of interest to be verified).

Typically, it preserves both infinite-horizon (long-run) properties, e.g., "the probability of eventually reaching an error state", finite-horizon (transient, or time-bounded) properties, e.g. "the probability of an error occurring within k time-steps", and, more generally, any property expressible in an appropriate

D. Bošnački and A. Wijs (Eds.): SPIN 2016, LNCS 9641, pp. 147–164, 2016.
DOI: 10.1007/978-3-319-32582-8_10

temporal logic such as PCTL [10]. It has been shown that, in contrast to non-probabilistic verification, the effort required to perform bisimulation minimisation can pay off in terms of the total time required for verification [12].

In this paper, we consider model reduction techniques for finite-horizon properties of Markov chains. We propose a *finite-horizon* variant of probabilistic bisimulation, which preserves stepwise behaviour over a finite number of steps, rather than indefinitely, as in standard probabilistic bisimulation. This permits a more aggressive model reduction, but still preserves satisfaction of PCTL formulae of bounded depth (i.e., whose interpretation requires only a bounded exploration of the model). Time-bounded properties are commonly used in probabilistic verification, e.g., for efficiency ("the probability of task completion within k steps") or for reliabilty ("the probability of an error occurring within time k").

We formalise finite-horizon probabilistic bisimulation, define the subset of PCTL that it preserves and then give a partition-refinement based algorithm for computing the coarsest possible finite-horizon bisimulation relation, along with a corresponding quotient model. The basic algorithm is limited by the fact it requires the full Markov chain to be constructed before it is minimised, which can be a bottleneck. So, we then develop on-the-fly approaches, which construct the quotient model directly from a high-level model description of the Markov chain, based on a backwards traversal of its state space. We propose two versions: one symbolic, based on SMT solvers, and one explicit-state.

We implemented all algorithms in PRISM and evaluated them on a range of examples. First, we apply the partition-refinement based approach to some standard benchmarks to investigate the size of the reduction that can be obtained in a finite-horizon setting. Then, we apply the on-the-fly approach to a class of problems to which it is particularly well suited: models with a large number of possible initial configurations, on which we ask questions such as "from which initial states does the probability of an error occurring within 10 s exceed 0.01?". We show that on-the-fly finite-horizon bisimulation can indeed provide significant gains in both verification time and scalability, demonstrated in each case by outperforming the existing efficient implementations in PRISM.

Related Work. For the standard notion of probabilistic bisimulation on Markov chains [18], various decision procedure and minimisation algorithms have been developed. Derisavi et al. [9] proposed an algorithm with optimal complexity, assuming the use of splay trees and, more recently, a simpler solution was put forward in [20]. Signature-based approaches, which our first, partition-refinement algorithm adapts, have been studied in, for example, [9,22]. Also relevant is the SMT-based bisimulation minimisation technique of [6] which, like our on-the-fly algorithm, avoids construction of the full model when minimising. Our SMT-based algorithm has an additional benefit in that it works on model descriptions with state-dependent probabilities. Other probabilistic verification methods have been developed based on backwards traversal of a model, for example for probabilistic timed automata [16], but this is for a different class of models and does not perform minimisation. Della Penna et al. considered finite-horizon verification of Markov chains [7], but using disk-based methods, not model reduction.

2   Preliminaries

We start with some background on probabilistic verification of Markov chains.

2.1   Discrete-Time Markov Chains

A discrete-time Markov chain (DTMC) can be thought of as a state transition system where transitions between states are annotated with probabilities.

Definition 1 (DTMC). *A DTMC is a tuple* $\mathcal{D} = (\mathcal{S}, \mathcal{S}_{init}, \mathbf{P}, \mathcal{AP}, \mathcal{L})$, *where:*

- $\mathcal{S}$ *is a finite set of states and* $\mathcal{S}_{init} \subseteq \mathcal{S}$ *is a set of initial states;*
- $\mathbf{P} : \mathcal{S} \times \mathcal{S} \to [0, 1]$ *is a transition probability matrix, where, for all states* $s \in \mathcal{S}$, *we have* $\sum_{s' \in \mathcal{S}} \mathbf{P}(s, s') = 1$;
- $\mathcal{AP}$ *is a set of atomic propositions and* $\mathcal{L} : \mathcal{S} \to 2^{\mathcal{AP}}$ *is a labelling function giving the set of propositions from* $\mathcal{AP}$ *that are true in each state.*

For each pair s, s' of states, $\mathbf{P}(s, s')$ represents the probability of going from s to s'. If $\mathbf{P}(s, s') > 0$, then s is a predecessor of s' and s' is a successor of s. For a state s and set $C \subseteq \mathcal{S}$, we will often use the notation $\mathbf{P}(s, C) := \sum_{s' \in C} \mathbf{P}(s, s')$.

A path σ of a DTMC $\mathcal{D}$ is a finite or infinite sequence of states $\sigma = s_0 s_1 s_2 \ldots$ such that $\forall i \geq 0$, $s_i \in \mathcal{S}$ and $\mathbf{P}(s_i, s_{i+1}) > 0$. The ith state of the path σ is denoted by $\sigma[i]$. We let $Path^{\mathcal{D}}(s)$ denote the set of infinite paths of $\mathcal{D}$ that begin in a state s. To reason formally about the behaviour of a DTMC, we define a probability measure Pr_s over the set of infinite paths $Path^{\mathcal{D}}(s)$ [14]. We usually consider the behaviour from some initial state $s \in \mathcal{S}_{init}$ of $\mathcal{D}$.

2.2   Probabilistic Computation Tree Logic

Properties of probabilistic models can be expressed using *Probabilistic Computation Tree Logic* (PCTL) [10] which extends Computation Tree Logic (CTL) with time and probabilities. In PCTL, state formulae Φ are interpreted over states of a DTMC and path formulae ϕ are interpreted over paths.

Definition 2 (PCTL). *The syntax of PCTL is as follows:*

$$\Phi ::= \text{true} \mid a \mid \neg \Phi \mid \Phi \wedge \Phi \mid \mathsf{P}_{\bowtie p}[\phi]$$
$$\phi ::= \Phi_1 \, \mathsf{U}^{\leq k} \, \Phi_2$$

where a *is an atomic proposition,* $\bowtie \in \{<, \leq, \geq, >\}$, $p \in [0, 1]$ *and* $k \in \mathbb{N} \cup \{\infty\}$.

The main operator in PCTL, in addition to those that are standard from propositional logic, is the probabilistic operator $\mathsf{P}_{\bowtie p}[\phi]$, which means that the probability measure of paths that satisfy ϕ is within the bound $\bowtie p$. For path formulae ϕ, we allow the (bounded) until operator $\Phi_1 \, \mathsf{U}^{\leq k} \, \Phi_2$. If Φ_2 becomes true within k time steps and Φ_1 is true until that point, then $\Phi_1 \, \mathsf{U}^{\leq k} \, \Phi_2$ is true. In the case where k equals ∞, the bounded until operator becomes the unbounded until operator and is denoted by U. For simplicity of presentation, in this paper, we omit the next ($\mathsf{X}\,\Phi$) operator, but this could easily be added.

Definition 3 (PCTL Semantics). *Let* $\mathcal{D} = (\mathcal{S}, \mathcal{S}_{init}, \mathbf{P}, \mathcal{AP}, \mathcal{L})$ *be a DTMC. The satisfaction relation* $\vDash_{\mathcal{D}}$ *for PCTL formulae on* $\mathcal{D}$ *is defined by:*

- $s \vDash_{\mathcal{D}} true \qquad \forall s \in \mathcal{S}$
- $s \vDash_{\mathcal{D}} a \qquad\qquad iff\ a \in \mathcal{L}(s)$
- $s \vDash_{\mathcal{D}} \neg\Phi \qquad\quad iff\ s \nvDash_{\mathcal{D}} \Phi$
- $s \vDash_{\mathcal{D}} \Phi_1 \wedge \Phi_2 \quad\ iff\ s \vDash_{\mathcal{D}} \Phi_1\ and\ s \vDash_{\mathcal{D}} \Phi_2$
- $s \vDash_{\mathcal{D}} \mathsf{P}_{\bowtie p}[\phi] \qquad iff\ Pr_s\{\sigma \in Path^{\mathcal{D}}(s) \mid \sigma \vDash_{\mathcal{D}} \phi\} \bowtie p$
- $\sigma \vDash_{\mathcal{D}} \Phi_1 \mathsf{U}^{\leq k} \Phi_2 \quad iff\ \exists i \in \mathbb{N}.(i \leq k \wedge \sigma[i] \vDash_{\mathcal{D}} \Phi_2 \wedge (\forall j.0 \leq j < i.\sigma[j] \vDash_{\mathcal{D}} \Phi_1))$

For example, a PCTL formula such as $\mathsf{P}_{<0.01}[\neg fail_1 \mathsf{U}^{\leq k} fail_2]$ means that the probability of a failure of type 2 occurring within k time-steps, and before a failure of type 1 does, is less than 0.01. Common derived operators are $\mathsf{F}\,\Phi \equiv true\,\mathsf{U}\,\Phi$, which means that Φ eventually becomes true, and $\mathsf{F}^{\leq k}\,\Phi \equiv true\,\mathsf{U}^{\leq k}\,\Phi$, which means that Φ becomes true within k steps.

2.3   Probabilistic Bisimulation

Larsen and Skou [18] defined (strong) *probabilistic bisimulation* for discrete probabilistic transition systems, which is an equivalence relation used to identify states with identical labellings and (probabilistic) step-wise behaviour.

Definition 4 (Probabilistic Bisimulation). *Let* $\mathcal{D} = (\mathcal{S}, \mathcal{S}_{init}, \mathbf{P}, \mathcal{AP}, \mathcal{L})$ *be a DTMC and* $\mathcal{R}$ *an equivalence relation on* $\mathcal{S}$. *Then* $\mathcal{R}$ *is a (strong) probabilistic bisimulation on* $\mathcal{D}$ *if, for* $(s_1, s_2) \in \mathcal{R}$:

$$(i)\ \mathcal{L}(s_1) = \mathcal{L}(s_2)\ \ and\ (ii)\ for\ all\ C\ \in \mathcal{S}/\mathcal{R}:\ \mathbf{P}(s_1, C) = \mathbf{P}(s_2, C)$$

where $\mathcal{S}/\mathcal{R}$ *denotes the set of equivalence classes of set* $\mathcal{S}$ *by relation* $\mathcal{R}$. *States* s_1, s_2 *are bisimilar if there exists a bisimulation on* $\mathcal{D}$ *containing* (s_1, s_2).

Two states that are probabilistically bisimilar will satisfy the same properties, including both infinite-horizon (long-run) and finite-horizon (transient) properties. Aziz et al. [3] proved that any property in the temporal logic PCTL is also preserved in this manner. Thanks to these results, the analysis of the original Markov chain, such as probabilistic model checking of PCTL, can be equivalently performed on the *quotient* Markov chain, in which equivalence classes of bisimilar states are lumped together into a single state.

Usually, we are interested in the coarsest possible probabilistic bisimulation for a DTMC $\mathcal{D}$ (or, in other words, the union of all possible bisimulation relations). We denote the coarsest possible probabilistic bisimulation by $\sim$. The quotient model $\mathcal{D}/\sim$ derived using this relation is defined as follows.

Definition 5 (Quotient DTMC). *Given DTMC* $\mathcal{D} = (\mathcal{S}, \mathcal{S}_{init}, \mathbf{P}, \mathcal{AP}, \mathcal{L})$, *the quotient DTMC is defined as* $\mathcal{D}/\sim = (\mathcal{S}', \mathcal{S}'_{init}, \mathbf{P}', \mathcal{AP}, \mathcal{L}')$ *where:*

- $\mathcal{S}' = \mathcal{S}/\sim = \{[s]_\sim \mid s \in \mathcal{S}\}$
- $\mathcal{S}'_{init} = \{[s]_\sim \mid s \in \mathcal{S}_{init}\}$
- $\mathbf{P}'([s]_\sim, [s']_\sim) = \mathbf{P}(s, [s']_\sim)$
- $\mathcal{L}'([s]_\sim) = \mathcal{L}(s)$

and $[s]_\sim$ *denotes the unique equivalence class of relation* $\sim$ *containing* s.

3   Finite-Horizon Bisimulation

We now formalise the notion of *finite-horizon bisimulation*, a step-bounded variant of standard probabilistic bisimulation for Markov chains [18]. We fix, from this point on, a DTMC $\mathcal{D} = (\mathcal{S}, \mathcal{S}_{init}, \mathbf{P}, \mathcal{AP}, \mathcal{L})$. Intuitively, a *k-step finite-horizon bisimulation*, for non-negative integer k, preserves the stepwise behaviour of $\mathcal{D}$ over a finite horizon of k steps. We use the following inductive definition.

Definition 6 (Finite-Horizon Bisimulation). *A k-step finite-horizon bisimulation, for $k \in \mathbb{N}_{\geq 0}$, is an equivalence relation $\mathcal{R}_k \subseteq \mathcal{S} \times \mathcal{S}$ such that, for all states $(s_1, s_2) \in \mathcal{R}_k$, the following two conditions are satisfied:*

(i) $\mathcal{L}(s_1) = \mathcal{L}(s_2)$;
(ii) $\mathbf{P}(s_1, C) = \mathbf{P}(s_2, C)$ for each equivalence class $C \in \mathcal{S}/\mathcal{R}_{k-1}$,

where $\mathcal{R}_{k-1}$ is a $(k-1)$-step finite-horizon bisimulation. A 0-step finite-horizon bisimulation is an equivalence relation $\mathcal{R}_0$ satisfying only condition (i) above.

Definition 7 (Finite-Horizon Bisimulation Equivalent). *We say states s_1, s_2 are (k-step) finite-horizon bisimulation equivalent (bisimilar), denoted $s_1 \sim_k s_2$, if there exists a k-step finite-horizon bisimulation $\mathcal{R}_k$ such that $(s_1, s_2) \in \mathcal{R}_k$.*

Two states s_1 and s_2 satisfying $s_1 \sim_k s_2$ have the same stepwise behaviour over k steps. The following simple, but useful, properties hold.

Proposition 1. *Let $s_1, s_2 \in \mathcal{S}$ be two states. Then:*

(a) if $s_1 \sim_k s_2$, then $s_1 \sim_j s_2$ for any $0 \leq j \leq k$.
(b) if $s_1 \sim s_2$, then $s_1 \sim_k s_2$ for any $k \geq 0$.
(c) if $s_1 \sim_k s_2$ and $s_1 \to s_1'$, then $s_1' \sim_{k-1} s_2'$ for some state s_2' such that $s_2 \to s_2'$.

From a model checking perspective, if $s_1 \sim_k s_2$, then s_1 and s_2 satisfy the same PCTL formulae up to a bounded depth k. We formalise this as follows.

Definition 8 (Formula Depth). *The depth of a PCTL formula Φ, denoted $d(\Phi)$, is a value in $\mathbb{N} \cup \{\infty\}$ defined inductively as follows:*

- $d(\mathrm{true}) = d(a) = 0$ *for atomic proposition a;*
- $d(\neg\Phi) = d(\Phi)$;
- $d(\Phi_1 \wedge \Phi_2) = \max(d(\Phi_1), d(\Phi_2))$;
- $d(\mathrm{P}_{\bowtie p}[\Phi_1 \, \mathsf{U}^{\leq j} \, \Phi_2]) = j + \max(d(\Phi_1) - 1, d(\Phi_2))$.

For example, if a and b are atomic propositions, we have $d(\mathrm{P}_{\bowtie p}[\mathrm{true}\,\mathsf{U}^{\leq 5} a]) = 5$, $d(\mathrm{P}_{\bowtie p}[\mathrm{true}\,\mathsf{U}^{\leq 5} a] \wedge \mathrm{P}_{\bowtie p}[\mathrm{true}\,\mathsf{U}^{\leq 6} a]) = 6$, and $d(\mathrm{P}_{\bowtie p}[\mathrm{true}\,\mathsf{U}^{\leq 5} \mathrm{P}_{\bowtie p}[a\,\mathsf{U}^{\leq 3} b]]) = 8$.

If states s_1 and s_2 are (k-step) finite-horizon bisimilar, then they satisfy exactly the same PCTL formulae of depth at most k.

Theorem 1. *Let s_1 and s_2 be two states such that $s_1 \sim_k s_2$, and Φ be a PCTL formula with depth $d(\Phi) \leq k$, then $s_1 \models \Phi$ if and only if $s_2 \models \Phi$.*

Proof. We prove the result by induction over the structure (see Definition 2) of PCTL formula Φ. Propositional operators are straightforward since s_1 and s_2 satisfy the same atomic propositions, by the definition of $\sim_k$, and, for $\Phi = \neg\Phi_1$ or $\Phi = \Phi_1 \wedge \Phi_2$, the subformulae Φ_1 and Φ_2 have depth at most k so, by induction, we can assume that $s_1 \models \Phi_i \Leftrightarrow s_2 \models \Phi_i$ for $i \in \{1,2\}$.

The remaining case to consider is $\Phi = \mathsf{P}_{\bowtie p}[\Phi_1 \, \mathsf{U}^{\leq j} \, \Phi_2]$. We know, from Definition 8, that the depths $d(\Phi_1)$ and $d(\Phi_2)$ of the two subformulae are at most $k - j + 1$ and $k - j$. From the semantics of PCTL, we have that, for any state s:

$$s \models \mathsf{P}_{\bowtie p}[\Phi_1 \, \mathsf{U}^{\leq j} \, \Phi_2] \;\Leftrightarrow\; Pr_s(\Phi_1 \, \mathsf{U}^{\leq j} \, \Phi_2) \bowtie p$$

which means it suffices to show that:

$$Pr_{s_1}(\Phi_1 \, \mathsf{U}^{\leq j} \, \Phi_2) = Pr_{s_2}(\Phi_1 \, \mathsf{U}^{\leq j} \, \Phi_2) \tag{1}$$

We in fact show this to be true for any states s_1, s_2, values $j \leq k$ and PCTL subformulae Φ_1, Φ_2 satisfying $s_1 \sim_k s_2$ and $\max(d(\Phi_1) - 1, d(\Phi_2)) \leq k-j$, which we prove inductively over j. From the model checking algorithm for PCTL [10], we know that, for any state s:

$$Pr_s(\Phi_1 \, \mathsf{U}^{\leq j} \, \Phi_2) = \begin{cases} 1 & \text{if } s \models \Phi_2 \\ 0 & \text{if } s \models \neg\Phi_1 \wedge \neg\Phi_2 \\ 0 & \text{if } s \models \Phi_1 \wedge \neg\Phi_2 \text{ and } j = 0 \\ \sum_{s' \in S} \mathbf{P}(s, s') Pr_{s'}(\Phi_1 \, \mathsf{U}^{\leq j-1} \, \Phi_2) & \text{if } s \models \Phi_1 \wedge \neg\Phi_2 \text{ and } j > 0. \end{cases}$$

For the base case $j = 0$, only the first three cases of the definition above can apply, and we know that $s_1 \models \Phi_i \Leftrightarrow s_2 \models \Phi_i$ for $i \in \{1,2\}$, so we have that $Pr_{s_1}(\Phi_1 \, \mathsf{U}^{\leq 0} \, \Phi_2) = Pr_{s_2}(\Phi_1 \, \mathsf{U}^{\leq 0} \, \Phi_2)$. For the inductive case, where $j > 0$, we can assume that $Pr_{s_1}(\Phi_1 \, \mathsf{U}^{\leq j-1} \, \Phi_2) = Pr_{s_2}(\Phi_1 \, \mathsf{U}^{\leq j-1} \, \Phi_2)$, as long as $s_1 \sim_{j-1} s_2$. Considering again the possible cases in the above definition, the first two follow as for $j = 0$ and the third cannot apply since $j > 0$. For the fourth case, since $j > 0$, we know there exists a $(j-1)$-step finite-horizon bisimulation $\mathcal{R}_{j-1}$. Let us further assume an (arbitrary) function $rep : \mathcal{S}/\mathcal{R}_{j-1} \to \mathcal{S}$, which selects a unique representative from each equivalence class of $\mathcal{R}_{j-1}$. We have:

$$
\begin{aligned}
&Pr_{s_1}(\Phi_1 \, \mathsf{U}^{\leq j} \, \Phi_2) \\
&= \sum_{s' \in \mathcal{S}} \mathbf{P}(s_1, s') Pr_{s'}(\Phi_1 \, \mathsf{U}^{\leq j-1} \, \Phi_2) && \text{by definition} \\
&= \sum_{C \in \mathcal{S}/\sim_{j-1}} \sum_{s' \in C} \mathbf{P}(s_1, s') Pr_{s'}(\Phi_1 \, \mathsf{U}^{\leq j-1} \, \Phi_2) && \text{since } \sim_{j-1} \text{ partitions } \mathcal{S} \\
&= \sum_{C \in \mathcal{S}/\sim_{j-1}} Pr_{rep(C)}(\Phi_1 \, \mathsf{U}^{\leq j-1} \, \Phi_2) \sum_{s' \in C} \mathbf{P}(s_1, s') && \text{by induction on } j \\
&= \sum_{C \in \mathcal{S}/\sim_{j-1}} Pr_{rep(C)}(\Phi_1 \, \mathsf{U}^{\leq j-1} \, \Phi_2) \mathbf{P}(s_1, C) \\
&= \sum_{C \in \mathcal{S}/\sim_{j-1}} Pr_{rep(C)}(\Phi_1 \, \mathsf{U}^{\leq j-1} \, \Phi_2) \mathbf{P}(s_2, C) && \text{since } s_1 \sim_j s_2 \\
&= \sum_{C \in \mathcal{S}/\sim_{j-1}} Pr_{rep(C)}(\Phi_1 \, \mathsf{U}^{\leq j-1} \, \Phi_2) \sum_{s' \in C} \mathbf{P}(s_2, s') \\
&= \sum_{C \in \mathcal{S}/\sim_{j-1}} \sum_{s' \in C} \mathbf{P}(s_2, s') Pr_{s'}(\Phi_1 \, \mathsf{U}^{\leq j-1} \, \Phi_2) && \text{since } s' \sim_{j-1} rep(C) \\
&= \sum_{s' \in \mathcal{S}} \mathbf{P}(s_2, s') Pr_{s'}(\Phi_1 \, \mathsf{U}^{\leq j-1} \, \Phi_2) && \text{since } \sim_{j-1} \text{ partitions } \mathcal{S} \\
&= Pr_{s_2}(\Phi_1 \, \mathsf{U}^{\leq j} \, \Phi_2) && \text{by definition}
\end{aligned}
$$

which proves (1), as required, and concludes the proof. $\square$

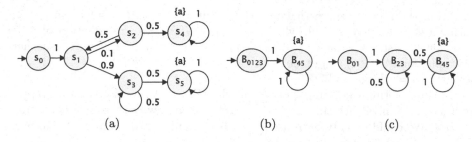

Fig. 1. (a) Example DTMC; (b–c) Finite-horizon quotient DTMCs for $k = 0, 1$.

In similar fashion to the standard (non-finite-horizon) case, we are typically interested in the *coarsest possible* k-step finite-horizon bisimulation relation for a given DTMC (labelled with atomic propositions) and time horizon k, which we denote by $\sim_k$. We can also define this as the union of all possible k-step finite-horizon bisimulation relations. Furthermore, for $\sim_k$ (or any other finite-horizon bisimulation relation), we can define a corresponding *quotient* DTMC, whose states are formed from the equivalence classes of $\sim_k$, and whose k-step behaviour is identical to the original DTMC $\mathcal{D}$.

This is similar, but not identical, to the process of building the quotient Markov chain corresponding to a full minimisation (see Definition 5). We must take care since, unlike for full bisimulation, given a state $B \in \mathcal{S}/\sim_k$ of the quotient model, the probabilities $\mathbf{P}(s, B')$ of moving to other equivalence classes $B' \in \mathcal{S}/\sim_k$ can be different for each state $s \in B$ (according to the definition of $\sim_k$, probabilities are the same to go states with the same $(k-1)$-step, not k-step, behaviour). However, when they do differ, it suffices to pick an arbitrary representative from B. We formalise the quotient DTMC construction below, and then present some examples.

Definition 9 (Finite-Horizon Quotient DTMC). *If* $\mathcal{D} = (\mathcal{S}, \mathcal{S}_{init}, \mathbf{P}, \mathcal{AP}, \mathcal{L})$ *is a DTMC and* $\sim_k$ *is a finite-horizon bisimulation on* $\mathcal{D}$, *then a quotient DTMC can be constructed as* $\mathcal{D}/\sim_k = (\mathcal{S}', \mathcal{S}'_{init}, \mathbf{P}', \mathcal{AP}, \mathcal{L}')$ *where:*

- $\mathcal{S}' = \mathcal{S}/\sim_k = \{[s]_{\sim_k} \mid s \in \mathcal{S}\}$
- $\mathcal{S}'_{init} = \{[s]_{\sim_k} \mid s \in \mathcal{S}_{init}\}$
- $\mathbf{P}'(B, B') = \mathbf{P}(rep(B), B')$ *for any* $B, B' \in \mathcal{S}'$
- $\mathcal{L}'(B) = \mathcal{L}(rep(B))$ *for any* $B \in \mathcal{S}'$,

where $rep : \mathcal{S}/\sim_k \to \mathcal{S}$ *is an* arbitrary *function that selects a unique representative from each equivalence class of* $\sim_k$, *i.e.,* $B = [rep(B)]_{\sim_k}$ *for all* $B \in \mathcal{S}'$.

Example 1. Figure 1 illustrates finite-horizon bisimulation on an example DTMC, shown in part (a). Figure 1(b) and (c) show quotient DTMCs for 0-step and 1-step finite-horizon bisimulation minimisation, respectively, where quotient state names indicate their corresponding equivalence class (e.g., B_{23} corresponds to DTMC states s_2 and s_3). For 2-step minimisation (not shown), blocks B_{23} and B_{01} are both split in two, and only the states s_4 and s_5 remain bisimilar.

From the above, we see that $s_2 \sim_1 s_3$, but $s_2 \not\sim_2 s_3$. Consider the PCTL formula $\Phi = \mathrm{P}_{\bowtie p}[\text{true}\,\mathsf{U}^{\leq k}\,a]$, which has depth $d(\Phi) = k$. Satisfaction of Φ is equivalent in states s_2 and s_3 for $k = 1$, but not for $k = 2$. To give another example, for $\Phi' = \mathrm{P}_{>0}[\mathrm{P}_{>0.5}[\text{true}\,\mathsf{U}^{\leq 2}\,a]\,\mathsf{U}^{\leq 1}\,a]$, which has $d(\Phi') = 1 + 2 - 1 = 2$, we have $s_3 \models \Phi'$, but $s_2 \not\models \Phi'$.

In constructing the 1-step quotient model (Fig. 1(c)), we used s_1 as a representative of equivalence class $B_{01} = \{s_0, s_1\}$, which is why there is a transition to B_{23}. We could equally have used s_0, which would yield a different quotient DTMC, but which still preserves 1-step behaviour.

4   Finite-Horizon Bisimulation Minimisation

Bisimulation relations have a variety of uses, but our focus here is on using them to minimise a probabilistic model prior to verification, in order to improve the efficiency and scalability of the analysis. More precisely, we perform *finite-horizon bisimulation minimisation*, determining the coarsest possible finite-horizon bisimulation relation $\sim_k$, for a given k, and then constructing the corresponding quotient Markov chain. Theorem 1 tells us that it is then safe to perform verification on the smaller quotient model instead.

We begin, in this section, by presenting a classical *partition-refinement* based minimisation algorithm, which is based on an iterative splitting of an initially coarse partition of the state space until the required probabilistic bisimulation has been identified. In the next section, we will propose on-the-fly approaches which offer further gains in efficiency and scalability.

4.1   A Partition-Refinement Based Minimisation Algorithm

The standard approach to partition refinement is to use *splitters* [9,19], individual blocks in the current partition which show that one or more other blocks contain states that should be split into distinct sub-blocks. An alternative approach is to use a so-called *signature-based* method [8]. The basic structure of the algorithm remains the same, however the approach to splitting differs: rather than using splitters, a *signature* corresponding to the current partition is computed at each iteration for each state s. This signature comprises the probability of moving from s in one step to each block in the partition. In the next iteration, all states with different signatures are placed in different blocks.

Because each iteration of the signature-based algorithm considers the one-step behaviour of every state in the model, it is relatively straightforward to adapt to finite-horizon bisimulation minimisation. Algorithm 1 shows the finite-horizon minimisation algorithm MINIMISEFINITEHORIZON. It takes a DTMC $\mathcal{D}$ and the time horizon k as input. The partition Π is first initialised to group states based on the different combinations of atomic propositions, i.e., states with identical labellings are placed in one block.[1] The partition is then repeatedly split, each time by computing the signatures for each state and splitting

---

[1] In the algorithm, we store the signatures with the partition, so Π is a list of pairs of blocks (state-sets) and signatures (distributions).

accordingly. The loop terminates either when k iterations have been completed or no further splitting is possible. Finally, the quotient model is constructed, as described in the previous section.

Correctness. The correctness of MINIMISEFINITEHORIZON, i.e. that it generates the coarsest k-step finite-horizon bisimulation, can be argued with direct reference to Definition 6. For $k = 0$, only the initialisation step at the start of the algorithm is needed. For $k > 0$ the ith iteration of the loop produces a partition Π which groups precisely the equivalence classes of $\sim_i$, which are constructed from those of $\sim_{i-1}$, as in Definition 6. It is also clear that we group *all* equivalent states at each step, yielding the coarsest relation. If the algorithm terminates early, at step j, then $\sim_i = \sim_k$ for all $j \leq i \leq k$.

Algorithm 1. MINIMISEFINITEHORIZON

Data: $\mathcal{D} = (\mathcal{S}, \mathcal{S}_{init}, \mathbf{P}, \mathcal{AP}, \mathcal{L})$, k

$\Pi, \Pi' := \emptyset$;   // Initialise partition

for $A \subseteq \mathcal{AP}$ **do**
$\quad$ $B_A := \{s \in \mathcal{S} \mid L(s) = A\}$
$\quad$ **if** $B_A \neq \emptyset$ **then** $\Pi := \Pi \cup \{(\{B_A\}, \langle\rangle)\}$;

$i := 1$;   // Splitting loop
while $i \leq k \wedge \Pi \neq \Pi'$ **do**
$\quad$ $\Pi' := \Pi$; $\Pi := \emptyset$
$\quad$ **for** $s \in \mathcal{S}$ **do**
$\quad\quad$ $Sig := \langle\rangle$;   // Compute signature
$\quad\quad$ **for** $B \in \Pi'$ **do** $Sig(B) := 0$;
$\quad\quad$ **for** $s \to s'$ **do**
$\quad\quad\quad$ $B_{s'} :=$ block of Π' containing s'
$\quad\quad\quad$ $Sig(B_{s'}) := Sig(B_{s'}) + \mathbf{P}(s, s')$

$\quad\quad$ $B_s :=$ block of Π' containing s
$\quad\quad$ **if** $\exists (B', Sig) \in \Pi \wedge B' \subseteq B_s$ **then**
$\quad\quad\quad$ $B' := B' \cup \{s\}$;   // New blocks
$\quad\quad$ **else**
$\quad\quad\quad$ $\Pi := \Pi \cup \{(\{s\}, Sig)\}$
$\quad$ $i := i + 1$

$\mathcal{S}' := \emptyset$; $\mathcal{S}'_{init} := \emptyset$;   // Build quotient
for $(B, Sig) \in \Pi$ **do**
$\quad$ $\mathcal{S}' := \mathcal{S}' \cup \{B\}$
$\quad$ **if** $B \cap \mathcal{S}_{init} \neq \emptyset$ **then** $\mathcal{S}'_{init} := \mathcal{S}'_{init} \cup \{B\}$;
$\quad$ $\mathbf{P}'(B, \cdot) := Sig$
$\quad$ $\mathcal{L}'(B) := \mathcal{L}(s)$ for any $s \in B$

return $\mathcal{D}' = (\mathcal{S}', \mathcal{S}'_{init}, \mathbf{P}', \mathcal{AP}, \mathcal{L}')$

---

5   On-the-Fly Finite-Horizon Minimisation

A key limitation of the partition-refinement approach presented in the previous section is that it takes as input the full DTMC to be minimised, the construction of which can be expensive in terms of both time and space. This can remove any potential gains in terms of scalability that minimisation can provide.

To resolve this, we now propose methods to compute a finite-horizon bisimulation minimisation in an *on-the-fly* fashion, where the minimised model is constructed directly from a high-level modelling language description of the original model, bypassing construction of the full, un-reduced DTMC. In our case, the probabilistic models are described using the modelling language of the PRISM model checker [15], which is based on guarded commands.

Our approach works through a backwards traversal of the model, which allows us to perform bisimulation minimisation on the fly. For simplicity, we focus on preserving the subclass of PCTL properties comprising a single P operator, more precisely, those of the form $P_{\bowtie p}[\, b_1 \, U^{\leq k} \, b_2\,]$ for atomic propositions b_1 and b_2. This is the kind of property most commonly found in practice.

5.1   The On-the-Fly Minimisation Algorithm

The basic approach to performing finite-horizon minimisation on the fly is shown as FINITEHORIZONONTHEFLY, in Algorithm 2. This takes *model*, which is a description of the DTMC, B_1 and B_2, the sets of states satisfying b_1 and b_2, respectively, in the property $P_{\bowtie p}[\, b_1 \, U^{\leq k} \, b_2\,]$, and the time horizon k. The algorithm does not make any assumptions about how sets of states are represented or manipulated. Below, we will discuss two separate instantiations of it.

The algorithm is based on a backwards traversal of the model. It uses a separate algorithm FINDMERGEDPREDECESSORS(*model, target, restrict*), which queries the DTMC (*model*) to find all (immediate) predecessors of states in *target* that are also in *restrict* (the *restrict* set will be used to restrict attention to the set B_1 corresponding to the left-hand side b_1 of the until formula). The algorithm also groups the predecessor states in blocks according to the probabilities with which they transition to *target* and returns these too. As above, each instantiation of Algorithm 2 will use a separate implementation of the FINDMERGEDPREDECESSORS algorithm.

The main loop of the algorithm iterates backwards through the model: after the ith iteration, it has found all states that can reach the target set B_2 within i steps with positive probability. The new predecessors for each iteration are stored in a set of blocks P. A separate set P' is used to store predecessors of blocks in P, which will then be considered in the next iteration.

More precisely, P (and P') store, like in Algorithm 1, a list of pairs (B, D) where B is a block (a set of states) and D is a (partial) probability distribution storing probabilities of outgoing transitions (from B, to other blocks). The set Π, which is used to construct the partition representing the finite-horizon bisimulation relation, is also stored as a list of pairs.

Algorithm 2. FINITEHORIZONONTHEFLY

Data: $model$, B_1, B_2, k

$P := \{\text{FINDMERGEDPREDECESSORS}(model, B_2, B_1)\}$; $P' := \emptyset$
$\Pi := \{(B_2, \langle\rangle)\}$

$i := 1$
while $P \neq \emptyset \wedge i \leq k$ **do**

    $(B, D) := \text{pop}(P)$;   // block B, (sub)distribution D
    for $(B', D') \in \Pi \wedge B \neq \emptyset$ **do**

        if $B' \cap B \neq \emptyset$ **then**

            replace (B', D') in Π with $(B' \setminus B), D')$ and $(B' \cap B, D' \cup D)$
            $B := B \setminus B'$
            refine all $(B'', D'') \in \Pi$ and (B, D) with respect to the split of B'
        end

    end

    if $B \neq \emptyset$ **then**

        $\Pi := \Pi \cup \{(B, D)\}$
        $P' := P' \cup \{\text{FINDMERGEDPREDECESSORS}(model, B, B_1)\}$
    end

    if $(P = \emptyset \wedge P' \neq \emptyset)$ **then**

        $P := P'$; $P' := \emptyset$
        $i := i + 1$
    end

end

return FINITEHORIZONQUOTIENT(Π)

Algorithm 3. FINITEHORIZONQUOTIENT

Data: Π

$\mathcal{S}' := \{B_{sink}\}$; $\mathcal{L}'(B_{sink}) = \emptyset$; $\mathcal{S}'_{init} := \emptyset$; $\mathbf{P}'(B_{sink}, \cdot) := \langle B_{sink} \to 1 \rangle$;
for $(B, D) \in \Pi$ **do**

    $\mathcal{S}' := \mathcal{S}' \cup \{B\}$
    if $B \cap \mathcal{S}_{init} \neq \emptyset$ **then** $\mathcal{S}'_{init} := \mathcal{S}'_{init} \cup \{B\}$;
    $p_{sink} = 1 - \sum_{(B', D') \in \Pi} D(B')$
    $\mathbf{P}'(B, \cdot) := D \cup \langle B_{sink} \to p_{sink} \rangle$
    $\mathcal{L}'(B) := \mathcal{L}(s)$ for any $s \in B$
end
return $\mathcal{D}' = (\mathcal{S}', \mathcal{S}'_{init}, \mathbf{P}', \mathcal{AP}, \mathcal{L}')$

Algorithm 2 begins by finding all immediate predecessors of states in B_2 that are also in B_1 and putting them in P. In each iteration, it takes each block-distribution pair (B, D) from P one by one: it will add this to the current partition Π. But, before doing so, it checks whether B overlaps with any existing blocks B' in Π. If so, B' is split in two, and the overlap is removed from B. At this point, the partition Π is refined to take account of the splitting of block B'. We repeatedly recompute the probabilities associated with each block in Π and, if these are then different for states within that block, it is also split.

Each iteration of the main loop finishes when all pairs (B, D) from P have been dealt with. If $i < k$, then newly found predecessors P' are copied to P and the process is repeated. If $i = k$, then the time horizon k has been reached and the finite-horizon bisimulation has been computed.

Finally, the quotient model is built. The basic construction is as in Algorithm 1 but, since on-the-fly construction only partially explores the model, we need to add an extra sink state to complete the DTMC.

Computing Predecessors. One of the main challenges in implementing the on-the-fly algorithm is determining the predecessors of a given set of states from the high-level modelling language description. The PRISM language, used here, is based on guarded commands, for example:

$$c > 0 \; \rightarrow \; c/K \; : \; (c' = c - 1) \; + \; 1 - c/K \; : \; (c' = c + 1);$$

The meaning is that, when a state satisfies the *guard* $(c > 0)$, the *updates* (decrementing or incrementing variable c) can be executed, each with an associated probability $(c/K$ or $1 - c/K)$. We assume here a single PRISM *module* of commands (multiple modules can be syntactically expanded into a single one [23]).

In the following sections, we describe two approaches to finding predecessors: one *symbolic*, which represents blocks (sets of states) as predicates and uses an SMT (satisfiability modulo theories) [5] based implementation; and one *explicit-state*, which explicitly enumerates the states in each block.

5.2 Symbolic (SMT-Based) Minimisation

Our first approach represents state sets (i.e., blocks of the bisimulation partition) *symbolically*, as predicates over PRISM model variables. If *target* is a predicate representing a set of states, their predecessors, reached by applying some guarded command update *update*, can be found using the *weakest precondition*, denoted **wp**(*update, target*). More precisely, if the guard of the command is *guard*, and *bounds* represents the lower and upper bounds of all model variables, the following expression captures the set of states, if any, that are predecessors:

$$bounds \; \wedge \; guard \; \wedge \; \mathbf{wp}(update, \; target)$$

We determine, for each guarded command update in the model description, whether states can reach *target* via that update by checking the satisfiability of the expression above using an SMT solver. FINDMERGEDPREDECESSORS (see Algorithm 4) is used to determine predecessors in this way. It also restricts attention to states satisfying a further expression *restrict*.

The probability attached to an update in a guarded command is in general a state-dependent expression *prob* (see the earlier example command) so this must be analysed when FINDMERGEDPREDECESSORS groups states according to the probability with which they transition to *target*. If the SMT query in the algorithm is satisfiable, a valid probability is also obtained from the corresponding valuation (p' in Algorithm 4). The conjunction of the expression *predecessor* and

---

Algorithm 4. FINDMERGEDPREDECESSORS (SMT-based)

Data: *model, target, restrict*

$P := \emptyset$
bounds := variable bounds from *model*

foreach $(guard, updates)$ *in model* **do**
    foreach $(prob, update)$ *in updates* **do**
        predecessor := *restrict* $\wedge$ *bounds* $\wedge$ *guard* $\wedge$ $\mathbf{wp}(update, target)$
        query := *predecessor* $\wedge$ $(p = prob)$
        while *query is satisfiable* **do**
            $p' :=$ value of p in *query*
            if $(B, \langle target \rightarrow p' \rangle) \in P$ *for some* B **then**
                replace $(B, \langle target \rightarrow p' \rangle)$ in P with
                  $(B \vee predecessor, \langle target \rightarrow p' \rangle)$
            else
                $P := P \cup \{(predecessor, \langle target \rightarrow p' \rangle)\}$
            end
            query := *query* $\wedge$ $(prob \neq p')$
        end
    end
end
return P

$p = prob$ denotes the set of predecessors with the same probability. To obtain all such probabilities, the algorithm adds a *blocking expression prob* $\neq p'$ to the query and repeats the process.

SMT-based methods for probabilistic bisimulation minimisation have been developed previously [6]. One key difference here is that our approach handles transition probabilities expressed as state-dependent expressions, rather than fixed constants, which are needed for some of the models we later evaluate.

5.3   Explicit-State Minimisation

As an alternative to the symbolic approach using SMT, we developed an explicit-state implementation of finite-horizon minimisation in which the blocks of equivalent states are represented by explicitly listing the states that comprise them. As in the previous algorithm, the blocks are refined at each time step such that states residing in the same block have equal transition probabilities to the required blocks. To improve performance and store states compactly, we hash them based on the valuation of variables that define them. This is done in such a way that the hash values are bi-directional (one-to-one).

The algorithm explicitly computes the predecessor state for each update and each state in the set *target*, the transition probability is then computed for each predecessor state and these are collected in order to group states into sets. The set *restrict* is not stored explicitly, but rather as a symbolic expression which is then evaluated against each state's variable values to compute the intersection.

6   Experimental Results

We have implemented the bisimulation minimisation techniques presented in this paper as an extension of the PRISM model checker [15], and applied them to a range of benchmark models. For both the partition-refinement based minimisation of Sect. 4, and the on-the-fly methods in Sect. 5, we build on PRISM's "explicit" model checking engine. For the SMT-based variant, we use the Z3 solver [4], through the Z3 Java API. All our experiments were run on an Intel Core i7 2.8 GHz machine, using 2 GB of RAM.

Our investigation is in two parts. First, we apply the partition-refinement algorithm to several DTMCs from the PRISM benchmark suite [17] to get an idea of the size of reductions that can be obtained on some standard models. We use: *Crowds* (an anonymity protocol), *EGL* (a contract signing protocol) and *NAND* (NAND multiplexing). Details of all models, parameters and properties used can be found at [24]. A common feature of these models is that they have a single initial state, from which properties are verified. Since on-the-fly approaches explore backwards from a target set, we would usually need to consider time horizons k high enough such that the whole model was explored.

So, to explore in more depth the benefits of the on-the-fly algorithms, we consider another common class of models in probabilistic verification: those in which we need to exhaustively check whether a property is true over a large set of possible configurations. We use *Approximate majority* [2], a population protocol for computing a majority value amongst a set of K agents, and two simple models of *genetic algorithms* [21] in which a population of K agents evolves over time, competing to exist according to a fitness value in the range $0, \ldots, N-1$. In the first variant, *tournament*, the agent with the highest value wins; in the second, *modulo*, the sum of the two scores is used modulo N. Again, details of all models, parameters and properties used can be found at [24].

6.1   The Partition-Refinement Algorithm

Figure 2 shows results for the partition-refinement algorithm. The top row of plots shows the number of blocks in the partition built by finite-horizon bisimulation minimisation for different values of k on the first three benchmark examples. For the largest values of k shown, we have generated the partition corresponding to the full (non-finite-horizon) bisimulation. In most cases, the growth in the number of blocks is close to linear in k, although it is rather less regular for the *NAND* example. In all cases, it seems that the growth is slow enough that verifying finite-horizon properties for a range of values of k can be done on a considerably smaller model than the full bisimulation.

The bottom row of plots shows, for the same examples, the time required to perform bisimulation minimisation and then verify a k-step finite-horizon property (details at [24]). The black lines show the time for finite-horizon minimisation, the grey lines for full minimisation. The latter are relatively flat, indicating that the time for verification (which is linear in k) is very small compared to the time needed for minimisation. However, we see significant gains in the total time required for finite-horizon minimisation compared to full minimisation.

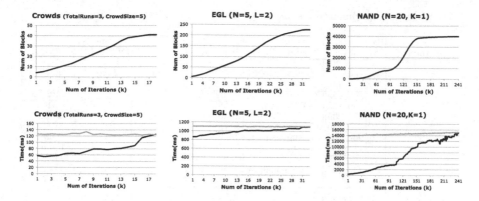

Fig. 2. Results for partition-refinement. Top: quotient size for varying time horizon k. Bottom: time for finite-horizon (black) and full (grey) minimisation/verification.

However, despite these gains, the times to minimise and verify the quotient model are still larger than to simply build and verify the full model. This is primarily because the partition refinement algorithm requires construction of the complete model first, the time for which eclipses any gains from minimisation. This was the motivation for the on-the-fly algorithms, which we evaluate next.

6.2 On-the-Fly Algorithms

Table 1 shows model sizes and timings for the on-the-fly algorithms on a range of models and scenarios. The left four columns show the model (and which on-the-fly algorithm was used), any parameters required (N or K) and the time horizon k. Next, under the headings 'Full Red.' and 'Finite Horiz.', we show the reductions in model size obtained using full (non-finite-horizon) and finite-horizon minimisation (for several k), respectively. In the first case, 'States' and 'Blocks' show the size of the full DTMC and the fully reduced quotient model, respectively. For the second case, 'Blocks' is the size of the finite-horizon quotient model and, to give a fair comparison, 'States' is the number of states in the full DTMC that can reach the target of the property within k steps (i.e., the number of states across all blocks). The rightmost three columns show the time required to build the model in three scenarios: 'Finite Horiz.' uses the on-the-fly approach over k steps; 'Full Red.' builds the full (non-finite-horizon) quotient by repeating the on-the-fly algorithm until all states have been found; and 'PRISM' builds the full model using its most efficient (symbolic) construction engine.

First, we note that finite-horizon minimisation yields useful reductions in model size in all cases, both with respect to the full model and to normal (non-finite horizon) minimisation. Bisimulation reduces models by a factor of roughly 2 and 5, for the *Approximate majority* and *Modulus* examples, respectively. For *Tournament*, a very large reduction is obtained since, for the property checked, the model ends up being abstracted to only distinguish two fitness values. Finite-horizon minimisation gives models that are smaller again, by a factor of between

Table 1. Experimental results for on-the-fly bisimulation minimisation.

Model (method)	N	K	k	Full Red. States	Full Red. Blocks	Finite Horiz. States	Finite Horiz. Blocks	Time (s) PRISM	Time (s) Full Red.	Time (s) Finite Horiz.
Approx. majority (explicit)	n/a	100	20	20300	10201	242	122	11.0	14.2	0.2
			40			882	442			0.3
			60			1922	962			0.4
		150	100	45450	22801	5202	2602	46.1	83.1	1.2
			150			11552	5777			5.1
			200			20402	10202			15.6
		200	250	80600	40401	31752	15877	memout	293.5	40.8
			300			45602	22802			93.9
			350			61952	30977			180.8
		250	375	125750	63001	71064	35533	memout	773.5	247.8
			400			80802	40402			323.2
			425			91164	45583			416.6
Genetic alg. tournament (explicit)	8	22	8	1184040	22	6435	10	19.2	5.3	0.3
			9			11440	11			0.4
			10			19448	12			0.4
		23	8	1560780	23	6435	10	31.1	7.0	0.3
			9			11440	11			0.4
			10			19448	12			0.4
	10	21	8	10015005	21	24310	10	59.0	43.6	0.5
			9			48620	11			0.6
			10			92378	12			0.7
		22	8	14307150	22	24310	10	61.3	51.3	0.5
			9			48620	11			0.6
			10			92378	12			0.7
Genetic alg. tournament (SMT)	4	9	3	165	9	20	5	0.03	155	4.5
			4			35	6			11.1
			5			56	7			23.5
		10	3	220	10	20	5	0.03	215	9.3
			4			35	6			15.1
			5			56	7			31.1
	5	9	3	330	9	35	5	0.04	723.4	22.1
			4			70	6			70.7
			5			126	7			180.9
		10	3	495	10	35	5	0.04	1998.7	48.8
			4			70	6			82.0
			5			126	7			233.7
Genetic alg. modulus (explicit)	7	19	8	177100	29565	22179	3638	0.4	475.3	6.8
			9			39404	6491			21.6
			10			66002	10914			64.3
		20	8	230230	38431	22179	3637	0.5	778.6	6.9
			9			39404	6488			20.3
			10			66068	10914			65.9
	9	11	6	75582	12707	24822	3435	0.3	79.9	7.7
			7			51756	8084			32.3
			8			70448	11745			58.3
		12	6	125970	21145	24906	3450	0.3	253.5	7.8
			7			54440	8482			37.4
			8			88642	14207			102.4

2 and 10 on these examples, even for relatively large values of k on the *Approximate majority* models. Comparing columns 7 and 8 in Table 1 shows that much of the reduction is indeed due to merging of bisimilar states, not just to a k-step truncation of the state space from the backwards traversal.

Regarding performance and scalability, we first discuss results for the SMT-based implementation. We were only able to apply this to the *Tournament* example, where a very large reduction in state space is achieved. On a positive note, the SMT-based approach successfully performs minimisation here and gives a symbolic (Boolean expression) representation for each block. However, the process is slow, limiting applicability to DTMCs that can already be verified without minimisation. Our experiments showed that the slow performance was largely caused by testing for overlaps between partition blocks resulting in a very large number of calls to the SMT solver.

The explicit-state on-the-fly implementation performed much better and Table 1 shows results for all three models. In particular, for the *Tournament* example, finite-horizon minimisation and verification is much faster than verifying the full model using the fastest engine in PRISM. This is because we can bypass construction of the full models, which have up to 14 million states for this example. For the *Modulus* example, the model reductions obtained are much smaller and, as a result, PRISM is able to build and verify the model faster. However, for the *Approximate Majority* example, the minimisation approach can be applied to larger models than can be handled by PRISM. For this example, although the state spaces of the full model are manageable, the models prove poorly suited to PRISM's model construction implementation (which is based on binary decision diagram data structures).

7   Conclusions

We have presented model reduction techniques for verifying finite-horizon properties on discrete-time Markov chains. We formalised the notion of k-step finite-horizon bisimulation mininisation and clarified the subset of PCTL that it preserves. We have given both a partition-refinement algorithm and an on-the-fly approach, implemented in both a symbolic (SMT-based) and explicit-state manner as an extension of PRISM. Experimental results demonstrated that significant model reductions can be obtained in this manner, resulting in improvements in both execution time and scalability with respect to the existing efficient implementations in PRISM.

Future work in this area will involve extending the techniques to other classes of probabilistic models, and adapting the on-the-fly approaches to preserve the full time-bounded fragment of PCTL, including nested formulae.

Acknowledgements. This work has been supported by the EU-FP7-funded project HIERATIC.

References

1. Aljazzar, H., Fischer, M., Grunske, L., Kuntz, M., Leitner, F., Leue, S.: Safety analysis of an airbag system using probabilistic FMEA and probabilistic counterexamples. In: Proceedings of the QEST 2009 (2009)
2. Angluin, D., Aspnes, J., Eisenstat, D.: A simple population protocol for fast robust approximate majority. Distrib. Comput. **21**(2), 87–102 (2008)
3. Aziz, A., Singhal, V., Balarin, F., Brayton, R.K., Sangiovanni-Vincentelli, A.L.: It usually works: the temporal logic of stochastic systems. In: Wolper, P. (ed.) CAV 1995. LNCS, vol. 939, pp. 155–165. Springer, Heidelberg (1995)

4. de Moura, L., Bjørner, N.: Z3: an efficient SMT solver. In: Ramakrishnan, C.R., Rehof, J. (eds.) TACAS 2008. LNCS, vol. 4963, pp. 337–340. Springer, Heidelberg (2008)
5. De Moura, L., Bjørner, N.: Satisfiability modulo theories: introduction and applications. Commun. ACM **54**(9), 69–77 (2011)
6. Dehnert, C., Katoen, J.-P., Parker, D.: SMT-based bisimulation minimisation of Markov models. In: Giacobazzi, R., Berdine, J., Mastroeni, I. (eds.) VMCAI 2013. LNCS, vol. 7737, pp. 28–47. Springer, Heidelberg (2013)
7. Della Penna, G., Intrigila, B., Melatti, I., Tronci, E., Zilli, M.V.: Finite horizon analysis of Markov chains with the murϕ verifier. STTT **8**(4–5), 397–409 (2006)
8. Derisavi, S.: Signature-based symbolic algorithm for optimal Markov chain lumping. In: Proceedings of the QEST 2007, pp. 141–150. IEEE Computer Society (2007)
9. Derisavi, S., Hermanns, H., Sanders, W.H.: Optimal state-space lumping in Markov chains. Inf. Process. Lett. **87**(6), 309–315 (2003)
10. Hansson, H., Jonsson, B.: A logic for reasoning about time and reliability. FAC **6**(5), 512–535 (1994)
11. Heath, J., Kwiatkowska, M., Norman, G., Parker, D., Tymchyshyn, O.: Probabilistic model checking of complex biological pathways. In: Priami, C. (ed.) CMSB 2006. LNCS (LNBI), vol. 4210, pp. 32–47. Springer, Heidelberg (2006)
12. Katoen, J.-P., Kemna, T., Zapreev, I., Jansen, D.N.: Bisimulation minimisation mostly speeds up probabilistic model checking. In: Grumberg, O., Huth, M. (eds.) TACAS 2007. LNCS, vol. 4424, pp. 87–101. Springer, Heidelberg (2007)
13. Katoen, J.P., Zapreev, I.S., Hahn, E.M., Hermanns, H., Jansen, D.N.: The ins and outs of the probabilistic model checker MRMC. Perform. Eval. **68**(2), 90–104 (2011)
14. Kemeny, J., Snell, J., Knapp, A.: Denumerable Markov Chains, 2nd edn. Springer, Heidelberg (1976)
15. Kwiatkowska, M., Norman, G., Parker, D.: PRISM 4.0: verification of probabilistic real-time systems. In: Gopalakrishnan, G., Qadeer, S. (eds.) CAV 2011. LNCS, vol. 6806, pp. 585–591. Springer, Heidelberg (2011)
16. Kwiatkowska, M., Norman, G., Sproston, J., Wang, F.: Symbolic model checking for probabilistic timed automata. Inf. Comput. **205**(7), 1027–1077 (2007)
17. Kwiatkowska, M., Norman, G., Parker, D.: The PRISM benchmark suite. In: Proceedings of the QEST 2012, pp. 203–204 (2012)
18. Larsen, K.G., Skou, A.: Bisimulation through probabilistic testing. Inf. Comput. **94**(1), 1–28 (1991)
19. Paige, R., Tarjan, R.E.: Three partition refinement algorithms. SIAM J. Comput. **16**(6), 973–989 (1987)
20. Valmari, A., Franceschinis, G.: Simple $O(m \log n)$ time Markov chain lumping. In: Esparza, J., Majumdar, R. (eds.) TACAS 2010. LNCS, vol. 6015, pp. 38–52. Springer, Heidelberg (2010)
21. Vose, M.: The Simple Genetic Algorithm: Foundations and Theory. MIT Press, Cambridge (1999)
22. Wimmer, R., Becker, B.: Correctness issues of symbolic bisimulation computation for Markov chains. In: MüllerClostermann, B., Echtle, K., Rathgeb, E.P. (eds.) MMB & DFT 2010. LNCS, vol. 5987, pp. 287–301. Springer, Heidelberg (2010)
23. http://www.prismmodelchecker.org/doc/semantics.pdf
24. http://www.prismmodelchecker.org/files/spin16fh

Schedulability Analysis of Distributed Real-Time Sensor Network Applications Using Actor-Based Model Checking

Ehsan Khamespanah[1,2]([⊠]), Kirill Mechitov[3], Marjan Sirjani[2], and Gul Agha[3]

[1] School of ECE, University of Tehran, Tehran, Iran
e.khamespanah@ut.ac.ir
[2] School of Computer Science and CRESS,Reykjavik University, Reykjavik, Iceland
[3] OSL, University of Illinois at Urbana-Champaign, Champaign, USA

Abstract. Programmers often use informal worst-case analysis and debugging to ensure schedules that satisfy real-time requirements. Not only can this process be tedious and error-prone, it is inherently conservative and thus likely to lead to an inefficient use of resources. We propose to use model checking to find a schedule which optimizes the use of resources while satisfying real-time requirements. Specifically, we represent a *Wireless sensor and actuator network* (WSAN) as a collection of *actors* whose behavior is specified using a C-based actor language extended with operators for real-time scheduling and delay representation. We show how the abstraction and compositionality properties of the actor model may be used to incrementally build a model of a WSAN's behavior from node-level and network models. We demonstrate the approach with a case study of a distributed real-time data acquisition system for high frequency sensing using Timed Rebeca modeling language and the Afra model checking tool.

Keywords: Sensor network · Schedulability analysis · Actor · Timed Rebeca · Model checking

1 Introduction

Wireless sensor and actuator networks (WSANs) can provide low-cost continuous monitoring. However, building WSAN applications is particularly challenging. Because of the complexity of concurrent and distributed programming, networking, real-time requirements, and power constraints, it can be hard to find a configuration that satisfies these constraints while optimizing resource use. A common approach to address this problem is to perform an informal analysis based on conservative worst-case assumptions and empirical measurements. This can lead to schedules that do not utilize resources efficiently. For example, a workload consisting of two periodic tasks would be guaranteed to be safe only if the sum of the two worst-case execution times (WCET) were less

© Springer International Publishing Switzerland 2016
D. Bošnački and A. Wijs (Eds.): SPIN 2016, LNCS 9641, pp. 165–181, 2016.
DOI: 10.1007/978-3-319-32582-8_11

than the shorter period, whereas it is possible in practice to have many safe schedules violating this restriction.

A second approach is trial and error. For example, in [18], an empirical test-and-measure approach based on binary search is used to find configuration parameters: worst-case task runtimes, timeslot length of the communication protocols, etc. Trial and error is a laborious process, which nevertheless fails to provide any safety guarantees for the resulting configuration.

A third possibility is to extend scheduling techniques that have been developed for real-time systems [19] so that they can be used in WSAN environments. Unfortunately, this turns out to be difficult in practice. Many WSAN platforms rely on highly efficient event-driven operating systems such as TinyOS [12]. Unlike a real-time operating system (RTOS), event-driven operating systems generally do not provide real-time scheduling guarantees, priority-based scheduling, or resource reservation functionality. Without such support, many schedulability analysis techniques cannot be effectively employed. For example, in the absence of task preemption and priority-based scheduling, unnecessarily conservative assumptions must be used to guarantee correctness in the general case.

We propose an actor-based modeling approach that allows WSAN application programmers to assess the performance and functional behavior of their code throughout the design and implementation phases. The developed models are analyzed using model checking to determine the parameter values resulting in the highest system efficiency. Note that our use of model checking is similar to the work of Jorgerden et al. who use it to maximize the life-time of batteries in embedded systems [14].

We represent a WSAN application as a collection of *actors* [2]. The model can be incrementally extended and refined during the application design process, adding new interactions and scheduling constraints. We use Timed Rebeca [25] as the modeling language and its model checking tool Afra [1,15] for analysis of WSAN applications. Timed Rebeca is a high-level actor-based language capable of representing functionality and timing behavior at an abstract level. Afra supports modeling and analysis of both of Rebeca and Timed Rebeca models; we use the timed model checking engine. Afra uses the concept of Floating Time Transition System (FTTS) [15] for the analysis of Timed Rebeca models. FTTS significantly reduces the state space that needs to be searched. The idea is to focus on event-based properties while relaxing the constraint requiring the generation of states where all the actors are synchronized. As the examples in [16] suggest, this approach can reduce the size of the state space by 50 to 90 %. Using FTTS fits with the computation model of WSAN applications and the properties that we are interested in.

We present a case study involving real-time continuous data acquisition for structural health monitoring and control (SHMC) of civil infrastructure [18]. This system has been implemented on the Imote2 wireless sensor platform, and used in several long-term development of several highway and railroad bridges [29]. SHMC application development has proven to be particularly challenging: it has the complexity of a large-scale distributed system with real-time requirements, while having the resource limitations of low-power embedded

WSAN platforms. Ensuring safe execution requires modeling the interactions between the CPU, sensor and radio within each node, as well as interactions among the nodes. Moreover, the application tasks are not isolated from other aspects of the system: they execute alongside tasks belonging to other applications, middleware services, and operating system components. In the application we consider, all periodic tasks (sample acquisition, data processing, and radio packet transmission) are required to complete before the next iteration starts. Our results show that a guaranteed-safe application configuration can be found using the Afra model checking tool. Moreover, this configuration improves resource utilization compared to the previous informal schedulability analysis used in [18], supporting a higher sampling rate or a larger number of nodes without violating schedulability constraints.

Contributions. This paper makes the following contributions:

- We show how a WSAN application may be modeled naturally as a system of actors. The abstraction and modularity of the actor model makes the approach scalable.
- We present a real-world case study that illustrates the effectiveness of our approach for a real WSAN application.
- We show how model checking toolsets can be used for an efficient schedulability analysis of WSAN application. Our case study shows we can compare the effects of different communication protocols on system performance.

2   Preliminaries

A WSAN application is a distributed system with multiple sensor nodes, each comprised of the independent concurrent entities: CPU, sensor, radio system, and bridged together via a wireless communication device which uses a transmission control protocol. Interactions between these components, both within a node and across nodes, are concurrent and asynchronous. Moreover, WSAN applications are sensitive to timing, with soft deadlines at each step of the process needed to ensure correct and efficient operation.

Due to performance requirements, and latencies of operations on sensor nodes, sensing, data processing, and communication processes must be coordinated. In particular, once a sample is acquired from a sensor, its corresponding radio transmission activities must be performed. Concurrently, data processing tasks–such as compensating sensor data for the effects of temperature changes– must be executed. Moreover, the timing of radio transmissions from different nodes must be coordinated using a communication protocol.

2.1   The Actor Model of WSAN Applications

The Actor model is a well-established paradigm for modeling distributed and asynchronous component-based systems. This model was originally introduced by Hewitt as an agent-based language where goal directed agents did logical reasoning [11]. Subsequently, the actor model developed as a model of concurrent computation for open distributed systems where *actors* are the concurrently executing entities [2]. One way to think of actors is as a service oriented framework: each actor provides services that may be requested via messages from other actors. A message is buffered until the provider is ready to execute the message. As a result of processing a message, an actor may send messages to other actors, and to itself. Extensions of the actor model have been used for real-time systems, in particular: RT-synchronizer [24], real-time Creol [6], and Timed Rebeca [25].

The characteristics of real-time variants of the actor model make them useful for modeling WSAN applications: many concurrent processes and interdependent real-time deadlines. Observe that common tasks such as sample acquisition, sample processing, and radio transmission are periodic and have well-known or easily measurable periods. This makes analysis of worst-case execution times feasible. However, because of the event-triggered nature of applications, initial offsets between the tasks are variable.

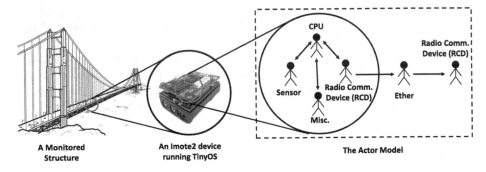

A Monitored Structure   An Imote2 device running TinyOS   The Actor Model

Fig. 1. Modeling the behavior of a WSAN application in its real-world installation in the actor model

We represent components of each WSAN node capable of independent action as an actor. Specifically, as shown in Fig. 1, a sensor node is modeled using four actors: `Sensor` (for the data acquisition) `CPU` (processor), `RCD` (a radio communication device) and `Misc` (carrying out miscellaneous tasks unrelated to sensing or communication). `Sensor` collects data and send it to `CPU` for further data processing. Meanwhile, `CPU` may respond to messages from `Misc` by carrying out other computations. The processed data is sent to `RCD` to forward it to a data collector node actor. We model the communication medium as an actor (`Ether`) and the receiver node also by the actor `RCD`. Using the actor `Ether` facilitates modularity: specifically, implementation of the Media Access Control (MAC) level details of communication protocols is localized, making it is easy to replace component sub-models for modeling different communication protocols without significantly impacting the remainder of the model. During the application design phase, different components, services, and protocols may be considered. For example, TDMA [8] as a MAC-level communication protocol may be replaced by B-MAC [23] with minimal changes.

Although schedulability analysis of WSAN applications can be challenging in the absence of a real-time scheduler, we reduce the problem of checking for deadline violations to the problem of reachability from a relatively small set of possible initial configurations. Model checking is the natural approach to this class of problems, and it is the approach we explore in this paper.

2.2 Timed Rebeca and the Model Checking Toolset

A Timed Rebeca (TR) model consists of reactive classes and a main program which instantiates actors (called *rebecs* in TR). As usual, actors have an encapsulated state, a local time, and their own thread of control. Each actor contains a set of state variables, methods and a set of actors it knows. An actor may only send messages to actor that it knows. Message passing is implemented by method calls: calling a method of an actor (target) results·in sending a message to the target. Each actor has a message bag in which arriving messages may be buffered; the maximum capacity of the bag is defined by the modeler.

Timing behavior in TR is represented using three timing primitives: `delay`, `after`, and `deadline`. A `delay` term models the passing of time for an actor. The primitives `after` and `deadline` can be used in conjunction with a message send: `after` n indicates it takes n time units for the message to be delivered to its receiver; `deadline` n indicates that if the message is not taken in n time units, it should be purged from the receiver's bag.

Afra 1.0 supports model checking of Rebeca models against LTL and CTL properties. Afra 2.0 supports deadlock detection and schedulability analysis of TR models; we use Afra 2.0 in this work. TR and Afra toolset have previously been used to model and analyze realtime actor based models such as routing algorithms and scheduling policies in NoC (Network on Chip) designs [26,27].

3 Schedulability Analysis of a Stand-Alone Node

We now illustrate our approach using a node-level TR model of a WSAN application to check for possible deadline violations. Specifically, by changing the timing parameters of our model, we find the maximum safe sampling rate in the presence of other (miscellaneous) tasks in the node. Then, we show how the specification of a node-level model can be naturally extended to network-wide specifications.

Following the mapping in Fig. 1, the TR model for the four different *reactive classes* in Fig. 2 through Fig. 4.

As shown in Fig. 2, the maximum capacity of the message bag of `Sensor` is set to 10, the only actor `Sensor` knows about is of type `CPU` (line 4), and `Sensor` does not have any state variables (line 5). The behavior of `Sensor` is to periodically acquire data and send it to `CPU`. `Sensor` is implemented using a message server `sensorLoop` (lines 13–17) which sends the acquired data to `CPU` (line 15). The sent data must be serviced before the start time of the next period, specified by the value of `period` as the parameter of `deadline`. Recall that there is a

```
 1 env int samplingRate = 25; // Hz
 2
 3 reactiveclass Sensor(10) {
 4   knownrebecs { CPU cpu; }
 5   statevars { }
 6
 7   Sensor() {
 8     self.sensorFirst();
 9   }
10   msgsrv sensorFirst() {
11     self.sensorLoop() after(?(10, 20, 30)); // ms
12   }
13   msgsrv sensorLoop() {
14     int period = 1000 / samplingRate;
15     cpu.sensorEvent() deadline(period);
16     self.sensorLoop() after(period);
17   }
18 }
```

Fig. 2. Reactive class of the Sensor

```
 1 env int sensorTaskDelay = 2; // ms
 2 env int miscTaskDelay = 10; // ms
 3 env int bufferSize = 3; // samples
 4
 5 reactiveclass CPU(10) {
 6   knownrebecs { RCD senderDevice, receiverDevice; }
 7   statevars { int collectedSamplesCounter; }
 8
 9   CPU() { collectedSamplesCounter = 0; }
10
11   msgsrv miscEvent() {
12     delay(miscTaskDelay);
13   }
14   msgsrv sensorEvent() {
15     delay(sensorTaskDelay);
16     collectedSamplesCounter += 1;
17     if (collectedSamplesCounter == bufferSize) {
18       senderDevice.send(receiverDevice, 1);
19       collectedSamplesCounter = 0;
20     }
21   }
22 }
```

Fig. 3. Reactive class of the CPU

nondeterministic initial offset after which the data acquisition becomes a periodic task. To represent this property, Sensor which sends a sendLoop message to itself; the message is nondeterministically delivered after one of 10, 20, and 30 (line 11). After this random offset, a sensor's periodic behavior is initiated (line 13). Note that in line 1, the sampling rate is defined as a constant. A similar approach is used in the implementation of the Misc reactive class.

The behavior of CPU as the target of Sensor and Misc events is more complicated (Fig. 3). Upon receiving a miscEvent, CPU waits for miscTaskDelay units of time; this represents computation cycles consumed by miscellaneous tasks. Similarly, after receiving the sensorEvent message from Sensor, CPU waits for sensorTaskDelay units of time; this represents cycles required for intra-node data processing. Data must be packed in a packet of a specified bufferSize. The number of collected samples + 1 is computed (line 16) and when the threshold is reached (line 17), CPU asks senderDevice, to send the collected data in one packet (line 18). As this is a node-level model, communication between nodes is omitted. The behavior of RCD is limited to waiting for some amount of time (line 6); this represents the sending time of a packet.

```
1  env int OnePacketTransmissionTime = 7; // ms
2
3  reactiveclass RCD (2) {
4    RCD() { }
5    msgsrv send(RCD receiverDevice, byte numberOfPackets) {
6      delay(OnePacketTransmissionTime);
7    }
8  }
```

Fig. 4. The node-level implementation of RCD

Note that computation times (delay's) depend on the low-level aspects of the system and are application-independent; they can be measured before the application design. For schedulability analysis, we set the deadline for messages in a way that any scheduling violations are caught by the model checker.

4 Schedulability Analysis of Multi-node Model with a Distributed Communication Protocol

Transitioning from a stand-alone node model a network model requires that the wireless communication medium Ether to be specified in order to model the communication protocol it supports. Then both the node-level and multi-node models must be considered. Recall that nodes in the multi-node model periodically send their data to an aggregator node (Fig. 1). The sending process is controlled by a wireless network communication protocol. The reactive class of Ether (Fig. 5) has three message servers: these are responsible for sending the status of the medium, broadcasting data, and resetting the condition of the medium after a successful transmission. Broadcasting data takes place by sending data to a RCD which is addressed by the receiverDevice variable. So, we can easily examine the status of the Ether using the value of receiverDevice (i.e., medium is free if receiverDevice is not null, line 13). This way, after sending data, the value of receiverDevice and senderDevice must be set to null to show that the transmission is completed (lines 28 and 29). Data broadcasting is the main behavior of Ether (lines 15 to 26). Before the start of broadcasting, the Ether status is checked (line 16) and data-collision error is raised in case of two simultaneous broadcasts (line 24). With a successful data broadcast, Ether sends an acknowledgment to itself (line 19) and the sender (line 20), and informs the receiver of the number of packets sent to it (line 21). In addition to the functional requirements of Ether, there may be non-functional requirements. For example, the Imote2 radio offers a theoretical maximum transfer speed of 250 kbps. When considering only the useful data payload (goodput), this is reduced to about 125 kbps.

We now extend RCD to support communication protocols. Figure 6 shows the model of TDMA protocol implementation. TDMA protocol defines a cycle, over which each node in the network has one or more chances to transmit a packet or a series of packets. If a node has data available to transmit during its alloted time slot, it may be sent immediately. Otherwise, packet sending is delayed until its next transmission slot. The periodic behavior of TDMA slot is handled by handleTDMASlot message server which sets and unsets inActivePeriod to show that whether the node is in its alloted time slot. Upon entering into it's slot, a device checks for pending data to send (line 31) and schedules handleTDMASlot message to leave the slot (line 30). On the other hand, when CPU sends a packet (message) to a RCD, the message is added to the other pending packets which are waiting for the next alloted time slot. tdmaSlotSize is the predefined size of the tdma slots, and currentMessageWaitingTime is the waiting time of this message in the bag of its receiver.

For the sake of simplicity, the details of RCD are omitted in Fig. 6. The complete source code (which implements the B-MAC protocol) is available on the Rebeca web page [1].

Once a complete model of the distributed application has been created, the Afra model checking tool can verify whether the schedulability properties hold in all reachable states of the system. If there are any deadline violations, a counterexample will be produced, indicating the path—sequence of states from an initial configuration—that results in the violation. This information can be helpful with changing the system parameters, such as increasing the TDMA time slot length, to prevent such situations.

5   Experimental Results and a Real-World Case Study

We examined the applicability of our approach using a WSAN model intended for use in structural health monitoring and control (SHMC) applications[1].

---

[1] The TR code of this case study, some complimentary shell scripts, the model checking toolset, and the details of the specifications of the state spaces in different configurations are accessible from the Rebeca homepage [1].

```
1  env int OnePacketTT = 7; // ms (transmission time)
2
3  reactiveclass Ether(5) {
4    statevars {
5      RCD senderDevice, receiverDevice;
6    }
7
8    Ether() {
9      senderDevice = null;
10     receiverDevice = null;
11   }
12   msgsrv getStatus() {
13     ((RCD)sender).receiveStatus(receiverDevice != null);
14   }
15   msgsrv broadcast(RCD receiver, int packetsNumber) {
16     if(senderDevice == null) {
17       senderDevice = (RCD)sender;
18       receiverDevice = receiver;
19       self.broadcastingIsCompleted() after(packetsNumber * OnePacketTT);
20       ((RCD)sender).receiveResult(true) after(packetsNumber * OnePacketTT);
21       receiver.receiveData(receiver, packetsNumber);
22     } else {
23       ((RCD)sender).receiveResult(false);
24     }
25   }
26   msgsrv broadcastingIsCompleted() {
27     senderDevice = null;
28     receiverDevice = null;
29   }
30 }
```

Fig. 5. Reactive class of the `Ether`

Wireless sensors deployed on civil structures for SHMC collect high-fidelity data such as acceleration and strain. Structural health monitoring (SHM) involves identifying and detecting potential damages to the structure by measuring changes in strain and vibration response. SHM can also be employed with *structural control*, where it is fed into algorithms that control centralized or distributed control elements such as active and semi-active dampers. The control algorithms attempt to minimize vibration and maintain stability in response to excitations from rare events such as earthquakes, or more mundane sources such as wind and traffic. The system we examine has been implemented on the Imote2 wireless sensor platform [18], which features a powerful embedded processor, sufficient memory size, and a high-fidelity sensor suite required to collect data of sufficient quality for SHMC purposes. These nodes run the TinyOS operating system, supported by middleware services of the Illinois SHM Services Toolsuite [13].

This flexible data acquisition system can be configured to support real-time collection of high-frequency, multi-channel sensor data from up to 30 wireless smart sensors at frequencies up to 250 Hz. As it is designed for high-throughput

```
1 env int OnePacketTT = 7; ms (transmission time)
2
3 reactiveclass RCD (3) {
4
5   knownrebecs { Ether ether; }
6
7   statevars {
8     byte id;
9     int slotSize;
10    boolean inActivePeriod;
11
12    int sendingPacketsNumber;
13    RCD receiverDevice;
14    boolean busyWithSending;
15  }
16
17  RCD(byte myId) {
18    id = myId;
19    inActivePeriod = false;
20    busyWithSending = false;
21    sendingPacketsNumber = 0;
22    receiverDevice = null;
23
24    if (id != 0) { handleTDMASlot(); }
25  }
26  msgsrv handleTDMASlot() {
27    inActivePeriod = !inActivePeriod;
28    if(inActivePeriod) {
29        assertion(tmdaSlotSize - currentMessageWaitingTime > 0);
30        self.handleTDMASlot() after(tmdaSlotSize -
               currentMessageWaitingTime);
31        self.checkPendingData();
32    } else {
33        self.handleTDMASlot() after((tmdaSlotSize * (numberOfNodes - 1))-
               currentMessageWaitingTime);
34    }
35  }
36
37  msgsrv send(RCD receiver, int packetsNumber) {
38    assertion(receiverDevice == null);
39    sendingPacketsNumber = packetsNumber;
40    receiverDevice = receiver;
41    self.checkPendingData();
42  }
43  msgsrv checkPendingData() { ... }
44
45  msgsrv receiveResult(boolean result) { ... }
46 }
```

Fig. 6. Reactive class of the RCD

sensing tasks that necessitate larger networks sizes with relatively high sampling rates, it falls into the class of *data-intensive sensor network applications*, where efficient resource utilization is critical, since it directly determines the achievable scalability (number of nodes) and fidelity (sampling frequency) of the data acquisition process. Configured on the basis of network size, associated sampling rate, and desired data delivery reliability, it allows for near-real-time acquisition of 108 data channels on up to 30 nodes—where each node may provide multiple sensor channels, such as 3-axis acceleration, temperature, or strain—with minimal data loss. In practice, these limits are determined primarily by the available bandwidth of the IEEE 802.15.4 wireless network and sample acquisition latency of the sensors. The accuracy of estimating safe limits for sampling and data transmission delays directly impacts the system's efficiency.

To illustrate the applicability of this work, we considered applications where achieving the highest possible sampling rate that does not result in any missed deadline is desired. This is a very common requirement in WSAN applications in the SHMC domain in particular. We begin by setting the value of `OnePacketTT` to 7 ms (i.e., the maximum transmission time of this type of applications) and fixed the value of `sensorTaskDelay`, `miscPeriod`, and `miscTaskDelay` to some predefined values. In addition to the sampling rate, the number of nodes in the network and the packet size remain variable. By assuming different values for the number of nodes and the packet size, different maximum sampling rates are achieved, shown as a 3D surface in Fig. 7. As shown in the figure, higher sampling rates are possible when the buffer size is set to a larger number (there is more space for data in each packet). Similarly, increasing the number of nodes decreases the sampling rate: in competition among three different parameters of Fig. 7, the cases with the maximum buffer size (i.e., 9 data points) and minimum number of nodes (i.e., 1 node) results in the highest possible maximum sampling rates. Decreasing the buffer size or increasing the number of nodes, non-linearly reduces the maximum possible sampling rate.

A server with Intel Xeon E5645 @ 2.40 GHz CPUs and 50 GB of RAM, running Red Hat 4.4.6-4 as the operating system was used as the model-checking host. We varied the size of the state space from < 500 to >140 K states, resulting in model checking times ranging from 0 to 6 s. Analyzing the specifications of the state spaces, some relations between the size of the state spaces and the configurations of the models are observed. For example, the largest state spaces correspond to configurations where `sensorTaskDelay`, `bufferSize`, and `numberOfNodes` are set to large values.

We also wanted to compare the effect of the communication protocol and the value of `sensorTaskDelay` in the supported maximum sampling rate, considering 648 different configurations. The maximum sampling rates found for each configuration is depicted in Fig. 8; they show that increasing the value of `sensorTaskDelay` as the representor of intra-node activities, decreases the sampling rate dramatically. They also show that using B-MAC results in achieving higher sampling rates in comparison to TDMA.

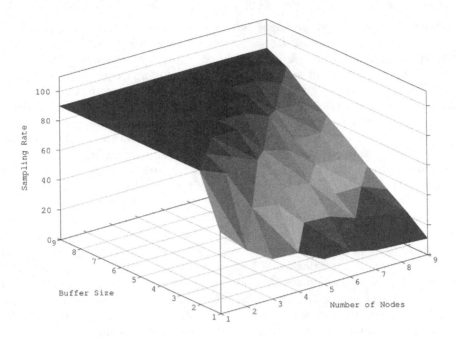

Fig. 7. The maximum sampling rate in case of using TDMA protocol and setting the value of `sensorTaskDelay` to 2 ms

The parameters used in our analysis of configurations were determined through a real-world installation of an SHMC application. Our results show that the current manually-optimized installation can be tuned to an even more optimized one: by changing the configuration, the performance of the system can be safely improved by another 7 %.

6 Related Work

Three different approaches have been used for analysis of WSANs: system simulation, analytical approach, and formal verification.

System Simulation. Simulation of WSAN applications is useful for their early design exploration. Simulation toolsets for WSANs have enabled modeling of networks [17], power consumption [28], and deployment environment [31]. Simulators can adequately estimate performance of systems and sometimes detect conditions which lead to deadline violations. But even extensive simulation does not guarantee that deadline misses will never occur in the future [5]. For WSAN applications with hard real-time requirements this is not satisfactory. Moreover, none of available simulators is suitable for the analysis WSAN application software.

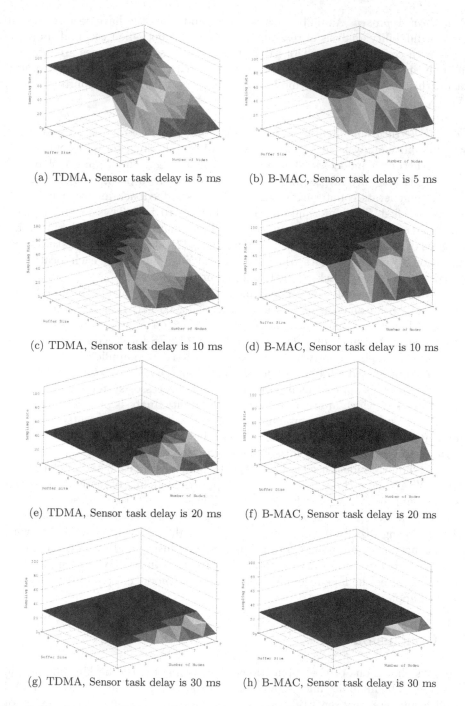

(a) TDMA, Sensor task delay is 5 ms   (b) B-MAC, Sensor task delay is 5 ms

(c) TDMA, Sensor task delay is 10 ms   (d) B-MAC, Sensor task delay is 10 ms

(e) TDMA, Sensor task delay is 20 ms   (f) B-MAC, Sensor task delay is 20 ms

(g) TDMA, Sensor task delay is 30 ms   (h) B-MAC, Sensor task delay is 30 ms

Fig. 8. Maximum possible sampling rate in case of different communication protocols, number of nodes, sensor internal task delays, and radio packet size

Analytical Approach. A number of algorithms and heuristics have been suggested for schedulability analysis of real-time systems with periodic tasks and sporadic tasks with constraints, e.g. [20]. Although these classic techniques are efficient in analyzing schedulability of real-time systems with periodic tasks and sporadic tasks, their lack of ability to model random tasks make them inappropriate for WSAN applications.

Formal Verification. Real-time model checking is an attractive approach for schedulability analysis with guarantees [5]. Model checking tools systematically check whether a model satisfies a given property [4]. The strength of model checking is not only in providing a rigorous correctness proof, but also in the ability to generate counter-examples, as diagnostic feedback in case a property is not satisfied. This information can be helpful to find flaws in the system. Norström et al. suggest an extension of timed automata to support schedulability analysis of real-time systems with random tasks [21]. Feresman et al. studied an extension of timed automata which its main idea is to associate each location of timed automata with tasks, called task automata [10].

TIMES [3] is a toolset which is implemented based on the approach of Feresman et al. [9] for analysis of task automata using UPPAAL as back-end model checker. TIMES assumes that tasks are executed on a single processor. This assumption is the main obstacle against using TIMES for schedulability analysis of WSAN applications, which are real-time distributed applications. De Boer et al. in [7] presented a framework for schedulability analysis of real-time concurrent objects. This approach supports both multi-processor systems and random task definition, which are required for schedulability analysis of WSAN applications. But asynchronous communication among concurrent elements of WSAN application results in generation of complex behavioral interfaces which lead to a state space explosion even for small size examples.

Real-Time Maude is used in [22] for performance estimation and model checking of WSAN algorithms. The approach supports modeling of many details such as communication range and energy use. The approach requires some knowledge of rewrite logic. Our tool may be easier to use by engineers unfamiliar with rewriting logic: our language extends straight-forward C-like syntax with actor concurrency constructs and primitives for sensing and radio communication. This requires no formal methods experience from the WSAN application programmer, as the language and structure of the model closely mirror those of the real application.

7   Conclusion

We have shown one of the applications of real-time model checking method in analyzing schedulability and resource utilization of WSAN applications. WSAN applications are very sensitive to their configurations: the effects of even minor modifications to configurations must be analyzed. With little additional effort required on behalf of the application developer, our approach provides a much more accurate view of an WSAN application's behavior and its interaction with the operating system and distributed middle-ware services than can be obtained by the sort of informal analysis or trial-and-error methods commonly in use today.

Our realistic—but admittedly limited—experimental results support the idea that the use of formal tools may result in more robust WSAN applications. This would greatly reduce development time as many potential problems with scheduling and resource utilization may be identified early.

An important direction for future research is the addition of probabilistic behavior analysis support to the tool. In many non-critical applications, infrequent scheduling violations may be considered a reasonable trade-off for increased efficiency in the more common cases. Development of a probabilistic extension is currently underway.

Acknowledgments. The work on this paper has been supported in part by the project "Timed Asynchronous Reactive Objects in Distributed Systems: TARO" (nr. 110020021) of the Icelandic Research Fund, by Air Force ResearchLaboratory and the Air Force Office of Scientific Research under agreement number FA8750-11-2-0084, and by National Science Foundation under grant number CCF-1438982. The U.S. Government is authorized to reproduce and distribute reprints for Governmental purposes notwithstanding any copyright notation thereon. The authors acknowledge the helpful comments by the anonymous referees and by Karl Palmskog.

References

1. Rebeca Formal Modeling Language. http://www.rebeca-lang.org/
2. Agha, G.A.: ACTORS - A Model of Concurrent Computation in Distributed Systems. MIT Press Series in Artificial Intelligence. MIT Press, Cambridge (1990)
3. Amnell, T., Fersman, E., Mokrushin, L., Pettersson, P., Yi, W.: TIMES: a tool for schedulability analysis and code generation of real-time systems. In: Larsen, K.G., Niebert, P. (eds.) FORMATS 2003. LNCS, vol. 2791, pp. 60–72. Springer, Heidelberg (2004)
4. Clarke, E.M., Grumberg, O., Peled, D.: Model Checking. MIT Press, Cambridge (1999)
5. David, A., Illum, J., Larsen, K.G., Skou, A.: Model-based framework for schedulability analysis using UPPAAL 4.1. In: Nicolescu, G., Mosterman, P.J. (eds.) Model-Based Design for Embedded Systems, pp. 93–119. CRC Press, Boca Raton (2010)
6. de Boer, F.S., Chothia, T., Jaghoori, M.M.: Modular schedulability analysis of concurrent objects in Creol. In: Arbab, F., Sirjani, M. (eds.) FSEN 2009. LNCS, vol. 5961, pp. 212–227. Springer, Heidelberg (2010)
7. de Boer, F.S., Jaghoori, M.M., Johnsen, E.B.: Dating concurrent objects: real-time modeling and schedulability analysis. In: Gastin, P., Laroussinie, F. (eds.) CONCUR 2010. LNCS, vol. 6269, pp. 1–18. Springer, Heidelberg (2010)
8. El-Hoiydi, A.: Spatial TDMA and CSMA with preamble sampling for low power ad hoc wireless sensor networks. In: Proceedings of the Seventh IEEE Symposium on Computers and Communications (ISCC 2002), 1–4 July 2002, Taormina, Italy, pp. 685–692. IEEE Computer Society (2002)

9. Fersman, E., Mokrushin, L., Pettersson, P., Yi, W.: Schedulability analysis of fixed-priority systems using timed automata. Theor. Comput. Sci. **354**(2), 301–317 (2006)
10. Fersman, E., Pettersson, P., Yi, W.: Timed automata with asynchronous processes: schedulability and decidability. In: Katoen, J.-P., Stevens, P. (eds.) TACAS 2002. LNCS, vol. 2280, pp. 67–82. Springer, Heidelberg (2002)
11. Hewitt, C., Bishop, P., Steiger, R.: A universal modular ACTOR formalism for artificial intelligence. In: Nilsson, N.J. (ed.) IJCAI, pp. 235–245. William Kaufmann (1973)
12. Hill, J., Szewczyk, R., Woo, A., Hollar, S., Culler, D., Pister, K.: System architecture directions for networked sensors. In: SIGPLAN Notices, vol. 35, pp. 93–104, November 2000
13. Illinois SHM Services Toolsuite. http://shm.cs.illinois.edu/software.html
14. Jongerden, M.R., Mereacre, A., Bohnenkamp, H.C., Haverkort, B.R., Katoen, J.-P.: Computing optimal schedules for battery usage in embedded systems. IEEE Trans. Industr. Inf. **6**(3), 276–286 (2010)
15. Khamespanah, E., Sirjani, M., Sabahi-Kaviani, Z., Khosravi, R., Izadi, M.-J.: Timed Rebeca schedulability and deadlock freedom analysis using bounded floating time transition system. Sci. Comput. Program. **98**, 184–204 (2015)
16. Khamespanah, E., Sirjani, M., Viswanathan, M., Khosravi, R.: Floating time transition system: more efficient analysis of timed actors. In: Braga, C., Ölveczky, P.C. (eds.) FACS 2015. LNCS, vol. 9539, pp. 237–255. Springer, Heidelberg (2016)
17. Levis, P., Lee, N., Welsh, M., Culler, D.E.: TOSSIM: accurate and scalable simulation of entire tinyos applications. In Akyildiz, I.F., Estrin, D., Culler, D.E., Srivastava, M.B. (eds.), Proceedings of the 1st International Conference on Embedded Networked Sensor Systems, SenSys 2003, Los Angeles, California, USA, 5–7 November 2003, pp. 126–137. ACM (2003)
18. Linderman, L., Mechitov, K., Spencer, B.F.: TinyOS-based real-time wireless data acquisition framework for structural health monitoring and control. Struct. Control Health Monit. (2012)
19. Lipari, G., Buttazzo, G.: Schedulability analysis of periodic and aperiodic tasks with resource constraints. J. Syst. Architect. **46**(4), 327–338 (2000)
20. Liu, J.W.S.: Real-Time Systems, 1st edn. Prentice Hall PTR, Upper Saddle River (2000)
21. Norström, C., Wall, A., Yi, W.: Timed automata as task models for event-driven systems. In: RTCSA, pp. 182–189. IEEE Computer Society (1999)
22. Ölveczky, P.C., Thorvaldsen, S.: Formal modeling, performance estimation, and model checking of wireless sensor network algorithms in real-time maude. Theor. Comput. Sci. **410**(2–3), 254–280 (2009)
23. Polastre, J., Hill, J.L., Culler, D.E.: Versatile low power media access for wireless sensor networks. In: Stankovic et al. [30], pp. 95–107
24. Ren, S., Agha, G.: RTsynchronizer: language support for real-time specifications in distributed systems. In: Gerber, R., Marlowe, T.J. (eds.) Workshop on Languages, Compilers and Tools for Real-Time Systems, pp. 50–59. ACM (1995)
25. Reynisson, A.H., Sirjani, M., Aceto, L., Cimini, M., Jafari, A., Ingólfsdóttir, A., Sigurdarson, S.H.: Modelling and simulation of asynchronous real-time systems using Timed Rebeca. Sci. Comput. Program. **89**, 41–68 (2014)
26. Sharifi, Z., Mohammadi, S., Sirjani, M.: Comparison of NoC routing algorithms using formal methods. In: Proceedings of PDPTA 2013 (2013, to be published)

27. Sharifi, Z., Mosaffa, M., Mohammadi, S., Sirjani, M.: Functional and performance analysis of network-on-chips using actor-based modeling and formal verification. In: ECEASST, vol. 66 (2013)

28. Shnayder, V., Hempstead, M., Chen, B.-R., Werner-Allen, G., Welsh, M.: Simulating the power consumption of large-scale sensor network applications. In: Stankovic et al. [30], pp. 188–200

29. Spencer Jr., B.F., Jo, H., Mechitov, K., Li, J., Sim, S.-H., Kim, R., Cho, S., Linderman, L., Moinzadeh, P., Giles, R., Agha, G.: Recent advances in wireless smart sensors for multi-scale monitoring and control of civil infrastructure. J. Civil Struct. Health Monit. 1–25 (2015)

30. Stankovic, J.A., Arora, A., Govindan, R. (eds.): Proceedings of the 2nd International Conference on Embedded Networked Sensor Systems, SenSys 2004, Baltimore, MD, USA, 3–5 November 2004. ACM (2004)

31. Sundresh, S., Kim, W.Y., Agha, G.: Sens: a sensor, environment and network simulator. In: Proceedings 37th Annual Simulation Symposium (ANSS-37 2004), 18–22 April 2004, Arlington, VA, USA, pp. 221–228. IEEE Computer Society (2004)

smid: A Black-Box Program Driver

Kareem Khazem[1]([✉]) and Michael Tautschnig[2]

[1] University College London, London, UK
karkhaz@karkhaz.com
[2] Queen Mary University of London, London, UK

Abstract. We aim to perform dynamic analysis at large scale and across a wide range of programs. A key problem to overcome is driving interactive programs effectively and efficiently. To address this problem, we developed SMID—an open-source tool that autonomously interacts with computer programs, based on a specification of which user interactions (key presses, mouse events) are valid. Users can define the space of valid user interactions as a state machine in the SMID language. SMID can then generate 'sensible' program runs (sequences of user interactions), which it sends to the target program. Runs can be saved and played back, facilitating the reproduction of bugs. We have used SMID to reproduce and help explain a bug in the CMUS music player. It is possible to use SMID to drive a wide variety of desktop programs, including those with a graphical, console, or even non-interactive user interface.

1 Introduction

Multiple efforts at automated *static* analysis of large software repositories exist, and have had a measurable impact on software quality. Notably, the experiment described in [9] has resulted in hundreds of bug reports, many of which have since been closed as fixed; and the Debile[1] effort has provided developers with the results of running several static analysers through a uniform interface.

We wished to have a tool with several features that would enable similar experiments to be run with *dynamic* program analyses. These features are:

Automation. We require the ability to automatically drive the user interfaces of computer programs.

Wide Applicability. We require that our tool can be used to drive a wide variety of software, regardless of the high-level user interface toolkit used.

Reproducibility. If a certain sequence of user inputs gives rise to an interesting behaviour (e.g. a crash), we require the ability to 'play back' that sequence in order to reproduce the behaviour.

Realism. We do not wish to spam target programs with random inputs, but would like to be able to exercise target programs with only those sequences of user inputs that a real user might issue.

Conciseness. On the other hand, we do not wish to define every possible use case as a set of user interaction 'scripts', but would rather have a concise definition of the desired user interactions with the target program.

---

[1] http://debile.debian.net.

© Springer International Publishing Switzerland 2016
D. Bošnački and A. Wijs (Eds.): SPIN 2016, LNCS 9641, pp. 182–188, 2016.
DOI: 10.1007/978-3-319-32582-8_12

1.1   Overview

We have implemented SMID (the *state machine interface driver*)—an open-source[2] tool that autonomously interacts with desktop computer programs, driving them with user input in the same way that a real user might. In this paper, we outline the aims and motivation of the tool in Sect. 1; describe SMID's input language in Sect. 2; and describe the tool's usage and how we used it to reproduce a bug in Sect. 3. A video demo of the tool can be viewed on YouTube[3].

With SMID, the space of valid interactions with a program is understood as a state machine—that is, a directed graph whose nodes are *states* and whose transitions are *sequences of user interactions*. A state is a point during the program's execution where a certain set of transitions are possible; these are often referred to as 'modes' in the user interaction literature [12].

Example: In a graphical web browser such as Firefox or Chromium, the main browser window, as well as each of the auxiliary windows (download window, print dialog, etc.) can be understood as states. Transitions (key presses and mouse events) may cause the state to remain the same (e.g. when pressing Ctrl+R to reload a web page), or change the state (e.g. clicking on the 'Options' menu item changes the state to the Options window). Different views in the same window may also be understood as separate states.

To use SMID, users describe such a state machine by writing a file in the SMID language. The file is parsed by the SMID tool, which outputs a single 'run' (a finite path through the state machine, from the initial to a final state). SMID then autonomously 'drives' the program by 'playing back' this run—that is, by sending the sequence of user interactions to the target program. By playing back a large number of runs, the target program can be rigorously tested.

1.2   Comparison with Existing Tools

Tools that we have explored, both in academia and in the wider software development community, fell short of one or more of the requirements listed above.

In both academia and industry, the majority of black-box driving tools are only able to interact with programs using one particular user interface toolkit (UIT). The tools Selenium [15], Mozmill [14], Watir [11] and Canoo [8] can only be used to autonomously interact with web applications. EXSYST [7] is a Java GUI automator, although its search-based technique is not limited to Java programs. A tool that does not have the single-UIT limitation is Jubula [16], which is able to drive applications using one of several web and desktop UITs.

Jubula and the web application drivers mentioned above work by executing a 'script' of user interactions, which corresponds to a single use case. To test the target program on all use cases, one must write a large number of scripts; changes in the underlying program then require updates to all affected scripts. We find this method to be fragile, and mention how SMID negates the need for redundant

---

[2] https://github.com/karkhaz/smid.

[3] https://www.youtube.com/watch?v=x45jjr5dIiY&feature=youtu.be.

specification in Sect. 3. There has been some work in academia on *automatically* determining the behaviour of the target program. Amalfitano et al. [1,2] describe techniques for determining the behaviour of Android applications and web applications, respectively. A formal approach to designing, specifying, and subsequently generating tests for graphical user interfaces is described in [3]. There has also been work to automatically understand user interface behaviour using techniques from artificial intelligence [10] or machine learning [5]. Nevertheless, these techniques have each been implemented for only a single UIT. One possibility for future work is to use the Linux Desktop Testing Project [4] (LDTP) to provide the highly semantic information that is needed for these 'behaviour-learning' tools, for a wide range of UITs and platforms.

In contrast, SMID allows the specification of the set of user interactions that are sensible for the target program using the language described in Sect. 2, without burdening the user with writing interaction 'scripts' and repeatedly specifying common interaction sequences. The fact that SMID sends events directly to the X Window System—which underlies all graphical user interface toolkits on desktop Linux and BSD operating systems—means that SMID is able to drive all interactive desktop applications, as well as console-based applications (through interaction with a terminal emulator), that run on an X-based operating system. The SMID language itself is UIT-agnostic, and we hope to use LDTP in the future in order to provide SMID users with interactions that are more semantic than raw interactions with X—for example, by specifying graphical widgets by name rather than by coordinate.

1.3   Scope and Limitations

SMID is aimed at running experiments on the large body of software supplied with a Linux distribution. Accordingly, while the language described in Sect. 2 is UIT-agnostic, our implementation of SMID targets desktop applications; we did not attempt to implement driving of touch- or voice-based user interfaces. The back-end to our tool is XDOTOOL [13], an API for sending events to an X server, but we expect that SMID can be modified to use a different back-end (like LDTP) in order to make it usable on other systems. While SMID is used to drive target programs toward error states, SMID does not implement any error detection itself; we leave application-specific error-detection to the user.

2   The SMID Language

The SMID language is used to describe a user interface as a state machine. Files written in the SMID language consist mostly of transition statements; in this section, we describe the various forms that transitions can take, as well as other features of the SMID language. The most up-to-date guide to the language is the reference manual[4] found on the SMID web site.

---

[4] http://karkhaz.com/smid/refman.html.

Figure 1 is a minimal SMID file. It shows the five kinds of statements in the SMID language: *initial* and *final* state declarations, a *transition* (containing *actions*), and *region* declarations. The states in the state machine are all states declared as the start or end state of a transition (i.e., SMID checks that there is a path from the initial state to a final state through every state)—in Fig. 1, those are nice_state and boring_state.

```
initial nice_state
final boring_state

nice_state --
   keys  [ Control+b Return ]
   text  "A random string"
   move  zork
   click (1 right)
--> boring_state

region zork = ( 30 110 50 145 )
```

Fig. 1. A minimal SMID file

The indented lines from nice_state to boring_state in Fig. 1 describe a transition. The syntax for transitions is start_states -- list of actions --> end_state. At any point during SMID's execution, SMID has a 'current state'. At each step of the program run, SMID chooses a random transition enabled at the current state; it then performs the actions of that transition, and then changes the current state to be the end state of the transition. The possible actions include keys, text and line for sending keypresses to the target program; move, move-rel, click and scroll for mouse events; as well as actions for switching windows, executing shell code, and changing the probability of following transition (SMID performs a random walk over the state machine by default). Complex user interfaces beget large numbers of similar transitions, so the SMID language includes syntactic sugar to make it possible to represent several transitions in a single statement—shown in Figs. 2 and 3. This allows us to specify large state machines using fewer statements, as noted in Sect. 3.

```
all -- keys [ q ] --> quit

foo -- keys [ q ] --> quit
bar -- keys [ q ] --> quit
baz -- keys [ q ] --> quit
```

Fig. 2. The first line is equivalent to the next three taken together, if foo, bar, baz and quit are the only states in the state machine and quit is a final state.

```
foo bar -- keys [ r ] --> stay

foo -- keys [ r ] --> foo
bar -- keys [ r ] --> bar
```

Fig. 3. The first line is equivalent to the next two taken together.

3   SMID Usage and Case Study

Given a SMID file with the syntax described in Sect. 2, one can use the SMID tool for several functions:

Visualising the State Machine. SMID can generate a diagram representing the state machine described by a SMID file. Figure 5 shows a state machine diagram generated from the SMID file in Fig. 4.

Generating a Run. SMID can output a list of user actions, called a 'run,' by accumulating the actions along a finite-length walk of the state machine.

Playing Back a Run. SMID can read a run and sends the specified interactions to the target program. Thus, given a run, SMID can autonomously interact with the target program in the same way a real user might.

```
initial new_window
final quit

all -- keys [ Control+Q ] --> quit
all -- keys [ Control+N ] --> new_window

all-except print_dialog -- keys [ Control+P ] --> print_dialog

new_window load_window --
  move url_bar
  click (1 left)
  line "URLs.txt"
  keys [ Return ]
--> load_window

load_window -- keys [ Control+S ] --> save_dialog
save_dialog -- keys [   Return  ] --> new_window
save_dialog -- keys [   Escape  ] --> load_window

region url_bar = (30 5 200 15)
```

Fig. 4. A SMID file containing several states.

In this section, we describe using SMID to pinpoint crashes in the target program.

We wrote a SMID file (available on GitHub[5]) for the CMUS[6] console music player. This file had 25 transitions, which SMID expanded into a 103-transition state machine. Hence, we find that the SMID language allows us to specify a wide range of behaviour in a concise format and with little redundancy.

We used this SMID file to reproduce a reported[7] segmentation fault. The bug report suggested that the bug was triggered when playing MP4-encoded media files. We set up a large library of audio and video containers, and a SMID specification designed to hone in on the reported bug. SMID caused CMUS to browse to one of the media files, seek to a random point in the file, and play the

---

[5] https://github.com/karkhaz/smid/blob/master/state-machines/cmus.sm.

[6] https://cmus.github.io.

[7] https://github.com/cmus/cmus/issues/204.

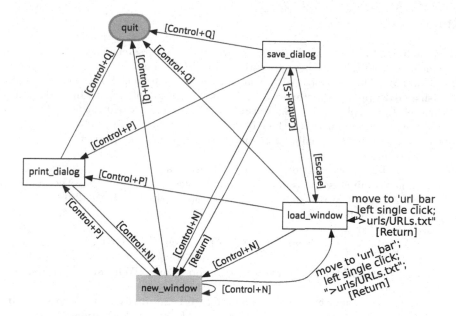

Fig. 5. State machine diagram corresponding to the SMID file in Fig. 4.

data for several seconds. Using this setup, SMID triggered the segfault in many of the several hundred runs that we ran.

By logging CMUS using the SYSTEMTAP [6] instrumentation framework while running it with SMID, we were able to discover several scenarios under which this bug was triggered, but which were not described in the original bug report. This demonstrates the utility of our approach—namely, sending a diverse range of inputs to the target program, from the space of 'sensible' user interactions.

4   Conclusions

The SMID language, described in Sect. 2, is UIT and platform agnostic. The current implementation of the SMID tool uses this fact to drive programs by sending user interactions directly to the underlying window system, rather than to a specific UIT. This means that we are able to drive the large variety of applications that can render a window under the X Window System.

Existing approaches either try to learn the state machine—tying them down to particular UITs, or drive the interface using a script—an approach which is not scaleable. The case study in Sect. 3 shows the value of our approach: by specifying all reasonable behaviours of the target program, we were able to quickly hone in on a bug without spamming the target program with unrealistic inputs.

Acknowledgements. We thank Carsten Fush and Tyler Sorensen, as well as several anonymous reviewers, for constructive feedback.

References

1. Amalfitano, D., Fasolino, A.R., Tramontana, P.: Reverse engineering finite state machines from rich internet applications. In: WCRE (2008)
2. Amalfitano, D., Fasolino, A.R., Tramontana, P., Carmine, S.D., Memon, A.M.: Using GUI ripping for automated testing of Android applications. In: ASE (2012)
3. Berstel, J., Crespi-Reghizzi, S., Roussel, G., Pietro, P.S.: A scalable formal method for design and automatic checking of user interfaces. In: ICSE (2001)
4. Chen, E., LDTP contributors: Linux desktop testing project. http://ldtp. freedesktop.org/
5. Dan, H., Harman, M., Krinke, J., Li, L., Marginean, A., Wu, F.: Pidgin crasher: searching for minimised crashing GUI event sequences. In: Goues, C., Yoo, S. (eds.) SSBSE 2014. LNCS, vol. 8636, pp. 253–258. Springer, Heidelberg (2014)
6. Eigler, F.C., Stone, D., Stone, J., Wielaard, M., SystemTap contributors: System-Tap. https://sourceware.org/systemtap/
7. Gross, F., Fraser, G., Zeller, A.: EXSYST: search-based GUI testing. In: ICSE (2012)
8. Huber, M., Schlichting, M., Canoo contributors: Canoo WebTest. http://webtest. canoo.com/
9. Kroening, D., Tautschnig, M.: Automating software analysis at large scale. In: Hliněný, P., Dvořák, Z., Jaroš, J., Kofroň, J., Kořenek, J., Matula, P., Pala, K. (eds.) MEMICS 2014. LNCS, vol. 8934, pp. 30–39. Springer, Heidelberg (2014)
10. Memon, A.M., Pollack, M.E., Soffa, M.L.: Using a goal-driven approach to generate test cases for GUIs. In: ICSE (1999)
11. Pertman, J., McHowan, H., Rodionov, A.: Watir. http://watir.com/
12. Raskin, J.: The Humane Interface: New Directions for Designing Interactive Systems. ACM Press/Addison-Wesley Publishing Co., New York, NY (2000)
13. Sissel, J.: xdotool–fake keyboard/mouse input, window management, and more. http://www.semicomplete.com/projects/xdotool/
14. Skupin, H., Hammel, J., Rogers, M., Mozmill contributors: Mozmill. https:// developer.mozilla.org/en-US/docs/Mozilla/Projects/Mozmill
15. Stewart, S., Selenium contributors: Selinium WebDriver. http://www.seleniumhq. org/projects/webdriver/
16. Tiede, M., Struckmann, S., Mueller, M., Jubula contributors: The Jubula functional testing tool. http://www.eclipse.org/jubula/

On-the-Fly Model Checking for Extended Action-Based Probabilistic Operators

Radu Mateescu[1,2]([✉]) and José Ignacio Requeno[1,2]

[1] Inria, CNRS, LIG, 38000 Grenoble, France
radu.mateescu@inria.fr
[2] University of Grenoble Alpes, LIG, 38000 Grenoble, France

Abstract. The quantitative analysis of concurrent systems requires expressive and user-friendly property languages combining temporal, data-handling, and quantitative aspects. In this paper, we aim at facilitating the quantitative analysis of systems modeled as PTSs (*Probabilistic Transition Systems*) labeled by actions containing data values and probabilities. We propose a new regular probabilistic operator that computes the probability measure of a path specified by a generalized regular formula involving arbitrary computations on data values. This operator, which subsumes the Until operators of PCTL and their action-based counterparts, can provide useful quantitative information about paths having certain (e.g., peak) cost values. We integrated the regular probabilistic operator into MCL (*Model Checking Language*) and we devised an associated on-the-fly model checking method, based on a combined local resolution of linear and Boolean equation systems. We implemented the method in the EVALUATOR model checker of the CADP toolbox and experimented it on realistic PTSs modeling concurrent systems.

1 Introduction

Concurrent systems, which are becoming ubiquitous nowadays, are complex software artifacts involving qualitative aspects (e.g., concurrent behaviour, synchronization, data communication) as well as quantitative aspects (e.g., costs, probabilities, timing information). The rigorous design of such systems based on formal methods and model checking techniques requires versatile temporal logics able to specify properties about qualitative and quantitative aspects in a uniform, user-friendly way. During the past two decades, a wealth of temporal logics dealing with one or several of these aspects were defined and equipped with analysis tools [3,8]. One of the first logics capturing behavioral, discrete-time, and probabilistic information is PCTL (*Probabilistic CTL*) [16].

In this paper, we propose a framework for specifying and checking temporal logic properties combining actions, data, probabilities, and discrete-time on PTSs (*Probabilistic Transition Systems*) [21], which are suitable models for representing value-passing concurrent systems with interleaving semantics. In PTSs, transitions between states are labeled by actions that carry, in addition to probabilistic information, also data values sent between concurrent processes during handshake communication. Our contributions are twofold.

© Springer International Publishing Switzerland 2016
D. Bošnački and A. Wijs (Eds.): SPIN 2016, LNCS 9641, pp. 189–207, 2016.
DOI: 10.1007/978-3-319-32582-8_13

Regarding the specification of properties, we propose a new regular probabilistic operator, which computes the probability measure of a path (specified as a regular formula on actions) in a PTS. Several probabilistic logics have been proposed in the action-based setting. PML (*Probabilistic Modal Logic*) [21] is a variant of HML with modalities indexed by probabilities, and was introduced as a modal characterization of probabilistic bisimulation. GPL (*Generalized Probabilistic Logic*) [9] is a probabilistic variant of the alternation-free modal μ-calculus, able to reason about execution trees, and equipped with a model checking algorithm relying on the resolution of non-linear equation systems. Compared to these logics, our probabilistic operator is a natural (action-based) extension of the Until operator of PCTL: besides paths of the form $a^*.b$ (the action-based counterpart of Until operators), we consider more general paths, specified by regular formulas similar to those of PDL (*Propositional Dynamic Logic*) [13]. To handle the data values present on PTS actions, we rely on the regular formulas with counters of MCL (*Model Checking Language*) [27], which is an extension of first-order μ-calculus with programming language constructs. Moreover, we enhance the MCL regular formulas with a generalized iteration operator parameterized by data values, thus making possible the specification of arbitrarily complex paths in a PTS.

Regarding the evaluation of regular probabilistic formulas on PTSs, we devise an on-the-fly model checking method based on translating the problem into the simultaneous local resolution of a linear equation system (LES) and a Boolean equation system (BES). For probabilistic operators containing dataless MCL regular formulas, the sizes of the LES and BES are linear (resp. exponential) w.r.t. the size of the regular formula, depending whether it is deterministic or not. In the action-based setting, the determinism of formulas is essential for a sound translation of the verification problem to a LES. For general data handling MCL regular formulas, the termination of the model checking procedure is guaranteed for a large class of formulas (e.g., counting, bounded iteration, aggregation of values, computation of costs over paths, etc.) and the sizes of the equation systems depend on the data parameters occurring in formulas. It is worth noticing that on-the-fly verification algorithms for PCTL were proposed only recently [22], all previous implementations, e.g., in PRISM [19] having focused on global algorithms. Our method provides on-the-fly verification for PCTL and its action-based variant PACTL, and also for PPDL (*Probabilistic PDL*) [18], which are subsumed by the regular probabilistic operator of MCL. We implemented the method in the EVALUATOR [27] on-the-fly model checker of the CADP toolbox [15] and experimented it on various examples of value-passing concurrent systems.

The paper is organized as follows. Section 2 defines the dataless regular probabilistic operator and Sect. 3 presents the on-the-fly model checking method. Section 4 is devoted to the data handling extensions. Section 5 briefly describes the implementation of the method within CADP and illustrates it for the quantitative analysis of mutual exclusion protocols. Finally, Sect. 6 gives concluding remarks and directions of future work.

2   Dataless Regular Probabilistic Operator

As interpretation models, we consider PTSs (*Probabilistic Transition Systems*) [21], in which transitions between states carry both action and probabilistic information. A PTS $M = \langle S, A, T, L, s^i \rangle$ comprises a set of states S, a set of actions A, a transition relation $T \subseteq S \times A \times S$, a probability labeling $L : T \to (0, 1]$, and an initial state $s^i \in S$. A transition $(s_1, a, s_2) \in T$ (also written $s_1 \xrightarrow{a} s_2$) indicates that the system can move from state s_1 to state s_2 by performing action a with probability $L(s_1, a, s_2)$. For each state $s \in S$, the probability sum $\sum_{s \xrightarrow{a} s'} L(s, a, s') = 1$.

A path $\sigma = s(= s_0) \xrightarrow{a_0} s_1 \xrightarrow{a_1} \cdots \xrightarrow{a_{n-1}} s_n \cdots$ going out of a state s is an infinite sequence of transitions in M. The i-th state and i-th action of a path σ are noted $\sigma[i]$ and $\sigma_a[i]$, respectively. An interval $\sigma[i, j]$ with $0 \leq i \leq j$ is the subsequence $\sigma[i] \xrightarrow{a_i} \cdots \xrightarrow{a_{j-1}} \sigma[j]$, which is empty if $i = j$. The suffix starting at the i-th state of a path σ is noted σ_i. The set of paths going out from s is noted $paths_M(s)$. The probability measure of a set of paths sharing a common prefix is defined as $\mu_M(\{\sigma \in paths_M(s) \mid \sigma[0, n] = s_0 \xrightarrow{a_0} \cdots \xrightarrow{a_{n-1}} s_n\}) = L(s_0, a_0, s_1) \times \cdots \times L(s_{n-1}, a_{n-1}, s_n)$.

The regular probabilistic operator that we propose computes the probability measure of paths characterized by regular formulas. For the dataless version of the operator, we use the regular formulas of PDL (*Propositional Dynamic Logic*) [13], defined over the action formulas of ACTL (*Action-based CTL*) [28]. Figure 1 shows the syntax and semantics of the operators.

Action formulas α are built over the set of actions by using standard Boolean connectors. Derived action operators can be defined as usual: true $= \neg$false, $\alpha_1 \wedge \alpha_2 = \neg(\neg\alpha_1 \vee \neg\alpha_2)$, etc. Regular formulas β are built from action formulas by using the testing (?), concatenation (.), choice (|), and transitive reflexive closure (∗) operators. Derived regular operators can be defined as usual: nil $=$ false∗ is the empty sequence operator, $\beta^+ = \beta.\beta^*$ is the transitive closure operator, etc. State formulas φ are built from Boolean connectors, the possibility modality ($\langle \ \rangle$) and the probabilistic operators ({ }$_{\geq p}$ and { }$_{>p}$) containing regular formulas. Derived state operators can be defined as usual: true $= \neg$false, $\varphi_1 \wedge \varphi_2 = \neg(\neg\varphi_1 \vee \neg\varphi_2)$, and $[\beta] \varphi = \neg\langle\beta\rangle\neg\varphi$ is the necessity modality.

Action formulas are interpreted on the set of actions A in the usual way. A path satisfies a regular formula β if it has a prefix belonging to the regular language defined by β. The testing operator specifies state formulas that must hold in the intermediate states of a path. Boolean connectors on states are defined as usual. A state s satisfies the possibility modality $\langle\beta\rangle\varphi_1$ (resp. the necessity modality $[\beta] \varphi_1$) iff some (resp. all) of the paths in $paths_M(s)$ have a prefix satisfying β and leading to a state satisfying φ_1. A state s satisfies the probabilistic operator $\{\beta\}_{\geq p}$ iff the probability measure of the paths in $paths_M(s)$ with a prefix satisfying β is greater or equal to p (and similarly for the strict version of the operator). A PTS $M = \langle S, A, T, L, s^i \rangle$ satisfies a formula φ, denoted by $M \models \varphi$, iff $s^i \models_M \varphi$ (the subscript $_M$ will be omitted when it is clear from the context).

Action formulas:
$$\alpha ::= a \qquad\qquad b \models_A a \qquad\quad \text{iff } b = a$$
$$\mid \mathsf{false} \qquad\quad b \models_A \mathsf{false} \qquad \text{iff false}$$
$$\mid \neg\alpha_1 \qquad\quad\; b \models_A \neg\alpha_1 \qquad \text{iff } b \not\models_M \alpha_1$$
$$\mid \alpha_1 \vee \alpha_2 \qquad b \models_A \alpha_1 \vee \alpha_2 \text{ iff } b \models_M \alpha_1 \text{ or } b \models_M \alpha_2$$

Regular formulas:
$$\beta ::= \alpha \qquad\qquad \sigma[i,j] \models_M \alpha \qquad \text{iff } i+1 = j \text{ and } \sigma_a[i] \models_A \alpha$$
$$\mid \varphi? \qquad\quad\; \sigma[i,j] \models_M \varphi? \qquad \text{iff } \sigma[i] \models_M \varphi$$
$$\mid \beta_1.\beta_2 \qquad \sigma[i,j] \models_M \beta_1.\beta_2 \text{ iff } \exists k \in [i,j].\sigma[i,k] \models_M \beta_1 \text{ and } \sigma[k,j] \models_M \beta_2$$
$$\mid \beta_1\mid\beta_2 \qquad \sigma[i,j] \models_M \beta_1\mid\beta_2 \text{ iff } \sigma[i,j] \models_M \beta_1 \text{ or } \sigma[i,j] \models_M \beta_2$$
$$\mid \beta_1^* \qquad\quad \sigma[i,j] \models_M \beta_1^* \qquad \text{iff } \exists k \geq 0.\sigma[i,j] \models_M \beta_1^k$$

State formulas:
$$\varphi ::= \mathsf{false} \qquad\quad s \models_M \mathsf{false} \qquad \text{iff false}$$
$$\mid \neg\varphi_1 \qquad\quad s \models_M \neg\varphi_1 \qquad \text{iff } s \not\models_M \varphi_1$$
$$\mid \varphi_1 \vee \varphi_2 \qquad s \models_M \varphi_1 \vee \varphi_2 \text{ iff } s \models_M \varphi_1 \text{ or } s \models_M \varphi_2$$
$$\mid \langle\beta\rangle\,\varphi_1 \qquad\; s \models_M \langle\beta\rangle\,\varphi_1 \text{ iff } \exists\sigma \in paths_M(s).\exists i \geq 0.$$
$$\sigma[0,i] \models_M \beta \text{ and } \sigma[i] \models_M \varphi$$
$$\mid \{\beta\}_{\geq p} \qquad\; s \models_M \{\beta\}_{\geq p} \text{ iff } \mu_M(\{\sigma \in paths_M(s) \mid \sigma \models_M \beta\}) \geq p$$
$$\mid \{\beta\}_{>p} \qquad\; s \models_M \{\beta\}_{>p} \text{ iff } \mu_M(\{\sigma \in paths_M(s) \mid \sigma \models_M \beta\}) > p$$

Fig. 1. Modal and probabilistic operators over regular paths

The operator $\{\beta\}_{\geq p}$ generalizes naturally the Until operators of classical probabilistic branching-time logics. The Until operator of PCTL [16], and probabilistic versions of the two Until operators of ACTL are expressed as follows:

$$[\varphi_1 \; \mathsf{U} \; \varphi_2]_{\geq p} = \{(\varphi_1?.\mathsf{true})^*.\varphi_2?\}_{\geq p} \qquad \begin{aligned} \left[\varphi_{1\alpha_1} \; \mathsf{U} \; \varphi_2\right]_{\geq p} &= \{(\varphi_1?.\alpha_1)^*.\varphi_2?\}_{\geq p} \\ \left[\varphi_{1\alpha_1} \; \mathsf{U}_{\alpha_2} \; \varphi_2\right]_{\geq p} &= \{(\varphi_1?.\alpha_1)^*.\varphi_2?.\alpha_2.\varphi_2?\}_{\geq p} \end{aligned}$$

In addition, regular formulas are strictly more expressive than Until operators, enabling to specify more complex paths in the PTS. For example, the formula:

$$\Psi_1 = \{send.(\mathsf{true}^*.retry)^*.recv\}_{\geq 0.9}$$

unexpressible in P(A)CTL due to the nested $*$-operators, specifies that the probability of receiving a message after zero or more retransmissions is at least 90 %.

3 Model Checking Method

We propose below a method for checking a regular probabilistic formula on a PTS on the fly, by reformulating the problem as the simultaneous resolution of a linear equation system (LES) and a Boolean equation system (BES). The method consists of five steps, each one translating the problem into an increasingly concrete intermediate formalism. The first four steps operate syntactically on formulas and their intermediate representations, whereas the fifth step makes use of semantic information contained in the PTS. A detailed formalization of the first four steps, in a state-based setting, can be found in [24]. We illustrate the method by checking the formula Ψ_1 on the PTS of a very simple communication protocol adapted from [3, Chap. 10], shown in Fig. 2(a).

1. Translation to PDL with Recursion. To evaluate an operator $\{\beta\}_{\geq p}$ on a PTS $M = \langle S, A, T, L, s^i \rangle$ on the fly, one needs to determine the set of paths going out of s^i and satisfying β, to compute the probability measure of this set, and to compare it with p. For this purpose, it is more appropriate to use an equational representation of β, namely PDLR (*PDL with recursion*), which already served for model checking PDL formulas in the non-probabilistic setting [26]. A PDLR specification is a system of fixed point equations having propositional variables $X \in \mathcal{X}$ in their left hand side and PDL formulas φ in their right hand side:

$$\{X_i = \varphi_i\}_{1 \leq i \leq n}$$

where φ_i are modal state formulas (see Fig. 1) and X_1 is the *variable of interest* corresponding to the desired property. Since formulas φ_i may be open (i.e., contain occurrences of variables X_j), their interpretation is defined w.r.t. a propositional context $\delta : \mathcal{X} \to 2^S$, which assigns state sets to all variables occurring in φ_i. The interpretation of a PDLR specification is the value of X_1 in the least fixed point $\mu\Phi$ of the functional $\Phi : (2^S)^n \to (2^S)^n$ defined by:

$$\Phi(U_1, ..., U_n) = \langle [\![\varphi_i]\!] \, \delta[U_1/X_1, ..., U_n/X_n] \rangle_{1 \leq i \leq n}$$

where $[\![\varphi_i]\!] \delta = \{s \in S \mid s \models_\delta \varphi_i\}$, and the interpretation of φ_i (see Fig. 1) is extended with the rule $s \models_\delta X = s \in \delta(X)$. The notation $\delta[U_1/X_1, ..., U_n/X_n]$ stands for the context δ in which X_i were replaced by U_i.

In the sequel, we consider PDLR specifications in *derivative normal form* (RNF), which are the modal logic counterparts of Brzozowski's (generalized) derivatives of regular expressions [5]:

$$\{X_i = \bigvee_{j=1}^{n_i} (\varphi_{ij} \wedge \langle \beta_{ij} \rangle X_{ij}) \vee \varphi_i\}_{1 \leq i \leq n}$$

where φ_{ij} and φ_i are closed state formulas. Note that, in the right hand side of equation i, the same variable $X_{ij} \in \{X_1, ..., X_n\}$ may occur several times in the first disjunct. Intuitively, a variable X_i denotes the set of states from which there exists a path with a prefix satisfying some of the regular formulas β_{ij} and whose last state satisfies X_{ij}. This is formalized using *path predicates* $P_i : \text{paths}_M \to \text{bool}$, defined by the following system of equations:

$$\{P_i(\sigma) = \bigvee_{j=1}^{n_i} \exists l_{ij} \geq 0.(\sigma[0] \models \varphi_{ij} \wedge \sigma[0, l_{ij}] \models \beta_{ij} \wedge P_{ij}(\sigma_{l_{ij}})) \vee \sigma[0] \models \varphi_i\}_{1 \leq i \leq n}$$

More precisely, $(\mu\Phi)_i = \{s \in S \mid \exists \sigma \in \text{paths}_M(s).P_i(\sigma)\}$.

The PDLR specification in RNF associated to a formula β is defined below:

$$\{X_1 = \langle \beta \rangle X_2 \qquad X_2 = \text{true}\}$$

in which the variable of interest X_1 denotes the PDL formula $\langle\beta\rangle$true, expressing the existence of a path with a prefix satisfying β and leading to some final state denoted by X_2. The corresponding path predicates are:

$$\{P_1(\sigma) = \exists l \geq 0.(\sigma[0,l] \models \beta \wedge P_2(\sigma_l)) \qquad P_2(\sigma) = \mathsf{true}\}$$

According to the interpretation of regular formulas (see Fig. 1), the path predicate $P_1(\sigma)$ holds iff $\sigma \models \beta$, and also $(\mu\Phi)_1 = \{s \in S \mid \exists\sigma \in paths_M(s).\sigma \models \beta\}$.

2. Translation to HML with Recursion. To bring the PDLR specification closer to an equation system suitable for verification, one must simplify it by removing the regular operators occurring in modalities. This yields a HMLR (*HML with recursion*) specification [20], which contains only HML modalities on action formulas. Regular operators can be eliminated by applying the following substitutions, which are valid equalities in PDL [13]:

$$\langle\varphi?\rangle X = \varphi \wedge \langle\mathsf{nil}\rangle X \qquad \langle\beta_1.\beta_2\rangle X = \langle\beta_1\rangle X' \quad \text{where } X' = \langle\beta_2\rangle X$$
$$\langle\beta_1|\beta_2\rangle X = \langle\beta_1\rangle X \vee \langle\beta_2\rangle X \qquad \langle\beta^*\rangle X = \langle\mathsf{nil}\rangle X' \quad \text{where } X' = \langle\mathsf{nil}\rangle X \vee \langle\beta\rangle X'$$

The rules for the '.' and '*' operators create new equations, necessary for maintaining the PDLR specification in RNF (the insertion of $\langle\mathsf{nil}\rangle X$ modalities, which are equivalent to X, serves the same purpose). The rule for the '|' operator creates two occurrences of the same variable X, reflecting that a same state can be reached by two different paths. These rules preserve the path predicates P_i associated to the PDLR specification, and in particular $P_1(\sigma)$, which specifies that a path σ satisfies the initial formula β.

The size of the resulting HMLR specification (number of variables and operators) is linear w.r.t. the size of β (number of operators and action formulas). Besides pure HML modalities, the HMLR specification may also contain occurrences of $\langle\mathsf{nil}\rangle X$ modalities, which will be eliminated in the next step.

3. Transformation to Guarded Form. The right hand side of an equation i of the HMLR specification may contain modalities of the form $\langle\alpha_{ij}\rangle Y_{ij}$ and $\langle\mathsf{nil}\rangle Y_{ij}$ (equivalent to Y_{ij}), which correspond to *guarded* and *unguarded* occurrences of variables Y_{ij}, respectively. To facilitate the formulation of the verification problem in terms of equation systems, it is useful to remove unguarded occurrences of variables. The general procedure for transforming arbitrary μ-calculus formulas to guarded form [17] can be specialized for HMLR specifications by applying the following actions for each equation i: (a) Remove the unguarded occurrences of X_i in the right hand side of the equation by replacing them with false, which amounts to apply the μ-calculus equality $\mu X.(X \vee \varphi) = \mu X.\varphi$. (b) Substitute all unguarded occurrences of X_i in other equations with the right hand side formula of equation i, and rearrange the right hand sides to maintain the equations in RNF. This produces a guarded HMLR specification:

$$\{X_i = \bigvee_{j=1}^{n_i}(\varphi_{ij} \wedge \langle\alpha_{ij}\rangle X_{ij}) \vee \varphi_i\}_{1 \leq i \leq n}$$

which is the exact modal logic counterpart of Brzozowski's derivatives of regular expressions [5] defined on the alphabet of action formulas. The transformation

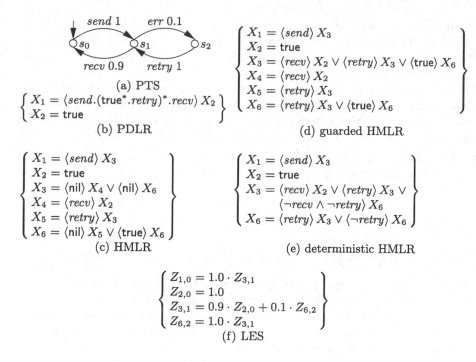

Fig. 2. Model checking formula ψ_1 on a PTS

to guarded form keeps the same number of equations in the HMLR specification, but may increase the number of operators in the right hand sides.

4. Determinization. A HMLR specification may contain, in the right hand side of an equation i, several modalities $\langle \alpha_{ij} \rangle X_{ij}$ whose action formulas are not disjoint, i.e., they can match the same action. This denotes a form of nondeterminism, meaning that the same transition $s \xrightarrow{a} s'$ can start a path σ satisfying the path predicate $P_i(\sigma)$ in several ways, corresponding to alternative suffixes of the initial regular formula β. To ensure a correct translation of the verification problem into a LES, it is necessary to determinize the HMLR specification. This can be done by applying the classical subset construction, yielding a deterministic HMLR specification defined on sets of propositional variables:

$$\{ X_I = \bigvee_{\emptyset \subset J \subseteq alt(I)} ((\bigwedge_{k \in J} \varphi_k) \wedge \langle \bigwedge_{k \in J} \alpha_k \wedge \bigwedge_{l \in alt(I) \setminus J} \neg \alpha_l \rangle X_J) \vee \bigvee_{i \in I} \varphi_i \}_{I \subseteq [1,n]}$$

where $alt(I) = \{ ij \mid i \in I \wedge j \in [1, n_i] \}$. Basically, each alternative $\varphi_{ij} \wedge \langle \alpha_{ij} \rangle X_{ij}$ in an equation $i \in I$ is combined with each alternative in the other equations having their index in I, taking care that the action formulas in the resulting modalities are mutually exclusive. As shown in [24] for a similar construction in the state-based setting, the determinization preserves the path predicate associated to the variables of interest X_1 and $X_{\{1\}}$ in the HMLR before and after determinization, i.e., $P_1(\sigma) = P_{\{1\}}(\sigma)$ for any path $\sigma \in paths_M$.

In the worst case, determinization may yield an exponential increase in the size of the HMLR specification. However, this happens on pathological examples of regular formulas, which rarely occur in practice; most of the time, the nondeterminism contained in a formula β is caused by a lack of precision regarding the iteration operators, which can be easily corrected by constraining the action formulas corresponding to iteration "exits". For example, the regular formula contained in Ψ_1 can be made deterministic by specifying precisely the retries and the fact that they must occur before receptions: $send.((\neg retry \wedge \neg recv)^*.retry)^*.recv$.

5. Translation to Linear and Boolean Equation Systems.

Consider a determinized HMLR specification in RNF corresponding to a regular formula β:

$$\{X_i = \bigvee_{j=1}^{n_i}(\varphi_{ij} \wedge \langle \alpha_{ij} \rangle X_{ij}) \vee \varphi_i\}_{1 \leq i \leq n}$$

where $\alpha_{ij} \wedge \alpha_{ik} = \mathsf{false}$ for each $i \in [1,n]$ and $j,k \in [1,n_i]$. The associated path predicates are defined as follows:

$$\{P_i(\sigma) = \bigvee_{j=1}^{n_i}(\sigma[0] \models \varphi_{ij} \wedge \sigma_a[0] \models \alpha_{ij} \wedge P_{ij}(\sigma_1)) \vee \sigma[0] \models \varphi_i\}_{1 \leq i \leq n}$$

They are related to the HMLR specification by $(\mu \Phi)_i = \{s \in S \mid \exists \sigma \in paths_M(s).P_i(\sigma)\}$, and to the initial regular formula β by $P_1(\sigma) = \sigma \models \beta$.

The last step of the model checking method reformulates the problem of verifying the determinized HMLR specification on a PTS in terms of solving a LES (*) and a BES (**) defined as follows:

$$
\begin{aligned}
Z_{i,s} = \ &\text{if } s \not\models X_i \text{ then } 0 \\
&\text{else if } s \models \varphi_i \text{ then } 1 \\
&\quad \text{else } \sum_{j=1}^{n_i} \text{if } s \not\models \varphi_{ij} \text{ then } 0 \\
&\qquad \text{else } \sum_{s \xrightarrow{a} s', a \models \alpha_{ij}} L(s,a,s') \times Z_{ij,s'}
\end{aligned}
\qquad (*)
$$

$$X_i^s = \bigvee_{j=1}^{n_i}(s \models \varphi_{ij} \wedge \bigvee_{s \xrightarrow{a} s'}(a \models \alpha_{ij} \wedge X_{ij}^{s'})) \vee s \models \varphi_i \qquad (**)$$

The LES (*) is obtained by a translation similar to the classical one defined originally for PCTL [16]. A numerical variable $Z_{i,s}$ denotes the probability measure of the paths going out of state s and satisfying the path predicate P_i. Determinization guarantees that the sum of coefficients in the right-hand side of each equation is at most 1. The BES (**) is produced by the classical translation employed for model checking modal μ-calculus formulas on LTSs [2,10]. A Boolean variable X_i^s is true iff state s satisfies the propositional variable X_i of the HMLR specification. The on-the-fly model checking consists in solving the variable Z_{1,s^i}, which denotes the probability measure of the set of paths going out of the initial state s^i of the PTS and satisfying the initial regular formula β. This is carried out using local LES and BES resolution algorithms, as will be explained in Sect. 5. The conditions $s \models X_i$ occurring in the LES (*) and the conditions $s \models \varphi_{ij}, s \models \varphi_i$ occurring in both equation systems are checked by applying the on-the-fly model checking method for solving the variable X_i^s of the BES (**) and evaluating the closed state formulas φ_{ij}, φ_i on state s.

By solving the LES obtained in Fig. 2(f), we obtain $Z_{1,0} = 1.0$, meaning that a message sent will be received (after zero or more retransmissions) with 100 % probability, and therefore the formula Ψ_1 is true on the PTS.

4   Extension with Data Handling

The regular formulas that we used so far belong to the dataless fragment [26] of MCL, which considers actions simply as names of communication channels. In practice, the analysis of value-passing concurrent systems, whose actions typically consist of channel names and data values, requires the ability to extract and manipulate these elements. For this purpose, MCL [27] provides action predicates extracting and/or matching data values, regular formulas involving data variables, and parameterized fixed point operators. The regular probabilistic operator $\{\beta\}_{\geq p}$ can be naturally extended with the data handling regular formulas of MCL, which enable to characterize complex paths in a PTS modeling a value-passing concurrent system.

To improve versatility, we extend the regular formulas of MCL with a general iteration operator "loop", which subsumes the classical regular operators with counters, and can also specify paths having a certain cost calculated from the data values carried by its actions. After briefly recalling the main data handling operators of MCL, we define below the "loop" operator, illustrate its expressiveness, and show how the on-the-fly model checking procedure previously described is generalized to deal with the data handling probabilistic operator.

4.1   Overview of Data Handling MCL Operators

In the PTSs modeling value-passing systems, actions are of the form "$C\ v_1 \ldots v_n$", where C is a channel name and $v_1, ..., v_n$ are the data values exchanged during the rendezvous on C. To handle the data contained in actions, MCL provides *action predicates* of the form "$\{C\ ...\ !e\ ?x{:}T\ \text{where}\ b\}$", where "..." is a wildcard matching zero or more data values of an action, e is an expression whose value matches the corresponding data value, x is a data variable of type T that is initialized with the corresponding data value extracted from the action, and b is an optional boolean expression (guard) typically expressing a condition on x. An action predicate may contain several clauses "$!e$" and "$?x{:}T$", all variables defined by "$?x{:}T$" clauses being visible in the guard b and also outside the action predicate. An action satisfies an action predicate if its structure is compatible with the clauses of the predicate, and the guard evaluates to true in the context of the data variables extracted from the action.

Regular formulas in MCL are built over action predicates using the classical operators shown in Sect. 2, as well as constructs inspired from sequential programming languages: conditional ("if-then-else"), counting, iteration ("for" and "loop", described in the next subsection), and definition of variables ("let"). The testing operator of PDL is expressed in MCL as $\varphi? = \text{if}\ \neg\varphi\ \text{then false end if}$.

Finally, the state formulas of MCL are built using modalities containing regular formulas, parameterized fixed point operators, quantifiers over finite domains, and programming language constructs ("if" and "let").

4.2   Generalized Iteration on Regular Formulas

The general iteration mechanism that we propose on regular formulas consists of three operators having the following syntax:

$$\beta ::= \ \text{loop} \ (x{:}T{:=}e_0) : (x'{:}T') \ \text{in} \ \beta \ \text{end loop} \ \mid \ \text{continue} \ (e) \ \mid \ \text{exit} \ (e')$$

The "loop" operator denotes a path made by concatenation of (zero or more) path fragments satisfying β, each one corresponding to an iteration of the loop with the current value of variable x. Variable x, which is visible inside β, is initialized with the value of expression e_0 at the first loop iteration and can be updated to the value of e by using the operator "continue (e)", which starts a new iteration of the loop. The loop is terminated by means of the "exit (e')" operator, which sets the return variable x', visible outside the "loop" formula, to the value of e'.

The iteration and return variables (x and x') are both optional; if they are absent, the "in" keyword is also omitted. For simplicity, we used only one variable x and x', but several variables of each kind are allowed. The arguments of the operators "continue" and "exit" invoked in the loop body β must be compatible with the declarations of iteration and return variables, respectively. Every occurrence of "continue" and "exit" refers to the immediately enclosing "loop", which enforces a specification style similar to structured programming.

For brevity, we define the semantics of the "loop" operator by translating it to plain MCL in the context of an enclosing diamond modality. The translation is parameterized by a profile $Z/x{:}T/x'{:}T'$, where x and x' are the iteration and return data variables of the immediately enclosing "loop", and Z is a propositional variable associated to it. We show below the translation of the three general iteration operators, the other regular operators being left unchanged.

$$\left(\left\langle \begin{array}{c} \text{loop} \ (x{:}T{:=}e_0) : (x'{:}T') \ \text{in} \\ \beta \\ \text{end loop} \end{array} \right\rangle \varphi \right)_{Z/x{:}T/x'{:}T'} \overset{\text{def}}{=} \mu W(x{:}T{:=}e_0).\langle (\beta)_{W/x{:}T/x'{:}T'} \rangle \varphi$$

$$(\langle \text{continue} \ (e) \rangle \varphi)_{Z/x{:}T/x'{:}T'} \overset{\text{def}}{=} Z(e)$$

$$(\langle \text{exit} \ (e') \rangle \varphi)_{Z/x{:}T/x'{:}T'} \overset{\text{def}}{=} \text{let} \ x'{:}T' := e' \ \text{in} \ \varphi \ \text{end let}$$

Basically, a possibility modality enclosing a "loop" operator is translated into a minimal fixed point operator parameterized by the iteration variable(s). The occurrences of "continue" in the body of the loop are translated into invocations of the propositional variable with the corresponding arguments, and the occurrences of "exit" are translated into "let" state formulas defining the return variables and setting them to the corresponding return values.

All iteration operators on MCL regular formulas can be expressed in terms of the "loop" operator, as shown in the table below. For simplicity, we omitted the definitions of $\beta\{e\}$ (iteration e times) and $\beta\{\dots e\}$ (iteration at most e times), which are equivalent to $\beta\{e \dots e\}$ and $\beta\{0 \dots e\}$, respectively.

Syntax	Meaning	Encoding using "loop"
β^*	≥ 0 times	loop exit | β . continue end loop
β^+	≥ 1 times	loop β . (exit | continue) end loop

$\beta\{e_1 \ldots e_2\}$	between e_1 and e_2 times	loop $(c_1$:nat $:= e_1, c_2$:nat $:= e_2 - e_1)$ in
		  if $c_1 > 0$ then β . continue $(c_1 - 1, c_2)$
		  elsif $c_2 > 0$ then exit | β . continue $(c_1, c_2 - 1)$
		  else exit end if
		end loop

for n:nat from e_1 to e_2
  step e_3 do
  β
end for
	stepwise	loop $(n$:nat $:= e_1)$ in
		  if $n < e_2$ then β . continue $(n + e_3)$
		  else exit end if
		end loop

To illustrate the semantics of general iteration, consider the formula $\langle\beta\{e\}\rangle$true stating the existence of a path made of e path fragments satisfying β. By encoding bounded iteration as a "loop" and applying the translation rules of general iteration, we obtain:

$$\langle\beta\{e\}\rangle\text{true} \ = \ \left\langle \begin{array}{l} \text{loop } (c\text{:nat} := e) \text{ in} \\ \quad \text{if } c > 0 \text{ then} \\ \qquad \beta \text{ . continue } (c-1) \\ \quad \text{else exit end if} \\ \text{end loop} \end{array} \right\rangle \text{true} \ = \ \begin{array}{l} \mu Z(c\text{:nat} := e). \\ \quad \text{if } c > 0 \text{ then } \langle\beta\rangle Z(c-1) \\ \quad \text{else} \\ \qquad \text{true} \\ \quad \text{end if} \end{array}$$

The bounded iteration operators $\beta\{e\}$, $\beta\{\ldots e\}$, and $\beta\{e_1 \ldots e_2\}$ are natural means for counting actions (ticks), and hence describing discrete-time properties. The full Until operator of PCTL, and its action-based counterparts derived from ACTL, can be expressed as follows ($t \geq 0$ is the number of ticks until φ_2):

$$[\varphi_1 \ \mathsf{U} \ \varphi_2]_{\geq p}^{\leq t} = \{(\varphi_1?.\text{true})\{0 \ldots t\}.\varphi_2?\}_{\geq p}$$
$$[\varphi_{1_{\alpha_1}} \ \mathsf{U} \ \varphi_2]_{\geq p}^{\leq t} = \{(\varphi_1?.\alpha_1)\{0 \ldots t\}.\varphi_2?\}_{\geq p}$$
$$[\varphi_{1_{\alpha_1}} \ \mathsf{U}_{\alpha_2} \ \varphi_2]_{\geq p}^{\leq t} = \{(\varphi_1?.\alpha_1)\{0 \ldots t\}.\varphi_1?.\alpha_2.\varphi_2?\}_{\geq p}$$

Besides counting, the general iteration operators are able to characterize complex paths in a PTS, by collecting the data values (costs) present on actions and using them in arbitrary computations (see the examples in Sect. 5).

4.3   Model Checking Method with Data Handling

The on-the-fly model checking method shown in Sect. 3 can be generalized to deal with the data handling constructs of MCL by adding data parameters to the various equation systems used as intermediate forms. We illustrate the complete method by checking the formula Ψ_2 on the PTS shown on Fig. 2:

$$\Psi_2 = \{ \ send.((\neg retry \wedge \neg recv)^*.retry)\{\ldots n\}.recv \ \}_{\geq 0.9}$$

Formula Ψ_2, which is a determinized data-based variant of Ψ_1, specifies that the probability of receiving a message after at most n retransmissions (where n is a parameter to be instantiated) is at least 90 %.

The various translation phases are illustrated on Fig. 3. The translation rules for standard regular operators given in Sect. 3 are applied for eliminating the "." operators in the PDLR specification (Fig. 3(c)). Then, the iteration at most n times is translated into a "loop" operator (Fig. 3(d)), and the corresponding modality is further refined using the semantics of "loop" defined in Sect. 4.2, yielding a HMLR specification parameterized by a counter (Fig. 3(e)). After bringing this specification to guarded form (Fig. 3(f)), a parameterized LES is produced (Fig. 3(g)) by the translation scheme given in Sect. 3, extended to handle data parameters. For instance, variable $Z_{5,1}(v)$ in the LES denotes the probability measure of the paths starting from state s_1 and satisfying the path predicate denoted by X_5 with the parameter c set to value v.

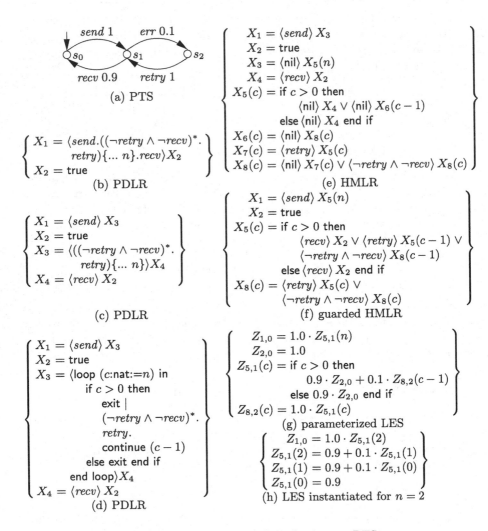

Fig. 3. Model checking formula ψ_2 on a PTS

Finally, a plain LES is generated (Fig. 3(h)) by instantiating $n = 2$ in the parameterized LES. Note that the guarded HMLR specification was already deterministic (since the regular formula in Ψ_2 was determinized), and hence the LES has a unique solution. By solving this LES (e.g., using substitution), we obtain $Z_{1,0} = 0.999$, which is the probability measure of the paths starting from the initial state s_0 of the PTS and satisfying the regular formula specified in Ψ_2. In other words, $n = 2$ retransmissions ensure that a message is received with 99.9% probability.

Termination. The presence of data parameters (with infinite domains) implies that the whole model checking procedure relies on the termination of the instantiation phase, which must create a finite LES solvable using numerical methods. This is in general undecidable, similarly to the termination of term rewriting [11]. Such situations happen for "pathological" formulas, which carry on divergent computations on data unrelated to the data values contained in the PTS actions. For example, the modality $\langle \mathsf{loop}\ (k{:}\mathsf{nat}{:}{=}0)\ \mathsf{in}\ a\ .\ \mathsf{continue}\ (k+1)\ \mathsf{end}\ \mathsf{loop}\rangle\mathsf{true}$ will not converge on the PTS consisting of a single loop $s \xrightarrow{a} s$, since it will entail the construction of an infinite LES $\{Z_s(0) = Z_s(1), Z_s(1) = Z_s(2), ...\}$. However, the model checking procedure terminates for most practical cases of data handling regular formulas (counting, accumulating or aggregating values, computing costs over paths).

5   Tool Support and Use

In this section, we show how the on-the-fly model checking method for the regular probabilistic operator works in practice. After briefly presenting the implementation of the method within the CADP toolbox [15], we illustrate its application for the quantitative analysis of shared-memory mutual exclusion protocols.

5.1   Implementation

We extended MCL with the general iteration operator "loop" on regular formulas and the regular probabilistic operator $\{\beta\}_{\bowtie p}$, where $\bowtie\ \in \{<, \leq, >, \geq, =\}$. Temporal and probabilistic operators can be freely combined, e.g., $[\beta_1]\{\beta_2\}_{\geq p}$ specifies that, from all states reached after a path satisfying β_1, the probability measure of an outgoing path satisfying β_2 is at least p.

We also enhanced the EVALUATOR [27] on-the-fly model checker with the translation of $\{\beta\}_{\bowtie p}$ formulas into BESs (for checking the existence of path suffixes) and LESs (for computing probability measures) as described in Sects. 3 and 4. The on-the-fly resolution of BESs is carried out by the algorithms of the CAESAR_SOLVE library [23], which already serves as verification back-end for (non-probabilistic) MCL formulas. For the on-the-fly resolution of LESs, we designed a local algorithm operating on the associated Signal Flow Graphs (SFG) [7], in a way similar to the BES resolution algorithms, which operate on the associated Boolean graphs [2]. The LES resolution algorithm consists of a forward exploration of the SFG to build dependencies between variables, followed by a backward variable elimination (a.k.a. substitution) and a final propagation to update the right-hand sides of equations with the solutions of variables. This substitution method, implemented with a careful bookkeeping of variable dependencies, performs well on the *very* sparse LESs resulting from $\{\beta\}_{\bowtie p}$ operators (typically, for a PTS with 10^6 states and a branching factor of 10, there are about $10^{-5} = 0.001\%$ non-null elements in the LES matrix). Connections to general purpose solvers for (less sparse) LESs are planned as future work.

5.2   Case Study: Analysis of Mutual Exclusion Protocols

We illustrate the application of the regular probabilistic operator by carrying out a quantitative analysis of several shared-memory mutual exclusion protocols, using their formal descriptions in LNT [6] given in [25]. We focus here on a subset of the 27 protocols studied in [25], namely the CLH, MCS, Burns&Lynch (BL), TAS and TTAS protocols, by considering configurations of $N \leq 4$ concurrent processes competing to access the critical section. Each process executes cyclically a sequence of four sections: non critical, entry, critical, and exit. The entry and exit sections represent the algorithm specific to each protocol for demanding and releasing the access to the critical section, respectively. In the PTS models of the protocols, all transitions going out from each state are assumed to have equal probabilities. We formulate four probabilistic properties using MCL and evaluate them on the fly on each LNT protocol description (for MCL formulas consisting of a single $\{\beta\}_{\bowtie p}$ operator, the model checker also yields the probability measure in addition to the Boolean verdict). For each property requiring several invocations of the model checker with different values for the data parameters in the MCL formula, we automate the analysis using SVL scripts [14].

Critical Section. First of all, for each $i \in [0, N-1]$, we compute the probability that process P_i is the first one to enter its critical section. For this purpose, we use the following MCL formula:

$$\{ (\neg\{CS\ !"ENTER"...\})^*.\{CS\ !"ENTER"\ !i\} \}_{\geq 0}$$

which computes the probability that, from the initial state, process P_i accesses its critical section before any (other) process. Symmetric protocols guarantee that this probability is equal to $1/N$ for all processes, while asymmetric protocols (such as BL) may favor certain processes w.r.t. the others. This is indeed reflected by the results of model checking the above formula for $N = 3$: for the BL protocol, which gives higher priority to processes of lower index, the probabilities computed are 72.59% (for P_0), 21.66% (for P_1), and 5.73% (for P_2), whereas they are equal to 33.33% for the other protocols, which are symmetric.

Memory Latency. The analysis of critical section reachability can be refined by taking into account the cost of memory accesses (e.g., read, write, test-and-set operations on shared variables) that a process P_i must perform before entering its critical section. The protocol modeling provided in [25] also considers non-uniform memory accesses, assuming that concurrent processes execute on a cache-coherent multiprocessor architecture. The cost c (or latency) of a memory access depends on the placement of the memory in the hierarchy (local caches, shared RAM, remote disks) and is captured in the PTS by actions "MU !c" [25].

The MCL formula aside computes the probability that a process P_i performs memory accesses of a total cost **max** before entering its critical section. The regular formula expresses that, after executing its non critical section for the first time, process P_i begins its entry section and, after a number of memory accesses, enters its critical section.

$$
\begin{aligned}
&\{ \ (\neg\{\text{NCS } !i\})^*.\{\text{NCS } !i\} \\
&\quad \text{loop } (\textit{total\_cost}:\text{nat}:=0) \text{ in} \\
&\qquad (\neg(\{\text{MU } ... \ !i\} \vee \{\text{CS } !"\text{ENTER}" \ !i\}))^* \\
&\qquad \text{if } \textit{total\_cost} < \textbf{max} \text{ then} \\
&\qquad\quad \{\text{MU } ... \ ?c:\text{nat } !i\} \\
&\qquad\quad \text{continue } (\textit{total\_cost} + c) \\
&\qquad \text{else exit end if} \\
&\quad \text{end loop} \\
&\quad \{\text{CS } !"\text{ENTER}" \ !i\} \\
&\}_{\geq 0}
\end{aligned}
$$

The "loop" subformula denotes the entry section of P_i and requires that it terminates when the cost of all memory accesses performed by P_i (accumulated in the iteration parameter $\textit{total\_cost}$) exceeds a given value **max**. The other processes can execute freely during the entry section of P_i, in particular they can overtake P_i by accessing their critical sections before it. Figure 4(a) shows the probability of entering the critical section for various values of **max**. Since the entry section contains waiting loops, the number of memory accesses of P_i before entering its critical section is unbounded (and hence, also the cost **max**). However, the probability that a process waits indefinitely before entering its critical section tends to zero in long-term runs of starvation-free protocols. This explains the asymptotic probability 1.0 observed in Fig. 4(a): a process has better chances to reach its critical section when the memory cost of its entry section increases.

Overtaking. Even if a mutual exclusion protocol is starvation-free, a process P_i that begins its entry section (and hence, starts requesting the access to the critical section) may be overtaken one or several times by another process P_j that accesses its own critical section before P_i does so. A qualitative measure of a starvation-free protocol is given by its *overtaking degree*, which is the maximum number of overtakes per couple of processes. This number should be as small as possible, and may vary among process couples for asymmetric protocols. A qualitative study of the overtaking degree was carried out in [25] using MCL regular formulas with counters. Here we use the same property in the probabilistic setting, which enables to compute the probability that process P_j overtakes P_i a given number of times. Figure 4(b) shows the results for the BL protocol, which outline its intrinsic asymmetry: lower index processes, with higher priority, also have better chances to overtake the other processes.

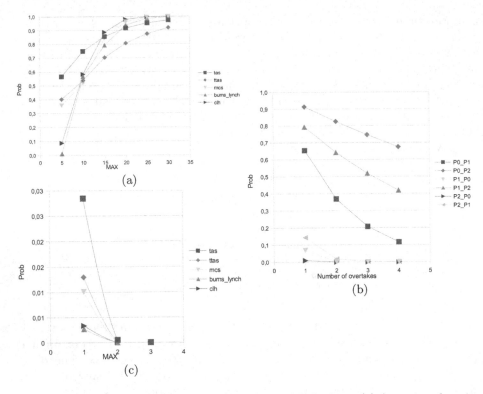

Fig. 4. Probabilities computed using on-the-fly model checking. (a) Accessing the critical section after memory accesses of cost MAX. (b) Overtaking of P_i by P_j ($P_j\_P_i$) in the BL protocol. (c) Standalone execution of P_i.

Standalone Execution. As opposed to overtaking, it is also interesting to examine the dual situation, in which a process P_i executes its cycle in standalone, i.e., without any interference with the other processes. This situation was explicitly formulated in [12] as the *independent progress* requirement, which should be satisfied by any mutual exclusion protocol. We can analyze this situation by computing the probability measure of a complete execution of process P_i without any other action being performed meanwhile by other processes.

This execution can be specified by the MCL formula aside, where **max** denotes the number of consecutive executions of P_i.

$$\{ \; ((\neg\{\mathsf{CS} \ldots ?j\text{:nat where } j \neq i\})^*.\{\mathsf{NCS} \; !i\}$$
$$(\neg\{\ldots ?j\text{:nat where } j \neq i\})^*.\{\mathsf{CS} \; !\text{"ENTER"} \; !i\}$$
$$(\neg\{\ldots ?j\text{:nat where } j \neq i\})^*.\{\mathsf{CS} \; !\text{"LEAVE"} \; !i\}$$
$$) \; \{\mathbf{max}\} \; \}_{\geq 0}$$

Figure 4(c) shows that the probability of standalone execution of P_i decreases with **max**, which reflects the starvation-free nature of the protocols.

Performance of Analysis. All model checking experiments have been carried out in a single core of an Intel(R) Xeon(R) E5-2630v3 @2.4 GHz with 128 GBytes of RAM and Linux Debian 7.9 within a cluster of Grid'5000 [4]. The sizes of the PTSs including the additional transitions of memory access costs (available in [25, Table 4]), range from 3 252 states and 6 444 transitions (for the TAS protocol) to 18 317 849 states and 31 849 616 transitions (for the CLH protocol).

The computing resources needed for on-the-fly verification depend on the complexity of the MCL regular formulas, and in particular the number and domains of their data parameters. For example, the analysis of the first access to the critical section takes between 3.25–5.5 s and 36.5–77 MBytes for all protocol configurations considered. For other properties, such as those concerning the memory latency or the overtaking, some peaks arrive up to 2–3 h and 12–14 GBytes because of the manipulation of data (cost of memory accesses) and iterations (number of overtakes). The analysis of the standalone execution of P_i may take up to 285 s and 1 230 MBytes for the BL protocol because of the complex cycles present in the PTS, while the same analysis takes less than 100 s (or even 10 s) for the other protocols.

6   Conclusion and Future Work

We proposed a regular probabilistic operator for computing the probability measure of complex paths in a PTS whose actions contain data values. Paths are specified using the action-based, data handling regular formulas of MCL [27] that we extended with a general iteration operator "loop" enabling the specification of arbitrarily complex paths. These new operators subsume those of P(A)CTL, and make possible the study of paths whose associated cost (calculated from the data values present on their actions) has a given value. We defined an on-the-fly model checking method based on reformulating the problem as the resolution of a linear equation system (LES) and a Boolean equation system (BES), and implemented it in the EVALUATOR model checker of the CADP toolbox.

To assess and finely tune our on-the-fly model checking method, we will experiment it on further examples and compare it (for properties expressible in PCTL) with explicit-state PRISM [19]. The on-the-fly analysis back-end (which is currently sequential) can be enhanced with distributed capabilities by connecting it with the MUMPS distributed solver [1] for sparse LESs. Finally, we will seek to extend our approach (which deals only with *finite* paths described using data-handling regular formulas) to handle infinite paths satisfying ω-regular properties, along the lines of [3, Chap. 10].

Acknowledgments. This work was supported by the European project SENSATION (*Self Energy-Supporting Autonomous Computation*) FP7-318490.

References

1. Amestoy, P.R., Duff, I.S., L'Excellent, J.-Y., Koster, J.: MUMPS: a general purpose distributed memory sparse solver. In: Sørevik, T., Manne, F., Moe, R., Gebremedhin, A.H. (eds.) PARA 2000. LNCS, vol. 1947, pp. 121–130. Springer, Heidelberg (2001)
2. Andersen, H.R.: Model checking and boolean graphs. TCS **126**(1), 3–30 (1994)
3. Baier, C., Katoen, J.-P.: Principles of Model Checking. MIT Press, Cambridge (2008)
4. Bolze, R., Cappello, F., Caron, E., Daydé, M.J., Desprez, F., Jeannot, E., Jégou, Y., Lanteri, S., Leduc, J., Melab, N., Mornet, G., Namyst, R., Primet, P., Quétier, B., Richard, O., Talbi, E.-G., Touche, I.: Grid'5000: a large scale and highly reconfigurable experimental grid testbed. IJHPCA **20**(4), 481–494 (2006)
5. Brzozowski, J.A.: Derivatives of regular expressions. JACM **11**(4), 481–494 (1964)
6. Champelovier, D., Clerc, X., Garavel, H., Guerte, Y., McKinty, C., Powazny, V., Lang, F., Serwe, W., Smeding, G.: Reference manual of the LNT to LOTOS translator (Version 6.2). Inria/Vasy and Inria/Convecs, p. 130 (2015)
7. Chua, L.O., Lin, P.M.: Computer Aided Analysis of Electronic Circuits. Prentice Hall, Upper Saddle River (1975)
8. Clarke, E., Grumberg, O., Peled, D.: Model Checking. MIT Press, Cambridge (2000)
9. Cleaveland, R., Iyer, S.P., Narasimha, M.: Probabilistic temporal logics via the modal μ-calculus. TCS **342**(2–3), 316–350 (2005)
10. Cleaveland, R., Steffen, B.: A linear-time model-checking algorithm for the alternation-free modal mu-calculus. FMSD **2**(2), 121–147 (1993)
11. Dershowitz, N.: Termination of rewriting. J. Symb. Comput. **3**(1), 69–115 (1987)
12. Dijkstra, E.W.: Solution of a problem in concurrent programming control. CACM **8**(9), 569 (1965)
13. Fischer, M.J., Ladner, R.E.: Propositional dynamic logic of regular programs. JCSS **18**(2), 194–211 (1979)
14. Garavel, H., Lang, F.: SVL: a scripting language for compositional verification. In: FORTE 2001, pp. 377–392. Kluwer (2001)
15. Garavel, H., Lang, F., Mateescu, R., Serwe, W.: CADP 2011: a toolbox for the construction and analysis of distributed processes. STTT **15**(2), 89–107 (2013)
16. Hansson, H., Jonsson, B.: A logic for reasoning about time and reliability. Formal Asp. Comput. **6**(5), 512–535 (1994)
17. Kozen, D.: Results on the propositional μ-calculus. TCS **27**, 333–354 (1983)
18. Kozen, D.: A probabilistic PDL. JCSS **30**(2), 162–178 (1985)
19. Kwiatkowska, M., Norman, G., Parker, D.: PRISM 4.0: verification of probabilistic real-time systems. In: Gopalakrishnan, G., Qadeer, S. (eds.) CAV 2011. LNCS, vol. 6806, pp. 585–591. Springer, Heidelberg (2011)
20. Larsen, K.G.: Proof systems for hennessy-milner logic with recursion. In: Dauchet, M., Nivat, M. (eds.) CAAP 1988. LNCS, vol. 299. Springer, Heidelberg (1988)
21. Larsen, K.G., Skou, A.: Bisimulation through probabilistic testing. Inf. Comput. **94**(1), 1–28 (1991)
22. Latella, D., Loreti, M., Massink, M.: On-the-fly fast mean-field model-checking. In: Abadi, M., Lluch Lafuente, A. (eds.) TGC 2013. LNCS, vol. 8358, pp. 297–314. Springer, Heidelberg (2014)
23. Mateescu, R.: Caesar_solve: a generic library for on-the-fly resolution of alternation-free boolean equation systems. STTT **8**(1), 37–56 (2006)

24. Mateescu, R., Monteiro, P.T., Dumas, E., de Jong, H.: CTRL: extension of CTL with regular expressions and fairness operators to verify genetic regulatory networks. TCS **412**(26), 2854–2883 (2011)
25. Mateescu, R., Serwe, W.: Model checking and performance evaluation with CADP illustrated on shared-memory mutual exclusion protocols. SCP **78**(7), 843–861 (2013)
26. Mateescu, R., Sighireanu, M.: Efficient on-the-fly model-checking for regular alternation-free μ-calculus. SCP **46**(3), 255–281 (2003)
27. Mateescu, R., Thivolle, D.: A model checking language for concurrent value-passing systems. In: Cuellar, J., Sere, K. (eds.) FM 2008. LNCS, vol. 5014, pp. 148–164. Springer, Heidelberg (2008)
28. R. De Nicola and F. W. Vaandrager. Action versus State Based Logics for Transition Systems. In Semantics of concurrency, LNCS vol. 469, pp. 407–419. Springer, (1990)

SymDIVINE: Tool for Control-Explicit Data-Symbolic State Space Exploration

Jan Mrázek, Petr Bauch, Henrich Lauko, and Jiří Barnat[✉]

Faculty of Informatics, Masaryk University,
Botanicka 68a, 602 00 Brno, Czech Republic
{xmrazek7,bauch,xlauko,barnat}@fi.muni.cz

Abstract. We present SymDIVINE: a tool for bit-precise model checking of parallel C and C++ programs. It builds upon LLVM compiler infrastructure, hence, it uses LLVM IR as an input formalism. Internally, SymDIVINE extends the standard explicit-state state space exploration with SMT machinery to handle non-deterministic data values. As such, SymDIVINE is on a halfway between a symbolic executor and an explicit-state model checker. The key differentiating aspect present in SymDIVINE is the ability to decide about equality of two symbolically represented states preventing thus repeated exploration of the state space graph. This is crucially important in particular for verification of parallel programs where the state space graph is full of diamond-shaped subgraphs.

1 Introduction

Automatic program analysis, e.g. detection of use of invalid memory or division by zero, is commonly used by both academia and industry for some time now. On the other hand, automatic program verification has not been widely accepted by the industry and remains mostly exclusively within the academic interest. This situation did not change even after the arrival of modern multi-core CPUs that made the concurrency related problems such as data races quite common, yet difficult to detect and solve by humans — an ideal opportunity for automated formal verification. The reasons for failure are numerous, however, the most tampering factor is the need for remodeling the input program in a modeling language of the model checker [1].

To address this specific issue, we present SymDIVINE– a tool for verification of real parallel C and C++ programs with non-deterministic inputs. The tool is built on top of the LLVM framework in order to avoid the need of modeling and, at the same time, to achieve precise semantics of C and C++ programming languages. SymDIVINE is motivated as an extension of our purely explicit model checker DIVINE [3] that is capable of handling full parallel C/C++ programs without inputs. To properly handle programs with inputs, SymDIVINE relies on Control-Explicit Data-Symbolic approach [2], which we detail below.

This work has been partially supported by the Czech Science Foundation grant No. 15-08772S.

D. Bošnački and A. Wijs (Eds.): SPIN 2016, LNCS 9641, pp. 208–213, 2016.
DOI: 10.1007/978-3-319-32582-8_14

2   Control-Explicit Data-Symbolic Approach

In the standard explicit state model checking, the state space graph of a program is explored by an exhaustive enumeration of its states. SymDIVINE basically follows the same idea, but it employs a *control-explicit data-symbolic* approach to alleviate the state space explosion caused by the non-deterministic input values. While a purely explicit-state model checker has to produce a new state for each and every possible input value, in SymDIVINE a set of states that differ only in data values is represented with a single data structure, the so called *multi-state*. Multi-state is composed of explicit control location and a set of program's memory valuations. The model checking engine in SymDIVINE operates on multi-states, which is the key differentiating factor of SymDIVINE if compared to other, purely explicit approaches. Relying on multi-states is computationally more demanding, but may bring up to exponential time and memory savings. See Fig. 1. Moreover, with an equality check for multi-states, we can easily mimic most explicit-state model checking algorithms – from simple reachability of error states to full LTL model checking [6].

DIVINE

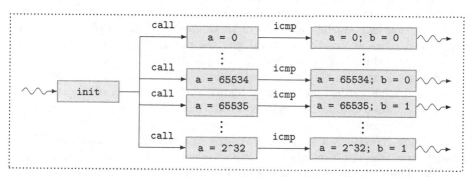

SymDIVINE

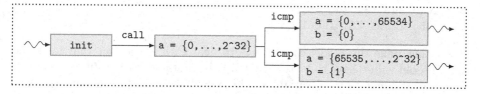

Fig. 1. The figure compares state exploration in the explicit approach of DIVINE and in the control-explicit data-symbolic approach of SymDIVINE on LLVM program example. From `init` state DIVINE explores states for every possible value of a (2^{32} values), hence exponentially expands state space. In contrast SymDIVINE approach of symbolic representation generates only two different states. One where the condition on branching ($a \geq 65535$) is satisfied and the other one where the condition is violated.

2.1   Representation of Multi-states

To perform verification of a program of size that is interesting from an industrial point of view, an efficient data structure for representation of multi-states is needed. While the representation of the explicit control-flow location is straightforward and easy, the representation of the set of program's variable valuations (the symbolic part) is rather challenging. We have tested several different representations during the development of SymDIVINE. Since our aim was to stick with a bit-precise verification, we only considered representations that were suitable for that. In particular, we dealt with binary decision diagrams, integer intervals and SMT formulae [4]. For the rest of the paper, we refer to the symbolic part as *symbolic data*.

In the current version of SymDIVINE, only quantified bit-vector SMT formulae are supported to represent symbolic data. The tool does not support dynamic memory allocation and manipulation at the moment, which makes the representation of symbolic data much simpler. Nevertheless, an unambiguous program variable naming scheme needs to be established so that different local variables with the same name are uniquely identified. Note that identifying variables with the index of a function they belong to, and an offset within the function in the LLVM bitcode is not satisfactory for the purpose of verification. In such scheme, we cannot differentiate the individual instances of the same variable within different function calls during recursion or in the presence of parallel threads. To deal with that we adopted the natural way the program's memory is organized – a stack divided into segments. Each function call made is linked with the corresponding segment on the stack, and so is every live instance of a variable. Therefore, individual instances can be identified by the index of the stack segment and an offset within that segment. Note that the first segment on the stack is reserved for global variables.

The code represents a simple LLVM program, where a is initialized with a non-deterministic 32-bit integer, then it is checked whether it is greater or equal to 65535. The result of the check is stored to b and used for branching.

```
%a = call i32 @__VERIFIER_nondet_int()
%b = icmp sge i32 %a, 65535
br i1 %b, label %5, label %6
```

Another issue the model checker has to deal with is the fact that for some variables, old values have to be remembered. To that end, SymDIVINE maintains the so called *generations* of variables. These are used to keep previous values of variables that have been redefined since the beginning of the execution of the program. Basically, each assignment to a variable generates a new generation of it. Consider, for example, the following C code: int x = 5; int y = x; x = 42; after execution of which the model checker have to remember that the variable y equals to an old value stored at the variable x.

Symbolic data part of a multi-state itself is further structured. In particular, it contains two sections – the so called *path condition* and *definitions*. The *path condition* is a conjunction of formulae that represents a restriction of the data that have been collected during the branching along the path leading to the current location. *Definitions*, on the other hand, are made of a set of formulae in the form *variable = expression* that describe internal relations among variables. *Definitions* are produced as a result of an assignment and arithmetic instructions. The structure of symbolic data representation allows for a precise description of what is needed for the model checking, but it lacks the canonical representation. As a matter of fact, the equality of multi-states cannot be performed as a syntax equality, instead, SymDIVINE employs an SMT solver and quantified formulae to check the satisfiability of a path condition and to decide the equality of two multi-states. For more details, we kindly refer to [2].

2.2 State Space Generation

SymDIVINE is built on top of the LLVM framework to simplify interpretation of complicated C/C++ semantics. To generate successors of a given multi-state we have implemented an interpreter of a subset of LLVM instructions. When generating new multi-states, the interpreter first checks if the input multi-state has a satisfiable path condition. If not, no successors are generated and the multi-state is marked as *empty* (invalid state). In the other case, the control location is systematically advanced for one of the threads, the corresponding instruction is executed and a new multi-state is emitted. After that the input multi-state is restored and the procedure is repeated for other threads. In this way, all thread interleavings are generated at the very fine-grained level of individual LLVM instructions. This would result in an enormous state space explosion unless SymDIVINE employed τ-reduction [7] to avoid emitting of invisible multi-states. With τ-reduction the penalty for fine-grained parallelism is eliminated. Moreover, to avoid repeated exploration of already visited states, a set of already seen symbolic data is maintained for each control location. Only new multi-states are further explored. Note that since there is no canonical representation for the symbolic data part, linear search is used to check for the presence of a multi-state in the list. At the moment, SymDIVINE relies on the Z3 SMT solver. To further reduce the length of symbolic data lists associated with the individual control-flow locations, SymDIVINE employs the so called *explication* [2]. If the definition part for a single variable leads to one single possible data value, the variable is removed from the symbolic data part of the multi-state and is treated as a regular explicit value. The process of explication is rather expensive, but it pays off, as it reduces the number of SMT calls made due to the multi-state equality tests.

As for interpretation of LLVM bitcode, most instructions (including arithmetic instructions) are implemented with the corresponding formula manipulation in the *definitions* section of a multi-state. Branching instructions for a condition φ always produce two succeeding states, where φ is conjuncted with the path condition of the first successor, and $\neg\varphi$ with the condition of the second successor. Function calls result in a initialization of a new stack segment, upon function return, the variables in the stack segment from where the function was called are substituted with the returned values and the corresponding stack segment is deleted. To support parallel C/C++ programs, SymDIVINE contains its own limited implementation of PThread library.

3   Using SymDIVINE

Given a C/C++ program, its verification using SymDIVINE is quite straightforward and simple. We adopted SV-COMP notation [5] to mark a nondeterministic input of the verified program. Using this notation a user can bring the input to the program by calling __VERIFIER_nondet_{type} function. We also support input assumptions, atomic sections, and asserts from SV-COMP notation. Beside this denotation of non-deterministic inputs, no other annotation is needed. To verify the annotated program, it has to be first compiled into the LLVM bitcode using Clang. The user can either do it manually with any compiler flags needed, or may use our script compile_to_bitcode to compile the program source code with the default compiler flags. After that the user has to choose if the program should be verified for an assertion safety or against an LTL property. To verify the program for the assertion safety, the user has to run ./symdivine reachability {program.ll}. Optional arguments verbose or vverbose can be used to track the progress of verification. If there is no run violating any assertion (both C and SV-COMP style) SymDIVINE responds that the model is safe. Otherwise, it outputs a single state in which the assertion is violated.

To verify the program against an LTL property, the user has to run ./symdivine ltl {property} {program.ll}. The LTL formula is passed as a plain text and is parsed by SymDIVINE internally. The format follows the standard LTL syntax. Atomic propositions are embedded into the formula and are bounded within square brackets. An atomic proposition can refer to any global variable in the verified program or a constant with a given bit-width. Since the support for debugging information in the bit code is not fully implemented yet, the global variables are referred to using their offset in a global segment (this offset can be read in the bitcode file). Note that for a bitcode file, Clang keeps the same order of variables as is the order of the variables in the source file. An example of LTL formula for SymDIVINE is as follows: !F(G[seg1_off0 = 0(32)]).

SymDIVINE does not currently support the debug information stored in bit code files, so all counterexamples are in the form of internal representation and with no link to the original source code file. However, since the internal representation follows strict and simple rules and the information obtained from the path condition is clearly readable, it is possible for a user to reconstruct the counterexample simply by following it in the source code file. This is currently the weakest part of SymDIVINE user interface.

4   Conclusions and Future Work

The main advantage of SymDIVINE is the fact that it performs a direct bit-precise verification of C/C++ programs with no need for modeling. Using a bit-vector theory, SymDIVINE can be bit-precise and handle bit-shifts, unsigned overflows, etc. Unlike symbolic executors or bounded model checkers, SymDIVINE also handles programs with infinite behavior, provided that the semi-symbolic state space is finite. The LLVM approach allows us to reflect compiler optimizations and architecture specific issues such as bit-width of variables. With a proper LLVM frontend, SymDIVINE is also applicable to various programming languages.

In the current state SymDIVINE is able to verify pieces of real world code. These pieces are, however, limited by the subset of LLVM instructions that is supported by our tool. The most limiting factor for SymDIVINE is the lack of support for dynamic memory. Besides that, our tool also misses advanced techniques that reduce resource usage and are incorporated within other tools, such as efficient memory compression. Absence of these techniques makes our tool more resource wasteful compared to the others. However, majority of the limitations are purely of technique nature and will be solved in the future. From the conceptional point of view, SymDIVINE approach does not deal well with cycles whose number of iterations depends on an input. SymDIVINE also cannot handle programs that run an infinite number of threads. However, this is not a limiting factor for real world use.

On the other hand, SymDIVINE demonstrates that the *Control-Explicit Data-Symbolic* approach can be used for verification of parallel programs with nondeterministic inputs, and we plan to further support it. SymDIVINE source code can be found at https://github.com/yaqwsx/SymDIVINE.

References

1. Alglave, J., Donaldson, A.F., Kroening, D., Tautschnig, M.: Making software verification tools really work. In: Bultan, T., Hsiung, P.-A. (eds.) ATVA 2011. LNCS, vol. 6996, pp. 28–42. Springer, Heidelberg (2011)
2. Barnat, J., Bauch, P., Havel, V.: Model checking parallel programs with inputs. In: 2014 22nd Euromicro International Conference on Parallel, Distributed and Network-Based Processing (PDP), pp. 756–759 (2014)
3. Barnat, J., et al.: DiVinE 3.0 – An explicit-state model checker for multithreaded C & C++ programs. In: Sharygina, N., Veith, H. (eds.) Computer Aided Verification (CAV 2013). LNCS, vol. 8044, pp. 863–868. Springer, Heidelberg (2013)
4. Bauch, P., Havel, V., Barnat, J.: LTL model checking of LLVM bitcode with symbolic data. In: Hliněný, P., Dvořák, Z., Jaroš, J., Kofroň, J., Kořenek, J., Matula, P., Pala, K. (eds.) MEMICS 2014. LNCS, vol. 8934, pp. 47–59. Springer, Heidelberg (2014)
5. Beyer, D.: Software verification and verifiable witnesses. In: Baier, C., Tinelli, C. (eds.) TACAS 2015. LNCS, vol. 9035, pp. 401–416. Springer, Heidelberg (2015)
6. Clarke Jr., E.M., Grumberg, O., Peled, D.A.: Model Checking. MIT Press, Cambridge (1999)
7. Ročkai, P., Barnat, J., Brim, L.: Improved state space reductions for LTL model checking of C and C++ programs. In: Brat, G., Rungta, N., Venet, A. (eds.) NFM 2013. LNCS, vol. 7871, pp. 1–15. Springer, Heidelberg (2013)

A Tool Integrating Model Checking into a C Verification Toolset

Subash Shankar[✉] and Gilbert Pajela

City University of New York (CUNY), New York, USA
subash.shankar@hunter.cuny.edu, gpajela@gradcenter.cuny.edu

Abstract. Frama-C is an extensible C verification framework that includes support for abstract interpretation and deductive verification. We have extended it with model checking based on counterexample guided refinement. This paper discusses our tool and outlines the major challenges faced here, and likely to be faced in other similar tools.

1 Introduction and Motivation

Program verification has a long history with a more recent growth in tools for semi-automatic and automatic verification, even though the general problem is undecidable. Three major underlying approaches are abstract interpretation [9], deductive verification based on Floyd-Hoare logic along with its weakest precondition interpretation [10–12], and model checking [7]. Unfortunately, no one approach can verify all programs in practice, with major tradeoffs including automatability, generality, scalability, and efficiency. In particular, while deductive verification techniques require deep user understanding to provide manual guidance (*e.g.*, to identify loop invariants) but can be used for all programs (given a suitably powerful theorem prover), model checking is completely automatic but suffers from state space explosion. Given the pros and cons of each technique, it is desirable to integrate them, enabling a 'verification engineer' to select tools as appropriate.

The Frama-C toolset is an extensible framework that integrates multiple static analysis techniques including abstract interpretation and deductive verification, for C programs. We have implemented a prototype model checking plugin to Frama-C that allows the user to mix-and-match all of these verification techniques. The end goal is to provide a software verification system that can exploit the benefits of all three underlying approaches in a convenient and integrated manner so program parts can be verified using the most appropriate approach, and the results integrated in a seamless fashion. We believe this is the first tool to combine these approaches.

2 Frama-C Overview

Frama-C is a platform for static analysis of C programs, and we outline the relevant parts in this section though the reader is referred to [13] for a more

© Springer International Publishing Switzerland 2016
D. Bošnački and A. Wijs (Eds.): SPIN 2016, LNCS 9641, pp. 214–224, 2016.
DOI: 10.1007/978-3-319-32582-8_15

extensive discussion. It is extensible through plugins that may share information and interact through a common interface. The plugins will typically interface with C Intermediate Language (CIL) and other tool results, as supported by the Frama-C kernel. All code is open-source and written in OCaml.

Frama-C analyses generally act on specifications written using the ANSI/ISO C Specification Language (ACSL) [1]. ACSL allows for specification of contracts on functions and statements (among other features), and we support three types of clauses in contracts:

- **requires**: pre-condition for the contract
- **ensures**: post-condition for the contract. When in a statement contract, it is conditional on normal termination; that is, not through a `goto`, `break`, `continue`, `return`, or `exit` statement (ACSL is a rich language that also includes analogs for the abnormal termination case, but we currently do not support these).
- **assigns**: The set of variables potentially modified by the statement/function (including those modified on abnormal execution paths). If there is no assign statement, any variable is assumed to be potentially modified.

Arguments for **requires** and **ensures** clauses are standard C expressions with numerous extensions to support simpler expression of properties. In particular, we support two functions:

- `\result`: evaluates to the return value of a function
- `\at(e,id)`: evaluates to the value of the expression `e` at label `id`, where the label may be in the C program or one of 6 ACSL-defined labels. We support 4 predefined labels:
  - `Pre`: The prestate of the function, when in a statement contract.
  - `Post`: The poststate of the contract (visible in ensures clauses).
  - `Old`: The prestate of the contract (visible in ensures clauses).
  - `Here`: the prestate when in a requires clause, and the poststate when in an ensures clause.

Frama-C comes with a number of plugins, and we are primarily interested in interfacing with two of these: **value** and **wp**. Value analysis applies forward dataflow analysis on domain-dependent abstract interpretation lattices to compute conservative approximations to all variable values. Some typical abstractions include intervals and mod fields for integers, intervals for reals, offsets into memory regions for pointers, etc. Loops must be unrolled by a constant user-selected number of iterations, which unfortunately may not be efficient for large iteration counts. It is possible to perform unbounded loop unrolling, but this results in a potentially non-terminating fixed point computation and is thus not recommended. The **wp** plugin performs deductive verification based on Dijkstra's weakest precondition calculus. As with all deductive verification techniques, there are limitations imposed by undecidability and the capabilities of underlying backend engines (SMT solvers and/or proof assistants). Additionally, loops are problematic since they require the manual identification of loop invariants, and it is generally recognized that software developers are not typically adept at identifying sufficiently strong invariants.

3   Model Checking for Software Verification

Traditional model checking automatically verifies liveness/reachability and safety properties expressed in temporal logic on a state machine representing the system being verified. Since an explicit representation of the state machine is often impractical, symbolic model checking uses a symbolic representation and has been used to verify very large systems [4]. However, even small programs lead to huge state spaces, and its direct use is thus limited. For example, a program with just 10 32-bit variables requires $\sim 10^{96}$ states, which approaches the limits of symbolic model checking.

Counter-example guided refinement (CEGAR) alleviates this problem by applying predicate abstraction to construct and verify a Boolean program abstracting the original program [6]. Initially, the predicates used for abstraction are typically either null (thus, abstracting the program into its control flow graph) or a subset of conditions in the program/contract. If the property is verifiable in the abstraction, it must be true; otherwise, the produced counterexample is validated on the original program. If validation fails (*i.e.*, the counterexample was spurious), the counterexample is analyzed to produce additional new predicates for refining the abstraction. This verify-validate-refine cycle is iterated until the property is proven (see Fig. 1), hopefully within a reasonable number of iterations.

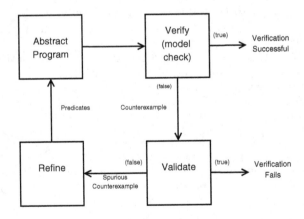

Fig. 1. CEGAR algorithm

There are several CEGAR-based tools for C program verification, with 2 common ones being SATABS [5] and Blast [2] which is now extended and embodied in the CPAchecker tool [3]. Both augment C with a __VERIFIER_assume(expr) statement that restricts the state space to paths in which expr is true (at the point of the statement), and both can be used to verify C assertions. CPAchecker is a configurable tool that allows for multiple analysis techniques, mostly related to reachability analysis. Configurations differ on underlying assumptions such as the approximation of C data types with mathematical types. CEGAR tool performances vary due largely to differing refinement strategies, and the approach in our plugin is to allow multiple user-selectable CEGAR backends. Since we wish to interact with other Frama-C tools that may be strict, we use a conservative configuration that does reachability analysis on bit-precise approximations (named `predicateAnalysis-bitprecise`), and all further mentions of CPAchecker in this paper should be understood to refer to this configuration.

4 The `cegarmc` Plugin

Our plugin, called `cegarmc`[1], verifies statements (which may of course contain arbitrarily nested statements) using SATABS and CPAchecker backends called through the Frama-C GUI. `Cegarmc` currently supports the following C99 and ACSL constructs:

- Variables/Types: Scalars including standard variations of integers and floats, arrays, structs/unions, and pointers (to these). Automatic and static storage classes are both supported. Type attributes (*e.g.*, for alignment, storage) are not supported.
- Statements: all constructs excluding exceptions. This includes function calls.
- ACSL: Statement contracts containing `ensures` and `requires` calls, with clauses that may be C expressions possibly using the ACSL functions mentioned in Sect. 2. For inter-procedural verification (discussed later), we also utilize function contracts in called functions along with assigns clauses. We do not verify function contracts themselves, since Frama-C can handle those given proofs of individual statement contracts.

These form a fairly complete C and ACSL subset, though there is in principle no reason why other constructs can't be supported (provided they have well-defined semantics across C standards, and a CEGAR backend supports them).

4.1 `Cegarmc` Implementation

`Cegarmc` functions by translating the CIL representation of the statement being verified along with its ACSL contract into an equivalent well-formed single-function C program that can be verified by SATABS or CPAchecker. Figure 2 illustrates the resulting architecture. Frama-C includes a mechanism for maintaining/combining validity statuses for contracts (possibly from multiple analyses) along with dependencies between contracts [8], and `cegarmc` emits a 'true' or 'dont know' status depending on results.

Figure 3 illustrates an abstract statement and its translation, where S' is essentially the CIL version of S. Each variable that appears in S is declared in the same order (thus ensuring parsability), though not necessarily contiguously

---

[1] The tool is open-source and available at http://www.compsci.hunter.cuny.edu/~sshankar/cegarmc.html.

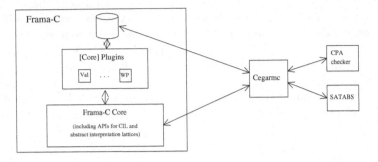

Fig. 2. System architecture

(see Sect. 4.2 for a discussion of resulting ramifications with respect to memory models). The labels CMCGOODEND and CMCBADEND capture normal and abnormal termination of S respectively, and S' also replaces abnormal terminations with branches to CMCBADEND (since ACSL statement contracts don't apply to abnormal terminations). Multiple requires clauses are translated to multiple assumes clauses. If there are multiple ensures clauses, this translation is repeated for each one, calling the CEGAR checker once per clause. It is easy to see that this simple translation is sound.

```
/*@ requires R;
      ensures E;
*/
S;
```

$\Rightarrow$

```
Declarations
__VERIFIER_assume(R);
S';
CMCGOODEND:
    assert(E);
CMCBADEND: return;
```

Fig. 3. Translation of statement

Inter-procedural verification is substantially more complicated. Model checkers require callee expansion, resulting in state space explosion. Assuming a contract can be written for the callee, our approach exploits this contract to implement a form of assume-guarantee reasoning, thus avoiding state space explosion. Our basic approach is to automatically replace function calls with assumes clauses capturing the corresponding contract. Figure 4 illustrates an abstract example of this translation for the non-void 1-argument side-effect-free case, where P[x:=y] is the substitution operator that replaces all free occurrences of x in P with y. If there are multiple [syntactic] instances of calls to foo in S, distinct identifiers are given to each call variable (e.g., CMCfoo1, CMC-foo2, ...) – note that multiple calls themselves (e.g., in a loop) are only given one variable since they are declared in a local scope/lifetime. The extensions to multi-argument and void functions are simple to see. Any proofs of S's contract are marked as conditional on foo's contract; thus, vacuous local proofs of S are possible, though the global proof would still fail since foo's contract would be false.

```
// S's body:
...
S1 // calls foo(actual);
...

/*@
  requires R2;
  assigns A2;
  ensures E2;
*/
SomeType foo(formal) {
  ...
};
```

$\Longrightarrow$

```
...
SomeType CMCfoo;
__VERIFIER_assume(
  !R2[formal:=actual] ||
  E2[\result:=CMCfoo]
     [\old(formal):=actual]
)
S1'[foo(actual):=CMCfoo]
...
```

Fig. 4. Inter-procedural translation of S

However, this is complicated by side-effects arising from interference between the statement and called function (*e.g.*, assigning of a static global variable). Cegarmc also checks for such interferences using ACSL assigns clauses to identify potentially modified variables and proceeds with the proof only if no potential interference is found. Additionally, if no assigns clause is present, cegarmc attempts to determine modified variables and marks resulting proofs conditional on independence (which may be proven separately).

Figure 5 illustrates the algorithm for handling such interferences, where $\Theta(S,C)$ denotes the transformation of S illustrated in Fig. 4. The algorithm works by first identifying which variables are modified by S and any functions called in S's body, in a manner consistent with ACSL semantics for assigns clauses. This essentially amounts to using the assigns clause when one is available, and analyzing the code to determine assigned variables otherwise. Then, it checks for side effects of called functions that may potentially interfere, and aborts if so (this case results in the desired property marked with a 'dont know' status). We currently do not support pointers in assigns clauses, though there may be side effects from, for example, static variables. Finally, it calls the CEGAR checker on the transformed program. Frama-C introduces the notion of emitters, whereby a proof is marked with the name of the supporting tool, and we exploit this to mark proofs as proven by MC or MC.ind depending on whether an independence assumption needed to be made. This latter case occurs when the called function has a null body (*i.e.*, it is a stub, declared in the caller as an extern) and no assigns clause. Of course, the user may later decide to supply more information and retry for an unconditional proof.

Figure 6 illustrates this translation on a simple interprocedural program containing a statement that repeatedly decrements a positive number s until it is zero[2]. In this case, id's function contract has neither an assigns clause nor a

---

[2] For readability reasons, only an abstracted translation is shown since the actual translation occurs at the CIL level.

Given the statement and functions (a schema is shown):

```
/*@                              /*@
   requires  R1;                   requires  R2;
   assigns  A1;                    assigns  A2;
   ensures  E1;                    ensures  E2;
*/                               */
S;  // calls foo                 foo(Formals) {  ...  };
```

Translation:

Rename multiple calls to the same function with distinct identifiers
IndepFlag ← false
if A1 = ∅ **then**
   A1 ← variables modified in S
end if
for all calls foo(actuals) ∈ S (denote the call C) **do**
   if foo's body is null and A2 = ∅ **then**
      IndepFlag ← true
   else if foo has a body and A2 = ∅ **then**
      A2 ← variables modified in foo
   end if
   if A1 ∩ A2 ≠ ∅ **then**
      abort "Interference with Called Function"
   end if
   S ← Θ(S, C)
end for
if not IndepFlag **then**
   Call CEGAR checker on program S with emitter MC
else
   Call CEGAR checker on program S with emitter MC.Ind
end if

Fig. 5. Translation for inter-procedural code

body, and `cegarmc` thus marks the proof with an MC.ind emitter. If the body for `id` (or an assigns clause) had been supplied, `cegarmc` would have been able to determine that there is no interference, and the proof would have been emitted with an MC emitter. In either case, the proof of the statement contract would be marked as conditional on the proof of `id`'s function contract, which could be proved using either `cegarmc` or other Frama-C tools such as `wp`.

4.2 Cegarmc Issues

Although `cegarmc`'s implementation is conceptually simple, there are numerous semantic issues to ensure soundness. Additionally, there are numerous complicating underlying issues, and we highlight the major ones below. We believe these issues are also likely to be faced by other such tools.

Sample Program	Translation

```
/*@ requires n>=0;
    ensures \result == n;
*/
int id (int n);

void main() {
  int s,k;
  /*@ requires s>0;
      ensures s==0;
  */
  {
    k=1;
    while (s>0)
      s = s-id(k);
  }
}
```

```
void main() {
  auto int s,k;
  __VERIFIER_assume(s > 0);
  k=1;
  while (s>0)
    int CMCid1;
    __VERIFIER_assume(
      (!(k >= 0) ||
        (CMCid1 == k)));
    s = s-CMCid1;
  }
CMCGOODEND:
  assert(s == 0);
CMCBADEND: return;
}
```

Fig. 6. Example program and (abstracted) translation

Tool Philosophy: Verification tools differ on whether analyses are guaranteed correct or merely approximations, and combination techniques additionally may be based on confidences/probabilities assigned to the tools. Frama-C's combination algorithm assumes all analyses are correct, and its analyses combination algorithms result in inconsistent statuses if, for example, two plugins emit different statuses for the same contract. In contrast, many CPAchecker analyses use approximations (*e.g.*, rationals for integers) for improved efficiency. Since cegarmc is intended to perform seamlessly in the Frama-C platform, it uses only sound tools/configurations where possible and provides feedback otherwise (though constrained by information available in tool documentation).

Language Semantics: Whereas Frama-C supports C99, SATABS and CPAchecker are based on ANSI C and C11, respectively. Cegarmc does not account for any resulting semantic issues, and is thus not suitable for verifying any program relying on the intricacies of a particular C standard. Syntactically, cegarmc only supports C99 constructs. This (typically unstated) issue is faced by all verification tools, and even within the CEGAR tools themselves since they may use other C-targeted tools.

Memory Model: Any analysis of programs with pointers (or more precisely, pointer arithmetic) is dependent on the underlying memory model. Cegarmc is by its nature restricted to supporting the most restrictive memory model of tools that it interfaces with. Thus, it uses the memory model of Frama-C's value analysis, which assumes that each declared variable defines exactly one distinct base address, and a pointer is not allowed to 'jump' across base addresses (though it may, of course, still point to different elements in the same array or struct/union). Value analysis also generates proof obligations capturing such conditions, which may be independently proven. CEGAR tools also make such assumptions, though they may simply produce unsound results or be unable to prove a valid contract instead of producing a proof conditional on the obligations. Note that with this memory model, `cegarmc` need not preserve relative memory addresses (as discussed with the translation algorithm).

Efficiency: Our goal in `cegarmc` (at least in the initial prototype) is to integrate existing CEGAR-based model checkers into a verification toolset, enabling further research in integrated multi-technique verification. Since model checking efficiency is determined primarily by the backend CEGAR tools, the appropriate measure of efficiency is the number of extra variables added by our translation. The only constructs for which extra variables are added are:

- Function calls: each function call results in one new variable of the return value type. Note that these variables may be local to a scope inside the verified statement, thus creating (and destroying) one new variable for each entry to the scope (*e.g.*, one per loop iteration).
- ACSL labels: For each supported label, one additional variable of the same type.

Thus, `cegarmc` is unlikely to significantly aggravate state space explosion.

4.3   Integration of Approaches

One of the major advantages of our approach is the integration of multiple verification techniques, and we believe our tool can provide a framework for research into various such types of integration. Indeed, the interprocedural approach outlined previously may be considered as a simple integration of deductive verification and model checking if the called function is verified using `wp` and the calling statement is verified using `cegarmc`.

We have also implemented one simple integration of abstract interpretation (`value`) and `cegarmc`, which we dub contextual verification. A function will typically contain multiple statements (say, statements $S_1, \ldots, S_n$), and the composition may not be provable (or take too long) using a pure CEGAR approach, partly because different predicate abstractions are needed for each constituent statement. However, value analysis may be used to determine the values of all variables in the initial state of S_k, and `cegarmc` can then be used to verify S_k's contract under this context. This is implemented through a user-selectable option, in which case `cegarmc` queries Frama-C's internal databases (see Fig. 2) for `value` results that can be used to compute S_k's initial state.

Strictly speaking, a statement contract is a standalone entity, and all information about the statement's initial state should be reflected in its requires clauses. Thus, we use a different emitter to indicate that the proof is contextual. When reviewing the final proof, a user must then ensure that value analysis was performed before the proof (or rerun value analysis and any `cegarmc` proofs marked as contextual).

5 Conclusions and Further Research

As mentioned earlier, the cegarmc prototype covers a fairly complete C subset. Its performance is almost completely dependent on that of the CEGAR model checker (which is in general highly variable), and cegarmc does not add significant inefficiencies. Although our primary goal is to enable the convenience of model checking in a powerful multi-approach system, we believe that we have also increased the power of CEGAR tools. In particular, contextual verification allows for CEGAR verification of program parts within procedures, while our inter-procedural approach enables verification without the typical state space explosion.

We believe that cegarmc is a framework for research into integrating verification approaches, both by us and others. In particular, we plan on integrating different verification approaches to: (1) more fully automate the integration of deductive verification and model checking, (2) exploit abstract interpretation and deductive verification techniques to configure CEGAR tools for better performance, and (3) combine partial results from different techniques for more complete verification.

Acknowledgements. This project was partially supported by Digiteo Foreign Guest Research Grant 2013-0376D and PSC-CUNY Grant 67776-00-45. Much thanks is due to Zachary Hutchinson, who contributed to some parts of the code. We would also like to thank the entire Frama-C team for invaluable guidance without which this tool would not have been possible.

References

1. Baudin, P., Cuoq, P., Filliâtre, J.-C., Marché, C., Monate, B., Moy, Y., Prevosto, V.: ACSL: ANSI/ISO C specification language, version 1.8
2. Beyer, D., Henzinger, T.A., Théoduloz, G.: Configurable software verification: concretizing the convergence of model checking and program analysis. In: Damm, W., Hermanns, H. (eds.) CAV 2007. LNCS, vol. 4590, pp. 504–518. Springer, Heidelberg (2007)
3. Beyer, D., Keremoglu, M.E.: CPAchecker: a tool for configurable software verification. In: Gopalakrishnan, G., Qadeer, S. (eds.) CAV 2011. LNCS, vol. 6806, pp. 184–190. Springer, Heidelberg (2011)
4. Burch, J., Clarke, E.M., McMillan, K., Dill, D., Hwang, L.: Symbolic model checking: 10e20 states and beyond. In: Proceedings of the Fifth Annual IEEE Symposium on Logic in Computer Science (LICS), pp. 428–439 (1990)
5. Clarke, E., Kroning, D., Sharygina, N., Yorav, K.: SATABS: SAT-based predicate abstraction for ANSI-C. In: Halbwachs, N., Zuck, L.D. (eds.) TACAS 2005. LNCS, vol. 3440, pp. 570–574. Springer, Heidelberg (2005)
6. Clarke, E.M., Grumberg, O., Jha, S., Lu, Y., Veith, H.: Counterexample-guided abstraction refinement. In: Emerson, E.A., Sistla, A.P. (eds.) CAV 2000. LNCS, vol. 1855, pp. 154–169. Springer, Heidelberg (2000)
7. Clarke, E.M., Grumberg, O., Peled, D.: Model Checking. MIT Press, Cambridge (1999)

8. Correnson, L., Signoles, J.: Combining analyses for C program verification. In: Stoelinga, M., Pinger, R. (eds.) FMICS 2012. LNCS, vol. 7437, pp. 108–130. Springer, Heidelberg (2012)

9. Cousot, P., Cousot, R.: Abstract interpretation: a unified lattice model for static analysis of programs by construction or approximation of fixpoints. In: Fourth ACM Symposium on Principles of Programming Languages (POPL), pp. 238–252 (1977)

10. Dijkstra, E.W.: Guarded commands, nondeterminacy, and formal derivation of program. Commun. ACM (CACM) 18(8), 453–457 (1975)

11. Floyd, R.: Assigning meanings to programs. Proc. Symp. Appl. Math. 19, 19–32 (1967)

12. Hoare, C.: An axiomatic basic for computer programming. Commun. ACM 12(10), 576–580 (1969)

13. Kirchner, F., Kosmatov, N., Prevosto, V., Signoles, J., Yakobowski, B.: Frama-c, a software analysis perspective. Form. Asp. Comput. 27, 573–609 (2015)

14. Shankar, S.: A tool for integrating abstract interpretation, model checking, and deductive verification (presentation). In: Clarke Symposium: Celebrating 25 Years of Model Checking, Pittsburgh (2014)

Fair Testing and Stubborn Sets

Antti Valmari[1](✉) and Walter Vogler[2]

[1] Department of Mathematics, Tampere University of Technology,
P.O. Box 553, 33101 Tampere, Finland
antti.valmari@tut.fi
[2] Institut für Informatik, University of Augsburg, 86135 Augsburg, Germany
walter.vogler@informatik.uni-augsburg.de

Abstract. Partial-order methods alleviate state explosion by considering only a subset of transitions in each constructed state. The choice
of the subset depends on the properties that the method promises to
preserve. Many methods have been developed ranging from deadlock-
preserving to CTL*- and divergence-sensitive branching bisimilarity
preserving. The less the method preserves, the smaller state spaces it
constructs. Fair testing equivalence unifies deadlocks with livelocks that
cannot be exited, and ignores the other livelocks. It is the weakest congruence that preserves whether the ability to make progress can be lost.
We prove that a method that was designed for trace equivalence also
preserves fair testing equivalence. We describe a fast algorithm for computing high-quality subsets of transitions for the method, and demonstrate its effectiveness on a protocol with a connection and data transfer
phase. This is the first practical partial-order method that deals with a
practical fairness assumption.

Keywords: Partial-order methods · Fairness · Progress · Fair testing
equivalence

1 Introduction

State spaces of systems that consist of many parallel components are often
huge. Usually many states arise from executing concurrent transitions in different orders. So-called *partial-order methods* [2,3,5–7,10,11,14,16–18,20] try
to reduce the number of states by, roughly speaking, studying only some orders
that represent all of them. This is achieved by only investigating a subset of
transitions in each state. This subset is usually called *ample*, *persistent*, or *stubborn*. In this study we call it *aps*, when the differences between the three do not
matter.

This intuition works well only with executions that lead to a deadlock.
However, traces and divergence traces, for instance, arise from not necessarily
deadlocking executions. With them, to obtain good reduction results, a constructed execution must often lack transitions and contain additional transitions
compared to the executions that it represents. With branching-time properties,
thinking in terms of executions is insufficient to start with.

© Springer International Publishing Switzerland 2016
D. Bošnački and A. Wijs (Eds.): SPIN 2016, LNCS 9641, pp. 225–243, 2016.
DOI: 10.1007/978-3-319-32582-8_16

As a consequence, a wide range of aps set methods has been developed. The simplest only preserve the deadlocks (that is, the reduced state space has precisely the same deadlocks as the full state space) [14], while at the other end the CTL* logic (excluding the next state operator) and divergence-sensitive branching bisimilarity are preserved [5,11,16]. The more a method preserves, the worse are the reduction results that it yields. The preservation of the promised properties is guaranteed by stating conditions that the aps sets must satisfy. Various algorithms for computing sets that satisfy the conditions have been proposed. In an attempt to improve reduction results, more and more complicated conditions and algorithms have been developed. There is a trade-off between reduction results on the one hand, and simplicity and the time that it takes to compute an aps set on the other hand.

Consider a cycle where the system does not make progress, but there is a path from it to a progress action. As such, traditional methods for proving liveness treat the cycle as a violation against liveness. However, this is not always the intention. Therefore, so-called *fairness assumptions* are often formulated, stating that the execution eventually leaves the cycle. Unfortunately, how to take them into account while retaining good reduction results has always been a problem for aps set methods. For instance, fairness is not mentioned in the partial order reduction chapter of [2]. Furthermore, as pointed out in [3], the most widely used condition for guaranteeing linear-time liveness (see, e.g., [2, p. 155]) often works in a way that is detrimental to reduction results.

Fair testing equivalence [12] always treats this kind of cycles as progress. If there is no path from a cycle to a progress action, then both fair testing equivalence and the traditional methods treat it as non-progress. This makes fair testing equivalence suitable for catching many non-progress errors, without the need to formulate fairness assumptions; for an application, see Sect. 7.

Fair testing equivalence implies trace equivalence. So it cannot have better reduction methods than trace equivalence. Fair testing equivalence is a branching time notion. Therefore, one might have guessed that any method that preserves it would rely on strong conditions, resulting in bad reduction results. Suprisingly, it turned out that a 20 years old trace-preserving stubborn set method [16] also preserves fair testing equivalence. This is the main result of the present paper. It means that *no reduction power is lost* compared to trace equivalence.

Background concepts are introduced in Sect. 2. Sections 3 and 4 present the trace-preserving method and discuss how it can be implemented. This material makes this publication self-contained, but it also contains some improvements over earlier publications. Section 5 discusses further why it is good to avoid strong conditions. The proof that the method also applies to fair testing equivalence is in Sect. 6. Some performance measurements are presented in Sect. 7.

2 Labelled Transition Systems and Equivalences

In this section we first define labelled transition systems and some operators for composing systems from them. We also define some useful notation.

Then we define the well-known trace equivalence and the fair testing equivalence of [12]. We also define tree failure equivalence, because it is a strictly stronger equivalence with a related but much simpler definition.

The symbol τ denotes the *invisible action*. A *labelled transition system* or *LTS* is a tuple $L = (S, \Sigma, \Delta, \hat{s})$ such that $\tau \notin \Sigma$, $\Delta \subseteq S \times (\Sigma \cup \{\tau\}) \times S$ and $\hat{s} \in S$. The elements of S, Σ, and Δ are called *states, visible actions*, and *transitions*, respectively. The state $\hat{s}$ is the *initial state*. An *action* is a visible action or τ.

We adopt the convention that, unless otherwise stated, $L' = (S', \Sigma', \Delta', \hat{s}')$, $L_i = (S_i, \Sigma_i, \Delta_i, \hat{s}_i)$, and so on.

The empty string is denoted with ε. We have $\varepsilon \neq \tau$ and $\varepsilon \notin \Sigma$.

Let $n \geq 0$, s and s' be states, and $a_1, \ldots, a_n$ be actions. The notation $s - a_1 \cdots a_n \to s'$ denotes that there are states $s_0, \ldots, s_n$ such that $s = s_0$, $s_n = s'$, and $(s_{i-1}, a_i, s_i) \in \Delta$ for $1 \leq i \leq n$. The notation $s - a_1 \cdots a_n \to$ denotes that there is s' such that $s - a_1 \cdots a_n \to s'$. The set of *enabled* actions of s is defined as $\mathsf{en}(s) = \{a \in \Sigma \cup \{\tau\} \mid s - a \to\}$.

The *reachable part* of L is defined as the LTS $(S', \Sigma, \Delta', \hat{s})$, where

- $S' = \{s \in S \mid \exists \sigma \in (\Sigma \cup \{\tau\})^* : \hat{s} - \sigma \to s\}$ and
- $\Delta' = \{(s, a, s') \in \Delta \mid s \in S'\}$.

The *parallel composition* of L_1 and L_2 is denoted with $L_1 \parallel L_2$. It is the reachable part of $(S, \Sigma, \Delta, \hat{s})$, where $S = S_1 \times S_2$, $\Sigma = \Sigma_1 \cup \Sigma_2$, $\hat{s} = (\hat{s}_1, \hat{s}_2)$, and $((s_1, s_2), a, (s'_1, s'_2)) \in \Delta$ if and only if

- $(s_1, a, s'_1) \in \Delta_1$, $s'_2 = s_2 \in S_2$, and $a \notin \Sigma_2$,
- $(s_2, a, s'_2) \in \Delta_2$, $s'_1 = s_1 \in S_1$, and $a \notin \Sigma_1$, or
- $(s_1, a, s'_1) \in \Delta_1$, $(s_2, a, s'_2) \in \Delta_2$, and $a \in \Sigma_1 \cap \Sigma_2$.

That is, if a belongs to the alphabets of both components, then an a-transition of the parallel composition consists of simultaneous a-transitions of both components. If a belongs to the alphabet of one but not the other component, then that component may make an a-transition while the other component stays in its current state. Also each τ-transition of the parallel composition consists of one component making a τ-transition without the other participating. The result of the parallel composition is pruned by only taking the reachable part.

It is easy to check that $(L_1 \parallel L_2) \parallel L_3$ is isomorphic to $L_1 \parallel (L_2 \parallel L_3)$. This means that $\parallel$ can be considered associative, and that $L_1 \parallel \cdots \parallel L_n$ is well-defined for any positive integer n.

The *hiding* of an action set A in L is denoted with $L \backslash A$. It is $L \backslash A = (S, \Sigma', \Delta', \hat{s})$, where $\Sigma' = \Sigma \backslash A$ and $\Delta' = \{(s, a, s') \in \Delta \mid a \notin A\} \cup \{(s, \tau, s') \mid \exists a \in A : (s, a, s') \in \Delta\}$. That is, labels of transitions that are in A are replaced by τ and removed from the alphabet. Other labels of transitions are not affected.

Let $\sigma \in \Sigma^*$. The notation $s = \sigma \Rightarrow s'$ denotes that there are $a_1, \ldots, a_n$ such that $s - a_1 \cdots a_n \to s'$ and σ is obtained from $a_1 \cdots a_n$ by leaving out each τ. We say that σ is the *trace* of the path $s - a_1 \cdots a_n \to s'$. The notation $s = \sigma \Rightarrow$ denotes that there is s' such that $s = \sigma \Rightarrow s'$. The set of *traces* of L is

$$\mathsf{Tr}(L) = \{\sigma \in \Sigma^* \mid \hat{s} = \sigma \Rightarrow\}.$$

The LTSs L_1 and L_2 are *trace equivalent* if and only if $\Sigma_1 = \Sigma_2$ and $\mathsf{Tr}(L_1) = \mathsf{Tr}(L_2)$.

Let L be an LTS, $K \subseteq \Sigma^+$, and $s \in S$. The state s *refuses* K if and only if for every $\sigma \in K$ we have $\neg(s = \sigma \Rightarrow)$. For example, $\hat{s}$ refuses K if and only if $K \cap \mathsf{Tr}(L) = \emptyset$. Because $s = \varepsilon \Rightarrow$ holds vacuously for every state s, this definition is equivalent to what would be obtained with $K \subseteq \Sigma^*$. The pair $(\sigma, K) \in \Sigma^* \times 2^{\Sigma^+}$ is a *tree failure* of L, if and only if there is $s \in S$ such that $\hat{s} = \sigma \Rightarrow s$ and s refuses K. The set of tree failures of L is denoted with $\mathsf{Tf}(L)$. The LTSs L_1 and L_2 are *tree failure equivalent* if and only if $\Sigma_1 = \Sigma_2$ and $\mathsf{Tf}(L_1) = \mathsf{Tf}(L_2)$.

To define the main equivalence of this publication, we also need the following notation: For $\rho \in \Sigma^*$ and $K \subseteq \Sigma^*$, we write $\rho^{-1}K$ for $\{\pi \mid \rho\pi \in K\}$ and call ρ a *prefix* of K if $\rho^{-1}K \neq \emptyset$.

Definition 1. *The LTSs L_1 and L_2 are* fair testing equivalent *if and only if*

1. $\Sigma_1 = \Sigma_2$,
2. *if $(\sigma, K) \in \mathsf{Tf}(L_1)$, then either $(\sigma, K) \in \mathsf{Tf}(L_2)$ or there is a prefix ρ of K such that $(\sigma\rho, \rho^{-1}K) \in \mathsf{Tf}(L_2)$, and*
3. *Part 2 holds with the roles of L_1 and L_2 swapped.*

If $K \neq \emptyset$, then the first option "$(\sigma, K) \in \mathsf{Tf}(L_2)$" implies the other by letting $\rho = \varepsilon$. Therefore, the "either"-part could equivalently be written as "$K = \emptyset$ and $(\sigma, \emptyset) \in \mathsf{Tf}(L_2)$". The way it has been written makes it easy to see that tree failure equivalence implies fair testing equivalence.

If L_1 and L_2 are fair testing equivalent, then $\sigma \in \mathsf{Tr}(L_1)$ implies by the definitions that $(\sigma, \emptyset) \in \mathsf{Tf}(L_1)$, $(\sigma, \emptyset) \in \mathsf{Tf}(L_2)$, and $\sigma \in \mathsf{Tr}(L_2)$. So fair testing equivalence implies trace equivalence and cannot have better reduction methods.

3   The Trace-Preserving Strong Stubborn Set Method

The trace-preserving strong stubborn set method applies to LTS expressions of the form

$$L = (L_1 \| \cdots \| L_m) \backslash A.$$

To discuss the method, it is handy to first give indices to the τ-actions of the L_i. Let $\tau_1, \ldots, \tau_m$ be symbols that are distinct from each other and from all elements of $\Sigma = \Sigma_1 \cup \cdots \cup \Sigma_m$. For $1 \leq i \leq m$, we let $\bar{L}_i = (S_i, \bar{\Sigma}_i, \bar{\Delta}_i, \hat{s}_i)$, where

- $\bar{\Sigma}_i = \Sigma_i \cup \{\tau_i\}$ and
- $\bar{\Delta}_i = \{(s, a, s') \mid a \in \Sigma_i \wedge (s, a, s') \in \Delta_i\} \cup \{(s, \tau_i, s') \mid (s, \tau, s') \in \Delta_i\}$.

The trace-preserving strong stubborn set method computes a reduced version of

$$L' = (\bar{L}_1 \| \cdots \| \bar{L}_m) \backslash (A \cup \{\tau_1, \ldots, \tau_m\}).$$

For convenience, we define

- $\bar{L} = \bar{L}_1 \| \cdots \| \bar{L}_m,$

- $V = \Sigma \backslash A$ (the set of *visible* actions), and
- $I = (\Sigma \cap A) \cup \{\tau_1, \ldots, \tau_m\}$ (the set of *invisible* actions).

Now we can write $L' = (\bar{L}_1 \parallel \cdots \parallel \bar{L}_m) \backslash I = \bar{L} \backslash I$.

It is obvious from the definitions that L' is the same LTS as L. The only difference between $\bar{L}$ and $L_1 \parallel \cdots \parallel L_m$ is that the τ-transitions of the latter are τ_i-transitions of the former, where i reveals the L_i from which the transition originates. The hiding of I makes them τ-transitions again. We have $V \cap I = \emptyset$, $V \cup I = \bar{\Sigma} = \Sigma \cup \{\tau_1, \ldots, \tau_m\}$, and $\bar{L}$ has no τ-transitions at all (although it may have τ_i-transitions). Therefore, when discussing the trace-preserving strong stubborn set method, the elements of V and I are called *visible* and *invisible*, respectively.

The method is based on a function $\mathcal{T}$ that assigns to each $s \in S$ a subset of $\bar{\Sigma}$, called *stubborn set*. Before discussing the definition of $\mathcal{T}$, let us see how it is used. The stubborn set method computes a subset of S called S_r and a subset of Δ called Δ_r. It starts by letting $S_r = \{\hat{s}\}$ and $\Delta_r = \emptyset$. For each s that it has put to S_r and for each $a \in \mathcal{T}(s)$, it puts to S_r every s' that satisfies $(s, a, s') \in \bar{\Delta}$ (unless s' is already in S_r). Furthermore, it puts (s, a', s') to Δ_r (even if s' is already in S_r), where $a' = \tau$ if $a \in I$ and $a' = a$ otherwise. The only difference to the computation of L' is that in the latter, every $a \in \bar{\Sigma}$ is used instead of every $a \in \mathcal{T}(s)$.

The LTS $L_r = (S_r, \Sigma, \Delta_r, \hat{s})$ is the *reduced* LTS, while $L = L' = (S, \Sigma, \Delta, \hat{s})$ is the *full* LTS. We will refer to concepts in L_r with the prefix "r-", and to L with "f-". For instance, if $s \in S_r$ and $\neg(s = \sigma \Rightarrow)$ holds in L_r for all $\sigma \in K$, then s is an r-state and s r-refuses K. Because $S_r \subseteq S$ and $\Delta_r \subseteq \Delta$, every r-state is also an f-state and every r-trace is an f-trace. We will soon state conditions on $\mathcal{T}$ that guarantee that also the opposite holds, that is, every f-trace is an r-trace.

Typically many different functions could be used as $\mathcal{T}$, and the choice between them involves trade-offs. For example, a function may be easy and fast to compute, but it may also tend to give worse reduction results (that is, bigger S_r and Δ_r) than another more complex function. Therefore, we will not specify a unique function $\mathcal{T}$. Instead, in the remainder of this section we will only give four conditions that it must satisfy, and in the next section we will discuss how a reasonably good $\mathcal{T}$ is computed quickly.

A function from states to subsets of $\bar{\Sigma}$ qualifies as $\mathcal{T}$ if and only if for every $s \in S_r$ it satisfies the four conditions below (the first two are illustrated in Fig. 1):

Fig. 1. Illustrating D1 (left) and D2 (right). The solid states and transition sequences are assumed to exist and the condition promises the existence of the dashed ones. The yellow (grey in black/white print) part is in the reduced LTS, the rest is not necessarily

D1 If $a \in \mathcal{T}(s)$, $a_1, \ldots, a_n$ are not in $\mathcal{T}(s)$, and $s - a_1 \cdots a_n a \to s'_n$, then $s - a a_1 \cdots a_n \to s'_n$.

D2 If $a \in \mathcal{T}(s)$, $a_1, \ldots, a_n$ are not in $\mathcal{T}(s)$, $s - a \to s'$, and $s - a_1 \cdots a_n \to s_n$, then there is s'_n such that $s' - a_1 \cdots a_n \to s'_n$ and $s_n - a \to s'_n$.

V If $\mathcal{T}(s) \cap V \cap \mathrm{en}(s) \neq \emptyset$, then $V \subseteq \mathcal{T}(s)$.

S For each $a \in V$ there is an r-state s_a and an r-path from s to s_a such that $a \in \mathcal{T}(s_a)$.

Intuitively, D1 says two things. First, it says that a sequence of actions that are not in the current stubborn set ($a_1 \cdots a_n$ in the definition) cannot enable an action that is in the current stubborn set (a in the definition). That is, disabled actions in a stubborn set remain disabled while actions outside the set occur. Second, together with D2 it says that the enabled actions inside the current stubborn set are in a certain kind of a commutativity relation with enabled sequences of outside actions. In theories where actions are deterministic (that is, for every s, s_1, s_2, and a, $s - a \to s_1$ and $s - a \to s_2$ imply $s_1 = s_2$), the then-part of D2 is usually written simply as $s_n - a \to$. It, D1, and determinism imply our current version of D2. However, we do not assume that actions are deterministic.

Certain partial-order semantic models of concurrency use a so-called independence relation [9]. Unlike in the present study, actions are assumed to be deterministic. If a_1 and a_2 are independent, then (1) if $s - a_1 \to s_1$ and $s - a_2 \to s_2$, then there is an s' such that $s_1 - a_2 \to s'$ and $s_2 - a_1 \to s'$; (2) if $s - a_1 a_2 \to$ then $s - a_2 \to$; and (3) if $s - a_2 a_1 \to$ then $s - a_1 \to$. It is often claimed that ample, persistent, and stubborn set methods rely on an independence relation. This is why they are classified as "partial-order methods". In reality, they rely on various strictly weaker relations. For instance, even if determinism is assumed, D1 and D2 do not imply independence of a_1 from a, because they fail to yield (3).

The names D1 and D2 reflect the fact that together with a third condition called D0, they guarantee that the reduced LTS has precisely the same terminal states – also known as deadlocks – as the full LTS. D0 is not needed in the present method, because now the purpose is not to preserve deadlocks but traces. However, because we do not yet have an implementation that has been optimized to the present method, in our experiments in Sect. 7 we used a tool that relies on D0 and implements it. Therefore, we present its definition:

D0 If $\mathrm{en}(s) \neq \emptyset$, then $\mathcal{T}(s) \cap \mathrm{en}(s) \neq \emptyset$.

That is, if s is not a deadlock, then $\mathcal{T}(s)$ contains an enabled action. We skip the (actually simple) proof that D0, D1, and D2 guarantee that deadlocks are preserved, see [16].

The condition V says that if the stubborn set contains an enabled visible action, then it contains all visible actions (also disabled ones). It guarantees that the reduction preserves the ordering of visible actions, in a sense that will become clear in the proof of Lemma 3.

The function $\mathcal{T}_\emptyset$ that always returns the empty set satisfies D1, D2, and V. Its use as $\mathcal{T}$ would result in a reduced LTS that has one state and no transitions.

It is thus obvious that D1, D2, and V alone do not guarantee that the reduced LTS has the same traces as the full LTS.

The condition S forces the method to investigate, intuitively speaking, everything that is relevant for the preservation of the traces. It does that by guaranteeing that every visible action is taken into account, not necessarily in the current state but necessarily in a state that is r-reachable from the current state. Taking always all visible actions into account in the current state would make the reduction results much worse. The name is S because, historically, a similar condition was first used to guarantee the preservation of what is called safety properties in the linear temporal logic framework. Again, the details of how S does its job will become clear in the proof of Lemma 3.

If $V = \emptyset$, then $\mathcal{T}_\emptyset$ satisfies also S. Indeed, then $\mathsf{Tr}(L) = \{\varepsilon\} = \mathsf{Tr}(L_r)$ even if L_r is the one-state LTS that has no transitions. That is, if $V = \emptyset$, then $\mathcal{T}_\emptyset$ satisfies the definition and yields ideal reduction results.

No matter what V is, the function $\mathcal{T}(s) = \bar{\Sigma}$ always satisfies D1, D2, V, and S. However, it does not yield any reduction. The problem of computing sets that satisfy D1, D2, V, and S and do yield reduction will be discussed in Sect. 4. In Sect. 6 we prove that D1, D2, V, and S guarantee that the reduced LTS is fair testing equivalent (and thus also trace equivalent) to the full LTS.

4 On Computing Trace-Preserving Stubborn Sets

To make the abstract theory in the remainder of this publication more concrete, we present in this section one new good way of computing sets that satisfy D1, D2, V, and S. It is based on earlier ideas but has been fine-tuned for the present situation. We emphasize that it is not the only good way. Other possibilities have been discussed in [17,20], among others.

Because the expression under analysis is of the form $(\bar{L}_1 \parallel \cdots \parallel \bar{L}_m) \backslash I$, its states are of the form $(s_1, \ldots, s_m)$, where $s_i \in L_i$ for each $1 \le i \le m$. We employ the notation $\mathsf{en}_i(s_i) = \{a \mid \exists s_i' : (s_i, a, s_i') \in \Delta_i\}$, that is, the set of actions that are enabled in s_i in L_i. We have $\tau \notin \mathsf{en}_i(s_i) \subseteq \bar{\Sigma}_i = \Sigma_i \cup \{\tau_i\}$. Furthermore, if $a \notin \mathsf{en}(s)$, then there is at least one i such that $a \in \bar{\Sigma}_i$ and $a \notin \mathsf{en}_i(s_i)$. Let $\mathsf{dis}(s, a)$ denote the smallest such i.

We start by presenting a sufficient condition for D1 and D2 that does not refer to other states than the current.

Theorem 2. *Assume that the following hold for $s = (s_1, \ldots, s_m)$ and for every $a \in \mathcal{T}(s)$:*

1. *If $a \notin \mathsf{en}(s)$, then there is i such that $a \in \bar{\Sigma}_i$ and $a \notin \mathsf{en}_i(s_i) \subseteq \mathcal{T}(s)$.*
2. *If $a \in \mathsf{en}(s)$, then for every i such that $a \in \bar{\Sigma}_i$ we have $\mathsf{en}_i(s_i) \subseteq \mathcal{T}(s)$.*

Then $\mathcal{T}(s)$ satisfies D1 and D2.

Proof. Let $a_1 \notin \mathcal{T}(s), \ldots, a_n \notin \mathcal{T}(s)$.

Let first $a \notin \mathsf{en}(s)$. Obviously $s - a \rightarrow$ does not hold, so D2 is vacuously true. We prove now that D1 is as well. By assumption 1, there is i such that L_i

disables a and $\text{en}_i(s_i) \subseteq \mathcal{T}(s)$. To enable a, it is necessary that L_i changes its state, which requires that some action in $\text{en}_i(s_i)$ occurs. These are all in $\mathcal{T}(s)$ and thus distinct from $a_1, \ldots, a_n$. So $s - a_1 \cdots a_n a \rightarrow$ cannot hold.

Let now $a \in \text{en}(s)$. Our next goal is to show that there are no $1 \le k \le n$ and $1 \le j \le m$ such that both $a \in \bar{\Sigma}_j$ and $a_k \in \bar{\Sigma}_j$. To derive a contradiction, consider a counterexample where k has the smallest possible value. So none of $a_1, \ldots, a_{k-1}$ is in $\bar{\Sigma}_j$. If $s - a_1 \cdots a_n \rightarrow$, then there is s' such that $s - a_1 \cdots a_{k-1} \rightarrow$ $s' - a_k \rightarrow$. Obviously $a_k \in \text{en}_j(s'_j)$. This implies $a_k \in \text{en}_j(s_j)$, because L_j does not move between s and s' since none of $a_1, \ldots, a_{k-1}$ is in $\bar{\Sigma}_j$. By assumption 2, $\text{en}_j(s_j) \subseteq \mathcal{T}(s)$. This contradicts $a_k \notin \mathcal{T}(s)$.

This means that the L_j that participate in a are disjoint from the L_j that participate in $a_1 \cdots a_n$. From this D1 and D2 follow by well-known properties of the parallel composition operator. $\qquad\square$

Theorem 2 makes it easy to represent a sufficient condition for D1 and D2 as a directed graph that depends on the current state s. The set of the vertices of the graph is $\bar{\Sigma}$. There is an edge from $a \in \bar{\Sigma}$ to $b \in \bar{\Sigma}$, denoted with $a \rightsquigarrow b$, if and only if either $a \notin \text{en}(s)$ and $b \in \text{en}_i(s_i)$ where $i = \text{dis}(s, a)$, or $a \in \text{en}(s)$ and there is i such that $a \in \bar{\Sigma}_i$ and $b \in \text{en}_i(s_i)$. By the construction, if $\mathcal{T}(s)$ is closed under the graph (that is, for every a and b, if $a \in \mathcal{T}(s)$ and $a \rightsquigarrow b$, then $b \in \mathcal{T}(s)$), then $\mathcal{T}(s)$ satisfies D1 and D2.

It is not necessary for correctness to use the smallest i, when more than one L_i disables a. The choice to use the smallest i was made to obtain a fast algorithm. An alternative algorithm (called *deletion algorithm* in [17]) is known that exploits the freedom to choose any i that disables a. It has the potential to yield smaller reduced LTSs than the algorithm described in this section. On the other hand, it consumes more time per constructed state.

Furthermore, the condition in Theorem 2 is not the weakest possible, as shown by the following useful observation: Assume a writes to a finite-capacity fifo L_f, $\bar{a}$ reads from it, and they have no other L_i in common; although $\bar{\Sigma}_f$ links them, we need not declare $a \rightsquigarrow \bar{a}$ when a is enabled, and we need not declare $\bar{a} \rightsquigarrow a$ when $\bar{a}$ is enabled, since they commute if both are enabled. Trying to make the condition as weak as possible would have made it very hard to read.

It is trivial to also take the condition V into account in the graph representation of the stubborn set computation problem. It suffices to add the edge $a \rightsquigarrow b$ from each $a \in V \cap \text{en}(s)$ to each $b \in V$.

Let "$\rightsquigarrow^*$" denote the reflexive transitive closure of "$\rightsquigarrow$". By the definitions, if $a \in \bar{\Sigma}$, then $\{b \mid a \rightsquigarrow^* b\}$ satisfies D1, D2, and V. We denote it with $\text{clsr}(a)$. It can be computed quickly with well-known elementary graph search algorithms.

However, we can do better. The better algorithm is denoted with $\text{esc}(a)$, for "enabled strong component". Applied at some state s, it uses a as the starting point of a depth-first search in $(\bar{\Sigma}, \text{"}\rightsquigarrow\text{"})$. During the search, the strong components (i.e., the maximal strongly connected subgraphs) of $(\bar{\Sigma}, \text{"}\rightsquigarrow\text{"})$ are recognized using Tarjan's algorithm [4,13]. It recognizes each strong component at the time of backtracking from it. When $\text{esc}(a)$ finds a strong component C that contains an action enabled at s, it stops and returns C as the result; note that a might not be in C. In principle, the result should also contain actions that are reachable from C but are not in C. However, they are all disabled, so leaving them out does not change L_r, which we are really interested in. If $\mathsf{esc}(a)$ does not find such a strong component, it returns $\emptyset$.

Obviously $\mathsf{esc}(a) \subseteq \mathsf{clsr}(a)$. So $\mathsf{esc}(a)$ has potential for better reduction results. Tarjan's algorithm adds very little overhead to depth-first search. Therefore, $\mathsf{esc}(a)$ is never much slower than $\mathsf{clsr}(a)$. On the other hand, it may happen that $\mathsf{esc}(a)$ finds a suitable strong component early on, in which case it is much faster than $\mathsf{clsr}(a)$.

To discuss the implementation of S, let $V = \{a_1, \ldots, a_{|V|}\}$. Let $S(s,i)$ denote that there is an s_i and an r-path from s to s_i such that $a_i \in \mathcal{T}(s_i)$. Our algorithm constructs L_r in depth-first order. The *root* of a strong component C of L_r is the state in C that was found first. Our algorithm recognizes the roots with Tarjan's algorithm. In each root s_C, it enforces $S(s_C, i)$ for each $1 \leq i \leq n$ in a manner which is discussed below. This suffices, because if $S(s,i)$ holds for one state in a strong component, then it clearly holds for every state in the component.

Each state s has an attribute ν such that if $\nu > |V|$, then $S(s,i)$ is known to hold for $a_1, \ldots, a_{\nu-|V|}$. When a state is processed for the first time, its ν value is set to 1 and $\mathsf{esc}(a_1)$ is used as its stubborn set. When the algorithm is about to backtrack from a root s_C, it checks its ν value. The algorithm actually backtracks from a root only when $\nu = 2|V|$. Otherwise it increments ν by one. Then it extends $\mathcal{T}(s_C)$ by $\mathsf{esc}(a_\nu)$ if $\nu \leq |V|$, and by $\mathsf{clsr}(a_{\nu-|V|})$ if $|V| < \nu \leq 2|V|$. The extension may introduce new outgoing transitions for s_C, and s_C may cease from being a root. If s_C remains a root, then its ν eventually grows to $2|V|$ and S holds for s_C. The purpose of making $\mathcal{T}(s_C)$ grow in steps with esc-sets first is to obtain as small a stubborn set as possible, if s_C ceases from being a root.

During the depth-first search, information on ν-values is backward propagated and the maximum is kept. This way, if s_C ceases from being a root, the new root benefits from the work done at s_C. Furthermore, non-terminal strong components automatically get $\nu = 2|V|$. To exploit situations where $V \subseteq \mathcal{T}(s)$ by condition V, if a visible action is in $\mathsf{en}(s) \cap \mathcal{T}(s)$, then the algorithm makes the ν value of s be $2|V|$.

Unfortunately, we do not yet have an implementation of this algorithm. Therefore, in our experiments in Sect. 7 we used a trick. A system is *always may-terminating* if and only if, from every reachable state, the system is able to reach a deadlock. For each deadlock s, we can pretend that $\mathcal{T}(s) = \bar{\Sigma}$ and thus that $V \subseteq \mathcal{T}(s)$, because $\mathcal{T}(s)$ contains no enabled actions no matter how we choose it. This implies that S holds automatically for always may-terminating systems. In [18] it was proven that if, instead of S, the condition D0 is used, then it is easy to check from the reduced LTS whether the system is always may-terminating. So we will use the following new approach in Sect. 7:

1. Try to make the system always may-terminating.
2. Construct L_r' obeying D0, D1, D2, and V.
3. If L_r' is always may-terminating, then extract a reduced LTS for the original system from L_r' as will be described in Sect. 7. Otherwise, go back to 1.

Stubborn sets obeying D0, D1, D2, and V can be computed by, in each state that is not a deadlock, choosing an enabled a and computing $\mathsf{esc}(a)$.

5   On the Performance of Various Conditions

The goal of aps set methods is to alleviate the state explosion problem. Therefore, reducing the size of the state space is a main issue. However, if the reduction introduces too much additional work per preserved state, then time is not saved. So the cost of computing the aps set is important. Also the software engineering issue plays a role. Little is known on the practical performance of ideas that have the biggest theoretical reduction potential, because they are complicated to implement, so few experiments have been made. For instance, first big experiments on weak stubborn sets [17] and the deletion algorithm [17] appeared in [8].

Often a state has more than one aps set. Let T_1 and T_2 be two of them and let $\mathcal{E}(T_1)$ and $\mathcal{E}(T_2)$ be the sets of enabled transitions in T_1 and T_2. It is obvious that if the goal is to preserve deadlocks and if $\mathcal{E}(T_1) \subseteq \mathcal{E}(T_2)$, then T_1 can lead to better but cannot lead to worse reduction results than T_2. We are not aware of any significant result on the question which should be chosen, T_1 or T_2, if both are aps, $\mathcal{E}(T_1) \not\subseteq \mathcal{E}(T_2)$, and $\mathcal{E}(T_2) \not\subseteq \mathcal{E}(T_1)$. Let us call it the *non-subset choice problem*. Already [15] gave an example where always choosing the set with the smallest number of enabled transitions does not yield the best reduction result.

We now demonstrate that the order in which the components of a system are given to a tool can have a tremendous effect on the running time and the size of the reduced state space. Assume that $L_1 \parallel \cdots \parallel L_m$ has deadlocks. Consider $L_1 \parallel \cdots \parallel L_m \parallel L_{m+1}$, where $L_{m+1} = \overset{\curvearrowleft}{\circ}\,\tau$. This extended system has no deadlocks. If the deadlock-preserving stubborn set method always investigates L_{m+1} last, then it finds the deadlocks of the original system in the original fashion, finds that L_{m+1} is enabled in them, and eventually concludes that the system has no deadlocks. So it does approximately the same amount of work as it does with $L_1 \parallel \cdots \parallel L_m$. If, in the initial state $\hat{s}$, the method happens to investigate L_{m+1} first, it finds a τ-loop $\hat{s} - \tau \rightarrow \hat{s}$. D0, D1, and D2 do not tell it to investigate anything else. So it stops extremely quickly, after constructing only one state.

For this and other reasons, measurements are not as reliable for comparing different methods as we would like them to be.

Technically, optimal sets could be defined as those (not necessarily aps) sets of enabled transitions that yield the smallest reduced state space that preserves the deadlocks. Unfortunately, it was shown in [20] that finding subsets of transitions of a 1-safe Petri net that are optimal in this sense is at least as hard as testing whether the net has a deadlock. Another similar result was proven in [2, p. 154]. Therefore, without additional assumptions, optimal sets are too hard to find.

This negative result assumes that optimality is defined with respect to all possible ways of obtaining information on the behaviour of the system. Indeed, optimal sets can be found by first constructing and investigating the full state space. Of course, aps set methods do not do so, because constructing the full

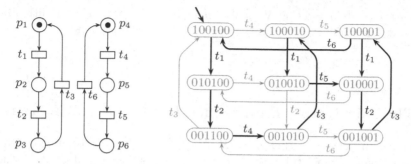

Fig. 2. Transitions are tried in the order of their indices until one is found that does not close a cycle. If such a transition is not found, then all transitions are taken

state space is what they try to avoid. In [20], a way of obtaining information was defined such that most (but not all) deadlock-preserving aps set methods conform to it. Using non-trivial model-theoretic reasoning, it was proven in [20] that, in the case of 1-safe Petri nets, the best possible (not necessarily aps) sets that can be obtained in this context are of the form $\mathcal{E}(T_s)$, where T_s is stubborn. In this restricted but nevertheless meaningful sense, stubborn sets are optimal.

The situation is much more complicated when preserving other properties than deadlocks. We only discuss one difficulty. Instead of S, [2, p. 155] assumes that the reduced state space is constructed in depth-first order and tells to choose an aps set that does not close a cycle if possible, and otherwise use all enabled transitions. Figure 2 shows an example where this condition leads to the construction of all reachable states, although the processes do not interact at all. The condition S is less vulnerable to but not totally free from this kind of difficulties. Far too little is known on this problem area.

The approach in Sects. 4 and 7 that does not use S is entirely free of this difficulty. This is one reason why it seems very promising.

In general, it is reasonable to try to find as weak conditions as possible in place of D1, V, S, and so on, because the weaker a condition is, the more potential it has for good reduction results. Because of the non-subset choice problem and other similar problems, it is not certain that the potential can be exploited in practice. However, if the best set is ruled out already by the choice of the condition, then it is certain that it cannot be exploited.

For instance, instead of V, [2, p. 149] requires that if $\mathcal{T}(s) \cap V \cap \text{en}(s) \neq \emptyset$, then $\mathcal{T}(s)$ must contain all enabled transitions. This condition is strictly stronger than V and thus has less potential for reduction. Furthermore, the algorithm in Sect. 4 can exploit the additional potential of V at least to some extent.

This also illustrates why stubborn sets are defined such that they may contain disabled transitions. The part $V \subseteq \mathcal{T}(s)$ in the definition of condition V could not be formulated easily, or perhaps not at all, if $\mathcal{T}(s)$ cannot contain disabled transitions. The following example reveals both that $V \cap \text{en}(s) \subseteq \mathcal{T}(s)$ fails (it loses the trace b) and that V yields better reduction than the condition in [2] ($\{a, b, u, \tau_2\}$ is stubborn, satisfies V, but $\tau_3 \in \text{en}(s) \not\subseteq \{a, b, u, \tau_2\}$):

$$\left(\underset{a}{\circ} \xrightarrow{a} \underset{u}{\circ} \xrightarrow{u} \underset{a}{\circ} \xrightarrow{a} \circ \parallel \circ \xrightarrow{u} \underset{\tau_2}{\circ} \xrightarrow{\tau_2} \underset{v}{\circ} \xrightarrow{v} \underset{b}{\circ} \xrightarrow{b} \circ \parallel \circ \xrightarrow{\tau_3} \underset{v}{\circ} \xrightarrow{v} \circ \right) \setminus \{u, v\}$$

6   The Fair Testing Equivalence Preservation Theorem

In this section we assume that $L_r = (S_r, \Sigma, \Delta_r, \hat{s})$ has been constructed with the trace-preserving strong stubborn set method, that is, obeying D1, D2, V, and S. We show that L_r is fair testing equivalent to L, where $L = (S, \Sigma, \Delta, \hat{s})$ denotes the corresponding full LTS, based on a series of lemmata. Lemma 4 shows that a trace leaving S_r can be found inside S_r, and Lemma 3 treats a step for this. Similarly, Lemmas 5 and 6 show how to transfer a refusal set in a suitable way.

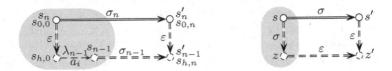

Fig. 3. Illustrating Lemma 3 (left) and Lemma 4 (right)

Lemma 3. *Assume that $n \in \mathbb{N}$, $s_n \in S_r$, $s'_n \in S$, $\varepsilon \neq \sigma_n \in V^*$, and there is an f-path of length n from s_n to s'_n such that its trace is σ_n. There are $s_{n-1} \in S_r$, $s'_{n-1} \in S$, $\lambda_{n-1} \in V \cup \{\varepsilon\}$, and $\sigma_{n-1} \in V^*$ such that $\lambda_{n-1}\sigma_{n-1} = \sigma_n$, $s_n = \lambda_{n-1}\Rightarrow s_{n-1}$ in L_r, $s'_n = \varepsilon\Rightarrow s'_{n-1}$ in L, and there is an f-path of length $n - 1$ from s_{n-1} to s'_{n-1} such that its trace is σ_{n-1}.*

Proof. Let $s_{0,0} = s_n$ and $s_{0,n} = s'_n$. Let the f-path of length n be $s_{0,0} - a_1 \cdots a_n \rightarrow s_{0,n}$. Because $\sigma_n \neq \varepsilon$, there is a smallest v such that $1 \leq v \leq n$ and $a_v \in V$. By S, there are $k \in \mathbb{N}$, $s_{1,0}, \ldots, s_{k,0}$, and $b_1, \ldots, b_k$ such that $a_v \in \mathcal{T}(s_{k,0})$ and $s_{0,0} - b_1 \rightarrow s_{1,0} - b_2 \rightarrow \cdots - b_k \rightarrow s_{k,0}$ in L_r. Let h be the smallest natural number such that $\{a_1, \ldots, a_n\} \cap \mathcal{T}(s_{h,0}) \neq \emptyset$. Because $a_v \in \mathcal{T}(s_{k,0})$, we have $0 \leq h \leq k$. By h applications of D2 at $s_{0,0}, \ldots, s_{h-1,0}$, there are $s_{1,n}, \ldots, s_{h,n}$ such that $s_{i,0} - a_1 \cdots a_n \rightarrow s_{i,n}$ in L for $1 \leq i \leq h$ and $s_{0,n} - b_1 \rightarrow s_{1,n} - b_2 \rightarrow \cdots - b_h \rightarrow s_{h,n}$ in L. If $b_i \in V$ for some $1 \leq i \leq h$, then $V \subseteq \mathcal{T}(s_{i-1,0})$ by V. It yields $a_v \in \mathcal{T}(s_{i-1,0})$, which contradicts the choice of h. As a consequence, $s_{0,0} = \varepsilon\Rightarrow s_{h,0}$ in L_r and $s_{0,n} = \varepsilon\Rightarrow s_{h,n}$ in L.

Because $\{a_1, \ldots, a_n\} \cap \mathcal{T}(s_{h,0}) \neq \emptyset$, there is a smallest i such that $1 \leq i \leq n$ and $a_i \in \mathcal{T}(s_{h,0})$. By D1 at $s_{h,0}$, there is s_{n-1} such that $s_{h,0} - a_i \rightarrow s_{n-1}$ in L_r and $s_{n-1} - a_1 \cdots a_{i-1}a_{i+1} \cdots a_n \rightarrow s_{h,n}$ in L. We choose $s'_{n-1} = s_{h,n}$ and let σ_{n-1} be the trace of $a_1 \cdots a_{i-1}a_{i+1} \cdots a_n$. If $a_i \notin V$, then we choose $\lambda_{n-1} = \varepsilon$, yielding $\lambda_{n-1}\sigma_{n-1} = \sigma_n$. If $a_i \in V$, then $V \subseteq \mathcal{T}(s_{h,0})$ by V, so none of $a_1, \ldots, a_{i-1}$ is in V, and by choosing $\lambda_{n-1} = a_i$ we obtain $\lambda_{n-1}\sigma_{n-1} = \sigma_n$. That $s_n = \lambda_{n-1}\Rightarrow s_{n-1}$ in L_r follows from $s_{0,0} = \varepsilon\Rightarrow s_{h,0} - a_i\rightarrow s_{n-1}$ in L_r. The rest of the claim is obtained by replacing s'_n for $s_{0,n}$ and s'_{n-1} for $s_{h,n}$ in already proven facts. $\square$

Lemma 4. *Let $n \in \mathbb{N}$. Assume that $s \in S_\mathsf{r}$, $s' \in S$, $\sigma \in V^*$, and $s = \sigma\Rightarrow s'$ in L due to an f-path of length n. Then there are $z \in S_\mathsf{r}$ and $z' \in S$ such that $s = \sigma\Rightarrow z$ in L_r, $z = \varepsilon\Rightarrow z'$ in L, and $s' = \varepsilon\Rightarrow z'$ in L.*

Proof. The proof is by induction on n. We start with the observation that, in case $\sigma = \varepsilon$, the claim holds with choosing $z = s$ and $z' = s'$. This settles the base case $n = 0$ and a subcase of the induction step, and it leaves us with the case $n > 0$ and $\sigma \neq \varepsilon$.

We apply Lemma 3 and get $s_1 \in S_\mathsf{r}$, $s'_1 \in S$, $\sigma_1 \in V^*$, and $\lambda_1 \in V \cup \{\varepsilon\}$ such that $\lambda_1\sigma_1 = \sigma$, $s = \lambda_1\Rightarrow s_1$ in L_r, and $s' = \varepsilon\Rightarrow s'_1$ in L. Furthermore, $s_1 = \sigma_1\Rightarrow s'_1$ in L due to an f-path of length $n - 1$, for which the lemma holds; hence, there are $z \in S_\mathsf{r}$ and $z' \in S$ such that $s_1 = \sigma_1\Rightarrow z$ in L_r, $z = \varepsilon\Rightarrow z'$ in L, and $s'_1 = \varepsilon\Rightarrow z'$ in L. Together, these also give $s = \lambda_1\Rightarrow s_1 = \sigma_1\Rightarrow z$ in L_r and $s' = \varepsilon\Rightarrow s'_1 = \varepsilon\Rightarrow z'$ in L, so we are done. $\square$

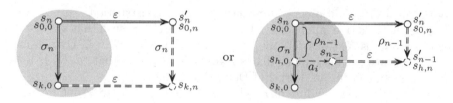

Fig. 4. Illustrating Lemma 5; a_i is invisible

Lemma 5. *Assume that $n \in \mathbb{N}$, $s_n \in S_\mathsf{r}$, $s'_n \in S$, $\sigma_n \in V^*$, $s_n = \sigma_n\Rightarrow$ in L_r, and there is an f-path of length n from s_n to s'_n such that its trace is ε. Either $s'_n = \sigma_n\Rightarrow$ in L or there are $s_{n-1} \in S_\mathsf{r}$, $s'_{n-1} \in S$, and ρ_{n-1} such that ρ_{n-1} is a prefix of σ_n, $s_n = \rho_{n-1}\Rightarrow s_{n-1}$ in L_r, $s'_n = \rho_{n-1}\Rightarrow s'_{n-1}$ in L, and there is an f-path of length $n - 1$ from s_{n-1} to s'_{n-1} such that its trace is ε.*

Proof. Let $s_{0,0} = s_n$ and $s_{0,n} = s'_n$. Let the f-path of length n be $s_{0,0} - a_1 \cdots a_n\rightarrow s_{0,n}$; obviously, the a_i are invisible. By the assumption, there is a path $s_{0,0} - b_1\rightarrow s_{1,0} - b_2\rightarrow \ldots - b_k\rightarrow s_{k,0}$ in L_r such that its trace is σ_n.

If $\{a_1, \ldots, a_n\} \cap \mathcal{T}(s_{i,0}) = \emptyset$ for $0 \le i < k$, then k applications of D2 yield $s_{1,n}, \ldots, s_{k,n}$ such that $s_{0,n} - b_1\rightarrow s_{1,n} - b_2\rightarrow \ldots - b_k\rightarrow s_{k,n}$ in L. This implies $s'_n = \sigma_n\Rightarrow$ in L.

Otherwise, there is a smallest h such that $0 \le h < k$ and $\{a_1, \ldots, a_n\} \cap \mathcal{T}(s_{h,0}) \neq \emptyset$. There also is a smallest i such that $1 \le i \le n$ and $a_i \in \mathcal{T}(s_{h,0})$. Applying D2 h times yields $s_{1,n}, \ldots, s_{h,n}$ such that $s_{0,n} - b_1\rightarrow \ldots - b_h\rightarrow s_{h,n}$ in L and $s_{h,0} - a_1 \cdots a_n\rightarrow s_{h,n}$ in L. By D1 there is s_{n-1} such that $s_{h,0} - a_i\rightarrow s_{n-1}$ in L_r and $s_{n-1} - a_1 \cdots a_{i-1}a_{i+1} \cdots a_n\rightarrow s_{h,n}$ in L. The claim follows by choosing $s'_{n-1} = s_{h,n}$ and letting ρ_{n-1} be the trace of $s_{0,0} - b_1 \cdots b_h\rightarrow s_{h,0}$. $\square$

Lemma 6. *Let $n \in \mathbb{N}$. Assume $K \subseteq V^*$, $\rho \in K$, $z \in S_r$, $z' \in S$, and $z = \varepsilon \Rightarrow z'$ due to an f-path of length n; assume further that z' f-refuses K and $z = \rho \Rightarrow$ in L_r. Then there exist $s \in S_r$ and a prefix π of K such that $z = \pi \Rightarrow s$ in L_r and s r-refuses $\pi^{-1}K$.*

Proof. The proof is by induction on n. The case $n = 0$ holds vacuously, since it would imply $z' = \rho \Rightarrow$, contradicting $\rho \in K$.

So we assume the lemma to hold for $n - 1$, and also the assumptions in the lemma for n. We apply Lemma 5 to z, z', and ρ. In the first case, we would again have the impossible $z' = \rho \Rightarrow$. So according to the second case, we have a z_1, z_1', and prefix ρ' of ρ and thus of K with $z = \rho' \Rightarrow z_1$ in L_r, $z' = \rho' \Rightarrow z_1'$ in L, and $z_1 = \varepsilon \Rightarrow z_1'$ due to an f-path of length $n - 1$.

Since z' f-refuses K, z_1' must f-refuse $\rho'^{-1}K$. If z_1 r-refuses $\rho'^{-1}K$, we are done. Otherwise, we can apply the induction hypothesis to $z_1 = \varepsilon \Rightarrow z_1'$ and $\rho'^{-1}K$. This results in an $s \in S_r$ and a prefix π' of $\rho'^{-1}K$ such that $z_1 = \pi' \Rightarrow s$ in L_r and s r-refuses $\pi'^{-1}\rho'^{-1}K = (\rho'\pi')^{-1}K$. We also have that $\rho'\pi'$ is a prefix of K and $z = \rho'\pi' \Rightarrow s$ in L_r, so we are done. $\square$

Theorem 7. *The LTS L_r is fair testing equivalent to L.*

Proof. Part 1 of Definition 1 is immediate from the construction.

Let (σ, K) be a tree failure of L_r. That is, there is $s \in S_r$ such that $\hat{s} = \sigma \Rightarrow s$ in L_r and s r-refuses K. Consider any $\rho \in V^*$ such that $s = \rho \Rightarrow$ in L. By Lemma 4, $s = \rho \Rightarrow$ also in L_r. This implies that s refuses K in L and that (σ, K) is a tree failure of L. In conclusion, Part 2 of Definition 1 holds.

Let (σ, K) be a tree failure of L. That is, there is $s' \in S$ such that $\hat{s} = \sigma \Rightarrow s'$ in L and s' f-refuses K. By Lemma 4 there are $z \in S_r$ and $z' \in S$ such that $\hat{s} = \sigma \Rightarrow z$ in L_r, $s' = \varepsilon \Rightarrow z'$ in L, and $z = \varepsilon \Rightarrow z'$ in L. Since s' f-refuses K, also z' f-refuses K.

Either z r-refuses K and we are done, or we apply Lemma 6, giving us an $s \in S_r$ and a prefix π of K such that $z = \pi \Rightarrow s$ in L_r and s r-refuses $\pi^{-1}K$. Hence, $(\sigma\pi, \pi^{-1}K) \in \mathsf{Tf}(L_r)$ and Part 3 of Definition 1 also holds. $\square$

Let us conclude this section with a counterexample that shows that the method does not preserve tree failure equivalence.

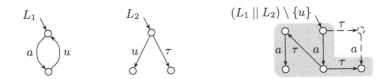

Fig. 5. A counterexample to the preservation of all tree failures. In $(L_1 \| L_2) \backslash \{u\}$, the solid states and transitions are in the reduced and the dashed ones only in the full LTS

Consider $(L_1 \| L_2) \backslash \{u\}$, where L_1 and L_2 are shown in Fig. 5 left and middle. Initially two sets are stubborn: $\{a\}$ and $\{a, u, \tau_2\}$. If $\{a\}$ is chosen, then the LTS is obtained that is shown with solid arrows on the right in Fig. 5. The full LTS also contains the dashed arrows. The full LTS has the tree failure $(\varepsilon, \{aa\})$ that the reduced LTS lacks.

7   Example

Figure 6 shows the example system used in the measurements in this section. It is a variant of the alternating bit protocol [1]. Its purpose is to deliver data items from a sending client to a receiving client via unreliable channels that may lose messages at any time. There are two kinds of data items: N and Y. To avoid cluttering Fig. 6, the data items are not shown in it. In reality, instead of sen, there are the actions senN and senY, and similarly with rec, d_0, $\bar{d}_0$, d_1, and $\bar{d}_1$.

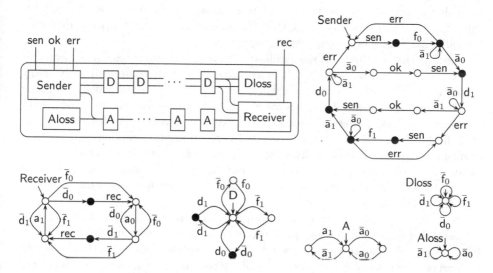

Fig. 6. The example system: architecture, Sender, Receiver, D, A, Dloss, and Aloss. Each sen, rec, d_0, d_1, $\bar{d}_0$, and $\bar{d}_1$ carries a parameter that is either N or Y. Each black state corresponds to two states, one for each parameter value. Each $\bar{x}$ synchronizes with x along a line in the architecture picture. The output of the rightmost D is consumed either by Receiver or Dloss, and similarly with the leftmost A

Because messages may be lost in the data channel, the alternating bit protocol has a timeout mechanism. For each message that it receives, the receiver sends back an acknowledgement message. After sending any message, the sender waits for the acknowledgement for a while. If it does not arrive in time, then the sender re-sends the message. To prevent the sender and receiver from being fooled by outdated messages, the messages carry a number that is 0 or 1.

The alternating bit protocol is impractical in that if either channel is totally broken, then the sender sends without limit in vain, so the protocol diverges.

The variant in Fig. 6 avoids this problem. For each sen action, Sender tries sending at most a fixed number of times, which we denote with ℓ. (In the figure, $\ell = 1$ for simplicity.) The protocol is expected to behave as follows. For each sen, it eventually replies with ok or err. If it replies with ok, it has delivered the data item with rec. If it replies with err, delivery is possible but not guaranteed, and it may occur before or after the err. There are no unsolicited or double deliveries. If the channels are not totally broken, the protocol cannot lose the ability to reply with ok.

After err, Sender does not know whether any data message got through and therefore it does not know which bit value Receiver expects next. For this reason, initially and after each err, the protocol performs a connection phase before attempting to deliver data items. It consists of sending a flush message and expecting an acknowledgement with the same bit value. When the acknowledgement comes, it is certain that there are no remnant messages with the opposite bit value in the system, so the use of that value for the next data message is safe. This is true despite the fact that the acknowledgement with the expected bit value may itself be a remnant message.

Assume that neither channel can lose infinitely many messages in a row. This is a typical fairness assumption. It guarantees that if there are infinitely many sen-actions, then infinitely many flush actions go through and infinitely many acknowledgements come back. However, it does not guarantee that any data message ever gets through. To guarantee that, it is necessary to further assume that if the acknowledgement channel delivers infinitely many messages, then eventually the data channel delivers at least one of the next ℓ messages that have been sent via it after the acknowledgement channel delivered a message. This assumption is very unnatural, because it says that the channels must somehow coordinate the losses of messages.

As a consequence, the traditional approach of proving liveness that is based on fairness assumptions is not appropriate for this protocol. On the other hand, fair testing equivalence can be used to prove a weaker but nevertheless useful property: the protocol cannot lose the ability to deliver data items and reply ok. This is why the protocol was chosen for the experiments in this section.

To implement Steps 1 and 3 in Sect. 4, we add to Sender a new state s_d and a transition labelled with t to s_d from each state that has an outgoing transition labelled with senN or senY. Let the resulting LTS be called Sender'. Clearly Sender $= ($Sender' $\|$ Block_t$)\backslash\{$t$\}$, where Block_t is the single-state LTS whose alphabet is $\{$t$\}$ and that has no transitions. After computing the reduced LTS L_r' using Sender' and treating t as visible, the final result is obtained as $(L_r' \| $ Block_t$)\backslash\{$t$\}$, which is trivial to compute from L_r'. This is correct, because fair testing equivalence is a congruence.

Table 1 shows analysis results obtained with the ASSET tool [18,19]. ASSET does not input parallel compositions of LTSs, but it allows to mimic their behaviour with C++ code. It also allows to express the "$\rightsquigarrow$" relation in C++ and computes stubborn sets with the esc algorithm. Thus it can be used to compute Step 2 of Sect. 4. ASSET verified that each LTS with the t-transitions is

Table 1. Each channel consists of c separate cells. Times are in seconds

c	Full LTS			Full, with t-transitions			Stubborn sets		
	States	Edges	Time	States	Edges	Time	States	Edges	Time
1	380	1068	0.0	440	1254	0.1	372	700	0.0
2	1880	6212	0.0	2224	7360	0.1	1234	1992	0.0
3	9200	34934	0.1	10976	41560	0.1	2986	4382	0.0
4	44000	188710	0.2	52672	224928	0.3	6104	8360	0.1
5	205760	983614	0.5	246656	1173536	0.6	11140	14494	0.1
6	944000	4977246	2.3	1132288	5941760	2.7	18726	23432	0.2
7	4263680	24582270	11.4	5115392	29357952	13.8	29578	35906	0.2
8	19013120	119011454	63.4	22813696	142177792	77.2	44496	52732	0.3
10							90150	103124	0.4
20							946520	1005784	3.6
30							4083190	4238144	18.8
40							11854160	12170204	68.2

Table 2. Each channel is a single reduced LTS

c	Full LTS			Full, with t-transitions			Stubborn sets		
	States	Edges	Time	States	Edges	Time	States	Edges	Time
10	42680	183912	0.3	51128	216300	0.4	16818	29756	0.2
20	287280	1278742	2.1	344568	1502900	2.4	84928	144116	0.7
30	913880	4112572	9.0	1096408	4831900	10.7	236438	391276	2.0
40	2102480	9513402	25.9	2522648	11175300	30.6	503348	819236	4.6
50	4033080	18309232	60.4	4839288	21505100	71.9	917658	1475996	9.3
60							1511368	2409556	17.7
70							2316478	3667916	29.1
80							3364988	5299076	45.9
90							4688898	7351036	70.3
100							6320208	9871796	102.8

indeed always may-terminating. To gain confidence that the modelling with C++ is correct, additional runs were conducted where the ASSET model contained machinery that verified most of the correctness properties listed above, including that the protocol cannot lose the ability to execute ok (except by executing t).

Table 1 shows spectacular reduction results, but one may argue that the model of the channels in Fig. 6 is unduly favourable to stubborn sets. The messages travel through the channels step by step. Without stubborn sets, any combination of empty and full channel slots may be reached, creating an exponential number of states. If a message is ready to move from a cell to the next one, then the corresponding action constitutes a singleton stubborn set.

Therefore, the stubborn set method has the tendency to quickly move messages to the front of the channel, dramatically reducing the number of constructed states.

To not give stubborn sets unfair advantage, another series of experiments was made where the messages are always immediately moved as close to the front of the channel as possible during construction of the full LTS. The fact about fifo queues and the "$\leadsto$" relation that was mentioned in Sect. 4 is also exploited. The results are shown in Table 2. Although they are less spectacular, they, too, show great benefit by the stubborn set method.

Acknowledgements. We thank the anonymous reviewers for their comments. Unfortunately, space constraints prevented us from implementing some of these.

References

1. Bartlett, K.A., Scantlebury, R.A., Wilkinson, P.T.: A note on reliable full-duplex transmission over half-duplex links. Commun. ACM **12**(5), 260–261 (1969)
2. Clarke, E.M., Grumberg, O., Peled, D.A.: Model Checking, p. 314. MIT Press, Cambridge (1999)
3. Evangelista, S., Pajault, C.: Solving the ignoring problem for partial order reduction. Softw. Tools Technol. Transf. **12**(2), 155–170 (2010)
4. Eve, J., Kurki-Suonio, R.: On computing the transitive closure of a relation. Acta Inform. **8**(4), 303–314 (1977)
5. Gerth, R., Kuiper, R., Peled, D., Penczek, W.: A partial order approach to branching time logic model checking. In: Proceedings of Third Israel Symposium on the Theory of Computing and Systems, pp. 130–139. IEEE (1995)
6. Godefroid, P.: Using partial orders to improve automatic verification methods. In: Proceedings of CAV 1990, AMS-ACM DIMACS Series in Discrete Mathematics and Theoretical Computer Science, vol. 3, pp. 321–340 (1991)
7. Godefroid, P. (ed.): Partial-Order Methods for the Verification of Concurrent Systems: An Approach to the State-Explosion Problem. LNCS, vol. 1032. Springer, Heidelberg (1996)
8. Laarman, A., Pater, E., van de Pol, J., Hansen, H.: Guard-based partial-order reduction. Softw. Tools Technol. Transf. 1–22 (2014)
9. Mazurkiewicz, A.: Trace theory. In: Brauer, W., Reisig, W., Rozenberg, G. (eds.) Petri Nets 1986. LNCS, vol. 255, pp. 279–324. Springer, Heidelberg (1987)
10. Peled, D.: All from one, one for all: on model checking using representatives. In: Courcoubetis, C. (ed.) CAV 1993. LNCS, vol. 697, pp. 409–423. Springer, Heidelberg (1993)
11. Peled, D.: Partial order reduction: linear and branching temporal logics and process algebras. In: Proceedings of POMIV 1996, Workshop on Partial Order Methods in Verification, DIMACS Series in Discrete Mathematics and Theoretical Computer Science, vol. 29, pp. 233–257. American Mathematical Society (1997)
12. Rensink, A., Vogler, W.: Fair testing. Inf. Comput. **205**(2), 125–198 (2007)
13. Tarjan, R.E.: Depth-first search and linear graph algorithms. SIAM J. Comput. **1**(2), 146–160 (1972)
14. Valmari, A.: Error Detection by reduced reachability graph generation. In: Proceedings of the 9th European Workshop on Application and Theory of Petri Nets, pp. 95–122 (1988)

15. Valmari, A.: State space generation: efficiency and practicality. Dr. Techn. thesis, Tampere University of Technology Publications 55, Tampere (1988)
16. Valmari, A.: Stubborn set methods for process algebras. Peled, D.A., Pratt, V.R., Holzmann, G.J. (eds.) Partial Order Methods in Verification: DIMACS Workshop, DIMACS Series in Discrete Mathematics and Theoretical Computer Science, vol. 29, pp. 213–231. American Mathematical Society (1997)
17. Valmari, A.: The state explosion problem. In: Reisig, W., Rozenberg, G. (eds.) APN 1998. LNCS, vol. 1491, pp. 429–528. Springer, Heidelberg (1998)
18. Valmari, A.: Stop it, and be stubborn! In: Haar, S., Meyer, R. (eds.) 15th International Conference on Application of Concurrency to System Design, pp. 10–19. IEEE Computer Society (2015). doi:10.1109/ACSD.2015.14
19. Valmari, A.: A state space tool for concurrent system models expressed in C++. In: Nummenmaa, J., Sievi-Korte, O., Mäkinen, E. (eds.) SPLST 2015 Symposium on Programming Languages and Software Tools, vol. 1525, pp. 91–105. CEUR Workshop Proceedings (2015)
20. Valmari, A., Hansen, H.: Can stubborn sets be optimal? Fundamenta Informaticae 113(3–4), 377–397 (2011)

Author Index

Printed in the United States
By Bookmasters